PATTERN OF CIRCLES

Pattern of Circles

An Ambassador's Story

JOHN E. DOLIBOIS

to Phelps,
with warm good wishes
in — kei —,
John E. Dolibois

THE KENT STATE UNIVERSITY PRESS
Kent, Ohio, and London, England

To Winnie

© 1989 by The Kent State University Press, Kent, Ohio 44242
All rights reserved
Library of Congress Catalog Card Number 89-8008
ISBN 0-87338-389-3 (cloth)
ISBN 10: 0-87338-702-3 (paper)
ISBN 13: 978-0-87338-702-6 (paper)
Manufactured in the United States of America
Second paper printing 2005.

07 06 05   7 6 5

Library of Congress Cataloging-in-Publication Data
Dolibois, John, 1918–
Pattern of circles : an ambassador's story / John E. Dolibois.
p. cm.
Includes index.
ISBN 0-87338-389-3 (cloth: alk. paper) ∞
ISBN 0-87338-702-3 (paper: alk. paper) ∞
1. Dolibois, John, 1918– . 2. Luxembourg Americans—Biography. 3. World War,
1939–1945—Personal narratives, American. 4. College administrators—Ohio—
Biography. 5. Ambassadors—United States—Biography. 6. Ambassadors—
Luxembourg—Biography. 7. Luxembourg—Biography. 8. United States—
Biography. I Title.
CT275.D835A3   1989
327.2'092—dc19
[B]
89-8008

British Library Cataloging-in-Publication data are available.

Contents

Foreword

MAY 31, 1982. A beautiful day in Western Europe! My wife and two daughters are seated with me among the dignitaries attending Memorial Day ceremonies at the American Military cemetery in the picturesque village of Hamm, Luxembourg.

Behind us stretch the rows and columns of 5,074 white marble crosses and Stars of David marking the graves of American World War II dead. Among them the grave of General George S. Patton, Jr., is distinguished from the others only by its solitary place in the cemetery's first row. A gentle breeze ruffles the small flags—American Stars and Stripes and Luxembourg tricolor—placed before each marker.

Before us stands the memorial shrine. Against a clear sky, its brilliant white and burnished bronze are dazzling in the morning sun. Lest the acres of graves be an inadequate reminder, one of the shrine's walls bears the inscription:

1941 - 1945
IN PROUD REMEMBRANCE
OF THE ACHIEVEMENTS OF HER SONS
AND IN HUMBLE TRIBUTE
TO THEIR SACRIFICES
THIS MEMORIAL HAS BEEN ERECTED BY
THE UNITED STATES OF AMERICA

But the people of Luxembourg need no reminders. Row upon row of folding chairs are occupied by citizens and officials of the Grand Duchy. All are here to commemorate the American liberation of their tiny country from the Nazi scourge.

On the plaza to the right of the chapel's entrance, beneath a blue and gold canopy, sit the participants in the day's proceedings. Among them are the Grand Duke and Grand Duchess of Luxembourg, the prime minister, the American ambassador, and a four-star general of the United States Air Force.

More than three dozen floral wreaths, each sponsored by a private, civic, or government organization, have been formally presented. With military precision each has been laid along the broad, terraced walkway leading to the shrine's entrance.

An expectant hush falls over the crowd. Even the breeze is still. The quiet is shattered by the thunderous roar of four U. S. Air Force F-15 fighters streaking, in tight formation, over the trees which guard the perimeter of the cemetery. With the scream of turbines pushed to full throttle one of the planes accelerates, negotiates a vertical climb, and disappears into the cloudless sky over Luxembourg. The three remaining jets continue in the broken-chevron, "missing flyer" formation.

We on the ground are deeply moved. Unexpectedly, this traditional flyers' tribute to their countrymen lost in battle has stripped us of the insulating mantle of time and insular concerns. Suddenly the emotions of World War II are thrust upon us. We are overwhelmed by the horrors, waste, and sacrifices of war. We grieve. We remember valor and heroism. We are proud. We exult in the triumph of a free people over their oppressors. We are thankful.

The jets' thunder fades. A bugler solemnly ascends the chapel's steps. He sounds taps. Hidden in the distant woods, a second trumpeter echoes the haunting melody.

At the podium the deputy chief of mission of the American embassy introduces the next speaker: "I now present his Excellency, the Ambassador of the United States of America, the Honorable John E. Dolibois. . . . "

My father steps to the microphone (despite the intimidating title, to me he's still just "Dad"). Obviously moved, he begins his first Memorial Day address as an American ambassador.

As Dad opens with formal greetings, I am proud to be in the audience. I sense that this place, this ceremony, and my father's role symbolize completion of another circuit of his life—a life characterized by multiple, interlocking circles. Many of the intersections among those circles are represented by nearby sites.

Less than two miles from the podium from which Dad speaks stands the house in which he was born on December 4, 1918. A corner of this now sacred cemetery was once a soccer field on which he played as a boy.

One hundred yards from the lectern is the grave of General George S.

Patton, Jr.—my father's wartime hero. It was from General Patton Dad received his army commission as a second lieutenant. Months later, under Patton's command, Dad would play a role in rescuing the famous Lipizzaner horses from Czechoslovakia—an adventure which, years later, would result in Dad's being honored by the Spanish Riding School in Vienna, and which Walt Disney would immortalize on film.

In December, 1945, Dad attended another ceremony at this same cemetery, General Patton's burial services.

A leisurely hour's drive from Hamm is the resort spa, Mondorf. It was there that the highest-ranking Nazis were interned after World War II as they awaited trial in Nuremberg. Lieutenant John E. Dolibois of U.S. Military Intelligence, native of Luxembourg, fluent in German, was their interrogator. During his many months in Mondorf, Dad maintained a diary; he compiled a scrapbook; he collected memorabilia. Often dismayed by those who would deny Hitler's Holocaust, Dad has frequently pledged to someday publicize his unique, firsthand impressions.

In the heart of nearby Luxembourg City is the Miami University European Center, a reminder of Dad's commitment to international education and a symbol of his thirty-four years on the staff of his alma mater in Oxford, Ohio. He began his years with Miami in 1947 as the university's first full-time alumni secretary. He went on to become vice president of Miami University and its chief development officer. As a result of his innovative fund-raising, scholarship, and building programs, Miami's development effort became a yardstick by which many other public institutions of higher education in the United States measured themselves. Several buildings on Miami's main campus, numerous research and educational grants, various endowed professorships, and many student scholarships owe their existence to Dad's tireless service to Miami University—now highly regarded among the "public ivys."

Presidents Richard Nixon and Gerald Ford consecutively appointed Dad to the prestigious Board of Foreign Scholarships which administers the Fulbright Cultural and Educational Exchange Program. He became the panel's senior member and a leader in international educational exchange. Accordingly, he was instrumental in establishing Miami's Center in Luxembourg.

Already considering early retirement from Miami in 1981, Dad and Mom were vacationing in Europe when the White House tracked them down and President Ronald Reagan requested Dad's services as United States ambassador to his native land of Luxembourg. Never before in American history had a naturalized American returned to the land of his birth in such a capacity. Dad said, "Yes. . . . "

With the triple retorts of a twenty-one-gun salute the 1982 Memorial Day ceremonies in Luxembourg are winding down. The American ambassador has concluded his brief remarks with the words: "Join with me in renewing our pledge to keep our two nations united, free, and at peace. There can be no better way of honoring our military heroes, both living and dead."

During the remaining three and one-half years of my father's tenure as United States ambassador to the Grand Duchy of Luxembourg he would approach his duties with the same tenacity, creativity, indefatigability, and loyalty which characterized his successes in the Boy Scouts during his "Americanization," his military service in the United States Army, and his many years at Miami University.

There would be formal visits to Luxembourg by high-ranking American officials. Never before had so many of such stature visited "little" Luxembourg. With Dad and Mom as host and hostess, Luxembourg's royal family—the Grand Duke and Grand Duchess—would visit the United States and be received at the White House during a formal State Visit, a first-time-ever event for them. In Luxembourg Dad and Mom would attend two royal weddings, a royal funeral, and meet the Pope during his State Visit to Luxembourg. These were but "bonuses" on the busy daily calendar of a full-time, working ambassador.

Dad resigned his post in Luxembourg after four years. He retired with a sincere sense of accomplishment. He had successfully placed Luxembourg on Washington's map of Europe. He brought credit to Miami University, in whose service he had dedicated a major segment of his life. He earned love, respect, and admiration among the citizens of the tiny, but proud, country of his birth. He continues to provide a model of integrity, honor, dedication, and loyalty for his three sons to emulate.

This book is John E. Dolibois's story.

For some, it will be the heartwarming tale of a youthful immigrant growing up in Akron, Ohio. He overcomes language and social barriers to become the first in his large family to attend a university. He succeeds in his chosen profession. Ultimately, he becomes a folk hero in the land of his birth when he returns as his adoptive country's highest representative.

Others might read this story as a firsthand, anecdotal history. It provides previously unpublished insights into the minds and machinations of the architects of Hitler's Third Reich. At the same time it offers its readers a rare and intriguing look at the inside workings of a contemporary American embassy in Europe.

Many may find this work a fascinating geography lesson. They will learn about one of Europe's oldest independent countries—the Grand

Duchy of Luxembourg. Founded in 963 A.D., Luxembourg was once the most impregnable fortress in Europe. Today, this tiny land is populated by a proud, industrious, and prosperous people. It enjoys one of the highest standards of living in the world. Highly industrialized, a major international banking center, and home to numerous international organizations, Luxembourg, like its larger neighbors—Belgium, France, and West Germany—has a full vote in the United Nations, NATO, and the European Community. As of this writing, it remains one of the United States' friendliest allies.

To his family and friends, this is the story of a humble, sensitive, perceptive, patriotic, and very human man. John E. Dolibois is a rare individual who, in his lifelong pursuit of excellence, has lived an American dream.

J. MICHAEL DOLIBOIS, M.D.
Oxford, Ohio

Acknowledgments

I AM GRATEFUL to a number of people who have shown an interest in the completion of this book. My friend of more than fifty-seven years, Francis J. "Grassy" Grassbaugh, provided the initial stimulus. Albert Stoltz, of Olingen, Luxembourg, prodded my memory and helped me recall scenes of our youth, and facts about the war. Our dear neighbor, Cissy Hoover, and our family doctor, Bill Beck, read the first draft and gave essential encouragement. William Beckett scrutinized my writing for the proper choice of words, and saved me from embarrassing errors. My former English professor and lifelong friend, Walter Havighurst, graded my effort and gave me an 'A.' Professor Dwight L. Smith literally opened the door that led to publication, and gave me much needed technical advice. Ethelwyn Fox Martello typed the manuscript with personal care and precision. Miami friend Harold Apel rendered yeoman service in reading proof.

Some of the photographs herein are courtesy of John Weyrich of the *Luxemburger Wort*. Others were taken by Claude Michels, our faithful embassy driver for four years. The official portrait of an ambassador in "grand tenue" is by Ron Stevens of Oxford.

My heartfelt thanks to Luxembourg artist Mars Schmit for the handsome watercolor on the front cover, and to Jack Steinman of Deluxe Engraving in Cincinnati for the color reproductions.

Dr. John T. Hubbell, director of the Kent State University Press, produced a penetrating critique of the first draft, and then guided the project to satisfying fulfillment. Editor Julia J. Morton contributed her exacting talent, tactful attention to detail, and, along with John Hubbell, heartwarming encouragement.

The most steadfast support came from my wife Winnie, friend, and critic. She endured my up-and-down moods, helped me recall incidents, and, in remembering, shared laughter or a tear with me.

Finally, Ralph and Bonnie Fey are very much a part of this story. We attended Miami University together. We enjoyed fraternal fellowship in Beta gatherings and at conventions. Together, we experienced campus trials and tribulations. We traveled all over Europe, celebrated mutual anniversaries. When Winnie and I came home again to Oxford in 1985, their loyal support helped us make the difficult adjustment. Their friendship inspired the writing of this memoir.

Ralph Norman Fey died in January 1989, exactly fifty years from the day on which we first met in Beta Theta Pi. Ours was a friendship that did "last through life." Vale, mi frater!

To the Boulevard
Emmanuel Servais

I'LL ALWAYS REMEMBER that day in Venice, June 2, 1981, even if it started badly. The personnel of the Gritty Palace Hotel went on strike right after breakfast. We were traveling with Barry and Marilee Levey, good friends from Middletown, Ohio. It was their first trip to Italy, and I wanted things to go right. Attorney Levey quickly solved a major problem. There were several unoccupied rooms with keys in the doors. In five minutes we had an ample supply of fresh linen and towels for the rest of our stay.

A Venetian sun warmed our stroll along the canals. We took dozens of pictures of ourselves feeding the pigeons on St. Mark's Square. A sudden noise would drive hundreds of them into the air, their droppings posing a challenge every time. I think there are more cats and dogs per sidewalk in Venice than anywhere else. Since sand and grass are scarce, the deposits of our feline and canine friends add to the hazard created by the pigeons. The sightseer has to look up, and down, as well as all around. I mention this only to explain why I needed to go back to our hotel for a change of shoes. I also wanted to take a short nap before dinner.

As I approached the Gritty Palace Hotel, the concierge pointed excitedly at me through the lobby window. "Oh hell," I thought to myself, "we've been robbed, or burned out, or something."

When I came face-to-face with the concierge, I detected a certain respect in his manner that had been lacking earlier. My Italian is limited, but I got the messagio: "Pregasi chiamare President Reagan in Washington White House."

Forget the elevator. I took the stairs to our room two at a time. I let myself in, reached for the phone and dialed 0. "I would like to talk to the president of the United States at the White House in Washington," I said to the hotel operator.

"Allo, so would I," came the cynical reply, punctuated by a busy signal.

Back downstairs I went for a talk with the concierge, who convinced the operator my request was serious.

A few minutes later we tried again, and made connection, but only with a White House secretary. "I'm sorry, Mr. Dolibois, the president had to leave for a luncheon engagement," she said, "will you be at this number for another hour or so?" I allowed that this could be arranged quite easily.

Off came my shoes, and I settled down for an hour's wait. Or longer. Meanwhile, my good wife Winnie and the Leveys came looking for me. When I told them what I was waiting for, Barry rushed to the portable fridge and opened a bottle of champagne. This had to be good news. The White House wouldn't track me down in Venice for any other reason.

At exactly eight o'clock the phone rang. Barry focused his camera and I picked up the receiver. My hand was shaking.

First the preliminaries of completing the connection. Then a secretary confirming my presence on the line, and next, the voice I'd heard on radio and TV so often.

"Well, what time is it over there?"

"It's eight o'clock in the evening, Mr. President."

"That's good," came the reply. "I called a guy in Australia yesterday, and got him out of bed at four in the morning. I didn't want to do that to you."

Now my shaking stopped. With a lot more confidence I said, "No problem, Mr. President. It's a beautiful evening here in Venice, and we're just getting ready to go have dinner at Harry's Bar. I wish you could join us."

"I wish that were possible," said Ronald Reagan, "but I called to make sure you don't like it too much in Italy. I have another place in mind for you."

Now I was relaxed. But good. "Mr. President, make me an offer I can't refuse." Winnie covered her ears.

"Hey, that's Italian. I saw *The Godfather* too," said the president with a chuckle.

Now we got down to business. Mr. Reagan said he wanted me to be his ambassador to Luxembourg. I didn't have to think about that very long. I accepted with a firm thank you and a pledge to serve to the best of my ability. The president assured me that he had full confidence in me, and added that I had been highly recommended.

At this point I was suddenly moved to blurt out, "Mr. President, I want to tell you that exactly fifty years ago this day, June 2, my father and I left Luxembourg to come to the United States as immigrants."

"I know that," said Ronald Reagan, "that's why I waited until today to call you."

I couldn't swallow the lump in my throat. The immigrant boy of half-century past was to become a United States ambassador, and, of all places, to Luxembourg. And I had actually talked to the president of the United States.

Winnie had been convinced that Ronald Reagan would find the story of my coming to the United States in 1931 romantic; and my return to Luxembourg to interrogate high-ranking Nazis dramatic. These tales, and more, would appeal to Ronald Reagan, the former actor and present chief executive.

In his last campaign speech in 1980 candidate Reagan had said that he would want a diplomatic corps whose members could speak the language, know the history, and understand the culture and the people of the country in which they served. Ohio Congressman Clarence "Bud" Brown, Jr., called me shortly after that speech was broadcast.

"Did you hear Reagan's speech?" Bud asked.

"Yes," I said, "and I think it was great."

"Well, I think he was talking about people with your qualifications," said he. "You're the only person I know who can speak the Luxembourg language. And you have the ideal background to be ambassador to Luxembourg. Shall I toss your hat in the ring?"

I was highly complimented, but convinced it would never fly. I was not a big contributor and had not been officially active in the Republican party.

"Bud," I said, "it's wonderful of you to think of me. I doubt if it'll work, but there's no harm in trying."

There were senators and congressmen who knew of my work on the Fulbright Board. Some of them were fraternity brothers in Beta Theta Pi. Prominent Miami University alumni in business and professions could be counted on to go to bat for me. Influential educators, with whom I had been associated for thirty-four years, would also have some influence. Bud Brown took all the names and went to work. Our own congressman, Tom Kindness, helped persuade the Ohio congressional delegation to endorse me.

Some friends had gotten in touch with Vice President Bush on my behalf. I had never met George Bush, but Winnie and I had known his wife Barbara for some time. Her father, Marvin Pierce, and her mother Pauline had graduated from Miami University. So did her brother Scott.

Like his father, he is a Beta fraternity brother. Scott still jokes about his student days when he was once a baby-sitter for our son Bob.

Marvin Pierce was one of Miami's outstanding alumni. He had earned four letters in each of the four major sports, and was a Phi Beta Kappa graduate and student leader. As president of the McCall Corporation, he had continued the leadership talents demonstrated at Miami, and he never forgot his alma mater. He was active in our alumni program and served as president of the Miami University Foundation when I was director of Development.

Mrs. Bush acknowledged her "Miami connection," and in public appearances in Ohio expressed her pride in her family and its relationship to Miami University. In the spring of 1981, Winnie and I had the pleasure of presenting Barbara Pierce Bush with an Honorary Lifetime Membership in the Miami University Alumni Association. Our personal friendship with Barbara's family aided my nomination.

There was much excitement back in Oxford when we returned from our vacation trip. Since the White House had first called my office at Miami University to locate me in Italy on June 2, everyone had jumped to the right conclusion. The good news had traveled fast.

But after the initial excitement, nothing. The summer passed slowly. I knew the various checks, disclosures, and clearances would drag on. But there were times when I thought I had dreamed the whole thing. I couldn't understand why it took so long to check on my financial status. That could have been done in five minutes.

On 28 July, the government of Luxembourg delivered its "agrément" of my appointment as ambassador, but it wasn't until mid-August that Congressman Kindness called. "Congratulations!" he said. "I'm happy to tell you that the president has forwarded your nomination to the Senate." At last, it was official, and public.

Area newspapers editorialized in my favor. There were TV and radio interviews, and the daily mail brought congratulatory letters and cards from near and far. It was heartwarming. Exciting. Barbara Bush wrote:

I am so thrilled about the good news for Luxembourg!! I can't think of a better family to represent us. You have to represent all that's good about America, and besides that, you know all about Luxembourg—a marriage made in Heaven—

Love and Congratulations to all—
Warmly,
Barbara

On August 18, I received an encouraging note from Senator Richard

G. Lugar of Indiana, who would conduct the confirmation hearings. Four trips to Washington were necessary. We needed to be trained and briefed. I had to be confirmed by the Senate, of course. There were all kinds of forms and documents to sign. And after that, I would be sworn in, and then get a rousing send-off with a visit to the Oval Office.

The confirmation hearing before the Senate Foreign Relations Subcommittee for Europe provided my first encounter with "media politics," or is it "investigative reporting?" On the way to the Capitol for the hearing, the State Department officer who escorted me showed me a copy of my curriculum vitae. He asked me to check it for errors and omissions. I found one immediately. Whoever prepared the material for submission to the committee and the press had completely ignored my membership on the Board of Foreign Scholarships. This was a presidential appointment, and I had been a senior member with eight years of service. During my tenure, I had arranged a retreat for the board and its staff members on the Miami University campus. I had developed the Fulbright alumni program. I had organized a regional conference in Oxford for foreign Fulbright scholars, and even brought the senator himself to Miami University for a commencement address and an honorary degree. It seemed to me this service should be mentioned as part of my qualifications.

The savvy gentleman who had shown me my file winked, and said, "Mr. Dolibois, do you want to be confirmed at a love feast, or do you want to be roasted in a controversy?"

I didn't understand. So he went on, "Who appointed you to the Board of Foreign Scholarships in 1968?"

"President Nixon," I said. And then it dawned on me. This hearing was public, televised, and covered extensively by the print media. Did I want to be identified as "another Nixon man in the Reagan administration?" No way. Forget I ever mentioned it.

The hearing did turn out to be a love feast. Five future ambassadors were being grilled by the committee, but all the attention centered on David Funderburk, slated for Romania. He was a Jesse Helms protégé, and the Democrats on the committee weren't about to give him an easy time. I think this took the heat off the rest of us. I had just come close to being controversial. The media would have had fun with that Nixon connection, innocuous as it was.

But then I did get some extra attention, after all. I had voiced the opinion that Luxembourg was important as a member of NATO and the European Community, as a center of influence. I also said Luxembourg was a good "listening post," by which I meant its being in the heart of Europe provided opportunity to hear all kinds of viewpoints in reaction to U.S. policies. But several reporters understood "listening post" as a potential center for espionage. They wanted to hear more about how I intended to involve the CIA and other intelligence agencies in my embassy program. That concern treated me to some corridor interviews, but I got only five seconds on TV news broadcasts. I ended up not being newsworthy after I explained my statement.

The fourth and final trip to Washington on October 9 was the first leg of our journey to the embassy residence at 22 boulevard Emmanuel Servais in Luxembourg. The one-day stopover was made for the purpose of meeting the president.

I had never been in the Oval Office; I had never met a president of the United States. Our son Bob and his wife Susie were also invited. Susie had worked in the White House for the Nixons and knew some of the staff people still there. This gave us some confidence.

President Reagan received us graciously, as if we were old friends. Other staff members were on hand, to keep things moving I guess. I was given a handsome set of cufflinks, and Winnie a stickpin, with the presidential seal. Official photos were taken, and as we were getting into position, the president said to me: "My appointment of you is meant to be a compliment to the people of Luxembourg. They sent us a boy, we made an American out of him, to come back fifty years later as the representative of the freedom and opportunity that is America."

At many speaking engagements in Luxembourg in the next four years, I shared this remark with my audiences. It always earned appreciative applause.

In the evening of that same October 9, Winnie and I boarded a TWA jumbo jet at Dulles International Airport. Bob and Susie and our two grandchildren, Ryan and Sara, had driven us to Dulles. As we said our tearful goodbyes, we realized, for the first time, that our new life had begun. The smooth flight to Paris—first class—was a good omen. And when the stewardess said, "Would you like another glass of champagne, your Excellency?" I knew that I was going to like this life.

We arrived in France bright and early the next morning and were the guests of the American ambassador, Arthur Hartmann, and his charming wife Donna. Our driver from Luxembourg was to pick us up the next day, Sunday, for the last leg of our journey.

We slept the sleep of the pampered. On Sunday morning, rested and refreshed, with a good breakfast under our belts, we ventured for a leisurely stroll along the Champs Élysées, and then went back to the embassy to get ready for our driver.

My predecessor, Ambassador Jim Lowenstein, had briefed me on the housekeeping staff. Our driver, whose name was Claude Michels, was the only native Luxembourger serving the residence. The other employees were French and Portuguese. The house manager called our room shortly after lunch to announce his arrival, and I went down to the lobby to meet him. There stood Claude, a young man of average height, neatly groomed, trim moustache, and a skeptical look on his face.

We shook hands, and Claude handed me my schedule for the week, a map of Luxembourg, and a list of all the employees and officers of the American embassy in Luxembourg. As I glanced at this material, I could sense Claude looking me over. Then he spoke for the first time to tell me about our departure and route. His English was halting, and he had trouble finding the right words. So I decided to answer him in Luxembourgish to help him out. I'll not forget his surprised grin. Ear to ear is no exaggeration. He'd been told I was born in Luxembourg, but never thought I could speak the language.

Paris was behind us shortly thereafter, and, as we started on to the Autoroute, Claude relaxed, ready for conversation. I answered his question about my background by telling him that I was born in the suburb of Bonnevoie. He nearly ran the car off the road. "That's fantastic," he said. "I *live* in Bonnevoie." He had just been married in the past year. He and his wife Jeanny, a hairdresser, had an apartment not far from where I lived as a boy.

As we got to know people later, it seemed that almost everybody in Luxembourg had a Bonnevoie connection. People would tell me they were also born there, or "my wife comes from Bonnevoie," or their parents, or in-laws. One even told me, "I once had a car accident in Bonnevoie."

Bonnevoie means "good road." Was this another good omen? Sure enough, my own "Bonnevoie connection" was to reap benefits at once. The first invitation we received after our arrival was from a Mr. Nic Mosar, a member of the Chamber of Deputies (comparable to our House of Representatives). The letter of invitation noted that he was born in Bonnevoie and was still living there. He was representing the people of the community in inviting us to be their guests of honor at a soiree arranged just for us. The event would be held in Bonnevoie and "all the people will be there."

Bonnevoie:
The Good Road

THAT PARTY IN BONNEVOIE was the perfect opener for our four years in Luxembourg. All the loose ends of my childhood, and subsequent relationship to my native country, started to come together on that memorable evening.

Luxembourg City, the city of a thousand years, is one of the crossroads of Europe. Its origin dates to 963, when a count of the Ardennes, Siegfried, built a feudal castle on a rock promontory. He named it "Lucilinburhuc," which became Luxembourg. The rock is now called "The Bock," which roughly translates into the hump, or the old goat. The river Alzette makes a loop around the northern, eastern, and southern flanks of that rock. At one time deep cliffs formed natural defenses on those three fronts; the western approaches of early Luxembourg were protected by walls and fortifications.

So Luxembourg was at first a castle, then a fortified city, and eventually a mighty fortress. It didn't become an open city until 1867 when the fortress was partially dismantled. A series of inner and outer walls, or line of palisades, had defended the approaches to the city. Today many of these walls, ruins of towers, and stockades still stand. Within the rock foundation of the city, a network of underground tunnels had been built. These tunnels and caves, called "Kasematten"—casemates—were part of the defense system in earlier years. In later wars these underground passages served as bomb shelters. They were also excellent hiding places for resisters, deserters, and escapees during the Nazi occupation. Art treasures and other valuables were hidden from the German occupiers in the casemates during both wars.

Down below, in the meandering valley of the Alzette, is the lower town of Luxembourg with the ancient suburbs of Grund, Pfaffenthal, and Clausen.

There's not much information about the lives of Siegfried, founder of the dynasty of Luxembourg, and his successors. We know that at one time Luxembourg was much bigger than it is now, and that counts of Luxembourg became emperors of the Holy Roman Empire, kings of Bohemia, and lords of many duchies, marquisades, counties, and smaller domains spread all over Europe.

After the middle of the fifteenth century, the city of Luxembourg was conquered by the troops of King Philippe of Burgundy. During the next four centuries, foreign rulers followed each other in efforts to transform the medieval city into a powerful fortress. After the Burgundians came the Spanish Hapsburg dynasty. Then Louis XIV of France in 1684. Spain dominated Luxembourg again until the Austrian Hapsburgs conquered it and ruled until 1795. The Austrians surrendered to the armies of the French Republic, and Luxembourg remained French until Napoleon's fall in 1814. In 1815, by decision of the Congress of Vienna, Luxembourg once more became the capital of an independent country, the Grand Duchy of Luxembourg.

That's enough history about my old homeland, except for the fact that today Luxembourg, the former "Gibraltar of the North," is not only the "Green Heart of Europe," it is the geographical and political heart as well.

In 1952, the Council of Ministers of the European Coal and Steel Community held its first meeting in Luxembourg. Since then, the High Court of Justice, the Secretariat of the European Parliament, the Common Market, Euratom, the European Investment Bank, and a number of other European institutions have located in Luxembourg.

On many evenings, from our bedroom in the embassy, we could see the setting sun reflected in the thousands of windows of the impressive buildings on the Kirchberg, the European Center. The high-tech Grand Duchess Charlotte Bridge, called "the Red Bridge" by Luxembourgers, leads to those starkly modern structures. The Red Bridge spans the dramatic valley and the suburb Pfaffenthal, which also provided us with spectacular views. At night we could hear the rumble of traffic crossing the bridge to the beginning of the Autobahn which takes it to Trier, Germany. The approaches to the suburbs Kirchberg, Weimershof, and Neudorf also begin at the other end of that tremendous bridge. The past and present have been fused in natural harmony in all sections and suburbs of Luxembourg City. Bonnevoie is the largest of the modern suburbs.

When Winnie and I arrived at the festival hall of Bonnevoie for the

"Dolibois Welcome Soiree," we were absolutely overwhelmed. A welcoming committee met us at the main door and led us into the auditorium. Nic Mosar, obviously a leading citizen of the community, headed the procession. He was relishing every moment of it, making political hay in the process.

Inside the hall, a big band, the Bonnevoie "Fanfare," was tootling away on a rousing Sousa march. The room was packed. There were at least three hundred people giving us an enthusiastic welcome.

A handsome little youngster about four years old presented Winnie with a huge bouquet of flowers. She instinctively leaned forward and kissed the boy on his cheeks—three times—the Luxembourg style. The audience burst into applause; the cameras clicked away. That picture became one of many in the years ahead. No matter where we went, there was always some cute child presenting flowers to "Madame."

The program that night began as soon as introductions were made. We sat in the place of honor, next to the parish priest. On his right sat a charming, elderly lady and her dignified son. I spotted a small cross on his lapel and knew he was also a priest. He was the Abbé André Heiderscheid, director of the *Luxemburger Wort*, a pro-American major newspaper in Luxembourg. He and his mother were there for a special reason. Madame Heiderscheid had been a close friend of my sister Agnes. At age fourteen, she often shared baby-sitter duties with her. I had been their charge. The dear lady was bursting with pride. She took my arm, pulled me toward her, and began crooning a lullaby. "That's what I used to sing to you," she said. Her son started making apologies, but she would have none of that.

"Of course, I call the ambassador by his pet name 'Hansi,' " she announced. "After all I changed his diapers and held him in my arms long before he was 'His Excellency.' " Nobody could argue with that.

Winnie and I were often entertained by the Heiderscheid family after that; the last time was in September 1986 when we were on a private visit to Luxembourg. A few weeks later, Mrs. Heiderscheid died of cancer at age eighty. She had shared her last social outing with us.

The Bonnevoie musicians had been rehearsing songs and music from *Oklahoma!* and *An American in Paris* for weeks. Irving Berlin, Stephen Foster, and John Philip Sousa were not overlooked. One speaker after another came to the podium and regaled the listeners, especially Winnie and me, with stories about the Dolibois family in Bonnevoie. I learned more about my mother and father, my brothers and sisters, in those two hours than I'd ever known before. It was an emotional high I'll never forget. Some of the photographs from that evening show Winnie dabbing her eyes, and I look a bit misty in one or two myself.

After the stories about my family, I was to have my turn. When I stepped up to the mike and tackled my first speech in Luxembourgish, I surprised myself. It came much easier than I ever expected, and, apparently the audience was ready to accept anything. Frankly, I don't remember what I said, and Winnie couldn't help me afterwards as she hadn't yet mastered her understanding of the language.

The speeches and songs ended, we were ushered to the social rooms for refreshments. And when we finally said goodnight, reluctantly and gratefully, we stepped into a miserably cold outside. I spotted two gendarmes patrolling the street and guarding our official car. They had been shivering out there for nearly four hours.

In my embarrassment, being responsible for their discomfort, I offered my hand in apology and appreciation. I learned later that this gesture was reported back to their colleagues. From then on, I was "Mr. Nice Guy" in the eyes of the police and the gendarmerie. We enjoyed special attention in the years ahead, were often treated to a special escort, a parking spot, or directed out of a traffic jam, above and beyond the customary diplomatic courtesy. I resolved to go that extra step whenever possible. I was learning diplomacy.

We carried home some nice mementos of that Bonnevoie soiree. One was a copy of my baptismal certificate, dated December 8, 1918. It was signed by M. Erasmy, the pastor of the parish who had presided at the marriages of four of my brothers and sisters, the baptism of two of us, and the burial of my mother. Twelve years after signing my baptismal certificate, he was the Dechant—the Dean—Erasmy; number one on my imaginary hit list for an offense I will share with you later.

I was born in Bonnevoie on December 4, 1918. My father was Karl Nikolas; my mother was the former Maria Winter. Her family had moved to the Saar from Hungary, my father's to the Saar from Paris. This explains the French name Dolibois, derived from something to do with chopping wood.

My parents grew up in the Saar. They were married in 1898. Six children had been borne by my mother by the time they moved to Luxembourg ten years later.

Papa ruled his family with an iron hand and, literally, put the fear of God into all our hearts. The Church was everything to him. He was highly respected in the community as a layman in the church and an honest hardworking tradesman, a plasterer. He came from a long line of plasterers and builders, and his reputation as a reliable craftsman had spread from the Saar into Luxembourg. He often did special jobs in Luxembourg for a builder named Devas. This meant commuting about 40 kilometers by train, and sometimes walking, pushing a handcart loaded with tools and materials ahead of him. Mr. Devas persuaded Papa Dolibois to settle in Luxembourg permanently. In 1908 Papa bought the construction business from Mr. Devas and my family made its home in Bonnevoie.

My "pattern of circles" came into play again when Winnie and I met the daughter of Mr. Devas in 1983. She was now Mme. Schockweiler, an elderly widow who remembered my family well. She took great pride in telling one and all about the smart thing her father did in bringing the Dolibois family to Luxembourg.

The seventh Dolibois child, my sister Elizabeth, "Liesel," was born in Luxembourg in 1910. I became number eight, three weeks after the signing of the armistice that ended World War I—the "war to end all wars."

The U.S. Army of Occupation was billeted in requisitioned Luxembourg homes, and our address was as good as any in Bonnevoie. Furthermore, my oldest sister Marie had turned an attractive nineteen, and had no trouble catching the eye of a soldier from Akron, Ohio. Their romance blossomed so well that by the time I was baptized, the family had consented to give me the same middle name as that of Albert Ernest Felton. Marie and Albert planned to get married and leave for America as soon as he was discharged.

Then tragedy struck. My mother died in the Spanish flu epidemic which ravaged Europe that winter. She was laid to rest in the cemetery of Bonnevoie just ten days after I was born. Her sudden death added heavy burdens to our family situation. Luxembourg had suffered the full effects of the wartime Allied blockade and my father found it difficult to provide for his large family. I'm told his hair turned white in less than a year, and his outlook on life was equally frosted during those postwar years. With Mother gone, farms destroyed, and the economy in shambles, milk for a newborn baby was almost impossible to find. The Yanks came to the rescue. Small cans of Carnation condensed milk began to arrive home each evening with my patron, Albert Felton. This American milk literally kept me alive.

Marie now bore primary responsibility for raising baby Jean—henceforth to be known as "Hansi." I've always had trouble with my name. Jean is French for Johannes, which is German. That becomes "Hans" for a nickname, and the diminutive "Hansi." I didn't get all that cleared up officially until I was naturalized in 1941. For one dollar extra, the court named me John.

Marie also cared for the younger brothers and sisters. Liesel was just eight. Kasi and Ted were ten and twelve. The teenagers were Heinrich at seventeen, Karl fifteen, and Agnes fourteen. I came to know my mother only through the eyes of my brothers and sisters. Papa never spoke of her. I learned that she was quiet and warmhearted and lived only for her husband and children. Her pictures show her as petite, black-eyed, and serious.

Albert Felton left without his Marie but came back to Luxembourg in 1929 to marry her and take her to America. Meanwhile, my brother Ted had taken to the road as soon as he was eighteen. He worked his way across the Atlantic and finally settled in Chicago where the trade he had learned from Papa served him well.

At an intersection of five streets in Bonnevoie-Sud stands the parish church. Papa decided to build a house for his family on what was to become rue Gounod, between the park and the church. My brothers had all taken up the building trade—plastering, stucco-work, bricklaying. All except Karl. He wanted to be a priest, the only other calling our Papa would respond to with favor. He wouldn't have allowed any other choice. Papa was the original author of "My way."

I can remember that house being built at number 8, rue Gounod. I think I was six years old when I started to help mix sand and cement, carried buckets of water, and stacked boards and bricks. I decided, then and there, the building trade was not for me.

I also remember that we always had boarders in our new house, cousins or in-laws from the Saar. They worked for my father and brothers during the building season. Room and board were part of their wages.

In 1925 I started school in Bonnevoie-Sud. My father's signature appears on each one of the trimester grade reports of the "Livret Scolaire." This green record-book of my educational progress shows what I studied and how well. It also tells about my conduct, orderliness, and application. It's a complete record of all six years in elementary school and it proves that I was one of the three best pupils in grades one and two of the school in Bonnevoie-Sud. Very early in my school years I had concluded that education was the best way out of inhaling plaster dust and lugging sand and cement the rest of my life.

Papa was of some consequence in Bonnevoie-Sud, the stately "Schweizer" of the parish. That translates into "Swiss" but I think deacon comes closer. Every Sunday, every Holy Day, and at every church function, Papa would don his flowing robe, in color with the religious event: purple during Advent; black for funeral masses and Good Friday; red on ordinary days. There was a beret, trimmed in gold, to match. He carried an imposing staff with a brass knob on the end. Papa also sported an impressive Hindenburg mustache, the kind that connects with the sideburns. He looked formidable, and terrified all the restless kids at mass. Papa's duty was to maintain *order*. He did it with dignity and pride. He'd police up and down the aisle, and squelch any squirm or whisper with a look that put the fear of God in all of us. Papa also had a twinkle in his eye which tempered the stern manner.

The Schweizer was at the head of every church procession. When the Parish of Bonnevoie made its annual pilgrimage to the Cathedral of Notre Dame in the city, on foot all the way, the Schweizer led the prayerful. Papa was all pomp and circumstance. For years after we came to the United States, a columnist of the *Luxemburger Wort*, whose pen name was Sylvester, wrote about my father. He paid his tributes on special holy days when Papa was missed. There are no such personages as Schweizer in Luxembourg churches today. I guess they could never find anyone to fill Papa's shoes.

Papa had no outside interests. No music, no sports, no theater. Vacations were not part of our life. My oft-repeated pleas for a bicycle always got the same answer, "A bicycle is unnecessary; you just pump your legs off to give your rear end a ride."

Besides being the church-Schweizer, Papa had only one other pastime, his Sunday afternoon pinochle game. For all my childhood years in Luxembourg, the Sunday schedule was always the same. I became an altar boy at a very early age, and never got by with just one mass. I served three or four each Sunday. After that I could pursue my own interests—until five o'clock. That's when I was due at the Café Birnbaum, where Papa and his pals were finishing their game. I was treated to a lemonade, and then Papa and I would walk home, hand in hand.

That Sunday evening walk home was always the highlight of the week for me, the only time Papa and I had a genuine father and son relationship. The rest of the time he paid little attention to me. He was a good man, honest to a fault. He was strict, quick to punish any wrong, but always fair. He was devoted to his family. But he wasn't much fun, and never gave advice or encouragement. He had his collection of sayings, such as, "God's mill grinds slowly, but surely," delivered with a stern look and a warning finger pointed toward heaven. Papa was especially good at warnings. When he said "Pass op!" (from the German "Pass Auf!") he meant you had now stretched his patience as far as it would go. "Watch out" was all the warning needed before his leather belt came off fast as lightning. He didn't encourage reading. "You'll ruin your eyes," he would say. But my boyhood stature was enhanced considerably by Papa's high standing in the community as a church leader. I was often elected captain of whatever was being organized.

Among my personal accomplishments, I was good at marbles. Ours were made of colored clay. The Luxembourg marble game started with a circle, three yards in diameter, drawn in hard dirt. In the middle of the circle was a hole about two inches deep and three inches wide. The marble was placed at the rim of the circle, and shot into the hole with thumb and forefinger. The one whose marble landed in the hole with the least number of shots won the game. A hole-in-one was super. The marble was called a jick, and if it got wet the color came off. Experienced marble shooters always had rainbow colored hands. Their pocket linings were also a mass of color.

Each kid carried a pocket knife—unless he was a sissy. Our version of mumblety-peg was similar to, but more deadly, than the U.S. version. A star player was one who could devise the most complicated flip of the knife blade into the grass, usually from a kneeling position. My best shot called for special talent. I started by holding my nose between thumb and forefinger of the left hand. This formed a loop into which I would place my right hand, holding the knife blade at the tip. Now I would flip my knife into the ground. If it stuck, I would get another turn, with an even more complicated shot.

The pocket knife came in handy for another great sport. This one called for a stick around three feet long and an inch thick. A piece, three inches long, was cut off the stick. We would then whittle a point at each end of the short peg. This was now called a "Vull"—a bird. The Vull was placed on the ground and whacked on one of the points with the stick. This would make the bird flip into the air, so that one could smack it with the stick and send it flying as far as possible. The guy who could whittle the best balance into his peg and hit it the farthest with the stick won the round.

That trusty pocket knife could get a boy in trouble, too. A cousin named Ewald was visiting us and cut his thumb severely while whittling. In those days, when little boys or girls had such accidents, they were encouraged to make "kaka." This would get rid of bad germs that cause infection. It would also calm the wounded and put his mind to other things. I can still see fat little Ewald sitting on the chamber pot in the middle of our kitchen. I swore I would never cut myself and be subjected to such indignity.

As 1927 rolled around, my brothers no longer saw any advantage in working for my father. One by one they broke away to try it on their own. Heinrich returned to the Saar, where he found a wife. Kasi did the same. Ted went to America, and Agnes moved to Paris where she became a seamstress.

My brother Karl had lost his interest in the priesthood and quit the seminary. Later he studied pharmacy, and branched out into photography. Eventually he would go to work for the Drogerie Bertogne—a drugstore on the main street in the city. Bertogne was the first to open a photo shop, and Karl was its manager.

Liesel had met a successful woodcarver of German descent. She was planning to marry him as soon as she could. So Papa decided to give up the big house in Bonnevoie, and move the rest of his dwindling family to a section of the city known as the Gare. We lived on the main avenue which leads to downtown Luxembourg, just on the other side of the viaduct across the Petrusse Valley. The viaduct is one of six major bridges connecting the city on the cliffs with its suburbs.

I was now attending the Neipperg School of Luxembourg-Gare. There were fifteen of us in the third grade, all boys. The fourth grade was a mixed class with twenty-seven boys and girls. I wasn't holding up too well against this new competition and had to struggle to keep my rank in the top third of the class.

Throughout elementary school in Luxembourg I shared my desk with the same boy, Jean Kayser, a likable fellow with great talent in math and art. Jean was blonde, blue-eyed, my size. I was dark-eyed, with brown hair. We made a good pair and became fast friends. Fifty years later, my neighbor across from the American embassy in Luxembourg was the same Jean Kayser, a retired architect. We saw each other often between 1981 and 1985, to trade memories as we once shared boyhood dreams.

In front of me sat René Kelsen, a feisty, highly competitive lad. We were always out-daring and outdoing each other, but our friendship was firm. During World War II, René was active in the Resistance, and served as an interpreter and guide for Third Army Reconnaissance. After the war he joined Goodyear in Europe and became a successful executive with that company. His final years before retirement were spent in Fulda, Germany. René and his wife Runnes went to Luxembourg when he retired in 1985, and we picked up our friendship where we left off fifty years earlier.

My father, sister Marie, and I lived in a second-story flat on the avenue de la Gare. In the building next to ours, the Bradtké family operated a well-known art and gift shop and a prominent art gallery. The Bradtké sons, Nikky and Paul, were my friends. The family more or less adopted me and gave me a taste of what could be obtained through greater knowledge and hard work. They thrilled me with my first automobile ride—in a Citröen—and a visit to their fabulous summer home in the northern part of Luxembourg. I was eleven years old.

When Albert Felton came to take his bride, my sister Marie, to Akron, Papa and I were alone. And times got worse as the Great Depression hit Luxembourg. Overcome by renewed difficulties, Papa became dispirited and discouraged. A cousin from the Saar, Brigitta, came to live with us and did the housework. We lived marginally. Barefoot in the summer, not by choice but necessity, dressed in hand-me-down clothes from my brothers, I still enjoyed my boyhood in Luxembourg. I look back on it now with only positive memories.

On occasion, my brothers Heinrich and Karl would see to it that I didn't miss out on a special event, like the traditional fair in August, or some religious festival or excursion. But most of the time I was on my own. I developed an assertive, competitive attitude. I was self-motivated, determined to never climb a ladder with a load of bricks or a sack of cement on my shoulders in order to make a living. I saw my white-haired Papa at age fifty-seven doing just that, day in and day out. It was not for me. And as my family was drifting apart, I began to depend on friends for affection and support. I formed and valued friendships that would last through life.

In all, I guess I was growing up a typical Luxembourger, stubborn, determined to succeed, with great pride in my country and its traditions. The Luxembourger knows where he comes from and is inspired to be worthy of his heritage and national motto: "Mir woelle bleiwen wat mir sin," "We want to remain what we are."

Luxembourg is great for those who love the outdoors. A part of the country about thirty minutes from the city is known as Little Switzerland. It offers the best of everything to the hiker. With its jumble of rock and woodland scenery, its curious rock formations, caves, gorges, and steep footpaths, this is part of the German-Luxembourg wildlife park. The castle of Beaufort, on the northern outskirts of this area, has special charm for young and old. The ruins are well-preserved. As one visits them it is easy to imagine life in that setting five hundred years ago. The chief attraction around the "Müllerthal" of Little Switzerland is Echternach. It was here that a thousand years ago St. Willibrord founded a monastery whose illuminated manuscripts were to become the most famous in Europe. A "dancing procession" in honor of St. Willibrord is unique in the world. It is held every Whit-Tuesday and brings thousands of pilgrims and tourist visitors from every country. Hundreds of parishes from all over Luxembourg participate in the dancing procession. It's so named because the participants—dancers, six-abreast—move to a repetitious, haunting melody. They dance in rhythm, three steps forward, two steps back, swaying from side to side. The music is provided by the village bands which accompany each group of pilgrims.

Whenever I could scrape up a few francs to pay the fare, I would make a trip on the "Jhangeli" to Little Switzerland, the Müllerthal, or Echternach. The Jhangeli, Luxembourgish for "little John," was the name of a unique train—two passenger cars drawn by a box-like, coal-fired locomotive. The latter spewed the blackest smoke imaginable in working up the power to haul the passengers from Luxembourg-Gare to Echternach through the beautiful countryside.

When we arrived at our destination on the Jhangeli two hours or more later, our faces and clothes were covered with a fine layer of soot. But we didn't mind that. Those holiday trips allowed for hiking, climbing, picnicking. We roasted potatoes and wieners over an open fire and fell in love over and over again with the beauty of the land.

Winnie and I never lost an opportunity to revisit those old haunts, to walk where I used to run. The Jhangeli is no more. The government has made a bicycle and hiking trail out of the road bed on which the tracks once led to Echternach. Along this trail there are still a few of the cafés which were rest stops for Jhangeli passengers. Now hikers rest on a terrace, drink a good Moselle wine or Luxembourg beer, and think of the good old days. Our favorite café was the Café Regenwetter, whose owner, the Widow Regenwetter, was visibly overcome with joy every time the American ambassador and his wife stopped at this lovely spot. My autographed photo hangs over her bar today. The dear lady, in her eighties, loved to speak of the days when she hid American and British pilots from the Germans. After the liberation, American GIs often came to the Café Regenwetter for relaxation.

Farther north in Luxembourg is the Ardennes region, the Oesling or "Êsleck" as the Luxembourgers call it. With its hillocks, its green forests of beech and fir, its slopes glowing with yellow gorse, and trout streams crystal clear, this heavenly landscape is what you dream about. It is dotted with ancient castles, none of which have lost their romantic charm. The wind-swept heights and sleepy valleys delighted me as a boy, and brought back vivid memories when I hiked them again as a man, fifty years later.

There was not much work in Luxembourg in depression days. Papa occasionally found odd jobs. We still owned our house in Bonnevoie, and the rent-income supplemented his earnings. We gave up the flat on the avenue de la Gare, and rented a small house in the Petrusse Valley. The Petrusse is a tiny stream that runs into the Alzette River a short kilometer from where Papa and I lived. Our house was in the shadow of the viaduct into the city. From my bedroom window I could see the steeples of the cathedral, the roof of the British embassy, and the walls which were part of the early fortifications of the city of Luxembourg.

On the far side of the Petrusse, opposite our house, loom the cliffs on which rests old and new Luxembourg City. The face of the cliffs is dotted with the openings that lead into the tunnels and caves of the casemates. The network of ancient passageways and chambers was our playground which we frequented almost daily in our search for adventure. Officially, they were off-limits. But that didn't stop us from scaling the walls to the nearest opening, crawling inside on our bellies far enough to reach the larger tunnels. From there we could walk upright and explore the maze of caves and connecting passages to our heart's content. Of course, we were always scared to death at what might lurk around the next corner. Flashlights were an unaffordable luxury. Candles and homemade torches lit our way. We invented all kinds of sporting events in those historic ramparts. We were Spaniards fighting Austrians, French warriors battling Spaniards, and Count Siegfried receiving the victors after each slaughter. We were early Christians holding forbidden masses in the catacombs, and dragon-slayers wrestling primeval underground beasts.

Certain tunnels and caves belonged to just our gang. Sometimes, our make-believe battles were set aside for real "wars," fought with gangs from other communities trying to muscle in on our territory. These fights never amounted to much more than confiscating candles and torches, raiding supplies, and scaring each other in the dark with blood-curdling screams.

Entering the casemates is now forbidden although a small section of the 16-kilometer networks of tunnels has been set aside as a tourist attraction. For a small admission fee one can walk around in the well-lighted passages and cavities. And chances are one would never run into "intruders" in the total darkness of a cave as we did on occasion. One time we came upon a man who was standing in the niche of a cave, his pants around his knees, exposing himself. When our torch lights fell on him, and our frightened screams echoed in the hollows, he took off in one direction, we in the other. After that incident none of us went near the caves for a long time.

Now and then we'd stumble onto young men and women who sought privacy in the casemates. We had little understanding of what they were doing, but our hooting and hollering would quickly break up their trysts.

Papa never talked to me about sex. Perish the thought! And there was no enlightenment on the street. Our strict Catholic upbringing made talking about such things a mortal sin. I suppose there wasn't much to arouse our curiosity, either. No magazine racks, TV, or sex education in the school. Nobody was playing doctor with the opposite sex in our gang of ten- to twelve-year-olds. Instead, we played "Holy Mass," vesting ourselves in capes, robes, and sheets, chanting in Latin, and holding confession.

But I did get a sex education. Alfonse, an elderly watchmaker and devout layman of St. Michael's Church, was in charge of the altar boys. We looked upon him as a holy man, obeyed his every command. One day Alfonse ordered me to meet him in the wardrobe of the municipal theater which he also supervised. Among the racks of dusty costumes and boxes of old hats and shoes, he sat on a single chair, held me on his lap, and solemnly explained how babies are made. I hadn't given the matter much thought before then, and after that was embarrassed every time I came near Alfonse.

The fathers of the Redemptorist Monastery let me be an altar boy in their beautiful church. For the rest of my boyhood in Luxembourg, I spent every Sunday morning with the padres. I served from three to six masses because each of them had to say his mass. I was working my way into heaven, and I think Papa was very proud of me, although he never said so. What I liked best was the generous breakfast the padres served us. We could use their library and watch movies in their theater in the afternoon. Thus I worshipped God in the morning; Tom Mix, Hoot Gibson, and Charlie Chaplin in the afternoon. Having been enlightened about sex by Alfonse, I could also enjoy the romancing of Willie Fritsch and Lillian Harvey.

I loved to read the books by Karl May, a German author who wrote stories about the American Wild West. In my fantasies I dealt with the rebellious Indians who were the enemies of my hero "Shatterhand." When my sister Marie sent me a cowboy outfit, I was the undisputed leader of the entire neighborhood.

Down in the Petrusse Valley, looking up at the spires of the church and the towers of the palace, I could dream of living in one of the villas on top of the cliff. Or riding in a limousine past the Grand Ducal Palace. But I knew it was only a dream, the impossible dream.

Yet, one day I did make contact with royalty. It was during the Christmas season. I recall the time of year because I was filled with a strong yearning for something that would prove there was a "Christkind"—a Christchild—who would not forget a poor boy in the valley. On my way home from church, I stopped to gawk at all the windows filled with toys and other goodies. The window at Namur's, the chocolate store on the Grand Rue, was particularly tempting. I gaped longingly at the display and then stepped away. Ouch! I had stepped on someone's toes. I looked up to apologize and stared right into the face of Her Royal Highness, Grand Duchess Charlotte of Luxembourg. I nearly fainted. Surely I would be packed off to jail immediately. The Grand Lady, in all her beauty, put her hand on my head and said, "D'ass gud, mei jong, neischt geschitt."

I've never forgotten that warm smile and that lovely voice telling me everything was "all right, my boy, no harm done." I recalled that smile and that voice when I had the privilege of representing the United States at her funeral in 1985. She had ruled Luxembourg forty-five years before abdicating in 1964 in favor of her son, the present Grand Duke Jean. I saw her in person only once after trampling on her foot so unceremoniously years ago. It was at the wedding of her grandaughter in 1982. Winnie and I were part of the Diplomatic Corps, sitting in the front rows. Grand Duchess Charlotte sat in place of honor next to her sister-in-law, the former Empress Zita of Austria.

That was a long way from the Petrusse Valley of 1931. To get from down below to the top of that cliff took fifty years, via Akron, Ohio, and across three thousand miles of Atlantic waters.

The Americanization of a Luxembourger

"THIS IS GOING TO BE a special day," I said to myself that Sunday morning in March 1931.

A warmer, brighter sun had awakened me before the old clock in our living room had struck six. Maybe I felt good because it was my turn to ring the bells at church. Furthermore, there would be a rare Pontifical Mass. The bishop was visiting the monastery. I dressed and wasted no time getting into town. I counted 139 steps climbing out of the Petrusse Valley to the Old Avenue, the main thoroughfare from the railroad station to the city. It was renamed Franklin D. Roosevelt Boulevard after World War II. I crossed it at the Cravat Hotel, turned up the rue Chimay to the rue des Capucins. The city was just coming to life. Early churchgoers were hurrying to St. Michael's Church, to the cathedral, or to the monastery church of the Redemptorists. I got there first.

Brother Nikolas was ready with instructions when I came into the sacristy. "Hansi, today you must ring the bell five minutes longer than usual," he said. "I hope you feel strong."

I rushed off to the bell tower. Instead of the usual three minutes, I was allowed five more. Great joy! The huge bell was attached to a heavy rope, about two inches thick. The rope hung from the belfry, and on its end was a big knot, a "seat" for the bellringer. I pulled the rope three or four times before any sound was heard. Then the bell was in full swing and the clapper connected for the first powerful "bong." After that, it was all in the rhythm: pull down and let up. Once we were on the right beat, I sat on the knot and rode up and down as the bell went through its arc. I was just the right weight for this job. How I loved to make that joyful sound! The whole city, and all the people in the suburbs of Grund, Pfaffenthal, and Clausen could hear my bell.

The morning got even better when Brother Nikolas assigned me to attend the bishop himself. But what made this Sunday in March so memorable didn't happen until I went to meet Papa at the Café Birnbaum in the afternoon.

I wondered why Papa seemed especially glad to see me. And why I was allowed to have a delicious tart with my usual lemonade. Papa sprang the big surprise on me as we were walking home. The sliver of a new moon was appearing in the darkening sky. We were just getting across the railroad bridge.

He stopped walking, held my hand tighter and took a deep breath. "We are going to America and live with Maria and Albert."

I was speechless. America! Cowboys and Indians! Skycrapers! Papa went on to tell me that my sister had written and it was final. He had already checked on immigration visas and all the other red tape involved. There was nothing to keep us in Luxembourg, except time. It would be months before everything was in order and I was not to tell anyone just yet.

Not telling anyone was the hardest part. I couldn't think about anything else in the days that followed. "Akron" was the first English word I put in my vocabulary. It is derived from the Greek "akros"—high place. It sure became that for me. As for our secret, I couldn't keep it after all. I needed a second opinion.

"Albert, I have something to tell you," I said to my good friend Albert Stoltz. We were sitting on the steps of his house after a soccer game. "But you must promise not to tell anyone," I added.

Albert could be trusted. I told him we were going to America, and then poured out my concerns and fears. I could speak no English. I had never even seen a real gun. How would I defend myself against the Indians? And they don't play soccer in Akron, Ohio, although my brother-in-law Albert had written to me about a game called baseball.

On and on I went. I was glad I told my friend Albert everything. He reassured me. He had come to Luxembourg from France. He had to learn Luxembourgish and had to make new friends too. It had all worked out for him, as it would work out for me. Albert was a good friend, and I would hate to leave him.

We didn't see each other again until fifty years later, when Albert heard about the new American ambassador in Luxembourg. His search for me had ended at last. "I kept looking for you in England, in France, and especially Luxembourg during the war," he told me. "I was sure our paths would cross somewhere."

Albert had been active in the Luxembourg Army and the Resistance organization, had worked with the Luxembourg government in exile, and was a close associate of His Royal Highness Prince Felix, the Prince Consort of the Grand Duchess Charlotte. When Luxembourg was liberated on September 10, 1944, Prince Felix was the first among Allied officers to set foot on Luxembourg soil. He associated often with Americans in Luxembourg after that, and Albert Stoltz had asked him to be on the lookout for a former Luxembourger named Dolibois. Ironically, Prince Felix and I met in the summer of 1945 when I was stationed in Mondorf, Luxembourg. He and his aide, Captain "Kit" Koch, came to Mondorf as guests of Col. B. C. Andrus, the commandant of the prison for the high-ranking Nazis. Andrus was my CO, and I was invited to the party. Unfortunately, I was using the name Gillen in place of Dolibois. If I had been using my right name, Prince Felix might have recognized it; Albert Stoltz would have been told that his onetime schoolmate of the Neipperg School had been found. Instead, another thirty-seven years passed before Albert and I could sit together again.

One other person knew our secret. M. Erasmy, the parish priest who had baptized me, left Bonnevoie sometime in 1929 to become the pastor of St. Michael's Church in the city. He had continued his close friendship with my father and Papa told him about our plans to emigrate to the United States. Eventually we decided that we shouldn't keep the secret any longer and in no time at all, my schoolmates and neighborhood friends were told of our intentions. Almost every occasion was now "the last time we'll be doing this together." I started to get cold feet. Did I really want to leave my friends, my home, my security? I began to hope something might happen to change our plans and we wouldn't have to leave after all. That hope almost became reality when an unpleasant incident came up.

Young and old of all the parishes in the Grand Duchy of Luxembourg make an annual pilgrimage to the Cathedral of Notre Dame. They do this during an eight-day festival in early May—the Octave. It is in honor of Mary, the patron saint of Luxembourg, the Consoler of the Afflicted. It is the principal religious event of the year. There are daily processions, prayerful gatherings, and inspirational high masses. It's a festive occasion, a centuries-old tradition.

To accommodate the many tourists and visitors, dozens of temporary restaurants and food stands are erected on the Place Guillaume, the market square near the cathedral. The smells of baked fish and pommes frites, sausages and sauerkraut, popcorn, chocolate, and nougat, mingle with that of waffles and cotton candy. There are vendors selling toys and balloons, religious statuary, rosaries, and blessed amulets. Barkers in

gaudy costumes promote their games of chance, shooting galleries, lot-
teries, and carousels. Ice creams for the young, beer and wine for the old.
Anything and everything. It's a super occasion. Only the big fair, the
Schobermesse, in August can surpass it.

Since I was leaving Luxembourg, I would never be able to go to an
Octave festival again. So this last time had to be special, and my friend
Jempy would see to it. Jempy (for Jean-Pierre) invited me to be his guest.
He had saved his allowance for the Octave, and he would pay for every-
thing all day long. I would remember him always over there in America.

On Octave Sunday we wandered from stand to stand, gorging ourselves on all the goodies, playing all the games, and shopping for souvenirs that would remind me of Jempy and Luxembourg.

On the day following, Jempy didn't come to school. Someone else did.
Schoolmaster Welfring (he looked like the movie star Adolphe Men-
jou), was taking us through the arithmetic lesson—in German—when
there was a knock on the door. A firm knock, ominous. Someone wanted
to see me, someone important. In the hall stood the curé of the souls of
the Dolibois family, the Monsignor M. Erasmy, dean of all the pastors.

"Gelobt Sei Jesus Christus," I gave the respectful greeting we'd been
taught to use in addressing a priest. I guess "Praise the Lord" comes
close to it. But I barely got the words out of my mouth before he had
grabbed me by the ear and forced me to my knees. Then he boxed my
ears right and left until I saw stars.

"You are a thief," he hissed. "You will go to prison. You will never go
to America; they don't want thieves over there. You are a disgrace to
your poor dead mother and your saintly father."

I had no idea what this was all about, and this deputy vicar of Christ
wasn't about to tell me. Mr. Welfring came out of the classroom, and the
pastor stopped whacking me. He pointed his finger at me and told the
schoolmaster why I was being punished.

My friend Jempy had stolen money from the cash register in his parents' store, and used it to entertain me at the festival. When the theft was
discovered, he claimed it had been my idea, that I had coerced him into
stealing the money. His mother reported my crime to Monsignor
Erasmy, who decided to take the law into his own hands.

Mr. Welfring had a sense of justice. He asked me if the charge was
true, and when I denied it, he believed me. He sent me back to class. My
ears and cheeks were fiery-red, but there were no tears. No one in my
class ever learned what happened. Mr. Welfring and Monsignor
Erasmy apparently worked out some way to resolve the matter, while I
lived in deadly fear the next two weeks, sure the police would come to
arrest me any moment. My generous friend Jempy avoided me when he

came to school a day later. We never spoke to each other again. As for Monsignor Erasmy, he and I would meet again some day under different circumstances.

I think the worst aspect of this episode was not having anyone in whom I could confide. I knew that Papa would never understand. I had to wrestle with my fears alone. So when Papa announced shortly after this incident that we were leaving Luxembourg by the end of the month, I was ready to go.

We crossed the tiny bridge over the Petrusse for the last time on June 2, 1931. My brother Karl and my sister Liesel walked behind us as we climbed the steps out of our valley and followed the Avenue de la Gare to the railroad station. My brother Heinrich had taken a longer way around, pushing a handcart with our suitcases up the winding road. No one spoke. We wouldn't see each other again, and we didn't know how to put our feelings into words. I was leaving everyone and everything I knew for a strange land, far across the sea. There was only one consolation. I would be with my sister (my "Mom") again, and I would have a real home and family.

In the weeks following, my mood must have been such that very little registered with me. I guess I wasn't even excited about the long train rides, the ocean voyage, and the prospect of seeing many new sights. I recall that Papa and I spent two weeks in the Saar with aunts, uncles, and cousins, with my brother Kasi and his wife Klärchen. My brother Heinrich stayed with us in the Saar and finally put us on the train to Antwerp, Belgium, for the first leg of our long journey to Ohio on June 17.

The SS *Lapland* of the Belgian Line was our ship of passage. It was a comfortable steamer, 18,600 tons. I remember seeing icebergs somewhere at sea, and I recall being seasick for several days. In short, the boat trip was memorable only in that it brought us safely across the Atlantic and ended on a special American holiday. It was the Fourth of July.

I was awakened by the sound of shooting and the tooting of horns. The shooting turned out to be fireworks; the horns and sirens were those of ships in New York Harbor. I had rushed to the deck to see the most breathtaking sight of my life. There stood the Statue of Liberty, with torch on high. "Welcome to the United States!" she seemed to be shouting.

And then I saw my first skyscrapers. I had never seen such tall buildings. For the first time I began to sense the adventure ahead. I was awed, scared, fascinated, thrilled.

The mood of celebration persisted all day. Since it was a holiday, our ship couldn't dock. We remained at anchor, a short distance from the Statue of Liberty, until the morning of July 5. We had a festive dinner on board the *Lapland*, a rousing welcome to America. We wore red, white, and blue hats, tossed streamers, and shouted goodwill messages in a dozen different languages. A fantastic fireworks display capped the evening. Thousands of torches lit up the Liberty statue. What a sight! What a welcome!

The moment Papa and I cleared customs and debarked our ship, we were in the hands of Travelers' Aid. We carried written instructions from my sister Marie and from our travel agency in Luxembourg. Our guide took us on a short tour of Manhattan, and then put us on the train to Ohio. I must have been in a state of shock. I don't remember anything of what I saw or what transpired.

I came to life only when we were just an hour or two out of Akron. Papa nudged me. "We'll soon be there," he said. He disappeared into the rest room with his suitcase, and reappeared some time later, dressed for an arrival in style. He was wearing the same suit he wore when he was married in 1898—morning coat, white starched collar, flowing necktie, and striped trousers. On his head, a white Panama hat. All this, along with his imposing mustache, identified Papa as someone to be reckoned with. He was all dignity, the Schweizer from Bonnevoie. I was wearing a suit, too, but with short pants. I had a visor cap to match.

Thus we stepped off the train in Akron, to be greeted by Maria and Albert, Albert's sister and her husband, and a band of neighbors. We were loaded into a big car, the biggest ever, and in no time at all I was in my new home on Spaulding Street. At the festive family reunion that evening, I felt far, far away from little Luxembourg.

Spaulding Street is at the foot of North Hill, off Tallmadge Avenue, near Cuyahoga Street. Our neighborhood was a hodgepodge of first generation Americans whose origins were Italy, Germany, Poland, England, and, of course, Luxembourg. I soon came to know Pete Vitto, Victor Roman, and Jack LaCause. My neighbors were Ted Modzeleski on one side and Franky Mabius on the other. There was Joe Patsy, John Urinski, and Roland Farwell; Cessie Murawski, Frances Paka, and Theresa Pescionere. I got to know them all in short time, by sign language mostly. I also learned that they were called Wops or Dagos, Polacks, and Jerries. I was soon dubbed Heinie or Krauthead. (Even today many Americans think Luxembourg is a city in Germany.) Nobody took offense at what we now call ethnic slurs. Life apparently was less complicated then.

Baseball! God, how would I ever master that difficult sport? And why does a football have pointed ends instead of being sensibly round? What were they saying to me? What did *that* mean? I was asking myself a hundred questions and I became more homesick for Luxembourg each passing day. Worst of all, I was now expected to go to school. It was September.

My sister Marie walked me up the hill to Findley School. I wasn't at all excited about the uncertainties ahead. The principal of Findley School was Miss Katherine B. Casswell. I could see the name and title on the big desk in her office.

"Now, you go on home, Mrs. Felton, and leave young John—is that the name you want us to use?—with us," she said to my sister, who told me about it later. Miss Casswell had also inquired about my age. Going on thirteen meant the seventh or eighth grade. "We'll test him first."

I stared at the test. I returned the paper, blank. My English vocabulary was a total of fifty words, some not for use in polite society. (I was a fast learner on Cuyahoga Street.) I went home heartbroken that afternoon. "They put me in kindergarten," I sobbed. "I'm thirteen years old. Everybody is laughing at me." It was a disaster.

But my brother-in-law Albert was philosophic about it. In his fine German, learned from his parents who were immigrants too, he explained that this was a challenge—an opportunity to learn English "the proper way" from the start. They were doing me a favor. It was not an insult. So back I went the next day. I buckled down, spent a few weeks in kindergarten, a few more at each of the next four levels, and by the end of the first semester, I was firmly settled in the sixth grade. The teachers in Findley School had done me a big favor. English was my best subject all through high school and college.

I got along well that first year in Findley School, but from time to time I was summoned to Miss Casswell's office for fighting. The best way to handle those who laughed at my accent or snickered when I opened the door instead of closing the window, was with my fists. As time went on, I got respect and saw less of the principal. I was becoming Americanized—slowly but surely. God's mill was grinding.

I had a home, a roof over my head and three meals a day. Albert Felton was a devoted hardworking husband and father who provided a good life for his family. He was always kind to me and willing to help in every way within his ability. Papa was comfortable, in good health, kept a fine vegetable garden, and did odd jobs around the house. Occasionally he would have a small cement or brick job in the neighborhood.

So my future was up to me. I was soon self-supporting as far as clothes and spending money were concerned. Albert owned four acres of strawberries, part of an old family farm where his brother lived. During strawberry season I was a champion picker, and in early evenings I went from house to house throughout the neighborhood peddling quarts of fresh strawberries out of the crates I hauled on my wagon.

I had another job. Every Saturday and Sunday morning and during vacations I helped Albert deliver milk on his Averill Dairy Company truck. It meant getting up at 4:00 A.M. to be at the dairy to load up by five. We worked as a team. Albert drove, and I ran the full bottles to the porches and brought the empties back. On the way home from work, Albert would teach me how to drive his Model T Ford.

I also washed windows and cars, and mowed lawns. So I earned enough to keep myself in decent clothes, pay my Scout dues, and handle a few pocket expenses. The Scout dues were an investment, the best I've ever made.

"To These Things You Must Return"

THE BOY SCOUTS OF AMERICA were made to order for someone in my shoes. When I hit my first home run in baseball, I felt I was well on the way to becoming an American, but it was the Boy Scout program that opened doors to growth and opportunity, changing my whole life.

Our doorbell rang one summer evening. My sister Marie answered the ring and was greeted by a tall, slender gentleman in well-tailored clothes. He took off his hat and started to speak with a strange accent, pleasing to my ears. At that time I was always conscious of how English was spoken. He introduced himself as Alfred Richmond, who represented American Legion Post number nineteen. They were organizing a new Boy Scout troop in our neighborhood, and I was on his list of boys being invited to join.

Soon thereafter, I became a charter member of troop 67 on North Hill. And Al Richmond became a second father, my counselor, benefactor, and friend. He hailed from Nashua, New Hampshire, which explained the accent I found so appealing. He was the chairman of the troop committee. The other members were Charlie Nutter and Norm Fuchs. All three had fought in France, and they had visited Luxembourg. They now took a special interest in the kid from the little country they had known. The committee selected Cliff Newhall to be the scoutmaster. The assistant scoutmaster was Jim Tucker. Cliff was a highway engineer; Jim a professional photographer.

Looking back on those years in troop 67, I realize that these five men contributed more to the shaping of my character than they ever realized. My family wanted the best for me, but couldn't point the way. I had to do it on my own, and I needed the guidance and support these volunteer leaders were giving so generously.

Al Richmond was an executive with the Ohio Edison Company. Charlie Nutter was a personnel officer for Goodrich Tire and Rubber Company, and Norm Fuchs was in research with General Tire. In troop meetings they could talk about the history of the flag of the United States of America with genuine pride and conviction. The Scout Oath and the Scout Law were more than just words to these men; they were rules to live by.

Naturally, I couldn't be a Scout in Akron without getting to know Camp Manatoc. The council's camp was located in Peninsula, north of Akron, and in all my travels I have never known a better place to hike and camp, to work and play, to learn, and yes, to worship. When we marched to the dining hall each evening, we sang our hearts out:

> Hit the trail never fail,
> And you'll live to tell the tale,
> It's the best camp that you'll ever know.

I was working on my first class rank when I first met Francis J. Grassbaugh, "Grassy," my best friend and confidant for over half a century. One of the requirements was to swim fifty yards, tread water for two minutes, and float motionless for sixty seconds. Grassy was a junior leader at the "Waterfront" and had to teach and test me. How I wished I could give commands in an authoritative voice such as his! And how I wished I could swim as fast and as far, and sit in a canoe as properly as he did! I was proud as punch when he called me by name the next time he saw me. We called him "Skipper." Ten years later he would be giving orders as a navy officer, a pilot, in the Pacific war.

Wednesday evenings were set aside for the main campfire program in the council ring. Jud Jusell, the professional Scout executive who was the camp director of Manatoc, became my role model the first time I saw him perform in front of the hundreds of campers, Scouts, parents, and visitors. I wanted to grow up and look like Jud, tall and tanned, charismatic. When he spoke in that deep rich voice and recited Indian lore and legend, I knew I wanted to be a professional Scout executive like him. In due time, he was transferred to another Scout council and I figured I would never see him again.

Twenty-five years later, I attended a Beta Theta Pi convention on Mackinac Island in Michigan. A venerable Beta named Charles Moderwell sat next to me at dinner one evening. I spotted a tiny Scout badge on his lapel. "Oh yes, I'm involved in Scouting," he replied to my question. "I've been active over fifty years. In fact, I designed the Scout uniform."

This led me to wonder if in his business with Scouting he had ever run across a Jud Jusell. "Of course I have," he said. "Jud Jusell is the Scout executive of Minneapolis, Minnesota right now."

I was determined to get in touch with my boyhood idol, and the chance came a few months later when Winnie and I went to Minneapolis for a Miami alumni dinner. We spent two days there, and were ready to go home again when Winnie pointed out that I hadn't called Jud Jusell.

To be honest, I had lost my nerve. I had been foolish to think the man would remember me after twenty-five long years. "He's met thousands of boys since leaving Akron and Manatoc," I said to Winnie. "Why would he remember me?" A "John who?" would be crushing. So I advised myself to leave well enough alone. But Winnie kept urging me on. A half hour before we were ready to leave town, I dialed the number of the Minneapolis Scout headquarters. It was Saturday morning; no one would be working anyway. The phone rang twice and then I heard the voice I had not forgotten.

"Jud Jusell speaking." The boss himself had answered the phone. Now I had to take the plunge.

"Mr. Jusell," I said, "this is John Dolibois. You probably don't remember me, but . . . ."

He interrupted. "Why, Johnny, of course I remember you. In fact, I'm looking at a picture of you right here under the glass top on my desk. You've got your mouth open, singing, on a boat to Kelleys Island."

What more can I say?

Jud and I have seen each other on various occasions since that phone call. He sends birthday wishes and holiday greetings with personal notes regularly. Now in his early eighties, he is enjoying retirement with his wife Elizabeth in Portland, Oregon. But I still see him, tall and stately, in front of the big campfire at Manatoc. He is wearing a colorful Indian headdress. He is intoning that bewitching "spell of Marnoc:"

> . . . these will draw you, ever draw you.
> For these things your heart shall yearn,
> For these things your soul shall burn,
> And in the end, friend, you will learn
> That to these things you must return.

I returned, of course. In a way, I never left.

When I was at camp, away from my family, I had no choice but to speak English. So I picked it up fast. I also learned many other things to help me grow, understand, appreciate. How to start a fire with only two matches, without paper or dry leaves. How to send smoke signals, use the Morse code with a flashlight, or send messages with flags and the semaphore code. I could identify at least twenty-five different trees by their bark or their leaves. I knew at least twenty-five birds by their shape, plumage, and call. I learned, and taught others, first aid and life saving. I wove leather belts and neckerchief slides, used colored beads to make headbands and wrist straps. My hunters' stew, and biscuits baked over the open fire with a reflector oven, were fit for a king, or a grand duke.

At Camp Manatoc I met a genuine American Indian, a Sioux, named Jimmy White Cloud. He taught me how to walk in the woods, noiselessly; how to find my way at night by following the stars. He also taught me a complicated ceremonial dance. Jimmy White Cloud was in charge of Indian lore at Camp Manatoc one summer, and I remember that summer as the best of all. I wrote Albert Stoltz, René Kelsen, and Nikky and Paul Bradtké all about it. How my friends back in Luxembourg must have envied me!

In 1936 I spent more nights at camp than in my bed at home. I was on the camp maintenance staff. I worked myself up the ladder, starting as a "honey dipper"—emptying the cesspools—for two dollars a week, plus room and board. After a stint on the road and bridge gang, I became the camp truck driver. On winter weekends we took turns manning the entrance gate to the camp, and policing the troop campsites.

Being song leader after supper in the messhall was my most rewarding assignment. I specialized in "Alouette," with a little hokum in French; and the "Schnitzelbank," with a genuine German accent. I could "Blow the Man Down" in a rousing sea chantey, and wail mournfully about my darling "Clementine."

Four years later I received my Eagle Scout badge on the stage of Central High School. The sponsor who pinned it on me was Mr. P. W. Litchfield, president of the Goodyear Tire and Rubber Company. This made a tremendous impression on me. I began to appreciate the fact that some things happen only in America. But there's more to the Eagle Scout story.

In 1956 I was the alumni director of Miami University. President John D. Millett, my boss, and I were in Akron for an alumni meeting. One of our hosts was Fred W. Climer, vice president of Goodyear, a 1918 graduate of Miami, and a member of our board of trustees. Fred Climer invited Dr. Millett and me to tour the Goodyear plant, after which he took us into what he called the "inner sanctum," the office of the retired chairman of the board of Goodyear. We were ushered into the biggest office I had ever seen, and we were presented to the old gentleman. Mr. Litchfield was confined to a wheelchair and retired, but he still came to his office for a few hours every day. I hung back as Mr. Climer and Dr. Millett conversed with him, but when we prepared to leave, I was moved to say something, too.

I told Mr. Litchfield that twenty years earlier he had pinned my Eagle Scout badge on me. I also told him the circumstances and what his part in that ceremony had meant to me. I won't ever forget his reaction. He gripped my arm with an arthritic, shaking hand and said: "Young man, let me tell you something. I'm considered to be very rich. I've been around the world eight or nine times. I can buy myself most anything I want. But nowadays, in my old age and in my condition, it takes a lot to make me happy. What you've just told me makes this the nicest day I've had in a long time. Thank you!"

There were tears in his eyes, and I knew he meant what he'd said. And I knew that I would want for myself the satisfaction of someday having someone say "thank you" to me under similar circumstances.

Being involved in Scouting and busy with part-time jobs, my years in Findley School went by quickly. September 1934 rolled around, and I was getting ready for high school—new faces, new names, new friends. But it was a lot easier than when I first enrolled in Findley School. The summers and the weekends at Camp Manatoc had helped the most. I spoke English with assurance, and could now concentrate on getting rid of my gutteral accent and the foreign idioms. In the troop I was Senior Patrol Leader, building confidence in myself, and gaining leadership experience.

So when I met Dr. Hugh C. Smith, principal of North High School, I didn't cringe. He was a giant of a man, with red hair, a mile-wide toothy grin, and a size fourteen shoe. I had heard that an angry Mr. Smith wouldn't hesitate to use that big foot on your behind. I stayed out of trouble and became a joiner instead: Hi-Y and Golden Key, the Drama and Glee clubs, the Algebra and Trigonometry Society. I was determined to be accepted, to be a real Yankee Doodle. But I didn't excel in sports. I wasn't big enough and I had started too late. No coordination. Except in track. I ran the 220- and the 100-yard dash, and I did well enough to qualify for the Mansfield Relays, the all-Ohio high school track meet. I got as far as the semifinals, and then piddled it away, literally. It happened on the starting line. We were on the mark, set to go, poised for the sound of the gun. Bang! The sprinters took off, all except me. I was still in the crouch, wetting my pants. The excitement had been too much.

They remembered me for a long time in North High track circles. After my "incident," Coach Bob White had put a big sign in the locker room, ordering all his runners to use the toilet before going out on the track. I understand the sign hung there for years.

Meanwhile, I decided to direct my talents into other channels. I fell in love. Her name was Marian Gallagher. She was the first girl I ever kissed (with genuine love), and I botched it.

We had been at the movies, the Nixon Theater, admission ten cents per person. I premeditated my strategy down to the last step on the way home. We detoured by way of Findley School grounds, and as we reached the darkest part of Cuyahoga Falls Avenue, under the trees, I took Marian into my arms. She responded. We kissed. Suddenly I heard a rustling in the hedges. Someone had spotted us. I didn't wait to find out who. I took off in a flash, leaving Marian standing there alone. I didn't stop running until I got home.

Marian forgave me. No one was in the bushes; it had been my imagination. Our romance blossomed and lasted nearly two years, but not without difficulty. Papa disapproved. Marian was a Protestant. Furthermore, she was a tap dancer, the star pupil and performer of the North Hill Dancing School. She appeared in tights and shorts, on the stage, in public. She was not the girl for me, and Papa raised hell about it every time I had a date with Marian. And every time he fussed, I loved Marian more. It was she who persuaded me to change my mind. She met someone she liked better, on a summer vacation, and she dumped me.

My heart was broken for a week or two, and then healed again. I was invited to lots of house parties, played spin-the-bottle and post office, and found out that little girls are made of sugar and spice. On Sunday afternoons we went to Summit Beach Amusement Park or swam in one of the many lakes around Akron. For a dollar a day we could rent a canoe and paddle around Turkeyfoot Lake. Al Richmond had a cottage on Turkeyfoot, and we were always welcome. Scoutmaster Cliff Newhall and his wife Betty organized parties for the older Scouts and their dates regularly. It was always a place to have fun without spending money, and that meant a lot in those depression years, especially in my circumstances.

I got my social security number during my senior year in high school. I needed it to start on my first regular job. My boss, Mr. Bill Strawn, also a member of American Legion Post number nineteen, owned a Pure Oil station on the corner of Tallmadge Avenue and North Main Street, just halfway between our house and North High School. I was hired to run the station from 9:00 P.M. to 6:00 A.M. five days a week. This paid ten dollars per week, plus any wash, wax or tire-changing job that came along during those hours. The occasional stretches between customers usually allowed time for a few catnaps in the early mornings. I could also find time to study. I became a member of the National Honor Society and was elected president of the senior class.

Al Richmond and the other members of our troop committee started talking "college education" to me, but when I tried out the idea at home, Papa looked at me blankly.

"Why?" he asked. "I never went to high school or college, and I've lived this long. Don't get such high and mighty ideas."

Marie and Albert thought it would be nice, but I'd have to find some way to do it on my own. They had their daughter Madeline, and their first obligation was to her. "Start looking for a real job," was the best advice I could get.

But there was plenty of talk about college at camp. Many of the camp leaders worked at Manatoc during summer vacations between college years. Ted Foley, Jr., son of the Scout executive, was a student at Miami University. So was Bill Yeck, for whom I worked as camp scoutmaster the summer after my junior year at North High. Bill's brother John was a senior leader when I first started going to Camp Manatoc. John was going into professional Scouting, and he was a Miami man, too.

I started hearing Miami over and over. The most ardent salesman for the university was Ken Gambee, scoutmaster of a West Hill troop, and president of the Miami University Alumni Club in Akron. He was always on the lookout for good students, and his enthusiasm for his alma mater was contagious. Ken was convinced I could get a scholarship, although there weren't many available. The best was the "open scholarship for men." This scholarship, subject to maintaining a B+ average, paid tuition and one hundred dollars cash each year for four years. "You can earn the rest of the money you need once you get to Oxford," Ken said convincingly. So I mailed my application, vowing to "help other people at all times" if this impossible chance were given me.

During spring vacation I received a letter from Miami University, advising that I was a semifinalist in the scholarship competition. I was invited to meet with the scholarship committee for a personal interview at the Leland Hotel in Mansfield at 9:00 A.M. the next Saturday morning. Mansfield was at least sixty miles away and no bus left early enough to get me there by nine in the morning. Al Richmond came to the rescue. He drove me to Mansfield. In a small hotel parlor I came face-to-face with three professors who immediately won me over: Dr. Marvin Peterson, economics; Dr. Walter C. McNelly, physiology; and Dr. William E. Anderson, mathematics. If these men were typical of Miami teachers, I wanted to go to Miami. The impossible wish now became an obsession. I had to find a way, scholarship or no.

Several weeks later, another letter from Miami. I was to meet Mr. Joseph W. Fichter, assistant vice president of the university, at the Mayflower Hotel in Akron. Wonder of wonders! Mr. Fichter told me that I was awarded the four-year open scholarship for men. He presented me with all kinds of material about Miami, all the information I needed as an entering freshman. I was being readied for what is known as "the Miami family."

Papa didn't understand what it was all about, but he seemed pleased and proud. By now he had come to recognize—and maybe appreciate— my determination to be more than a laborer, even though I respected and admired the hard work he had done all his life. Until his death in 1948, Papa never again objected to anything I wanted to do. He started to show his pleasure with any success I had. I know that he bragged about my accomplishments in his letters to our family and friends in Luxembourg. He just found it difficult to come right out and tell *me*.

In short, my family rejoiced with me and encouraged me, but they always reminded me that I would have to do it on my own. That didn't bother me; I knew I could make it. I had many friends pushing me on, and before too long I would meet someone who would share my dreams and aspirations, and influence my choices and decisions, in all the years ahead.

" 'Neath the Elms at Old Miami"

WORKING AT A GAS STATION back in the thirties was a lot different from what it is now. An all-night job wasn't so risky. Robberies were rare. Customers paid cash for their purchases and got full service. My boss was a strict taskmaster who insisted on a clean shop. The same was expected of employees. "Be Sure with Pure" was embroidered on my uniform jacket and on my cap.

I was pushing the broom around the mechanics' area when the bell signalled a customer at the pumps. The customer was Mary Kelly. Mary was a vice president of our high school senior class, and was the tallest and most popular girl. Mary had a friend sitting next to her in the car. The moment we were introduced, something clicked. The eyes got to me first, then the smile. I can even tell you now, fifty years later, what she was wearing. Her name was Winifred Helen Englehart, and I was destined to see a good deal more of her. And something else clicked. I remembered seeing her graduation picture in the *Akron Beacon Journal* a few days earlier. She was graduating from Sacred Heart Academy. It was plain that I would have to follow up this chance meeting. In school the next day, I persuaded Mary Kelly to invite Winnie Englehart to our commencement. Afterwards, we would celebrate the end of our high school careers with dinner and dance. To be sure (with Pure?) I urged Mary to come along, too. It worked.

Thus, on June 17, 1938, Winnie was subjected to hearing me speak on "What Price Peace?" It was the first of many speeches she would hear me deliver in the next five decades. My family was mighty proud of me that night. The kid who couldn't speak a word of English seven years earlier was now the spokesman for the class. Thank you, Mrs. Dambach, Mrs. Applebaum, and Miss Gertrude McBee of Findley School!

Herman Pirchner's Alpine Village was "located on the Playhouse Square in Cleveland, Ohio" according to the announcer who introduced their weekly radio program. They specialized in Wiener schnitzel and yodeling. They also took two weeks' of my gas station wages that commencement night. It was worth every penny. My two companions of the evening pretended to enjoy the clomping of the "Schuhplatterl" and the slapping on the Lederhosen. I was the worldly bon vivant, ordering food and drink in German, and even requesting a waltz which I couldn't dance. If only the Neipperg School gang could see me now, I thought.

I saw a lot of my new girl that summer, especially since I gave up working at the gas station to take a better paying job on a beer truck. Winnie's father was vice president of the Carmichael Construction Company. Carmichael owned and operated the Akron Brewing Company, and Dad Englehart was its chief executive officer. I became a helper on one of their delivery trucks, thus switching from former milkman to beer man. I wrestled cases and barrels of "White Crown Beer" during the day, and romped with Winnie's baby brother Jimmy in the evenings.

Meanwhile, preparations for my freshman year at Miami University were taking on a different perspective. Love blossomed. Winnie and I decided we should go to college together. It was up to me to persuade her parents to approve our plan. My old-fashioned approach to Dad Englehart worked wonders, not because I was persuasive, but because he had prepared himself for some bad news when I asked to see him.

He sat in his rocking chair in the living room, fidgeting; back and forth he rocked. I explained that Winnie and I were in love. He rocked faster. "We've decided we would like to go to Miami University together," I explained. "I'm studying to go into professional Scouting, and after we graduate we want to get married." I had laid it all out. The rocking stopped. So did the drumming of the fingers on the arms of the chair. Relief was spread all over his face. I'm sure he had feared that we wanted to get married right away. No wonder he had been nervous.

Dad Englehart was never one to waste words. He spelled out his answer in a few short sentences. Yes, he had noticed we had a crush on each other. He also thought we might demonstrate it less publicly—especially when the younger kids were around. As for college, he and Mother had planned to send Winnie to St. Mary's at Notre Dame. They were willing to go along with the Miami idea but not sure they could support it for a full four years. There were five more children to educate.

Winnie might have to help out by finding a job. Anyway, it was settled. I was treated like a member of the family from that day on and I've never regretted it.

Winnie couldn't start at Miami until the second semester in January as enrollment for September was closed. I would have to go to Oxford alone, and Winnie would catch up later. Meanwhile, she would work for her dad in the Carmichael office.

I was at Winnie's home saying my goodbyes when Ken Gambee knocked on the door. He felt obligated to give me some last-minute pointers on how to succeed at Miami. We sat on the curb in front of the house. Ken was stressing the importance of fraternity life at Miami. "To get the most out of college," he said, "you have to join a fraternity." He reached in his pocket and came up with his own pledge pin of Sigma Alpha Epsilon. "I want you to have this, John. I want the SAEs to pledge you. It would make me happy, and it will make you happy." I appreciated the sentiment behind this gesture, even though at that time I didn't have the faintest idea what fraternity affiliation was all about.

We said goodbye, Ken walked to his car, stopped and turned around. "You got any money?" he asked. I didn't have a cent. My earnings of the summer and my savings had been sent to Miami University to pay for my room and board. The one hundred dollars from my scholarship would pay lab fees, books, and incidental fees. I thought I wouldn't need anything else.

"You'll need spending money," Ken said. "You'll have to buy supplies, toothpaste, and you'll need a haircut from time to time." He reached in his pocket. "Here, take this, you'll need it." Noting my reluctance, he added, "Pay me back when you can. It's a loan." Then he drove off. In my hand I held a ten, five, and one dollar bill. I owed Ken Gambee sixteen dollars, and a lot more.

My friend Al Richmond had insisted on driving me to Oxford, a trip we would repeat several more times in the next four years. It gave us a chance to talk; the eager college student and the seasoned veteran. I voiced my hopes and impressions, he shared his experience and wisdom. Without Al Richmond I would never have been able to complete four years at Miami. I was the son he never had. He took the place of the father who couldn't cope with the ambitions and the needs of a boy in a new world.

I told Al about Ken Gambee's pledge pin. He agreed with Ken that I needed a fraternity to help me get the most out of college life. Then he proposed a plan. He would send me a check each month to cover my fraternity fees and dues. This was a business deal. I signed a note for an interest-free loan, to be paid back after graduation. The loan was repaid although it took a little longer than expected due to a world war, but I kept my end of the bargain.

I loved Miami the first time I laid eyes on the "crimson towers against the sky," the tall smokestack, the water tower, and the beautiful steeples of the Methodist Church. As you approached on Route 73, you could see them from far away. They disappeared from sight each time the car went down a dip in the road, and then reappeared as it rose up over another crest. And then, suddenly, you saw the sign, Oxford, "Home of Miami University, founded 1809." There were green open spaces between buildings erected in quadrangles. And trees, lots of trees. There were the beechwoods of Western College and the lower campus, and rows of elms on both sides of High Street. It was so green, like the "green heart of Europe"; I thought of Luxembourg's Gruenewald, of the copper beech trees, and the well-kept forests. I felt at home here. I started at once to put in my own roots that would hold me the rest of my life. I was assigned to room 210 Elliott Hall, the oldest—and finest—residence hall, right in the heart of the campus.

I soon learned that Miami was more than a meticulously planned conglomerate of colonial red brick buildings. It was people who gave Miami special distinction. People such as Walter Havighurst, my English professor and freshman adviser. He would become one of my cherished and respected friends. Forty years after my first day in his class, author Havighurst wrote a biography, *The Dolibois Years*. In it he pays tribute to my happy successes. He describes "the Dolibois journey, a pattern of circles," and recalls the first time we met. It was in his English class in room 105, Irvin Hall. I sat in the second seat, third row. In the book he quotes from the first theme I wrote for him in 1938.

Between 1947 and 1981, Professor Havighurst was actively involved in the alumni program which I directed at Miami University. He visited Winnie and me in Luxembourg during our embassy years. Our guest book shows an entry for June 28, 1982: "Gratefully, in Luxembourg at last—Walter Havighurst."

Miami was Walter Havighurst. It was Burton L. French and Marvin Peterson, Walter McNelly and William E. Anderson. Miami people who were my teachers, my friends, and, later, my colleagues. The Miami Family was unique. I was lucky indeed to be taken into it.

Joseph M. Bachelor taught us Shakespeare. His final exams lasted as long as four hours. I think my greatest scholastic achievement was being able to write five blue books in answer to his examination questions. I had learned something.

Joe Bachelor also taught "Words"—an etymology course—and in his teaching he taught about life. He was a philosopher and a poet, an adviser and an advocate. When our first son was born, Joe Bachelor sent instructions to us at Blue Ridge Summit, Pennsylvania: "Boil a page of Shakespeare in his milk each day. . . ." He meant it. When our second son was born, we named him Robert Joseph, his middle name in Joe Bachelor's honor.

"What we have here . . ." was a phrase Dr. Burton L. French always used whenever he introduced a new viewpoint or a favorite topic. He was our professor of political science and of parliamentary procedure. If he were alive today, and I were to visit his class, he would probably say: "What we have here is one of my former students who went on to become a United States ambassador." Then he would smile benignly, and ask, "Isn't that pleasing?" Dr. French was a gentleman through and through, an inspiring teacher.

Winnie came to see me several times during the first semester of my freshman year. We walked hand-in-hand down historic Slant Walk, past Thobe's Fountain, old Harrison Hall, and into the library. Arm-in-arm we strolled down High Street under the stately old elms, whose branches met from both sides of the street, forming a leafy canopy, a dark-green tunnel. The old elms started to die out in our senior year, and were completely gone when we returned after the war. In three years some 150 were removed, and I sensed the loss of cherished friends.

Winnie grew to love Miami during these campus visits, and by the time she registered for classes on February 1, was completely sold on the place. The Miami years were good years for us, filled with rich memories and lasting friendships. Winnie became a member of Delta Gamma Sorority and I joined Beta Theta Pi. Communications in Sigma Alpha Epsilon had apparently broken down. The SAEs didn't get the word about me until several days after I had pledged Beta. Too late. I returned Ken Gambee's pledge pin with genuine regret.

The Beta experience became an essential part of my college career. I needed to belong, to find my American identity. The idea of young men banding together in a common cause appealed to me. I liked being privy to a secret handshake, a lofty motto; ritual and mysticism had been part of my upbringing, and I was comfortable with it. But the best part was having so many close friends, "brothers" from whom I learned something every day. Fraternity life was different before the war. Good manners, proper dress, and decorum were expected: coats and ties for dinner; white tablecloths and linen napkins; waiters in white jackets. We sang the doxology before dinner and the "Loving Cup" after. Nobody came late or left early without permission from "Mom" Troth, our housemother. Mutual assistance toward the higher aspirations of life and cultivation of the intellect were more than high-sounding phrases, and I took it all in. For the kid from down in the valley in Luxembourg, it was heady stuff, and I needed all the help I could get. The good, rich gift of laughter was there, too. I loved the song sessions, the serenades. When I planted my Beta pin on Winnie, to let the world know that she was "the flower of my heart, my Beta Rose," I couldn't sleep for several nights. In those days, the entire chapter would serenade the girl who had just received a brother's pin, and the lucky lover himself had to sing a solo. That was a far cry from wailing "Oh my darling Clementine" for a bunch of Boy Scouts around the campfire. Besides that, the solo was extremely difficult, and even the best among the serenaders would crack on the high notes. All the girls in the dormitory would be at the windows to hear me do my solo, and if they started giggling, I'd be dead. I worried through it, but did fine.

On Saturday and Sunday evenings we were allowed to have open house and could bring girls to the Beta house to play bridge, or dance. The fraternity houses were off-limits to girls at any other time. We danced to records mostly and when the needle stuck on one of the scratchy old disks, the dancers would jump up and down making the dining room floor shake and vibrating the needle on to the next note.

It was the era of the big bands, and many of the famous ones came to Miami University for such formal events as the Freshman Strut, the Sophomore Hop, the Junior Prom, and the Senior Ball. A tuxedo was as necessary as saddle shoes or white bucks.

I was at the right place at the right time as far as my initiation into the fraternity was concerned. The Betas were founded at Miami University and celebrated their centenary during the summer of my freshman year. Eight young men had organized the fraternity in 1839, and in their honor eight Alpha Chapter pledges were initiated by the General Fraternity at the Centenary Convention. I was one of the eight, and that in itself was enough to put me on cloud nine.

On Centenary Day, August 8, 1939, hundreds of Betas of all ages, alumni and undergraduates from all parts of the United States, gathered in the Miami stadium for a convention photo. After that they lined up for a parade, singing all the way up High Street, under that canopy formed by those great elm trees, down Slant Walk to Harrison Hall in which the eight founders had formally established the fraternity a hundred years earlier. Someone had decided I should carry the American flag at the head of this parade. What a proud moment that was for me! I was reminded of Papa leading the procession of worshippers from Bonnevoie to the cathedral in the city of Luxembourg. The Beta Bells, to be housed in a Beta campanile, were rung during the ceremony, and I choked back a flood of memories in reaction.

"And now let hand grip into hand, and eye look into eye . . ." sang hundreds of voices. I was a Beta too now, and would be privileged to enjoy the friendships that would last through life. Among the nationally known personalities participating in the Centenary Convention was Wendell L. Willkie, who would become a candidate for the presidency of the United States a year later. I walked up to this great American and said, "Hello, Brother Willkie, I'm John Dolibois." He greeted me with warmth and a special grip of the hand. "They shine among the stars that grace the galaxy of Fame," are words of a Beta hymn I recall vividly.

William Warren Dawson was among the "Silver Grays" who initiated us eight neophytes into the fraternity on that memorable evening. Two years later, Bill Dawson was the president of the General Fraternity, and we met again. The Miami Betas had elected me president of the Alpha Chapter, and I was privileged to be a delegate to the general convention at Mackinac Island. He remembered me as one of the eight centenary initiates from Oxford. Bill Dawson was dean of the law school at Western Reserve University, and a highly respected lawyer. The Dawson family cook, one Aunt Lucinda, referred to her employer as "a extra average man!" I agreed with Aunt Lucinda.

Miami had a no-car rule which was strictly enforced during our student days. Only students with jobs requiring cars were given a special permit. Girls weren't allowed to ride in cars without written parental consent. We rebelled, but not vehemently. It was a good rule. It put all students, rich or poor, in the same social class, and they stayed in Oxford in the evenings and on weekends.

There was a no-drinking rule, too, but the innovative could always find a way to get around it. If you saw a group of students heading out of town for a picnic near the old covered bridge, or in the beechwoods near the Western campus, you would see them carrying a large milk can along with blankets, baskets of food, and a portable radio. The milk can would be filled with an exotic concoction known as "purple passion"— grape juice laced with gin.

I suffered no financial hardship during my four Miami years. My scholarship paid tuition and a hundred dollars each year and I supplemented that with all kinds of jobs. The first was in the Varsity Book Exchange in Harrison Hall. This was a student YMCA operation in which we bought and sold used textbooks, and offered candy bars and soft drinks for sale between classes. I washed windows and cars, mowed lawns, hung storm windows, and did other odd jobs for some of my profs. In my sophomore year, I hit on a brilliant scheme for even greater earnings. We were sitting on the Beta house porch one Friday afternoon, watching the pretty girls walk by on their way uptown. Many were carrying laundry kits. So were many of the male students. Laundromats hadn't been invented yet, and students sent their laundry home each week in special kits. This meant taking them to the post office at the far end of town. I started counting the number of laundry kits being carried past our house and thought to myself, "Boy, I'd like a quarter for each one of those being hauled uptown." And then it hit me. Why not?

Early the next morning I was at the Railway Express office. The manager was named Walter Winscott, a bean-pole type, who picked up and delivered Railway Express shipments. "Mr. Winscott, how much will you pay me if I double the number of shipments for you in one month?" I asked. He looked at me as if I were crazy. He also figured that if I succeeded, it would mean twice as much work for him. On the other hand . . . ? "Well now," he said, scratching his head, "I'll have to take that up with the head office in Indianapolis."

Several days later, I was called to the RE depot. One of their regional managers was there, and in no time at all, he made me an offer. They would pay me five cents for every shipment off the Miami campus. I borrowed twenty-five dollars and printed five thousand handbills: "Four reasons why you should send your laundry home by Railway Express." The best reason was pickup and delivery service. Winnie and I slipped a handbill under every door in every residence hall and fraternity house.

Six weeks later, Walter Winscott complained that he couldn't possibly handle all those laundry kits and trunks and suitcases by himself; for another five cents per shipment, would I tag them for him? We were in business. I never went hungry at Miami. This was indeed the land of opportunity, as long as you were willing to work, and use a little initiative.

The Boy Scouts weren't forgotten. If I was going into professional Scouting, I had to remain active. I organized a troop in Oxford, sponsored by the Kiwanis Club. The scoutmaster was John Wolford, a Kiwanis member and my geology professor. The troop met in his classroom in Brice Hall, the geology building, every Tuesday evening.

The Boy Scouts weren't integrated in Oxford in 1939, and a year later I found myself directing a troop for black boys, sponsored by the Oxford Colored Community Chorus. Frankly, I wasn't motivated by any special do-gooder spirit, and it wasn't fashionable to be "liberal" in that sense. Not yet. I just organized that troop because I was asked to do it, and because I felt all boys wanting to be Scouts should have that opportunity. I came to know a lot of nice families in Oxford. Ten years later my former Scouts, black and white, became neighbors, coworkers, and friends.

By now the Boy Scout headquarters in nearby Hamilton took notice of

me. I was approached by Carl Kobert, the Scout executive, and was hired
as summer camp director for the Fort Hamilton Council. I held that job
for two successive summers, and at the beginning of my junior year at
Miami, the council employed me as a part-time junior executive. I organized Cub packs around Hamilton and outlying districts, conducted
training courses for den mothers and pack leaders, and swept out the
Scout office. My earnings allowed me to buy my first car, a 1932 Chev-
rolet, which I needed in my work. No use writing to my friends in Luxembourg about this. They would never believe it.

Ruth Klug was one of two young ladies working in the Scout headquarters at the time. I decided she was just the girl for Grassy, my best
friend of Camp Manatoc days. Grassy, then a Navy pilot in Pensacola,
Florida, took my advice, met Ruth on his next leave, and in April 1942 I
proudly served as best man at their wedding.

Winnie and I were finishing our junior year at Miami when Hitler's
armies invaded Poland in September 1938. World War II was launched.
The following day, German armies stormed into Luxembourg, Belgium, and the Netherlands. Until then, neither young nor old in the
U.S. had given much thought to developments in Germany. "America
Firsters" were demonstrating for noninvolvement. President Roosevelt
was urged to keep us out of it. A lot of the neutralist sentiment was stirred
up by members of Hitler's "Fifth Column" operating in the United
States and other countries. Gustav Blanke, a German exchange student
living in the Beta house, was suspected of being a Nazi spy. At least he
was a good propagandist.

Our bull sessions lasted far into the night now as we argued the pros
and cons of America's involvement. Gus Blanke defended the viewpoint
of the Third Reich, but after Pearl Harbor, he quit Miami and returned
to Germany.

The Munich crisis should have alerted Americans about the Nazi
menace, but we continued to keep our heads in the sand. Many Americans still believed Hitler could be trusted; they urged "negotiation."
Cries for appeasement and concessions were heard across the land.
Meanwhile, Chamberlain returned from Munich, brandishing his um-
brella, promising "peace in our time."

More knowledgeable Americans could see the handwriting on the
wall. Stories about concentration camps, anti-Semitism, and Nazi atrocities became more common. Nevertheless, the prevailing sentiment was,
"stay out of it."

In my own family, concern grew day by day. Papa's last letter to my
brother Karl in Luxembourg was written in the spring of 1940 and returned, "addressee unknown." Correspondence with the rest of my

family in the Saar had deteriorated as early as 1935 when the Saar voted in a plebiscite to be a part of the Third Reich. People living in what was now Nazi Germany were not encouraged to write letters to America. Eventually all contact ceased. We wouldn't learn about the fate of my brothers and sisters until years later.

At Miami, students talked about the "phony war" and the "silent war," but not seriously. We became more concerned after the Battle of Dunkirk and the beginning of the London blitz. I was sure that U.S. involvement was inevitable, and began to change my plans for the future.

As a registered alien, I was required to carry an ID card at all times. I had registered for the draft and as soon as I was twenty-one I applied for American citizenship. Becoming an American citizen wasn't easy. The red tape stretched for miles, between Akron and Oxford, but by the fall of 1940 I was finally "processed." The induction ceremony was held in the Butler County courthouse in Hamilton, the Honorable Judge Peter Paul Boli presiding. I was one of a number of persons to be naturalized, and, like the others, I was given a miniature flag of my native country. I sat there clutching the tiny pennant, listening to patriotic speeches by several politicians, a representative of the D.A.R., and a member of the American Legion. And then the judge entered the courtroom. When my name was called I walked up to his bench. I had watched those before me. The judge would make a final check of the documents before him, sign the important certificate, and then administer the oath of allegiance. After that I would hand him my little Luxembourg flag and receive a small American flag in return, along with the naturalization certificate. I would return to my seat amidst polite applause and be the genuine article—an American citizen.

I got as far as the bench. The judge looked at my papers, and frowned.

"Son," he said, "your home is in Summit County, right?"

I said, "Yes, your Honor."

"Well," he said, "the law requires that you get your citizenship papers in the county where you have legal residence. You live in Butler County just a few months, as a student."

I was crestfallen. Then Judge Boli suggested that all was not lost. I needed certification of residence from Summit County; the signature of two witnesses to prove I had lived in the USA—Summit County—for at least one full year. Back to my seat I went, still holding on to my little Luxembourg flag, still a registered alien.

Months passed while the red tape unraveled. On June 6, 1941, I was called to the telephone at the Beta house. It was Judge Boli's secretary in Hamilton. My final papers had arrived. She wanted to know when I could come to the judge's office and get my naturalization certificate. Problems! School ended the next day. I was going home right after my last exam in the morning. She was sympathetic. She also didn't want to engage in further paper shuffling back to Summit County. "If you can get here before noon tomorrow," she said, "I think we can handle it here."

My exam was at 10:00 A.M. By the time I was on the road to Hamilton it was nearly 11:30. And when I got to the courthouse there was no place to park. It was Saturday morning, market time in Hamilton. There was plenty of nice fresh fruit, vegetables, eggs, and cheese, but no place to park. It was after twelve when I finally dashed into the judge's chamber.

"I'm so sorry," said his secretary. "The judge has left. But don't worry, he goes to the Y for his massage every Saturday, and if you go there right now, you can catch him."

I ran the two blocks to the YMCA. I located the steam baths and massage room in the basement, found a door ajar, and pushed it open. Behold, there was a stark naked judge of the Common Pleas Court lying on the table. He wore black socks—only. A beefy masseur was pounding on his back. The judge noticed me and motioned me in. I was expected.

"All right, son. Let's get it over with. Raise your right hand and repeat after me." Slap, pat, smack! I renounced all foreign potentates and pledged my allegiance. The judge signed the paper I had brought with me. Then he shook my hand and said, "Congratulations, young man. I know this is a funny way to get your citizenship. But you're an Eagle Scout and by now you know what being an American is all about." I sure as hell did. And I wasted no time getting back to the courthouse to claim my naturalization certificate. I checked it for accuracy. It notes a scar on the bridge of my nose under "visible distinctive mark." On the back of the certificate is a typed statement reading, "Name changed by order of court from *Jean* Ernest Dolibois to *John* Ernest Dolibois as a part of the naturalization." My Americanization was complete.

Winnie attended summer school in 1941, making up the courses she lacked by having started a semester later than I. When we returned to Oxford in September, we were both full-fledged seniors. I had decided to give up my plans to go into professional Scouting although I would continue my active service to Scouting as a volunteer. I wanted to start giving back, but meanwhile a job in industry would make more sense. So I concentrated on business courses during the next nine months. I decided to go into personnel management. However, more drastic changes were in store for me, and for everyone else in the country.

December 7, 1941. A thin layer of snow was on the ground, but that didn't deter us from plans to spend the afternoon in the country. Winnie and I had accepted an invitation from our good friend Dan Schisler and his girl Ginny Remke. Dan owned a handsome Pontiac, and a permit to use it. We were stretching the limitations of that permit by using the car for strictly personal pleasure. If we got caught we would throw ourselves on the mercy of the court. I had turned twenty-three just four days earlier, and Dan had already made plans to sign up for the U.S. Army Air Corps. Europe was at war, the future was uncertain. Surely there were more important things than a no-car rule violation. We dared. We enjoyed a drive through the countryside, the rolling hills of southwestern Ohio, and the music of the New York Philharmonic on the car radio. Then an announcer broke in to describe the disaster that had struck Pearl Harbor. The devastating news ended our pleasure ride. We returned to Oxford, dropped the girls off at their dorm, and rushed to the Beta house.

All the brothers were gathered around the radio in the living room. There were shouts of anger as more details of the treacherous Japanese attack were made known. There were tears even—of frustration, worry, and uncertainty.

On December 8, President Roosevelt addressed a joint session of Congress. "War Declared" read the black headlines. In no time at all, Miami became a wartime campus. War emergency courses were announced for the second semester. Several Beta brothers quit school immediately to join the armed forces. War savings stamps and bonds were being sold by student organizations and fund drives for the support of the Red Cross were organized. Maps of the Pacific Islands appeared on bulletin boards. And everybody talked war.

Winnie and I decided to get married. We discussed it with our families during the Christmas holidays; no opposition. Could we afford it? Yes, by pooling our resources, we were sure two could live more cheaply than one. College rules, banning married students, were suspended. On January 17, 1942, some of our professors dismissed their Saturday morning classes so they and our friends could join us in St. Mary's Church of Oxford. Even President and Mrs. Upham came to our wedding. Al Richmond wouldn't miss it for anything, and made the trip from Akron along with our families.

We had a splendid reception at the Beta house, a wedding breakfast for our families and the wedding party at Venn's Colonial Restaurant uptown, and then took off on our honeymoon—to Cincinnati. The honeymoon chariot was Dan Schisler's Pontiac which the Beta brothers had lavishly decorated.

We were back in Oxford thirty-six hours later, studied for final exams, and took the first on Monday morning. We both got A's.

We settled down for the final semester of our senior year. I served out the rest of my term as president of the Betas, and had a chance to appreciate what mutual assistance and unsullied friendship was about. Our efficiency apartment was one room with an in-a-door bed, a tiny, completely equipped kitchen, and a bath. All we needed was a table, two chairs, and a bookcase. The Betas in industrial arts put those items together. The table turned out sort of orange when Chuck Garrity tried to stain it maple, but we were broadminded. These were the best days in spite of the dark clouds of war over our heads.

Rather than wait to be drafted, I decided to sign up for the navy V-8 program. A college degree and two months of training would entitle me to a commission as an ensign. I got as far as being fitted for a uniform when a navy bureaucrat read the fine print on my "contract" and discovered I had only been a U.S. citizen for eight months. Navy commissions went only to *"real* Americans" according to the guy in the recruitment office. Nothing to do now but sweat out the draft. My neighbors on the draft board back in Akron didn't waste any time. "Greetings" and orders to report for the physical arrived on April 11. I was excused from my classes and headed for Akron. In two days I was back, and a week later I received notice that I had been classified 1-B. The vision in my left eye was defective, 20/400. They didn't need me to liberate Luxembourg after all.

So it was time to look for a job—a real one. I interviewed with Procter & Gamble in Cincinnati and was a management trainee by the middle of May.

On graduation day, Winnie followed me across the stage to receive our sheepskins. We had the same last name now. The commencement speaker was Admiral Watt Tyler Clevarious, a sign of the times. The baccalaureate speaker—they still had them before the war—was an Episcopalian bishop, a Beta. We were now ready for the big, bad, outside world.

We rented the furniture for our apartment on Bond Hill. We knew we wouldn't be using it long. Winnie immediately landed a job as receptionist for King Machine Tool Company, just down the hill from where we lived. I rode the bus to Ivorydale, and soon mastered the difference between edible and inedible products, Crisco and Ivory soap. Our happy state didn't last. The draft board in Akron ran through its 1-A's in a hurry, and around the end of October they got down to the 1-B's. My records were transferred to the greater Cincinnati area, and on November 12, I was in the army.

Saying goodbye was not as traumatic as I had expected. Splendid preparatory schooling had readied me for an equally outstanding high school experience. I had enjoyed absolutely fantastic adventures in the Boy Scouts. I worked my way through one of the finest universities in the country, and was privileged to belong to a great fraternity. I had a good position with a respected corporation, and that position would be waiting for me when I got back. And most of all, I had a wonderful wife. America had made all this possible for me. The time had come for me to start paying back. I was ready.

The Making
of an Interrogator

MY ARMY CAREER STARTED on a dreary November day when I climbed aboard a rickety olive-green bus in front of the post office in downtown Cincinnati. My fellow travelers were an odd assortment of characters, not a "soldier" among them. Some sat glumly staring out of the bus window. Others puffed away at cigarettes, assuming an "I-don't-give-a-damn" attitude. As we crossed the bridge over the Ohio into Kentucky, someone started singing:

> You're in the army now, you're not behind the plow;
> You son of a bitch, you'll never get rich;
> You're in the army now.

I didn't join in the raucous laughter. My mind was in a spin. I was thinking of Winnie, who had decided to stay in Cincinnati for the time being. I thought of my own army career, of where I could be most useful. My daydreaming was interrupted when the sergeant in charge was on his feet, calling for attention. "All right you guys! You're in Fort Thomas now. Haul ass outta this bus and form into two lines. Short guys in front. Get movin'!" I snapped out of my reverie, grabbed my small handbag, and stepped out of the bus. I got into line, in front.

We marched into a large barracks room, and were sworn in. Next, we were bored by a pep talk delivered in a nasal monotone by a major who had probably given that same talk a hundred times. We lined up again, marched to another building, and were issued uniforms, fatigues, and standard equipment. While cross-checking the receipt I had signed for this "U.S. property," I thought I heard my name. I almost didn't recognize it—"Doleebolos." When I finally identified myself I got some good advice: "Stay awake, Bub, and from now on answer pronto when you're called."

I also got a card with directions to another barracks building and to a large room on its second floor. There were two rows of double-decker bunks; at the foot of each bunk stood a large tin can of sand. "Oh my God . . . ," I thought at first, and then I realized the cans were for cigarette butts only.

A small, pimply-faced PFC pointed to one of the bunks, told me to hang my uniform and civilian clothes in the locker behind the bunk, and get into my fatigues. Then I was to grab a broom and start sweeping the floor. "Get movin'!" I saw two other newcomers sweeping the floor at the far side of the room. "You're in the army now!" I said to myself.

At eight o'clock the next morning I was standing in line for the third time since getting up at six. The first was a line to the latrine. The second was for breakfast—oatmeal, cold toast, and an orange, on a tin mess tray. And now I was lined up in the personnel section, waiting to be classified. Considering the seriousness of this matter, I thought the line was moving rather fast. Then I found out why. "O.K. Delappus, what can you do?" I was up front.

I made my first mistake in the army. I corrected the pronunciation of my name, ". . . like in Illinois," I said. A quick, silent shuffle of my papers, followed by a pearl of wisdom:

"Look, wise-ass, jest because youse went to college don't expect me to get literary at youse."

I got the message and humbly answered the previous question. "Well, I can speak French and German. I'd like to get into Military Intelligence."

"Did you ever drive a truck?"

"No sir," I lied (Camp Manatoc didn't count), "but I can speak German fluently."

"How about a bus or tractor, a plow, or something heavy with air brakes?"

I wasn't going to give up so easily. "No sir, but I can speak French and German."

By then my minute and a half was up. The "director of personnel," a balding corporal, made a check mark on my classification record, initialed it, and waved me on.

Two days later I was on a troop train to Fort Knox, Kentucky, where the army would make a tank driver out of me. Like everyone else I had taken a battery of aptitude and IQ tests *after* the interview. This didn't change the classification the corporal had already given me.

Looking back on those three days at Fort Thomas, I concluded the army needed bodies at the Armored Force Replacement Training Center, Fort Knox, on November 13, 1942. Maybe if I had been inducted two days later I would have been sent to the Cooks and Bakers School in Georgia. Who knows?

All right! I decided to turn obligation into opportunity. I learned to hurry up and wait. I got into shape in no time. The day began with calisthenics at 6:00 A.M., and usually ended with an increasingly longer run before supper. In between, I learned how to assemble and disassemble my pistol, my rifle, and eventually, a .30 caliber machine gun. I also learned to fire each of them. I drove a jeep, a ¾-ton, and then a 2½-ton truck. I failed miserably on the motorcycle, but performed well in a tank and the armored personnel carrier. By the time I was able to hike twenty-five miles with a full pack on my back, and no blisters on my feet, the three-month basic training period was over. I could lick my weight in wildcats. I had survived a beneficial kind of hell. I was proud of myself.

The first six weeks had been the worst because there was no free time off the base, not one furlough until just two days before Christmas. Then I got a forty-eight-hour pass to Louisville.

Winnie now worked at Shillito's Department Store in Cincinnati as a personal shopper. Her twenty-five dollars per week looked a lot better than my twenty-one dollars per month, but financially we were back to biting the bullet. Nevertheless, Winnie was overjoyed when I called to tell her we could meet in Louisville on Christmas Eve even if it meant a four-hour bus trip for her, after work.

There were about 150,000 troops in Fort Knox at that time. At least half that number would be in Louisville for Christmas. Where would we sleep? I didn't worry about it until I arrived in the big city. To get there, I had to share a cab with five other GIs. The cab service on weekends—a thirty mile trip at top speed—was how many Kentuckians supplemented their income.

The thought of being with Winnie in a few hours provided the only bit of Christmas spirit I could work up. But first I had to find a place for us to stay. I made the rounds of the downtown hotels. All I got was funny looks. There was no room at *any* inn; I was naive to think there might even be a slight chance. Just before resigning myself to our sitting up all night in the bus station, I made one more attempt. I located a tourist home in the phone book and called. Bingo! They'd just had a cancellation. If I came out at once I could have the room.

I never moved so fast in all my life. I walked and ran twenty-one blocks on Third Street from downtown Louisville to a picturesque Victorian mansion. A storybook "Southern Colonel" answered my ring. Black suit, string tie, snow-white hair, mustache and goatee. His voice could have soothed a rampant lion. I quickly explained why I was out of breath. He drew his own conclusions; I couldn't afford a taxi. The room cost three dollars, payable in advance, and I had four dollars. But the room was perfect, furnished in antiques, high ceilings, even a gas-burning fireplace.

I told the "Colonel" I would be back with my wife as soon as her bus arrived from Cincinnati. The kind old gentleman led me to the front door and then stopped. "Young man," he said, with a smile I don't think I'll forget, "you'll be needing some money to get a bite to eat, and do bring your lady out in a taxi. It's too far to walk from town." With that, he handed my three dollar deposit back to me. "You can pay for your room later," he said. Now, that was the nicest Christmas present anyone could have given me—trusting kindness, when I needed it most.

Winnie and I remember that Christmas as one of the best. We didn't have a tree or presents. We had each other and the true meaning of Christmas, revealed by that kind southern gentleman. We stayed at his tourist home as many weekends as possible after that. We'll always remember our special hideaway and Kentucky hospitality.

And I'll always remember how much my Boy Scout experience helped during the crucial three months of basic training at Fort Knox. Outdoor living was second nature to me. So was pitching a tent, cooking on bivouac, and assuring my comfort and well-being on long hikes. A Scout is helpful, friendly, courteous, kind. Believe me, the Scout law helped me adjust to this new environment. I could count the college graduates in our training battalion on the fingers of one hand. The illiteracy rate was high. If I wanted to have friends, I needed a lot of patience and tolerance.

David Del Pilar was my favorite sidekick. David came from the Philippines. He was as determined as I was to make the best of our situation. When basic training ended he and I were the only two from our company chosen for the Officers Candidate School. The next OCS class, the thirty-ninth of the Armored Force School at Fort Knox, didn't begin until two weeks after basic training. David and I were promoted to corporals, but during that two-week waiting period we went through hell. We were in limbo; no specific unit, no assignment. So we were on KP one day, barracks and latrine duty the next. Then back to KP again. I think I picked up at least two million cigarette butts in our barracks area in those two weeks. I peeled potatoes, scrubbed garbage cans, mopped latrine floors, and disinfected toilet bowls. And when all that was done, I scrubbed the siding of the barracks and washed dozens of windows. But the worst of all was putting up with abuse from the mess sergeant who supervised our chores.

Sergeant Elmer Beckler was an old timer, regular army. He was a big man, broad-shouldered, with gigantic paws for hands. He limped. He had been shot in the fanny in World War I. The old wound bothered him most on rainy days, and I dreaded KP when it rained. That's when Beckler was meaner than usual. I can still hear him bellow: "All right, Lootennant, get your finger outta your ass and start scrubbing those garbage cans." He made no bones about disliking officers, especially the "ninety-day wonders." It was a happy day when we finally assembled our gear to move to the Armored Force School. Sergeant Beckler came to see us off. He lumbered to my bunk while I was packing, held out his hand and said, "Lootennant, you're gonna be all right. You can take it. Good luck!" Then he saluted me and limped out of the barracks. Now that was a compliment I would remember for a long time.

I enjoyed the challenge of the Officers Candidate School. To become a "ninety-day wonder" in just ninety days called for concentrated effort. They threw everything at us: leadership techniques, gunnery, strategy, tactics, communications, current events; we hiked, drilled, read maps, and did our calisthenics, while noncoms and officers watched every move, day and night. A lot of the "discipline" was similar to fraternity hazing; twenty demerits and you were out on your ear. David and I were trying to set a new record. Neither of us had a single demerit the first eight weeks and we were getting cocky about it.

That's when we were told the joy ride would soon end. Major General George S. Patton, Jr., commanding the First Armored Corps, would conduct the midterm inspection, and everybody got demerits when Patton was on the job. David and I decided we weren't everybody; we would get through this inspection with a clean slate. General Patton couldn't scare us.

We worked on it and I did pass the barracks inspection without a demerit. My friend did not. When the general asked him how many pairs of socks were in his footlocker, he answered "seven." General Patton frowned. "There are nine pairs of socks," he snarled. "Two demerits. Incorrect inventory."

We both passed the uniform inspection, and then formed outside for the final phase, rifle inspection. I knew I had it made. You could have sucked a milkshake through the bore of my rifle. It was *clean*. When the general stepped in front of me, I snapped to "Present arms." He grabbed my rifle, slid back the bolt, spun the weapon high and looked through the open end of the barrel. I heard a slight grunt, and in a flash the rifle was back in my hands. I rammed the bolt-head forward to close it. It stuck. The nickel, which we always kept in the mechanism to hold down the spring of an unloaded rifle, had mysteriously popped out, and was lying at my feet.

"What is it, heads or tails?" barked the general. I looked down quickly. "Heads sir!"

"Two demerits; moving in ranks without permission," was the verdict. General Patton and his entourage moved to the next victim. Did I detect a self-satisfied smile on that stern face? I know the platoon sergeant who kept score on his clipboard was grinning. "Everybody gets demerits when General Patton is on the job," he'd been telling us all week!

On June 17, 1943 Patton was the speaker when our class was commissioned and he didn't spare the "blood and guts" in his address to the new lieutenants and their families. "Face a fear and it will disappear." "Grab 'em by the nose and kick 'em in the ass." The general explained that he used "the language of soldiers who are ready to kill." The language of war is not polite.

Forty years later I was reminded of that speech. Winnie and I were being shown around the Pescatore Foundation in Luxembourg City. The Pescatore is a retirement community for wealthy senior citizens. A bronze plaque on the front of the main building lets it be known that this was the headquarters of General George S. Patton, Jr., from December 1944 through March 1945. When we were there in 1982, our host led us into a small chapel, next door to the room Patton had used as an office.

"This is where General Patton offered his famous prayer [for good weather] during the Battle of the Bulge," he said with great pride as we entered the chapel. Sometime later, I located a copy of the Patton prayer in the archives and had it reproduced on parchment, and then framed. Winnie and I gave it to the Pescatore Foundation. It now hangs in the small chapel for all to appreciate. It begins with, "Lord, this is Patton speaking to you . . . ."

Ten members of our OCS class were commissioned cavalry. I was one of them. Patton distributed the crossed sabers insignia personally to the lucky ten. Winnie pinned the second lieutenant bars on my shoulders. Two days later I was crawling on my belly through acres of mud, under barbed wire fences, with live machine gun fire over my head. I learned to keep my head down. This was battle training, a whole month of it after graduating from OCS. The newly commissioned Mechanized Cavalry and Armored Infantry lieutenants were undergoing strenuous training under simulated battle situations. We lived in tents in bivouac areas. We tore up the countryside in tanks and armored cars. We fired all kinds of guns, and became accustomed to the sound of bullets splattering off the armor of the tanks in which we were riding. It came close to the real thing, and we bitched our heads off at the stupidity of it all. But when the four weeks ended, we were proud to have survived. We were ready to make the world safe for democracy.

However, the Armored Force had different ideas. My first assignment as a greenhorn lieutenant was not to combat duty, but to Camp Chaffee, Arkansas. I was attached to Troop A, Twenty-third Cavalry Reconnaissance Squadron, Mechanized, Sixteenth Armored Division, a new division just being formed. We were the cadre, which meant we would be in Arkansas for at least two years. It also meant fighting the boredom of routine army life, repetitious exercises and training in camp, on bivouac, and on maneuvers in the Ouachita and Ozark mountains. The most exciting thing that happened to me out there was discovering a tarantula one night in my bedroll.

Winnie joined me in Arkansas and we actually bought a house in Fort Smith, not far from Camp Chaffee. We shared the house with another couple and their seven-month-old baby. Our part ownership was assured with a one thousand dollar down payment. Again, we rented the furniture. Since we would be in Arkansas at least two years, we decided to enjoy whatever family life the war would permit.

Two months after arriving in Arkansas, I was ordered back to Fort Knox to attend an officers' communications course in the Armored Force School. We sold our share in the house, donated our pots and pans to our friends, and headed back to Kentucky. That was the bad news. The good news was that Winnie was going to have a baby. We were determined to make the best of it, to stay together as long as we could. The scuttlebutt was that upon completion of this communications course in three months, I would be shipped overseas, probably to the Pacific theater where light tanks and communication technology were in great demand. I had already decided they'd never send me to Europe; it would make too much sense.

Housing was in critically short supply around Fort Knox. Twenty miles away, on the outskirts of Elizabethtown, Kentucky, stood an old farmhouse, almost hidden from view by a bunch of scraggly pine trees and overgrown forsythia hedges. It was owned by an army captain's wife whose husband was somewhere in North Africa. She had two small children. She also had a spare bedroom at the top of the stairs. It didn't have a door and the bed sagged, but we could have it for sixty-five dollars a month if Winnie would look after the children when their mother had to go out, and if I would bank the furnace at night, and fire it in the morning. We signed a three-month contract.

I managed to buy into a share-the-ride deal for transportation back and forth.

The monotony of life for the next three months was almost unbearable. Up at 5:00 A.M., I stoked the furnace, shaved and dressed, gulped a glass of juice, and hiked two miles to an intersection where I met my ride to camp. After breakfast in the officers' mess, I went to class until six o'clock in the evening. Then back to Elizabethtown and our "home." Don't ask me what I studied or learned; I haven't the slightest idea. The communications equipment on which we were schooled was out of date by the time I ever had a chance to use it. The dots and dashes of the Morse code I still remembered from my Boy Scout Signalling Merit Badge. Our being together was the only thing that mattered to Winnie and me at this point.

New orders were issued a week before the officers' communications course ended. It was December 23, 1943. I opened my envelope with trembling hands, fully expecting to read of an assignment to somewhere in the Pacific. "By order of Brigadier General Holly, Commander of the Armored Force School," Second Lieutenant John E. Dolibois, 01018596, was "reld 31 Dec 1943 from further DS with TAS" and directed to travel, "as soon thereafter as practicable to his proper station." Back we went to the Twenty-third Cavalry Reconnaissance Squadron, Sixteenth Armored Division, Camp Chaffee, Arkansas.

It wasn't a joke. A reprieve maybe? We didn't stop to ask. Back to Fort Smith we went. This time we found a completely furnished duplex in a pleasant neighborhood and settled down once again as a happily married couple, awaiting the arrival of spring and our first child. I was appointed platoon commander, honing my technical and leadership skills, gaining confidence day by day. I had the valuable help of experienced noncoms who had seen action in North Africa. Our enlisted personnel were fed to us fresh from basic training. We were in the process of developing an efficient combat outfit.

Springtime in Arkansas is a special experience. The cold winds in the low hills soften to gentle breezes, bringing a freshness all their own. The sweet smell of blossoms and spring flowers is in the air. If you're going on an army bivouac, that's the time to do it. Our reconnaissance troop was in the field for an entire week, roaming the hills, simulating recon problems, scouting an imaginary enemy. At noon, on a Monday in late April, we were in position on a rocky slope overlooking a broad river valley. We decided to break for chow. I was sitting on the trunk of a fallen oak, balancing my messkit on my knees. My mind was on Winnie and the weeks ahead. The baby was due in three or four weeks and all was well.

"Hey Dolly!" I heard someone calling me by my army nickname. They had stopped struggling with Dolibois. It was Captain Kent Lawwill, from squadron headquarters. "I've got an urgent message for you," he said. "You're being shipped out; top speed."

My heart sank. "Not another fiasco like the Officers Communications School!" I prayed. There was no time to waste. I had to hurry up, *now*. The waiting would come later. Someone drove me to HQ at Camp Chaffee, and there I got the sketchy details. My orders were classified. I was to leave ASAP, which was *now*, on military air transport to Washington, D.C. My final destination would be revealed upon arrival in Washington.

I picked up my orders and travel authorization, and had a driver take me home. Winnie was out. I had no idea where she might be. I stuffed my clothes into a suitcase and the rest of my belongings in a duffel bag. I wrote a note to Winnie, promising to get in touch as soon as I could, and left the house with a heavy heart.

During the flight all kinds of wild, confusing thoughts ran through my mind. What was in store for me now? Why all this great rush, and all this secrecy? I got my answers just a few minutes after our arrival. The army had finally remembered that I could speak German. After eighteen months in the Armored Force, I was transferred to Military Intelligence. No one explained the need for all the hurry and the secrecy. I concluded that I probably was supposed to be somewhere at a specific time to accommodate a training schedule. I was right. And the secrecy had to do with where I was going.

I spent the night in temporary officers' quarters at Andrews Air Force Base, and then climbed into an olive-green bus—naturally—for a two-hour ride to Camp Ritchie, Maryland, eighty miles north of Washington.

Camp Ritchie had been the Maryland National Guard Camp for years. In 1943 it became the Military Intelligence Training Center. I was part of an odd assortment of mixed talent from all over the USA. Some came from foreign countries. There was a prince of Bourbon-Parma; an Italian count; there were former hotel managers, government officials, chefs, corporation executives, and prominent journalists. The inmates of Camp Ritchie were said to speak fifty languages—all, in fact, except good American English. Some wag had composed a poem which began:

Vas you effer at Camp Ritchie, der schoenste
Platz of all,
Where the sun comes up like Donder, mit recorded
bugle call?

I vividly remember that thunderous bugle call—reveille—blown out of a public address system. It echoed and reechoed through the Catoctin Mountains encircling the camp. I was to hear it day after day, in getting ready for my IPW class. The IPW stands for Interrogator Prisoners of War. That's what I was now being trained for. It was a two-month course, after which I would be assigned to an IPW team and shipped to Europe for service at battalion or regimental level, reporting to an S-2 or G-2 officer.

But first I had to worry about Winnie, back in Fort Smith. I found I didn't have to guard the secret of my whereabouts after all. That was more army bullshit. I called to tell her that I was in "der schoenste Platz of all" close to Blue Ridge Summit, Pennsylvania and not far from Hagerstown, Maryland, astride the Mason-Dixon Line. I would be there at least two months, and, God willing, I would find some way to get back to Fort Smith to see our baby before I was shipped overseas. Winnie was relieved to hear from me but not happy with the way things were shaping up. But she's half Irish. A week later I received a telegram:

Dear John. Dr. Jones advises trip to Maryland by Pullman would be safe. Have promises for every assistance in matter of Drs. in Hagerstown. Leave decision to you for you know situation better than I. Can handle things easily at this end if a reunion is possible. Will await reply from you. Love Winnie.

I knew her mind was made up. I went into high gear. The USO office steered me to a lady in Blue Ridge Summit who owned and operated the Locust Grove Inn, a complex of guest houses which used to accommodate Washingtonians vacationing in the mountains before the war. Nora B. Hoffmaster now rented rooms and apartments to military families stationed at Ritchie. I wasted no time seeing Mrs. Hoffmaster. She was a character. All business, but after a little snort from one of many liquor bottles she stored in her bathtub, she gave me bad news. She was terribly sorry, but she was all filled up. I turned on all my persuasive powers. I knew this old entrepreneuer would find a way if I could just convince her. I did. Her parlor was not in use, and she had an extra bed. She would set it up in the parlor if we were willing to share the kitchen and the bath with four other couples living in the main house. We were willing. It turned out to be some arrangement, especially with the refrigerator. Labels on everything. Amazingly, it worked with a minimum of friction.

My next step was to call on the only doctor in Blue Ridge Summit, Dr. Harvey Bridgers. Yes, he would accept Winnie as his patient, but she would have to see him as soon as she arrived. I wired the information to Winnie. Western Union brought her reply:

Dear John. Arrive Baltimore 9:45 Monday morning. Will see you at Locust Grove Inn Monday afternoon. Don't worry. Love Winnie.

I worried. She had to close out our living arrangements in Fort Smith, pack our meager belongings, and then travel twenty-two hours on a train from the western part of Arkansas to Baltimore, Maryland. The baby was due any day. When the local mountain train chugged into Blue Ridge Summit that Monday afternoon, I was mighty happy and relieved. At once we walked from the quaint old railroad station across the street to Dr. Bridger's office. The genial country doctor beamed. He found Winnie tired but healthy. There should be no problems.

Six days later, Winnie awakened me. The rising sun was beaming its way into our parlor-bedroom. It was Mothers' Day, May 14, and Winnie was ready to become a mother. Dr. Bridgers decided on the hospital in Waynesboro, Pennsylvania, as it was closer than the one in Hagerstown. So our son arrived north of the Mason-Dixon Line, the first native-born Yankee in the Dolibois family. We named him John Michael, and to avoid confusion, called him Johnny-Mike.

The First Training Battalion of Camp Ritchie went on bivouac the next day. Perfect timing! I didn't see Winnie and our baby son for five days while Military Intelligence hiked the Appalachian Trail. The exercise was to make combat soldiers out of the transfers from the Quartermaster and Supply Corps, the Cooks and Bakers Schools, the Signal Corps, and those who came direct from civilian occupations. I had an edge. After my training in the Armored Force, this program was a picnic.

In the classrooms of the Military Intelligence Training Center we learned about German Army Organization and the Order of Battle; we studied the rise of National Socialism, and the characteristics and personalities of high-ranking Nazis; we were thoroughly trained in the techniques of interrogation and the psychology of handling prisoners of war.

At night, at the Locust Grove Inn, I learned to cope with diapers and formula, and how to dress or undress a wiggling bundle of dynamite.

Nora B. Hoffmaster found a larger room for us, with private bath and cooking facilities. Things were looking up in Blue Ridge Summit.

In no time at all, my two months in the M.I.T.C. school came to an end. The Allied Forces had landed in Normandy and Brittany. We were on the Continent at last, prisoners were being taken, and IPW personnel were very much in demand. So were interpreters, counterintelligence, and photo intelligence people. The specialists trained in the cloak-and-dagger stuff were needed for operations behind enemy lines. Ritchie supplied them all. And within days after my class finished, I, too, was alerted to be shipped out. I was now an interrogator. Furthermore, Winnie and I were prepared for the inevitable. This time we could say the proper goodbyes and make provisions for the time when this war would be over.

I thought I was walking the mile from Blue Ridge Summit to Camp Ritchie for the last time. My destination was the auditorium, the alert center. I joined a solemn group of officers and enlisted personnel sitting on their duffel bags and foot lockers. The colonel in charge of the detachment was giving final instructions when the door opened for someone with a message for him.

"The following officers are herewith dis-alerted and will report to Colonel Warndorf, Chief of Section Five, immediately: Second Lt. Franz Brotzen, Second Lt. John E. Dolibois, Second Lt. Ulrich Landauer." This on-again-off-again business was nerve-racking. As I stood to retrieve my gear, someone next to me muttered, "You lucky bastard!"

Brotzen, Landauer, and I met at the door and walked the short distance to the offices of Section Five—the German Section. Colonel Warndorf greeted us warmly. We had been added to his section as instructors and would be training interrogators and teaching intelligence personnel about the German army and its political and military leaders. I was now an IPW officer in name only. It would be some time before I could use my newly acquired talent vis-à-vis a real German PW.

After the cordial welcome from Colonel Warndorf and Staff Sergeant Walter O. Schnyder, I stowed my gear and returned to Blue Ridge Summit as fast as my legs could carry me. Winnie was elated. We spent the rest of the day unpacking and rearranging our furnishings. When I told Mrs. Hoffmaster about my staying on as permanent cadre, she moved us into another building where a good-sized apartment had just been vacated. Our new home was called the "Martin House."

Our neighbors were Carl and Louise Doria and their baby daughter Karen, who was six months older than our Johnny-Mike. We became the best of friends immediately—a friendship that has now lasted more than forty years. The Dorias live in Milwaukee, and we have visited each other often since the end of the war. The pattern of circles, which describes my life, led to Paris in 1985 when Carl and Louise visited us in Luxembourg. Forty years earlier—almost to the day—Carl and I had begun our overseas duty in Paris. In 1985, as we strolled along the Seine with our wives, it seemed like only yesterday.

As a teacher one learns a helluva lot more than as a student. I stood before my first class just two days after my dramatic removal from the alert list. I enjoyed teaching. As I became more proficient, I began lecturing in German. I was familiar with weaponry and could describe the function of German arms, their tactical and strategic use. I taught German Order of Battle and the Nazi party organization to my S-2 and G-2 students, many of whom were field grade officers. Some were generals. I was still a second lieutenant. Being sent from one school to another, and transferred from one specialty to another, didn't give me a chance to work in grade long enough to earn a promotion. I was in charge, but every one of my students outranked me.

Being disalerted stirred up mixed emotions. On one hand I was elated to be able to stay longer with Winnie and Johnny-Mike. On the other hand, I was missing out on the chance to be useful in action overseas and getting ahead as an officer. I heard from a number of my former classmates in OCS and from former colleagues in the division. They were now captains and even majors. I didn't realize until later that my schooling and my teaching qualified me for the most unique opportunity of my life. In fact, I would benefit from these earlier experiences forty years later.

"Triumph des Willens" is a three-hour documentary film directed by Leni Riefenstahl, the well-known actress and director who rose to fame during the Nazi regime. The film features the Nazi party rallies in Nuremberg, the endless parades and the speeches, also endless, by top Nazi leaders: Hitler and Goering, Hess and Goebbels, and many others. By viewing this film we became thoroughly familiar with the Nazi personalities. We observed their manners of speech, their walk—or strut—their posturing and, especially, their fawning behavior toward Hitler. We identified uniforms and rank insignia of the leaders of the military and paramilitary organizations in this Nazi Rally—the annual "Parteitag" in Nuremberg, where tens of thousands idolized their Fuehrer. I showed that film to all students in the German section every Thursday afternoon for eight months. I could almost recite all the speeches myself.

I took it for granted that I wouldn't be sent overseas as a member of a regular IPW team, interrogating ordinary prisoners of war. I was sure something special would develop if my teaching at Ritchie should ever end. I didn't have long to wait.

One evening in early March, Carl Doria and I were bowling at the officers club on the post. A headquarters officer took me aside and confided that he'd seen my name on the list of those to be shipped out with the next detachment. When I pushed for more information, I learned that Carl Doria's name was on the same list. Our interest in bowling died quickly. Carl and I headed for home, rehearsing the best way to break the news to our wives.

Louise and Winnie met the test. They had known for some time that sooner or later our idyllic situation in charming old Blue Ridge Summit would come to an end. None of us could complain about the good fortune we'd enjoyed so far.

Troop movements from Camp Ritchie were no longer the secret events of earlier days. We got official alert notices with only the exact date of departure still classified. We were allowed ten days leave to get our affairs in order and to make our farewells. I made a quick trip to Akron.

Papa was in a dither. Not hearing from any of our family in Europe for more than five years had been hard on him. Now his youngest son was leaving for Europe, too. I had never seen my strict, self-disciplined father so upset. He couldn't be consoled. My promise to do everything possible to locate my brothers and sisters reassured and comforted Papa, and, as it turned out, finding my family after the war was an exciting, incredible undertaking.

Back in Blue Ridge Summit, we made the most of the last few days with our families. Carl and I found all kinds of ways to goldbrick, to avoid the Mickey Mouse activities that were routine at Camp Ritchie. On the night before Easter we combined our artistic talents to color the eggs which our kids would hunt the next morning.

But the army had different plans for us on Easter morning, April 1, 1945. By 7:00 A.M. Carl and I, and many more Ritchie-ites, were on a train to Camp Shanks, New York, the staging area for our military journey to Europe. Lieutenants Brotzen and Landauer from Section Five were with us, too. The war in Europe was drawing to a close. The German Section, along with Carl Doria's section, was being phased out. Ritchie would now concentrate on training intelligence personnel for the Pacific theater.

Our detachment spent three days at Camp Shanks, repacking, buying more clothing and equipment, and then we moved on to pier 86 in New York. We embarked immediately on Ship Number 605, formerly the French luxury liner *Ile de France*. It sailed out of New York harbor, past the Statue of Liberty, at exactly noon on Thursday, April 5. We lost sight of American shores three hours later.

Another life was now beginning for me. Fourteen years earlier, I had gazed upon these shores for the first time, a wide-eyed, innocent boy, credulous, naive. Now I was an officer in the United States Army, the beneficiary of the many opportunities the new world had made possible for me. An hour after we had entered the open sea, I was handed a telegram with good news. I was promoted to first lieutenant.

Those Dancing
White Horses

OFFICERS WERE QUARTERED in remodeled staterooms of the former luxury liner. We slept in double-decker bunks and enjoyed reasonably comfortable facilities. A severe storm broke out the fourth day at sea and threw us some eighty miles off course. I quickly lost interest in the shows a USO troupe put on for us every evening, the only entertainment on board. Things got more lively when a two-destroyer escort met us. There was talk about German submarines and when depth charges were set off at regular intervals everybody got excited. But nothing serious developed.

We saw land, the coast of Wales, on Friday, April 13, and when I awoke the next morning our ship was anchored off Gourock, West Scotland. The whole harbor was dotted with ships of all kinds. It was a thrilling sight, but each ship was flying its flag at half-mast. President Roosevelt had died the day before. It was a misty, dreary day, just right for this depressing news. We weren't given much time to dwell on it, however. Small barges took us down the bay into Grennock where we disembarked, glad to be on terra firma again. We filed into waiting trains, small English coaches, six men to a compartment. It was comforting to have Carl Doria as a traveling companion, to share impressions with him.

A fast fourteen-hour train ride took us across Scotland through Glasgow, Edinburgh, then south through the whole of England, including London. I saw the aftermath of the Battle of Britain, the effects of the bombing raids on London and adjacent cities. For the first time war became real to me. We had marveled at the cleanliness and the orderliness of Scotland and Northern England, the air raid shelters, the victory gardens, and the flowers everywhere. Now we were in the midst of appalling devastation, but still there was a sense or order. Here was the evidence of the indomitable spirit of the British. The rubble was neatly piled on both sides of the streets. Traffic was maintained, business as usual. But most impressive was the friendliness of the people themselves. They waved and cheered as our troop train passed; the two-finger "V" for victory sign was a standard greeting. I was sure that many similar trains had traveled the same route in previous weeks and months. And I'm sure the welcome for them was as cheerful and sincere as it was for us. I felt good about being in Great Britain.

It was Sunday afternoon when we arrived in Southampton. No Channel steamers to France were available. Two had been sunk by German subs in the last week. Not a pleasant prospect. So we spent three miserable days in a transient camp, sleeping in tents and eating C-rations. The only pastime was waiting for the rain to stop. We even tired of bitching.

At last, on the fourth day, we were taken to the Southampton docks. Our spirits rose considerably even though all kinds of scare stories about the Channel crossing and our destination were making the rounds.

I stayed awake all night and even ventured out on the blacked-out deck once. There was a bright full moon, and I was amazed to see a countless number of ships that had materialized during the night as part of a convoy. In the morning they had disappeared just as mysteriously. Our steamer was alone again. In a short while we approached the French coast, and entered the harbor of Le Havre.

The ruins were a depressing sight. There was barely enough room for our little steamer to pass into the harbor amidst the wreckage and the rubble. We docked at an improvised pier, grabbed our gear, and were hastily loaded into waiting trucks. Our next stop was another transient area, Camp Lucky Strike. Up until then our move from Ritchie to Le Havre had been well orchestrated. Now chaos set in.

After two boring days in Lucky Strike we were herded into windowless boxcars—a troop train—and subjected to a miserable, bumpy ride to an Infantry Replacement depot at Étampes, thirty miles south of Paris. It turned out that the Ritchie crowd got there by mistake. It took another three days to get it all straightened out. Then we were packed into a fast express which took us into Paris in thirty-five minutes—a journey which had lasted nine hours a few days earlier. At the Gare l'Est in Paris we were met by a bus which took us to the Paris suburb of Le Vésinet. I had never been in Paris before. I gawked like a real tourist, and loved it, even in a war atmosphere. Already I was hoping to have a long stay in the City of Light.

The SHAEF (Supreme Headquarters Allied Expeditionary Force) Military Intelligence headquarters was in Le Vésinet. We were billeted in a splendid villa, and immediately engaged in taking tests, being interviewed, classified, and assigned according to our specialties. We had time to see a bit of Paris, too. One could easily hitch a ride into town on a military vehicle, and then feast one's eyes on sights such as Montmartre, the Latin Quarter, the Arc de Triomphe, the Eiffel Tower. I was beginning to like "combat duty."

One evening Brotzen and Landauer invited me to join them on a visit to a family they knew in Paris. The visit flopped. Nobody home. We were stuck, without transportation, somewhere in Paris. But the night was young and so were we. We started to walk aimlessly down one street and up another. It didn't take long for us to be spotted as three little lambs who'd lost their way. A French entrepreneur approached us.

"Ah, mon Colonel," he said to Lieutenant Brotzen, who threw back his shoulders and assumed a new air of command. "Are the gentlemen officers looking for the VIP American Officers Club?" Of course we were. He would lead us to it.

Our guide took us around the block, to a shuttered, nondescript house, and knocked on the door. It opened. "Colonel" Brotzen offered a generous gratuity to our helpful citizen-guide. Then it dawned on me. This was my first encounter with a pimp, a French *procureur*. I quickly took all but one ten-franc note out of my billfold and tucked the rest of my money in an inside pocket. The hostess led us to the dimly lit bar of this "officers club," and seated us at a small, round table covered with a thick red velvet tablecloth. A bottle of champagne appeared from nowhere. So did three mademoiselles. We shook hands all around and added more chairs to the table. We didn't spill any military secrets in the meaningless conversation that followed, unless the brightness of the crescent moon, the evening temperature, and the direction to the Champs Elysées were classified information.

My lady friend was getting impatient. She put her hand on my knee and asked if I would like to see the rest of the house. Now I demonstrated my savoir faire. "Combien Mademoiselle?" I asked. She smiled generously. "Pour toi, Chérie, only twenty-five francs."

I reached for my billfold, opened it, and we both looked crestfallen at the lonely ten-franc note nestled in the fold.

The kind lady's tone was one of resignation. "C'est la fooking guerre!" she said and sashayed out of the room.

At about that same moment Brotzen came to life. He looked at his watch and announced that we were late for our important rendezvous.

He paid for the champagne, and we took off on the double. Out on the street, Landauer turned to me with the understatement of the month. "You know, I think that was a whorehouse."

It definitely was the end of our night-out-on-the-town. Older and wiser, we three sophisticated officers and gentlemen found our way to the Place de la Concorde, failed to locate transportation of any kind, and headed due west on foot to our home in Le Vésinet. It was a long, long walk by the light of a waning moon. It also turned out to be my last night in Paris. My new assignment was tacked to the door of my room when we got back to our billet.

The next morning I said goodbye to my buddy Carl Doria and other companions from Camp Ritchie. An afternoon express train took me to Rheims-Charleville where a vehicle met me and took me nineteen kilometers north to Revin. My new outfit was a detailed interrogation center for the Military Intelligence Service—6824 DIC (MIS). My commanding officer was Lieutenant Colonel T. C. Van Cleve. My quarters were in a requisitioned private home coded "Georgia." I would work in a building called "Arizona." The headquarters of the DIC was coincidentally named "Ohio." I was an interrogator at last. The prisoners were an assorted lot of general officers, politicians, scientists, and others with special backgrounds or knowledge of a nature that called for "detailed interrogation."

The PWs had been brought to the detailed interrogation center after having been screened by IPW teams in the field. The day after arriving in Revin I was ordered on just such a screening mission. It would take me to Bavaria, in the vicinity of Munich where I would find myself making contact with my own reconnaissance unit of the Sixteenth Armored Division from Camp Chaffee. My world was getting smaller.

I had a jeep and a driver, Corporal Clifford E. Burke. We had a generous supply of K-rations and C-rations, bedrolls, and all the time in the world. Our route was circuitous, through Metz, then south of Saarbrucken into Mannheim. We were inside Germany all right, but saw more GIs than Germans. In the course of our travels we could easily get a hot meal from an army field kitchen; lodging was wherever we could find a barn or grab a bed in a hotel or inn commandeered by our forces. We passed through areas where heavy fighting had ended just days before. Some buildings were still smoldering. Occasionally, we ran into gunfire. There were snipers along the route. The fear was unpleasant, but bearable. I saw my first grime-covered "dogfaces," men who had been in battle for several months. There was still a lot of action ahead, but you could tell that things were winding down.

On our way to Munich we traveled the famous Autobahn. I marveled at how the Germans had built the super highway so that it could be used as a runway for fighter aircraft. Along a stretch of several miles I saw camouflaged clearings in the woods where the planes had been hidden. But not too well. From the road we could see the wreckage of many that had been strafed or bombed in their hiding places. We also saw lots of guns out of action, wrecked vehicles of all kinds. I averted my eyes from the occasional corpse in the ditches.

I'm not very good at describing the horrors of war. Even now, forty-two years later, I can't find the words to tell you about Dachau, the infamous concentration camp. I arrived there on April 30, just two days after its liberation. I learned that Prince Felix of Luxembourg was there on April 29 to greet the liberated Luxembourg inmates at the camp gates. Those fortunates who had survived the ordeal would never forget that their own prince consort was among the Allies bringing them their freedom; actually saving their lives in the process. I wished I could have been there a day earlier and witnessed that memorable scene.

I was supposed to be on the lookout for German PWs who might be useful for detailed interrogation, but primarily I was to watch for high-ranking Nazis in disguise. We had reports that many of them were passing themselves off as ordinary German soldiers, thus hoping to be overlooked in the confusion and to disappear. We know now that many of them succeeded, eventually finding safe havens in Central and South America, and even in the United States. My orders indicated that I was traveling "for the purpose of carrying out the instructions of the Theater Commander." The last line, which read "BY COMMAND OF GENERAL EI-SENHOWER," assured us food, lodging, and gasoline when needed. So I decided to just play along. Whenever we came upon a unit with prisoners of war, I would question any who looked like good prospects or behaved suspiciously. If I was interested in a special prisoner, I would arrange for him to be sent to Seventh Army Interrogation Center in Augsburg. Later on, such PW would be moved to Revin.

Just outside of Munich I learned that the Sixteenth Armored Division was not in the Seventh Army sector; they were with Patton's Third Army around Nuremberg and Regensburg. So we changed course and headed northeast. While stopping for gas at a GI depot we learned the latest news. U.S. and Soviet armies had met somewhere on the Elbe; Mussolini had been executed by Italian partisans near Lake Como; the Russians were on the outskirts of Berlin. It was obvious that the war in Europe would end in a few weeks.

I wasn't prepared for the complete devastation I saw in Nuremberg, the site of the great Nazi party rallies. Somehow it seemed right to bomb hell out of the place. The beautiful medieval heart of Nuremberg, the old city, was almost leveled. We couldn't drive from one end of town to the other. Because of the ruins and rubble, we had to backtrack many times to find a way north. I remembered how often I had listened to Hitler speak in the film, "Triumph des Willens." "Give me ten years and you will not be able to recognize Germany," he said in 1933. Well, it was certainly not recognizable in 1945.

We followed the troops of the Second Armored Cavalry to the Czechoslovakian border. To my amazement, I ran into several men I knew back in Camp Chaffee. The Twenty-third Cavalry Reconnaissance Squadron was moving in the direction of Pilsen. I thought it a rather useless exercise since the war was nearly over. There was almost no resistance, except for isolated machine gun nests, some antitank guns, and a few snipers.

An estate belonging to the Skoda family in Zinkowy, on the edge of the Bohemian Forest, was headquarters of the cavalry group under the command of a Colonel Reed. The place was overrun with Polish DPs. There were a lot of German PWs who were allowed to roam freely over the area, apparently quite content to hang around the Americans, do some odd jobs, and pick up cigarettes and food. I made a few interrogations but learned nothing useful. It was easier to relax with a cup of coffee, and I was in the process of doing just that when the CO sent for me. A German captain stood before him, dressed in a Luftwaffe uniform. He identified himself as a member of a German Air Force Intelligence Unit located in a hunting lodge not far from our position. They called themselves *Dienststelle Ost* (Duty-Station East). It soon became clear to me that theirs was a detailed interrogation center very much like ours in Revin. For five years they had been gathering information about the Soviets. They interrogated prisoners, deserters, especially White Russians, and analyzed aerial photos and captured documents. Now they expected Russian troops to reach their hiding place soon. The captain had come forward as spokesman for the group. They preferred to be captured by the Americans.

My diary notes give this captain only the letter "O" as a name. I don't remember if that is because I never found out his whole name, or if there was some reason for coding his identity in my notes. At any rate, I saddled my jeep early the next morning. My driver, Captain "O," and I rode in it. A 2½-ton truck followed. In about ten minutes we pulled up to the rustic lodge, the *Dienststelle Ost.* I was greeted by Lt. Col. W. W. Holters, the commanding officer of the unit. He was a dapper gent, in full uniform, all spit and polish. He wasted no time telling me that he was a flyer in World War I, and had been a member of the famous Immelman Squadron.

He took his "surrender" quite seriously and ceremoniously directed the loading of boxes on our truck. They were full of interrogation reports, maps, and charts. Two junior officers and my Captain O got into their German command car. Ten enlisted men and noncoms climbed onto our truck, Holters joined me in my jeep, and we headed back to Zinkowy. The whole operation took less than twenty minutes. I suspected the good colonel was more worried about being spotted by the SS than he was about the Russians. He didn't begin to unwind until we were well out of sight of his abandoned headquarters.

Holters looked to be about fifty years old. A pince-nez, balding head, and well-groomed version of a Hitler mustache gave him a scholarly appearance. At first we circled each other warily in our conversation. He seemed to have something on his mind, and finally put out a feeler. "Do you like horses, Herr Oberleutnant?" Did I know anything about the famous Spanish Riding School of Vienna? The Lipizzaner stallions?

"Yes, I like horses," I said, "but I don't ride. I'm Mechanized Cavalry." I needed enlightenment about the Spanish Riding School. Colonel Holters explained the origins of the spectacular breed of horses and the famous school in which they have performed since the sixteenth century. The reason for the equestrian lecture soon became clear.

There was a breeding station, a stud, at an estate called Hostau near Zinkowy. Nearly 250 horses, stallions, mares, foals, and brood mares were at this stud. Most of the horses were Lipizzaner, although Gabardiner, a Caucasian breed, and other breeds helped to make up the lot. Some were privately owned, but most of them belonged to the government. The stud of the Spanish Riding School used to be located at Piber in Austria. It was taken over by the Germans after the annexation of Austria, and moved to Hostau in 1942. It was now under the control of the Ministry of Food and Agriculture. The Spanish Riding School had been placed under the command of the German army. Some of the performing school stallions had been brought to Hostau for breeding, and also for safety, when the bombing of Vienna became intense.

Holters said the Czechs didn't like the Germans and as soon as the war ended they would surely confiscate the horses. The Russians would butcher the valuable animals or use them as work horses. Fourteen beautiful Lipizzaners of the Spanish Riding School in Budapest had been shot by the Russians when the highly trained show horses had resisted all attempts at harnessing. Unless the stud were saved it would be the end of the centuries-old Spanish Riding School.

Colonel Holters had tears in his eyes as he told me all this. By now I was raring to do whatever needed to be done. Hostau was just five minutes south of the road we were traveling. I ordered the sergeant with the truck and our cooperative prisoners to proceed back to Colonel Reed's headquarters. Corporal Burke and I would make a short detour with Colonel Holters in our jeep.

On the way to Hostau I learned more about the Lipizzaners and became thoroughly fascinated. It seems that Baldur von Schirach, Hitler Youth leader and Gauleiter of Vienna, had insisted on keeping the Spanish Riding School operating in Vienna as a way of keeping up the morale of the people. Not until the air raids were increasing in number and severity, and the horses were in great danger, did he allow their evacuation. In March 1945 some of the stallions were taken to Hostau, but the top performers, a valuable sixty-two of them, were shipped by rail to St. Martin-im-Innkreis, in Upper Austria. The transport of those stallions from Vienna to St. Martin, a distance of only two hundred miles, took four days. On several occasions their train was caught in air raids but somehow they escaped disaster. They had been accompanied on this dangerous journey by the commander of the Spanish Riding School, Col. Alois Podhajsky. Apparently Podhajsky and Holters had become good friends since the stud at Hostau and the *Dienststelle Ost* were practically neighbors. Now we approached Hostau, and Holters would have to finish his fascinating story later.

What a sight met my eyes on this lovely, sunny day! Hundreds of horses were in the pasture. I had never seen such beautiful snow-white animals. But there were also blacks and grays. Holters explained that Lipizzaners are born with a black coat and turn white in their seventh or eighth year. Dozens of foals frolicked in the meadows and the gorgeous mares were grazing peacefully. The noble elegance of it all moved me deeply. My camera couldn't stop clicking.

I wasted no time moving on to Zinkowy to report to Colonel Reed. The name Podhajsky was familiar to him as his brother had been at the Cavalry School at Fort Riley, Kansas, and had ridden a horse by that name. So the colonel went into action at once. Approximately two hundred horses were herded from Hostau across the Czechoslovakian-German border to Schwarzenberg in Bavaria with a tank platoon providing an escort. Some German PWs were used in the roundup of the herd. Unfortunately, some of them were inexperienced riders. The stallions panicked and stampeded back to the stables. I understand about ten or twelve of them were never recaptured.

What happened to those top-performing school horses that had been brought to St. Martin? Colonel Podhajsky told me the story. On May 3 the command staff of the Twentieth Corps, Patton's Third Army, set up headquarters in the castle-estate of Count and Countess Arco-Valley in St. Martin. This was the farm to which the stallions of the Spanish Riding School had been brought. The corps commander, General Walton H. Walker, was intrigued with the idea of having the famous stallions in his headquarters and invited General Patton to fly from Frankfurt to see what had fallen into his care. A great show was arranged for Patton and the assistant secretary of war who accompanied him to St. Martin. An expert rider, Patton had competed for the Olympic crown in the military pentathlon in Stockholm in 1912. Podhajsky rode for the Olympics in Berlin in 1936. They now met at St. Martin, the victor and the vanquished. Patton was fascinated by the performance and agreed to place the Spanish Riding School under the special protection of the American army. Colonel Podhajsky was allowed to locate the stud and to get help in bringing the stallions and the stud together.

In the annals of the Spanish Riding School, General George S. Patton, Jr., is heralded as the savior of the illustrious, ancient institution. However, the record should show that when first told about the school he had snorted: "Why in the hell were fifty-five healthy men teaching horses how to dance instead of fighting in their Army?"

I still had the responsibility of getting Colonel Holters and the rest of my PW of the *Dienststelle Ost* moved out of the area. We arranged to transport them to Augsburg, to the Seventh Army interrogation center, and then to the 6824 DIC in Revin. Corporal Burke and I returned directly to Revin. After our exciting adventure, I was eager to settle down for a while.

On my first evening back in Revin, I was sitting in my room in "Georgia" writing to Winnie. Through the open window I heard someone tromping down the cobblestone street. He was whistling a tune that brought back vivid memories of our Miami days. It was a Beta song, "When Stars are Hiding." I rushed to the window and called out to the whistler. He was Lt. Malcolm M. Hilty, the only fraternity brother I met during all my overseas duty. Mal was a graduate of Carnegie Tech in Pittsburgh. He was an opera singer, a Wagnerian tenor. He had spent several years in Germany during the thirties and had occasionally sung before audiences that included high-ranking Nazis, especially Reichsmarschall Herman Goering.

Mal had also done some intelligence gathering for the USA. He had left Germany just before war was declared and now he was back, in uniform, serving as an IPW officer. We were destined to spend the next twelve months together on various exciting assignments.

Mal Hilty advised me that we would have a victory parade the next morning. General Alfred Jodl had signed the unconditional surrender in Rheims. I passed through that city on my way back to Revin. I thought if I had known, I might have arranged to get a glimpse of the infamous chief of operations of the German High Command. Of course, I had no way of knowing then that in less than four weeks I would come face to face with Oberstgeneral Jodl, and would spend almost every day of the next five months with him.

The 6824 DIC held its victory parade in little Revin. In full dress uniform, and to the beat of a single drum, we marched down the main street behind an American flag. The French citizens cheered us on. It wasn't a fancy parade by a long shot, but I'll always remember the overwhelming feeling of relief and pride that swept over me. Occasionally, some Frenchmen would call out "Vive l'Amerique" as we passed, and I'd throw back my shoulders and stick out my chin. We won!

Colonel Holters and his crew arrived in Revin a few days after our victory parade. Because of the unusual intelligence potential of the group, a small special unit was formed to work with them. My Ritchie colleagues, Brotzen and Landauer, arrived from another assignment. They, Lt. Paul Comstock, and I made up the unit. We were under the direction of Captain John Boker, who had also taught German army organization and tactics at Camp Ritchie. Outside of working hours, Colonel Holters continued to expand my appreciation of the Spanish Riding School. He even parted with one of his prize personal possessions, a book named "Maestoso Austria," the love story of two people and a horse—a Lipizzaner, naturally.

My adventure in the Bohemian Forest has a sequel. Under Colonel Podhajsky's continued direction, the Spanish Riding School had existed in exile in Wels, Austria since March 1945. In the years that followed, the dancing white horses had celebrated triumphs throughout the world. They had captivated audiences on two major tours to America and Canada. They had been admired and acclaimed in Great Britain, all over Europe, and particularly in the land of their forefathers—Spain. Not until nine and a half years after their departure from Vienna did they go back "home" again.

I had read all about the reopening of the Spanish Riding School in 1955 and for years had dreamed of seeing the Lipizzaner in action. I took Winnie and our youngest son Brian to Europe. The opening performance of the 1965 winter season was scheduled for September 12 and we planned our trip accordingly. But horrors! Our travel agent couldn't get tickets. Neither could the Hotel Sacher where we were staying. The Vienna office of tourism failed me, too. The performance had been sold out for months. I was desperate. As a last resort I wrote a letter to Colonel Podhajsky himself. I explained the situation, and for good measure, I enclosed the precious photo of him with me which Colonel Holters had taken of us at Hostau twenty years earlier.

Weeks went by; no answer. I gave up. Then, just three days before our departure for Europe, a letter arrived from the Spanish Riding School. Colonel Podhajsky had retired in January of that year and was on a trip around the world. My letter had caught up with him in Paris, and he had called the school from there. I was to present the letter from the school at the ticket window one hour before the performance on September 12; they were holding three tickets for us. My expectations were surpassed!

On the morning of September 12 in Vienna, I dashed to the Hofburg, the splendid complex of buildings which houses the Spanish Riding School. The magnificent bells of St. Stefan's cathedral were tolling nine o'clock. When I arrived at the square before the ticket office my heart sank. There was a line of people at least a block long. They were queing up for the "standing-room only" tickets that might become available at the last minute. If I waited in that line I'd never get my tickets before the start of the performance. I bravely crashed the line, stepped up to the window, getting some dirty looks on the way. I presented my letter which proved to be a magic wand. There was an envelope marked with my name and the cost of three tickets. Austrian efficiency. I paid, gladly, and clutching my booty, returned to our hotel to get Winnie and Brian.

We were back at the Hofburg in no time. Hundreds were already ahead of us. When the doors opened we followed the stream of people until we got to the usher. He glanced at my tickets and snapped his fingers. Another usher rushed over and invited us to follow him, away from the entrance. I began to panic. Had something gone wrong?

We were led ceremoniously to the State Box. We were VIPs. This wasn't merely a happy dream. We were in Vienna, front row center in the royal box of the magnificent Spanish Riding School. All the magic that had been present here for hundreds of years took hold of me. The great chandeliers gleamed in all their splendor. The music began as the doors to the elegant riding hall opened. The snow-white horses with their gold trappings entered the arena in single file. They walked up to the State Box. The riders bared their heads. We joined in the thunderous applause of all the spectators in the hall. The show began.

I still have the program of that memorable performance. It was auto-graphed for us by the chief rider, Irvinger, and the commander of the school, successor to Colonel Podhajsky. He was Lieutenant Colonel Handler. The stallions performed to music by Strauss, Mozart, Chopin, and Bizet; the steps and movements were breathtaking to watch.

I was most impressed by what is called the Capriole. The Lipizzaner leaps simultaneously with all four feet. At the height of the leap he kicks violently with the hind legs. Back in Hostau, Colonel Holters had told me this maneuver was often used in the early days in battles against foot soldiers. The rider directs his well-trained steed to kick out in the movement of the Capriole. I saw the colts doing this same stunt in the field, and I learned that this is a mannerism of the Lipizzaner. The trick is to get the horse to do it on command. For me, the Capriole was the highlight of the "school above the ground" movements of the performance.

And for us the memorable show ended all too soon. Afterwards we visited the stables in the Stallburg. We learned that every Lipizzaner stallion has a double name, each name revealing the line of descent. The first name is that of the sire, the second is the name of the dam. There are six dynasties, all of which go back to the founding sires. So every Lipizzaner stallion's name begins with one of those six, like Maestoso, Pluto, or Neapolitano.

In the stables I overheard someone ask, "What is the military value of the Spanish Riding School?" The Austrian rider's answer tells it all. "What is the military value of a ballet?"

When we left the Hofburg and the Spanish Riding School that sunny afternoon, we were both elated and sad. We didn't think we'd ever see those grand horses perform again. But we were wrong. In 1984, Winnie and I made a trip to Vienna from Luxembourg. We were visiting our friends Hubert and Marietta Feichtlbauer, whose friendship goes back to my affiliation with the Fulbright Program. We very much wanted to take in a performance of the Spanish Riding School, but again, tickets were impossible to get. Hubert, a well-known Austrian journalist, was aware of my wartime experiences. He called on Madame Podhajsky, the widow of the famous colonel, who was able to repeat her husband's kind act of twenty years earlier. We got tickets for the four of us, not in the State Box this time, but still among the best seats in the house. All the memories of 1945 and 1965 came rushing back to me. It was overpowering.

But let's go back to 1945 and Revin. With the war finally over, there was time to breathe. Our interrogation now was only of historic significance. The pressure was off. I had time to explore the area around Revin and enjoyed some good hiking in the surrounding hills. Rheims was a two-hour jeep ride away. Several times in the weeks that followed, Mal Hilty and I went there for the "Opera Comique" at the Grand Theatre. We saw *Faust*, a four-hour production with Mario Franzini as Mephistopheles. We enjoyed superb performances of *The Magic Flute* and *Madame Butterfly*.

Our special prisoner group from the *Dienststelle Ost* were soon shipped off to Washington, where their interrogation projects would be even more detailed than they had been at our DIC. I was sorry to lose my contact with Colonel Holters. I would always remember his introducing me to the Lipizzaner magic. I also had the feeling our intelligence operation in Revin was drawing to an end. So I quickly wangled orders for a visit to Luxembourg. I expected to be transferred one of these days soon, and I might never get another chance to make such a trip. Furthermore, I had promised Papa that I would do my best to find my brothers and sisters. My boss, Major Ivo V. Giannini, was sympathetic. I was authorized to "proceed on or about May 31, 1945 to Luxembourg City for the performance of a special mission." Mal Hilty was able to travel with me.

Fourteen years had passed since my father and I said goodbye to our family and friends in Luxembourg. I wondered what I would find now on my return. I expected no difficulty locating Heinrich, Karl, and Kasi, or my sisters Liesel and Agnes. I also hoped to find friends from the Neipperg School. It dawned on me how little I knew about happenings in Luxembourg since May 1940 when German armies overran the tiny Grand Duchy. I had many questions.

The Class of 1945

As MAL HILTY AND I steered our jeep across the French-Luxembourg border on a mild Sunday morning in May 1945, we were traveling the same route taken by General Lunsford E. Oliver and his Fifth Armored Division eight months earlier in their liberation of the Grand Duchy. The first American soldier to die on Luxembourg soil lost his life at an intersection we crossed right after we entered the little town of Pétange.

The people of Pétange later erected a monument to the unidentified American on the spot where he died. On the monument is inscribed "We Will Never Forget." On every September 9 since then, the people of the town gather at this monument to pay tribute to the American soldier who made the supreme sacrifice for their freedom. As ambassador, I was privileged to participate in this moving ceremony each year.

We headed into the city on the Route de Longwy. We saw much evidence of earlier fighting—shrapnel marks and bullet holes on the sides of houses and storefronts, piles of rubble and potholes in the streets, occasionally the remnants of a building that had been bombed. The houses still standing were drab, gray, depressing.

I remembered the Luxembourgers' love of tradition. I told Mal that we were just in time for a concert at the Place d'Armes. Sure enough, we were. For several hundred years the Place d'Armes had been a parade ground. It's a handsome square, lined with chestnut and linden trees. Row upon row of sidewalk cafés provide the beer, wine, and food at tables under the trees and around a bandstand. When I was a boy, I joined my school friends on the Place d'Armes after church. We'd walk arm in arm, sometimes in step to the band music, around the pavilion. We weren't there to hear the music, however. We came to watch the girls, who walked arm in arm in a counterclockwise direction. Thus, we'd meet face to face. We boys would strut; the girls would giggle. But that was all behind me now.

Mal and I seated ourselves at a table, and I noticed for the first time how many GIs were in the square. At a table next to ours sat two black soldiers. The waiter came to their table. I heard one of them give his order: "Zwé Humpen Béier wann Iech gelifft." I nearly fell off my chair. Here was the first Luxembourgish I heard in fourteen years. It came from a black American soldier. It hadn't taken long for our GIs to learn how to order "two steins of beer, please."

Upon hearing Luxembourgish spoken I was able to switch on my own speech processes. Words I thought I had forgotten came to me as readily as the taste for the Luxembourg brew.

Mal and I checked into the Alfa Hotel across from the railroad station. It was set aside for American officers. Immediately I made inquiries about my family, the name Dolibois. No success. There were no telephone directories, no information operators. And I didn't know until then that French-sounding names were "verboten" under the Nazi regime. I was told that Luxembourgers with foreign names were required to change them to German. This also explained why all the street names were German. Now that the Nazis had gone for good, the original names were returning.

We decided to spend the rest of the day sightseeing. On Monday, at the opening of business, I would begin my search in earnest. So Mal and I drove through the Petrusse Valley, past my old house, along the cliffs, and under the bridges. We visited my mother's grave in Bonnevoie, and my former school. The church in which I'd been baptized, and in which Papa had served as Schweizer had been hit during an air raid. My "homecoming" was not the joyful occasion I had expected. Of course, it was reassuring to be able to find my way around town, to locate so many familiar landmarks. But everything looked worn, drab, abysmally poor, despondent. I had little hope of finding my brothers and sisters. That night I went to bed with a heavy heart.

Early Monday morning I started out on my search, alone. First to the fishmarket, to St. Michael's church. I felt certain that Monsignor Erasmy, our former pastor and family friend, would know something about the Dolibois family. I hoped he was still around. I wanted that mean old character to see young "Hansi" in an American officer's uniform. He was the one who boxed my ears back in 1931, assuring me that I would not be welcome in America, thief that I was.

But St. Michael's church was locked. A passerby told me that Monsignor Erasmy was now the pastor of the new church on the Gare. It would have been my parish church if we still lived in the Petrusse Valley.

Back in my old neighborhood on the Gare, the monsignor recognized me at once. "Aus dem Haenschen ist ein Hans geworden," he exclaimed clapping his hands together in mock wonderment. Yes, the little boy had indeed grown into a man; "and with no help from you," I thought to myself. But let bygones be bygones!

Erasmy had no information about my family, not even a hint. He himself had been gone from the city for several years. He suggested the police might be able to help me. So I went to the Préfecture de Police. There were no records of any kind; not in city hall, either. But one policeman was helpful. "Why don't you try the Red Cross," he offered, "they've been quite successful in locating missing and displaced persons."

At the Red Cross a white-haired matron proved to be an angel. She asked the right questions, no bureaucratic nonsense. "Do you happen to know where your brother was working when you last heard from him?" she prodded. Yes, I remembered. It was a drogerie—a pharmacy—on the Grand Rue. Well, there were four such establishments on the Grand Rue. "Let's go alphabetically," she said, "start with B, Bertogne." Bingo! It was the first one.

"Yes, Karl Dolibois worked for me many years," said Mr. Pierre Bertogne, a sweet old gent with rosy cheeks and a wistful smile. "But he had to use his wife's maiden name, Bausch. It was the law, you know." And then he took my arm, patted me on the shoulder. My brother died in December 1942. He had trouble with the gestapo, resisted military conscription, was under arrest. He died of a ruptured appendix in the prison in the Grund. They had refused him medical care.

Mr. Bertogne directed me to the rue des Capucins where Karl's widow and little daughter lived. Number seven, a short block from the monastery church where I had served as altar boy. I climbed four flights of stairs to a top floor apartment. I knocked on the door. It opened and before me stood my sister-in-law, Karl's widow Rose. She gasped, her eyes opened wide, and before I could say anything she glided to the floor in a faint. A very frightened little girl stood in the middle of the room. She burst into tears, and I didn't know to whom I should give attention first. Fortunately, Rose came to at once. I didn't have to tell her who I was. It was my resemblance to my brother that had caused her reaction.

The little girl was Renée; five years old, she was adopted. Of course, that bit of news had never reached us back in the States during those years of no communication.

I resolved immediately to provide as much happiness as possible for my new-found niece. On my return visit the next day, I was able to bring her the first orange she had ever seen. Other goodies from the officers' mess at the Alfa Hotel brought great joy to these two members of my family, who were immediately renamed Dolibois.

I came up zero as far as my two brothers, Heinrich and Kasi, and my two sisters, Liesel and Agnes, were concerned. Rose had not seen or heard from any of them since Karl's burial in 1942. None of them was in Luxembourg anymore.

There was one bright note in our visit to my old stamping grounds. The Bradtké family was still in business on the avenue de la Gare. The parents, and the two boys, Nikky and Polo, were at home, in good health, and genuinely excited about seeing me again. They filled me in on the whereabouts and activities of some of our schoolmates. But the information was fragmentary. I promised to return as soon as possible, and to pick up where we left off.

As Mal Hilty and I drove back to Revin, I wasn't overly elated about my first Luxembourg visit. Writing to Papa and Marie about Karl's death wouldn't be easy, especially since I had absolutely no clue about the rest of the family.

Back in Revin, we settled into our routine again. Most of the time was spent on housekeeping duties, and speculating on when we would be sent to the Pacific, and why.

I reported to my CO, Major Giannini, after our return from Luxembourg. I shared with him my observations and the results of my visit. He was very sympathetic, and then broke into a broad grin.

He opened his desk drawer and pulled out a sheaf of papers. "Looks like you'll be leaving us in a day or two, Lieutenant. I have your new travel orders here," he said, still grinning. I wondered why he seemed so pleased with himself.

"Have you heard anything about CCPWE number thirty-two?" he asked.

"No, sir."

"Well, it's the Central Continental Prisoner of War Enclosure, number thirty-two. It's also known as 'Ashcan' for some reason or other." His grin became broader. "Does Mondorf-les-Bains mean anything to you?"

"Yes sir, it's a small resort town in southern Luxembourg, right on the French border."

"I've never heard of it myself," said the major, "but that's where you are going. It beats the Philippine Islands."

I couldn't believe my ears. Somebody must have screwed up the works, but good. How could they ever have come up with Luxembourg as my next assignment? That just isn't the way the army does things. But I kept my mouth shut. Leave well enough alone.

The orders contained more good news. My friend Mal Hilty would be in the same place. Our "chief" would be Captain Herbert Sensenig, with whom both of us had worked before. And Sensenig reported to our former CO, Colonel T. C. Van Cleve, who had left Revin for an unknown destination a few weeks earlier. This Central Continental Prisoner of War Enclosure was just being established.

I learned that the 6824 DIC (MIS) was being moved from Revin to Oberursel-im-Taunus, not far from Frankfurt, Germany. SHAEF, Supreme Headquarters Allied Expeditionary Force, was being abolished. Our new command would be USFET, United States Forces European Theater. All that was of no consequence to me at the moment. I was too excited about being assigned to Luxembourg, even though I had no idea what the new job was about.

Master Sergeant Amos M. Francischelli and PFC Richard D. Vine were my travel companions from Revin to Luxembourg. We headed directly to Mondorf, a pleasant little Spa on the French-Luxembourg border. I remembered it for its beautiful park, a quiet stream on which one could row a boat, lots of old trees, and acres of flowers. There were many hotels and inns, a clinic, and the special facilities that go with a health resort—a "watering place." The Romans had developed Mondorf-les-Bains more than a thousand years ago. The dominant feature of the town was a large four-story structure—the Palace Hotel. I knew of it from my childhood days, but as we approached the building in 1945, I found it drastically altered.

Our jeep came around the bend and halted at an enormous gate, part of a fifteen-foot high barbed wire fence that stretched around the main building, a driveway, and gardens. On each corner of the fence stood a guard tower. Two soldiers and a very visible machine gun ominously occupied each tower. Camouflage nets and large planes of canvas hung on trees and posts all around the place. It was to prevent anyone from seeing what went on inside that fence. There were huge klieg lights overhead. I discovered later that two strands of wire on that fence were electrified. None of the PW enclosures in which I had worked were protected as heavily as this one.

Sergeant-of-the-guard Robert Bock sat in a jeep in front of the gate as I climbed out of mine. He and his driver wore MP armbands. Their shiny helmet liners also sported the white letters "MP." I returned their salute. "Good afternoon, Sergeant," I said. "I'm reporting for duty here. What kind of place is this? What's going on in there?"

His answer was typical of the hardbitten combat sergeant, the military policeman. "Hell, Lieutenant, I don't know. I've been here two weeks and I haven't been inside yet. To get in here you need a pass signed by God, and then somebody has to verify the signature."

Well, I had the right papers. I walked about one hundred meters to the entrance of the imposing Palace Hotel and was greeted by two guards stationed at the front door. In the lobby sat a noncom who was expecting me. Captain Sensenig would meet me at the Schleck Hotel around five o'clock. Lieutenant Hilty had arrived two days ago and was on a mission in Germany. I was the only other Military Intelligence officer assigned here, and I should leave my gear in room 30, up one flight of stairs.

That's all I learned from the staff sergeant, who wore the patch of the 391st Anti-Aircraft Battalion. I climbed up the stairs, located room 30 and let myself in with the key he had given me. It was an ordinary hotel room, with rather noisy wallpaper. A table and two chairs, and a folding army cot made up the furnishings. I started to unpack my duffel bag when I heard a knock on the door. Thinking this might be Captain Sensenig or one of the guard officers, I opened the door and got the surprise of my life. Before me stood a stout man, about five foot ten inches, dressed in a natty pearl-gray uniform, gold braid on the collars, gold insignia of rank on the shoulders. He clicked his heels, bobbed his head once, and said, "Goering, Reichsmarschall!" I gave a damn poor impression of an intelligence officer. My mouth fell open. Quickly, I gathered my wits and asked the man to step inside. He came to the point at once. On his arm he held a pair of uniform trousers which he handed to me. Then he explained that this was a pair he had "overlooked" when told the day before that he could have only one suit and one extra pair of trousers. "Since I am determined to be a model prisoner," he explained, "I thought I should bring this surplus item to you." I think I detected a note of sarcasm.

Goering then planted his feet apart, put his hands behind his back, and lodged his first complaint. He had been "misled" by the American officers to whom he had surrendered, "voluntarily." At Augsburg he had been told that he was going to a palatial spa and would be treated royally, as deserving the ex-commander in chief of the German Luftwaffe, a marshal of the Reich. He had arrived with all his finery, eleven suitcases. All this had been confiscated. He was extremely nervous and agitated, breathing hard and rapidly. But I was more nervous. For the first time I realized that my new assignment in Mondorf obviously had to do with high-ranking Nazis. It explained the security precautions around the building. I was in for the experience of a lifetime, eager to get my briefing from Captain Sensenig, and to get started on the right foot.

At this point, Goering himself pointed the way. It occurred to me that his knocking on my door was not due to his anxiety about having too many trousers. He could have given that extra pair to a guard just as easily. He had seen me walk into the compound. He was curious about me and the trousers became an excuse to find out for himself who I might be.

"You're such a young man, Herr Leutnant. What will be your duty in this 'elegant' establishment?"

Then he answered his own question. "Are you by chance a welfare officer who will see to it that we are treated correctly, according to the Articles of War?"

I decided I could answer that question in part truthfully. So I said, yes, I would be working along those lines. Goering was pleased. I found later that he took it upon himself to inform the other prisoners about my arrival and my responsibilities.

Our conversation was ended. He had satisfied his curiosity. He made a great show again of heel-clicking, bowing, and taking his 280 pounds out of my room.

I sat down and replayed this surprising incident in my mind, recalling the brief conversation for later guidance. This was going to be a challenging and exciting adventure. I needed to know all about "Ashcan" as soon as possible.

Captain Sensenig was waiting for me at the Hotel Schleck. The comfortable, small hotel, just two short blocks from the detention center, was the officers' mess, the temporary billet, and the office of the commandant of the prison. He was Col. Burton C. Andrus, cavalry, and I was presented to him at once. His eyes lit up when he saw the crossed sabres on my lapels. He quizzed me about my background. I passed the test. Colonel Andrus was quite a character. I would get to know him well in the months ahead. He prided himself on his own military—cavalry— experience. He was a flashy dresser; his helmet liner lacquered to a high polish in Patton fashion. His trim mustache and clipped speech identified him as a rather vain person. He obviously relished his important position of command. He didn't walk, he marched. And as long as you let him know that you knew he was in charge, you would have no problem with him. But he managed to cause a few problems for us, by the way he ran his tight ship.

Sensenig and I talked far into the night as he outlined the mission of the Central Continental Prisoner of War Enclosure, number 32—code name "Ashcan"—under the direction of Military Intelligence. Everything was still in the startup stage. A lot of details had to be clarified. This installation had been ordered into being by Allied Command as a processing station and interrogation center. We were representing the interests of Military Intelligence Service, SHAEF G-2. Eventually, a number of high-ranking Nazis would be processed through this detention center. So far, each day had brought its own surprises.

For several months in early 1945, the Palace Hotel had been used as a billet for American troops being readied for the invasion of Germany. The Moselle River and the German border were less than five miles east of Mondorf. In late April, forty-two German prisoners of war, who had been held at Mailly-le-Camp in the French Department de l'Aube, were brought to Mondorf. They were specially selected as cooks, bakers, waiters, and handy men. The group included a barber, a dentist, a doctor, and even a hotel manager. It was their job to prepare the Palace Hotel as a prison and to staff it under the supervision of American personnel.

First they moved all the fancy hotel furniture into storage at a nearby cloister. Each "guest room" was then equipped with a folding army cot, two GI blankets, a chair, and a table. Eventually, the windows would be replaced with fiberglass and iron bars. These German prisoners of war considered themselves very fortunate. They were well-fed, comfortably housed, and enjoyed more freedom and privileges than the field marshals, generals, admirals, Gauleiters, and government bigwigs who had been pushing them around for more than a dozen years. Now they could look *down* on what they called the "Bonzen"—the big wheels.

Captain Sensenig described the first few days of the Ashcan operation to me. He said the first important prisoner to arrive was Arthur Seyss-Inquart, the man who betrayed Austria and later became the Reichs-kommissar of Holland. The lord mayor of Stuttgart, Dr. Karl Stroelin, arrived after Seyss-Inquart, along with Wilhelm Frick, a former minister of the Interior, and, most recently, the Reichsprotektor of Bohemia-Moravia. That same afternoon, General Field Marshal Wilhelm Keitel checked in with his aide, Colonel von Freyend, and Corporal Oskar Moench, his batman. This posed problem number one, what to do with aides and batmen? Sensenig decided to treat the officers as prisoners, and assign enlisted men to the regular PW labor cadre. For a while at least, it was agreed to allow one batman or valet for every six generals and admirals. General Eisenhower issued a declassification order a few days later which changed all that.

Field Marshal Albert Kesselring was delivered to the Palace Hotel with a serious headwound from an auto accident. He was extremely upset about his detention, and made all kinds of demands for his physical comfort. Another problem. If all PW were to be treated alike, how could pillows be provided for some and not for others? If we wanted them to cooperate fully in interrogation, we had to keep up their morale. Colonel Andrus and the guard element of the detention center didn't agree with "special favors" and "sympathetic treatment." The problem would plague us on and on.

Hans Frank, better known as "the butcher of Poland" for the extermination orders he gave while he was governor general of Poland, made a spectacular entrance in his silk pajamas. Frank had been arrested on April 30 and tried to commit suicide by slashing his neck, left wrist and arm, and his left side with a knife. He was carried into the Palace Hotel and placed under twenty-four-hour guard, one guard in his room, another outside the door. Frank wasn't going anywhere, especially since he had no clothing other than his pajamas.

Reichsmarschall Hermann Goering brought not only eleven suitcases, but also his valet to the CCPWE number 32. Captain Sensenig said it took a whole afternoon to list his valuables and search his luggage. It took an equally long time to pacify him. His hand shook so he could barely sign his name. The shaking was from his addiction to narcotics. On his person and in his luggage were found large quantities of small white pills which were identified as paracodin, the chemical name for which is Dihydrocodeine. Goering was in the habit of taking twenty in the morning and twenty in the evening. The German doctor among the labor PW, Dr. Ludwig Pfluecker, started at once in getting Goering to cut down on his intake. As I got to know Goering better, I found it interesting that he took great pride in cooperating in this endeavor. Later on, our own American doctor, Captain William J. Miller, took charge of the program. The prisoner of war rations and the routine the doctors prescribed resulted in Goering's losing considerable weight and becoming healthier than he had been for some time. It was the one development about which the former Reichsmarschall did not complain. His vanity was being aroused. He fancied looking like the hero of the Luftwaffe again, the highly decorated ace of the famous Richthofen Squadron of World War I.

In the course of my briefing by Captain Sensenig, I told him about Goering's visit to my room earlier in the afternoon. He suggested enthusiastically that I should indeed play the role of a welfare officer for getting information. He and Hilty would handle the more formal interrogations; I would be responsible for "morale," but in the process keep accurate records of what the prisoners said to me. I would visit prisoners in their rooms, chat with them at chance meetings in the building, and invite them to my own room for informal discussions. I might even give them English lessons if they were interested. Any excuse to make conversation. It turned out to be an effective ploy.

We also agreed that I should not use my last name, since I had relatives in Germany, and one never knows what paths one might cross. I chose to be known to the Nazi leaders as Lieutenant John Gillen. This was a Luxembourg name that occurred to me, and I used it from that time on.

As word got around that Lieutenant Gillen was a sympathetic sort of guy who was willing to listen to complaints and even translate letters or try to locate families, I never lacked for company. The gossipping, the backbiting, and the eagerness to shift blame to another led to revelations that proved very useful. Gradually, a pattern evolved. An interrogator would work with a prisoner. Later I might drop in on the prisoner to inquire about his health or to check if he needed anything. With the interrogation fresh in his mind, the internee often felt compelled to talk about it, to set the record straight. He might recall something he had wanted to tell his interrogator. Or, he would complain that the facts had been distorted by someone else, a colleague or fellow officer. Soon I would get his opinion of that particular "informer."

In short, my gossip file and collections of off-the-cuff remarks got bigger and better. I came up with some great information and character-izations that proved useful in rounding out an interrogation report. I was grateful to Goering for suggesting the cover I could use in my work at Ashcan. Later, once my role was fixed in the prisoners' minds, I was able to take on regular interrogations on historic or military matters that were not controversial.

Sensenig, Hilty, and I were joined by two more interrogators, Captain Kurt R. Wilheim and Lieutenant John G. Ziegler. We had a fine cadre of enlisted men who helped out with research, preparation of reports, and even taking on interrogations when suitable. Meanwhile, more and more prisoners arrived on the scene. Some stayed with us for the next three months. Others were held at the Mondorf center for a few days or weeks, and then were hustled off to agencies in London, Paris, or Wies-baden. The British had an interrogation center which was coded "Dust-bin." Who said there is no humor in bureaucracy? The person who picked the codenames "Ashcan" and "Dustbin" must have given some thought to how much trash we hauled from one to the other.

Shortly after I joined the Mondorf installation, an efficient system of processing arriving prisoners was established by Captain Hubert Biddle of the Guard Battalion. Biddle, from Columbus, Ohio, demonstrated good Midwestern sense in setting up the procedure. Arriving PW would be brought to the Military Intelligence office first. While they stepped into a bathroom where the doctor would examine them, a guard searched their clothes thoroughly. They then dressed and went to an interrogation room for processing. Next came the room assignment.

Meanwhile, their baggage was searched and the items allowed were returned to them. The rest was put in storage. Kurt Daluege, former Generaloberst of the German police, was the first prisoner subjected to this effective system. The search revealed two phials of poison in brass containers, the first of many such discoveries.

Soon we added Robert Ley, the leader of the Reichsarbeitsdienst, (the labor service organization of the Third Reich), and the foreign minister, Joachim von Ribbentrop, to our roster. Then came Jakob Nagel, state secretary for the German Postal Service; the minister of Labor and Social Policy, Franz Seldte; even the president of German breweries, Franz Schwarz.

We held former ambassadors and officials in the German Foreign Office, such as Franz von Papen, Schwerin von Krosigk, and Admiral Nicholas von Horthy, the regent of Hungary. For some reason these "vons" were housed exclusively in a separate villa just behind the Palace Hotel. We referred to it as the "*von* Annex." A baron was added, Baron Gustav Adolf Steengracht, state secretary in the Foreign Office. Then came a couple of commoners, Hjalmar Schacht, finance minister, and Richard Walther Darré, the Reichsminister of Food and Agriculture. At first I thought well of Darré, because his ministry had the responsibility for the Lipizzaner stud in Czechoslovakia. Then I learned that he was also an SS Obergruppenfuehrer.

On one day early in June, a shipment of twenty-four prisoners arrived. The enrollment now stood at fifty-one, and the atmosphere in Ashcan changed considerably. Until then, Captain Sensenig had been fighting a constant battle with Colonel Andrus over the treatment of the prisoners. Military Intelligence wanted the internees treated with fairness and consideration. This would keep them in a cooperative mood, important to effective interrogation. But Colonel Andrus appeared to have passed judgment already, on one and all. They were war criminals, and he was meting out punishment. Prisoners, regardless of rank, were to snap to attention when the colonel appeared. One general who failed to do so ended up in a basement room on bread and water for a day or two. This helped enforce discipline, but sure as hell didn't get much cooperation in an interrogation session.

Albert Speer, Hitler's chief architect and Reichsminister for Armaments stayed with us for just a few days. Apparently he was much in demand at higher levels. He was moved to Paris, came back for a day or two, and then was shipped off to London. I saw him again in Nuremberg two months later.

But Grand Admiral Karl Doenitz, the commander of submarines and then commander in chief of the German navy, arrived with Generaloberst Alfred Jodl, chief of operations of the Armed Forces High Command. These two, along with Field Marshal Wilhelm Keitel, and several other members of the German General Staff, would be with us from beginning to end. Hitler had designated Doenitz president of the Reich and commander in chief of the armed forces. It was in fact Doenitz who had formally ended the war.

As the number of our "guests" increased, I became more and more intrigued. It seemed that every Nazi ever mentioned in the news during the late thirties and early forties was here under one roof in little Luxembourg. Alfred Rosenberg, the Nazi philosopher, Walther Funk, the president of the Reichsbank; a bevy of Gauleiters and military officers of varying ranks, joined those who had come earlier. One of the last arrivals—we called each newcomer a "gain"—was none other than Julius Streicher, the notorious Jew-baiter, editor of the pornographic, anti-Semitic newspaper, *Der Stuermer*. Streicher had also been the Gauleiter of Franken.

His brass-knuckle type of anti-Semitism had become offensive even to some of the most ardent Nazis. Streicher had taken great pleasure in the destruction of synagogues, the smashing of storefronts, the beatings, and finally, the pits and gas chambers. He had always wanted the Jews exterminated. He preached what all the party members agreed on: "The Jew was the main cause of the troubles Germany faced after World War I." But his vicious, unsavory character had repelled many of them.

When he showed up at Mondorf his former colleagues objected to his presence. They threatened to leave the dining room if he entered it. Colonel Andrus loved this protest. It provided another opportunity for him to let the "Bonzen" know who was running this show. A meeting was called at which Andrus made it clear that they were all in the same category, and they would all be treated alike.

Nevertheless, we decided that it would be best for Streicher to be lodged on another floor. So, the "Jew-baiter" was given a private room, number 59, a floor below the others. When he entered the dining room, no one spoke to him. For a few days he ate by himself. Then he was joined by Robert Ley, the Labor Front leader. The two became inseparable. We called them the Bobbsey Twins. They had a lot in common.

It became obvious after the first week or two that cliques were forming, actually three distinct social circles. On one hand were the members of the German General Staff: Field Marshal Wilhelm Keitel, chief of the Armed Forces High Command (OKW); Generaloberst Alfred Jodl, his chief of operations; General of the Artillery Walter Warlimont, Jodl's deputy; Field Marshal Albert Kesselring, once chief of Armed Forces Italy and later the Supreme Commander West; and Generals

Friedrich von Boetticher, Hermann Reinecke, Johannes Blaskowitz, and others. In the same group were the admirals, Eric Raeder and Doenitz. Here were the guys who had helped Hitler plan and execute World War II. While they favored Germany's military power, some of them were not necessarily in sympathy with the Nazi way of doing things. Most of them vehemently denied any knowledge of the atrocities, the conspiracy, and even the violent anti-Semitism of the Nazi regime. Later they were joined on our roster by Field Marshals Gerd von Rundstedt and Werner von Blomberg; Generals Heinz Guderian and Sepp Dietrich; and a few more admirals. The German General Staff group hung together. They wanted as little as possible to do with the other prisoners. And they were quite willing to denounce their fellow inmates in the course of interrogations and discussions.

In the second circle or clique were the real Nazi gangsters. They were the "alte Kaempfer"—the old fighters—who had been with Hitler at the beginning of his rise to power. Some had participated in the attempted "Beer Hall Putsch" in Munich in 1923. Some had been in prison with him at Landsberg. After Hitler became the chancellor, they were rewarded with the positions that held the powers of life and death. Julius Streicher and Robert Ley stood out in this group of street brawlers. Among others were Hans Frank, Alfred Rosenberg, Seyss-Inquart, Wilhelm Frick, and Walter Buch. Hermann Goering belonged to this group, but was shunned by them, as he was by most of his former colleagues. Rudolf Hess, still interned in England, would not join us until Nuremberg.

These were the Nazi "Bonzen"—the persons largely responsible for the inhuman atrocities associated with the Nazi leadership. The General Staff group avoided them, with disdain. In turn, they blamed the generals for losing their glorious war and the Thousand Year Reich. No love was lost between those two groups.

The members of the third social circle were united by what they had in common—the bureaucracy of the Third Reich. Otto Meissner, president of the presidial chancellery, stuck with Hans Heinrich Lammers, Reichminister and chief of the Chancellery. Graf Lutz Schwerin von Krosigk was the former finance minister, designated foreign minister by Hitler in his last will and testament. Certainly Franz von Papen, Schacht, and Nicholas von Horthy fitted into this third category. As did Franz Seldte, minister for Labor and Social Policy, Wilhelm Stuckart, secretary in the Ministry of the Interior, and a dozen more. They were the "statesmen"—the career public service officers. Some of them had been in the government during the Weimar Republic. They changed their political colors to be acceptable to Hitler's regime. They were opportunists of the highest order.

It's noteworthy that only two of this group were tried in the first session of the International War Crimes Trials, Schacht and von Papen. Both were acquitted, along with Hans Fritzsche, the assistant to Goebbels in the Propaganda Ministry. Some of these "public servants" were indicted and tried in subsequent trials. In Mondorf they were helpful sources of information in the preparation of the cases against the twenty-two major Nazi war criminals.

Goering didn't fit into any one of these three categories. He was not German General Staff even though he held the highest military rank as commander of the Luftwaffe. As "Reichsmarschall" he ranked higher than a five-star general. His erstwhile Nazi colleagues did not respect him as chief of the Luftwaffe, and as Hitler had turned against him, he was not acceptable to them either. The government officials didn't welcome him, although he was president of the Reichstag, and held other high government positions.

Goering considered himself the number one personage at the detention center, so he attempted to be the chief spokesman, with or without their consent. He fancied himself the captain of the team. He tried to organize a joint defense, to be the aggressive cheerleader. But feelings were bitter. Judgment was passed by one on the other. Thus Goering was, after all, alone, sitting by himself during mealtimes or reading in his favorite cane chair on the Palace Hotel veranda.

We continued to experience growing pains as the CCPWE was getting organized. A verbal order by telephone came from SHAEF G-2 after the Nazi leader of the Sudeten Germans, Konrad Henlein, committed suicide while a prisoner of the Americans. Watch crystals, razors and razor blades, glassware of all kinds, shoelaces, neckties, and belts, were to be confiscated. Eyeglasses could be used only under guard. Problems! The removal of window panes without barring the window opening would only expedite suicides. The prisoner could simply throw himself out of the window. It was decided to quietly disobey the order until things were under better control.

A few days later we started to get metal bars, a sort of powerful wire mesh. This obstruction was built into the window frames, and then the window glass was knocked out. There was broken glass all over the place. The Nazis laughed themselves silly. They called the exercise "Kristallnacht"—crystal night—in reference to the night in 1938 when the windows of Jewish shopkeepers and homes were smashed as part of the Nazi's anti-Semitic pogrom. The ironic aspect of it all was the presence of broken glass everywhere. Any internee who wanted to commit suicide could have picked up a piece of glass and cut himself to shreds.

When Captain Sensenig briefed me about the start-up of activities at Ashcan, he didn't hide the fact that we would have problems with the people responsible for guarding the prisoners. Especially Colonel Andrus. He loved strutting around the halls and making the inmates bow and scrape whenever they passed him. Almost daily he issued new orders dictating their behavior and outlining new rules. Fortunately, he couldn't speak German, so one of us had to interpret his mandates for him. Sometimes it was difficult to keep from joining the high-ranking Nazis in their covert laughter. He kept insisting that we inform the prisoners over and over that he was their commanding officer. They were to come to attention whenever he appeared. Infringement would result in disciplinary action. The PW were duly informed and accepted this as a matter of course.

But after the word got around they started playing games. They treated all of us with the same deference Colonel Andrus demanded, knowing it would make us uncomfortable. For instance, if I walked into the building while they were sitting on the veranda, they would all rise in unison, stand at rigid attention, and chant "Guten Morgen Herr Leutnant!" Having marshals, generals and admirals snap-to whenever I came around was a little more than my ego needed. Eventually, and fortunately, they tired of their game and the atmosphere became more relaxed.

A visit from the American provost marshal, General Record, resulted in a somewhat less rigid situation. The prisoners were given three blankets instead of two, and mattresses and pillows were issued to each internee. The prisoners were allowed a fair amount of clothing. This was especially important to Hans Frank, who was still in his pajamas.

It was also decided the prisoners should have something to do to pass the time. Reading material was provided—books, newspapers, and magazines. A chess set and a checker board were available in the reading room. They could listen to the Armed Forces radio at regular times.

We even arranged for "extra-short" shoestrings, without which some of them couldn't stay in their shoes. It would have been difficult for any one of them, no matter how scrawny, to hang or strangle himself on a four-inch shoestring.

At about the same time, an order from General Eisenhower was issued to all PW installations clarifying the status of the high-ranking Nazis. They were to be treated as declassified prisoners of war, all of equal rank. They were to be addressed only as "Mister," with no military rank or official title or exchange of salutes. Those still wearing uniforms were required to remove all insignia of rank and all decorations. Their daily rations were those prescribed by the Geneva Convention for all prisoners of war, sixteen hundred calories per day.

Apparently, this order was the result of much confusion at different processing centers. It may also have been prompted by the letters General Eisenhower was receiving. Admiral Doenitz, Field Marshal Keitel, Goering, and others, refused to be declassified prisoners. They insisted they were heads of state, commanders in chief. They demanded respectful, dignified treatment. They wrote letters to General Eisenhower, the secretary of war, the secretary of state and even to President Truman. At Mondorf our job was to translate those letters and send them on through channels.

Following the visit of the provost marshal and receipt of General Eisenhower's special order, Colonel Andrus decided to draft a message that would make things clear once and for all. It was read to all assembled prisoners:

> Whereas I do not desire to stand in the way of your writing letters concerning alleged theft of property or other violations of human rights, writing letters about the inconveniences or lack of convenience or about your opinions as to any indignity or deference due you is fruitless and apt to only disgust those in authority. Since, as you know, I am subject to frequent inspections by representatives of the highest authority some changes have been made as a result of these inspections. The letters you have written have not yet reached these authorities, but are still on their way through subordinate channels.
>
> The commandant, his superiors, the Allied Governments, and the public of the nations of the world, are not unmindful of the atrocities committed by the German government, its soldiers, and its civil officials. Appeals for added comfort by the perpetrators and parties to these conditions will tend only to accentuate any contempt in which they are already held. Therefore it is my duty to suggest that all refrain from writing letters borne solely of personal vanity.

The message was read in German by Captain Sensenig and punctuated by Colonel Andrus with occasional whacks on the table with his swagger stick.

I'm not sure this message made things clear after all. The less important internees, and even those who felt some guilt, must have wondered why and how they were found guilty without first being tried.

The interrogation officers appealed to Colonel Van Cleve to talk to Colonel Andrus and settle the conflict once and for all. The CCPWE number 32 was a processing/interrogation center, not a penal institution. The guard element was to provide security and to maintain discipline—to prevent escape, suicides, and/or a possible attack on the detention center. Military Intelligence was to gather information. We couldn't work at cross-purposes and succeed. I think Andrus got the message. He gradually recognized and appreciated our objective and became less imperious. In time, the prisoners stopped mocking him as a Chaplinesque figure of authority. For my part, I liked the old boy. We became good friends, and I ended up admiring his attention to duty and his conscientious performance. It wasn't easy being responsible for some sixty or more prisoners whom most of the world despised.

The prisoners were allowed to leave their rooms at certain hours. They could sit on the veranda, in the reading room, or walk around the gardens inside the barbed wire enclosure under the watchful eyes of the guards. I don't think I ever got used to going up the stairs or walking down a hall of the Palace Hotel and bumping into the Reichsmarschall of the Third Reich or the commander in chief of the German navy. Meeting a Nazi Gauleiter or the successor to Adolf Hitler, so casually, was unreal. I didn't realize the historic significance of what I was doing until much later. I concentrated mostly on getting enough points to go home to my family.

When the Mondorf detention center was first opened in late May, its location was a well-guarded secret. The out-of-the-way health resort was to provide a site where the pretrial interrogation and processing could be handled without disturbance and very little interruption. But it couldn't last. A worldwide press was determined to solve the mystery of "Whatever happened to the big Nazis?" The secret was "leaked." Reporters and photographers moved into Mondorf, clamoring for interviews and pictures. Colonel Andrus decided only he would grant interviews. Only influential newsmen would be allowed to visit inside the enclosure, and no individual photographs of any kind could be taken. One group picture was permitted. We gathered all of our inmates on the front steps of the Palace Hotel. *Time* magazine published the full-page portrait and titled it "The Class of 1945."

Indeed, it looked like a class picture. Front row center, stern and regal, was the president of the class, Reichsmarschall Hermann Goering. On his right, Ritter von Epp, governor of Bavaria; on his left, Franz Xaver Schwarz, Nazi party treasurer. Robert Ley refused to look at the "birdie," glumly staring into the distance over his left shoulder. Von Ribbentrop frowned at the photographer on the edge of the group. Streicher had his arms folded against his chest, defiant as ever. Oddly enough, most of the field marshals, generals, and admirals—Keitel, Jodl, Kesselring, Doenitz, and Raeder—stood inconspicuously in the back rows. Nobody was smiling.

There was a gap in the very last row. If I had stood up straight, my face would have been in the portrait, too. I had been in charge of lining up the "class of 1945," and ducked down when the photographer was ready. I've regretted my shyness of the moment ever since.

Life in Ashcan

CONFUSION OVER TERMINOLOGY reigned at Ashcan. Were our "guests" inmates, internees, prisoners of war, criminals? It all depended on whom you asked. To Colonel Andrus they were criminals, one and all. Captain Sensenig preferred the term "PW," and the plural Ps/W. Mal Hilty and I called them internees and addressed them with "mister." In our interrogation reports they were identified as "subject." And the German PW labor cadre used "Bonzen."

The Luxembourgers had other names for them, some unprintable. We found that out when 176 Luxembourg citizens were brought to Mondorf from the Dachau concentration camp.

Luxembourg government authorities decided to bring persons liberated from various concentration camps to the health resort for recuperation. The mineral baths, the beautiful park, and the restful atmosphere would certainly help in the rehabilitation of those who had suffered so much. It was a form of beneficial quarantine, but it posed new problems for us. Behind the barbed wire fence and the camouflage nets were the very persons responsible for what those Luxembourgers had endured at Dachau, Buchenwald, and other camps.

Colonel Andrus, Captain Sensenig, and I met with representatives of the displaced persons and assured them that the Nazis were not living in luxury, that ours was an interrogation center in preparation for the International War Crimes Trials. I think it helped for me to be able to explain these things in Luxembourgish. However, the Luxembourgers had already done their own checking on life inside Ashcan.

I was told that if you walked to the top of the road skirting the Palace Hotel grounds, and then climbed about ten feet up the bank next to the road, you could get a clear view of the terrace, the grounds, and the entrance to the hotel. Looking over the canvas hangings and the camouflage nets, the Luxembourgers could see the "héicht Déier"—the big wigs—shuffling along in tie-less shoes and slippers. They spotted the shabby castoff clothing many wore, and they had already observed the subdued behavior of the internees. They knew from the way American officers were greeted as they entered and left the building, that those Nazis were not being treated as honored guests.

The Luxembourgers hated the Germans and made no effort to hide their feelings. The German forces had invaded Luxembourg in the early morning of May 10, 1940. Luxembourg's army of some four hundred men didn't try to stop them. In fact, there were no casualties except for two customs officers who had tried to hold them up at the border. Naively it was thought the Maginot Line would stop the advancing Germans, and the Belgian and French armies would soon drive them back into Germany.

German soldiers didn't harm the Luxembourgers, although they cleaned out the shops, especially food and clothing stores. Misery for the Luxembourgers began when Gustave Simon, the Gauleiter, arrived. Luxembourg was "reunited" with Germany, annexed as Gau Moselland. Young Luxembourgers had to join the Hitler Youth; the older persons became "Volksdeutsche." Those who didn't join lost their jobs or weren't allowed in schools. If Luxembourgers lost their jobs, they were sent to Germany and assigned work. French-sounding words in the Luxembourg language were verboten. Streets and public places were renamed. The Luxembourg flag was illegal; the Grand Ducal family was forced into exile.

Things really started to go sour when Luxembourg Jews were forced to wear the yellow stars of David, and subjected to the same persecution as the Jews in Germany. Eventually those Jews who had not managed to escape from Luxembourg were interned in concentration camps and many were executed. Young Luxembourgers born between 1915 and 1926 were forced into the German army. Those who deserted could be executed as traitors or their families sent to concentration camps.

Life under the Nazis became a living hell, and a very active underground organization of resisters developed. The bravery and the sacrifices of the resisters and fighters is well documented. Many aligned themselves with the Armée Blanche in Belgium or the FFI in France, while others served their country in the various Luxembourg underground movements. Some five hundred Luxembourgers escaped to England, struggling through Belgium, Holland, France, and Portugal. They were in constant danger, and endured great hardships. Their objective was to join the British, French, U.S., and other allied armies, including the Foreign Legion. They sought to fight for their country's freedom. Many of them succeeded, including my Neipperg schoolmate Albert Stoltz. I've had the good fortune to spend hours on end with veterans of these various exploits who proudly relive their experiences and religiously take part in reunion and commemorative events forty years later.

Luxembourg humor always plays a role in the recounting of such adventures. The German bosses in Luxembourg demanded the "Heil Hitler!" of all citizens, as they did in Germany. The traditional greetings were not permitted. The Nazi greeting was required upon entering a public place. Typically, Luxembourgers outsmarted the SS and the collaborators by rapidly saying, "Drei Liter!" (three liters) which sounded so much like Heil Hitler the Germans never knew the difference. Sabotage, active and passive resistance, made things difficult for the Germans. A general strike by Luxembourgers was punished with mass arrests and executions. No wonder Luxembourgers regard Americans not only as soldiers who drove the occupying Germans out of Luxembourg, but also as liberators who restored to them their freedom, their sovereignty, and their very existence. Looking back on those years of horror, it is surprising that Ashcan wasn't stormed by the Luxembourg people during the three months the Nazi bigwigs were in Mondorf.

We did have other "invaders" of Ashcan—inspectors. It seemed every branch of service and every allied nation wanted to have a piece of the action—or maybe just to satisfy their curiosity. Not a day passed without high-ranking officers, or a team of officers, or politicians from every nook and cranny, coming to inspect the facilities. Each inspection took us away from our scheduled interrogations and just screwed up the works.

We had a two-fold mission at this PW enclosure. Briefs and questionnaires from the Paris office of the Nazi War Crimes Commission came to us regularly. Supreme Court Justice Robert Jackson was to serve as the prosecutor for the United States at the four-power international War Crimes Tribunal in Nuremberg. We were charged with getting the information he and his staff needed. There was much to learn about the personalities and characteristics of the Nazi leaders. We knew little about the roles many of them played in the conspiracy with which they would be charged. Who gave orders to execute prisoners of war? Who was responsible for the "final solution?" What did the people know about concentration camps? Slave labor? How did the paramilitary and political organizations and institutions function in making up the cadre of the military power that enabled Hitler and his cohorts to launch World War II? What lessons could we learn from all this?

Every agency of government was compiling reports and histories. The War Department History Section wanted to know all about strategy, order of battle, the role played by members of the elite German General Staff. Other departments of our government got involved, too. Labor wanted to know about the German Labor Front, Ley's "Reichsarbeits-dienst." Commerce and Treasury had a lot of questions to be asked German ministers of Trade and Finance. Agriculture sent question-naires aimed at Darré, the minister of Food and Agriculture, and another agency was interested in social policy and public housing. As the number of prisoners swelled, so did the traffic of questionnaires. Just interrogating on the basis of the written briefs was a round-the-clock job.

Our second mission was that of coordinating the visits of interrogation teams from allied nations and our own government. France, Belgium, England, and quite frequently the Soviet Union, sent teams of military officers or civilian government officials to interrogate certain prisoners. We had to fit such visits into our own interrogation schedules. We often sat in on their interviews to make sure our procedural rules were ob-served. Since we were responsible for these world-renowned personali-ties, we made sure nobody was going to twist arms, pull fingernails, or squeeze testicles. But I will say that I wouldn't have blamed representa-tives of some of these victimized nations if they had administered a swift kick to some of the Nazi leaders' behinds.

Things really got hectic when visiting VIPs wanted to be entertained. The Soviets particularly. They worked hard when they worked, but when the day was done, they wanted to eat and drink. I should say drink and eat. They supplied their own vodka, and they were insistently gen-erous in sharing the vast supply. They were insulted if you held back on matching their frequent toasts.

Working with the Soviets was challenging in other ways. Sometimes we wondered if they came to Mondorf to interrogate Nazis or to check on us Americans. Invariably they would pretend they couldn't speak German and needed one of us to interpret. In such cases their team in-cluded an English-speaking officer, always a woman. The seemingly endless inquisition would start with a Russian question, translated into English by their officer. Then I would repeat it in German for the pris-oner. The answer would then go back the same route, into English, then Russian. It wouldn't take us long to figure out that some of their team could speak better German than we could. It really got hairy if the Nazi prisoner could speak English and got into the game by pretending otherwise.

More often, the Soviets spoke German but pretended none of them could handle English. In the "post-interrogation" gatherings, when the vodka popped out of their handy vodka-valise, we had to be careful about what we said to each other. The Cold War had already begun.

The Russians seemed to be interested in military personnel only. Doenitz, Keitel, Jodl, and Goering were almost always on their list.

Of course, there were American VIPs too, and most of the time I would be charged with entertaining them. A jeep tour around Luxembourg was always on the itinerary. I became well acquainted with Luxembourg restaurants, especially around the Moselle. The charming country inns of the North, in the Ardennes and "Little Switzerland," were open again. Forty years later as ambassador I could return to some of those special places. On the Moselle, the charming Hotel Simmer in Ehnen was one of the establishments I visited often in 1945. During embassy years its present owners Arsène and Adeline Millim became our best friends. We dined sumptuously with them and other friends on many occasions.

One day two FBI officials arrived to interview several of our prisoners. One of the agents suggested it might be interesting to have a souvenir of Reichsmarschall Hermann Goering in the FBI museum. I decided to ask Goering for such a contribution. He was absolutely delighted. Slapping his fat thighs he roared: "Imagine my being featured in the famous FBI museum with the gun of John Dillinger and the mask of Baby-Face Nelson. It's a fantastic idea!" Then he went on, "Aha, I'm already indicted. A notorious criminal. American children in the future will shudder when they see a souvenir of the vicious Reichsmarschall in the FBI collection."

Sarcasm was one of Goering's best tools. He was willing to part with one of his gold "Schulterklappen"—the epaulets of his rank as Reichsmarschall. It depicted crossed batons, the laurel wreath of victory with a swastika in its center, and the gothic German eagle, all resting on gold braid. He had cut them off his uniform a week earlier when the declassification order came in. He accompanied me to the storeroom where we removed an epaulet from one of his bags and made note of the action on his inventory list. Then he turned to me and said, "Would you like to have the other one, Herr Leutnant? I won't have any more use for it."

I didn't have a single souvenir of my adventure, and I didn't want the old boy to start twisting my arm. I've never visited the FBI museum to see if his epaulet is on display and frightening little children. But the one I have is a special memento, framed with the autograph "Hermann Goering, Reichsmarschall."

Goering was in an expansive mood the day he gave me his gold-encrusted insignia of rank. I saw him again later in the afternoon and he showed me a little booklet in which he meticulously had written jokes being told in Germany about himself and other Nazis. Of course, these had to be "underground jokes." A person could end up in prison if overheard telling one. But on this day, Goering showed me another side of himself—his sense of humor, which I would learn to appreciate in the months that followed. His enormous ego still allowed him to laugh at himself.

On this particular day, he wanted to share one of his favorite stories making the rounds in Germany. But first he elaborated on National Socialism as the Germans knew it. Nazism was not an idea, an organization, a party, or even an institution. No, it was a *movement*, a movement that would sweep over the entire world. The National Socialist Movement—a "Bewegung." With that lecture concluded, he told his story.

It seems the Reichsmarschall had been on an extensive tour of all the fronts, including North Africa. He had been gone nearly a month. Upon his return he prepared his reports, made his official calls, and finally retired to his private quarters where his beautiful wife Emmy awaited him. He took her in his arms, looked deep into her eyes, and said, "Ach Emmy, Liebling, when I'm with you I can forget everything. I forget the SS, the NSKK, the War, even the Fuehrer." Emmy pinched him lovingly and replied, "Hermann, whatever you do, don't forget the movement." Goering laughed loudest, well pleased with himself, the charming raconteur.

Everybody who came to Ashcan wanted to interview Goering. Sometimes he would be very cooperative and turn on all his charm. On other occasions he would balk, pouting, protesting at being at everyone's beck and call. Then it would be necessary to stroke his ego. "No wonder, Herr Goering, after all, you are the highest ranking of all officials in this prison. You are the official spokesman for the Third Reich, the most knowledgeable. . . ." He would eat it up; his chest swelling. Thoughtfully, he would nod in agreement. But I also sensed that he was chuckling to himself. I don't think we fooled him one bit.

Goering was afraid of thunderstorms. During one particularly vicious storm, we thought he was having a heart attack. He was a strange mixture, sometimes almost childish, other times full of snarling, vicious sarcasm. Then witty, again moody, to the point at which he would freeze into stubborn silence. He was not a coward, as he has often been pictured. He proved his bravery during World War I when he was one of Germany's leading aces, among the most decorated of the famous Richthofen air circus. And he was no dumbbell by a long shot. Goering had the third highest IQ of the major Nazi war criminals.

In Mondorf, what he feared most was being sent to Russia, and being interrogated by a Russian team. We exploited that fear. When Goering became uncooperative, we needed only to suggest that we might as well ship him "to the other side," since he wasn't willing to work with us. This technique was probably the most cruel we employed.

We didn't use drugs or torture of any kind in getting information from the Nazis. Not even secret recording devices. It annoys me nowadays when I talk of my experiences to young people that they seem more concerned with our methods of getting information than with the history and the objectives of the War Crimes Trials. They've heard so much about the handling of PW by North Koreans and Vietnamese. They've watched spies and counterspies, and James Bond, on television. They have a warped idea of our working methods in 1945. Some even seem concerned about the rights of the Nazis.

We didn't have to use artificial devices to get our prisoners to talk. We sometimes had trouble getting them to shut up. Almost all of the men in Ashcan were eager to talk. They felt neglected if they hadn't been interrogated by someone for several days. If you were interrogated a lot, it meant you were important, and we, the enemy, realized your importance. Some were motivated by guilt feelings; they wanted to get things off their chests. The favorite pastime was casting blame. In anticipation of events to come, some prisoners were ready to tell all they knew to someone else. It was almost an unconscious form of plea-bargaining.

So our biggest challenge was not getting them to tell us more than name, rank, and serial number. Our challenge was trying to find out who was telling the truth and who was lying. Cross-examination. Playing one prisoner off against the other. We were certain we were right in allowing them to eat together; giving them the freedom to visit each other in their rooms, to sit or walk together in their social grouping. It stimulated conversation, even led to arguments. And often I was taken into their confidence when they needed a "shoulder to cry on."

General "Wild Bill" Donovan, director of the OSS (the Office of Strategic Services, which was the forerunner of the CIA), spent a lot of time with us. He stressed the techniques of getting and evaluating information. We were urged time and time again to study closely the personal relations of the various internees with a view of playing them off against each other. The War Crimes Commission planned to prove that the accused Germans conspired to seize power in Germany, then gain control in Europe. Proof of any overt act carried out to further this conspiracy would aid in convicting them. My role as "welfare officer" was becoming useful in this effort.

General Donovan's participation in our interrogation program helped to convince Colonel Andrus of the importance of compromise and occasional leniency, even the pretense of sympathy. The punishment would come later, ordered and administered by those ordained to judge and mete it out. We had to constantly remind Andrus that the prisoners we were holding in Ashcan had not yet been tried, found guilty, and sentenced. We needed the information they could give us.

The greater number of the Nazi leaders could not believe they would be tried as war criminals. They honestly felt that they were being held as prisoners of war, out of action, until victory was nailed down and the conquerors were sure there would be no resumption of fighting. Sometimes they joked about their predicament. "Herr Leutnant, why don't you tell General Eisenhower that I don't plan to reorganize the Waffen SS? I just want to go to my lovely house on the Chiemsee and bounce my grandchildren on my knee."

It was easy to initiate an interrogation of most of the internees. "I sent for you today because we have received a request from an agency for more information about a specific incident. Can you enlighten me?" This question would serve me as an opener. Invariably, the interview would then lead into personalities. Most of the time I would end up with more information than I originally asked for or needed.

They had questions for me, too. "How did you learn to speak German so well?" I stuck to the truth. I told them I was born in Luxembourg, had emigrated to the United States, and had continued my studies of German in the university. It was easier to be as honest as possible about my own background. It sure helped to avoid confusion in trying to keep track of lies. My real name leaked out anyway several months later when I was on a special mission. In the long run, the Nazis weren't stupid, either. They knew I was in Military Intelligence. I simply gave the impression of being a soft touch; I would treat them right. Two of my fellow interrogators developed their own techniques for getting information, based on the prisoners' awareness of their being Jewish. These two officers were admirably correct and restrained, often under trying circumstances. I admired them greatly, and I'm sure the Nazis couldn't help but respect them, too.

After a couple of weeks in the Palace Hotel, we were provided with much more attractive quarters. A short distance from the entrance to Ashcan was the Pension Wellkomm, a three-story guest house owned by the Wiltgen family. Their son, my age, had been shipped off somewhere by the Germans. His two-year-old daughter "Rollo" was the pride and joy of her grandfather, who was my father's age. Being in the same house with that little girl made my separation from Winnie and my own son, Johnny-Mike, more tolerable. Whenever possible, I would take Rollo on short walks in her stroller and tell her the children's stories I wished I could be telling my own son. The environment at the Pension Well-komm was homey; a respite from the depressing hours spent in Ashcan.

At least once every two weeks I managed to spend an hour or so with my brother's widow and little Renée. Those were never joyful visits, although my bringing all kinds of food and snacks made me a welcome visitor. Rose was still in mourning. Her health was not good. She worked hard at sewing and ironing for other people to supplement her meager pension. Renée reminded me of a little fawn, with big eyes and a very shy nature. She was obviously starved for love as well as for decent food. I was able to help a little bit. But our conversation was never earth-shaking. Rose couldn't describe the occupation years without bursting into tears. I stopped asking questions; we had so little in common.

When we finally settled into a routine, it was possible to find free Sunday afternoons and evenings in the city. The trick was being able to commandeer a jeep or command car for such an occasion. Seeing the Bradtké family regularly allowed me to renew my boyhood friendship with Nikky and Paul. Other friends of the Neipperg School were still "at large." It was difficult to locate people when mail delivery, telephone services, and transportation were far from normal. Many Luxembourgers hadn't returned to their homes from exile, prison camps, refugee centers, and processing areas for displaced persons. It would be years before everyone was back in place, if at all.

Letters from my father and my sister Marie arrived at regular intervals. Each one was more persistant in inquiring about my brothers and sisters. The news of Karl's death was quite a shock to them, and they feared the worst about the others as well.

One Sunday afternoon, Rose came running out to my jeep before I even had a chance to turn off the engine. She had been expecting my visit, watching at the window for my coming all day. In her hand she held a letter from my sister Agnes. She and her husband Gustav and their two children Marianne and Ilse were living in Sindlingen, Germany, not far from Frankfurt. They owned a "Gasthaus"—mit Unterkunft—a restaurant with guest rooms. Luxembourgers on their way home from places in Germany had stayed in their inn and were kind enough to bring a message to Rose from my sister Agnes. I was elated. At least one of my family was found. I resolved to make a trip to Frankfurt at the earliest opportunity.

It came sooner than expected. Mal Hilty and I were assigned to take a prisoner, General Blaskowitz, and some intelligence reports to our special detention center in Wiesbaden. This was a unit at which Lieutenants Brotzen and Landauer from Section Five at Camp Ritchie were stationed. It was a pleasure to see my former colleagues and travel companions again. We relished swapping stories, recalling our uneventful, but memorable visit to the "VIP Officers Club" in Paris. We bitched about all the snafus in our respective missions, and put a bottle of whiskey to rest. Then we found bunks for ourselves. In the morning, Hilty and I headed in the direction of the River Main to the small town of Sindlingen. It is next to Hoechst where the I. G. Farben chemical plant was located. This facility had suffered almost no bombing damage during the heavy raids and the costly fighting around Frankfurt. I suspect this was by design. The I. G. Farben offices now served as headquarters for General Eisenhower's USFET command.

Mal and I attracted considerable attention as we drove through the cobblestone streets of Sindlingen in our command car. No GIs were stationed in this town. We were a novelty. My sister's "Gasthaus zum Stern" wasn't hard to find. Mal waited in the car while I went to the front door. I remember it was a full-length glass door, giving Agnes a first look at me as she came to answer the bell. I heard a loud cry and footsteps running down the hall. She had recognized me at once, even though I was fourteen years older than when she last saw me.

Now I was in an American officer's uniform. I was totally unexpected. It was hysteria! Uncontrollable laughter and crying, a most intense reaction.

My two nieces were a surprise, too. I had known Agnes's husband in Luxembourg, but we did not know about the girls. This would be great news for the folks back in Akron.

Mal Hilty was ushered into the family reunion at once. A grand dinner was put together in no time. We contributed our rations to the best my sister could hustle out of her cellar. A neighbor had watched our arrival from her window across the street. She appeared with the gift of a sausage. This was also a good excuse to find out about all the excitement. Nonfraternization was still the rule, and two American officers were hardly entitled to such an enthusiastic welcome. My sister's stock in the neighborhood rose to great heights when it became known that one of them was her brother.

I should explain that I was carrying an official certificate identifying me as a member of Military Intelligence, with authorization to "apprehend, speak to, enter homes of and transport any German national as is necessary in the performance of his duties." That would come in handy in case an MP should see me fraternize.

This first reunion with my family was a great success, not only because we saw each other again, but also because Agnes had the address of our sister Liesel. She had a daughter, Inge, who would be four years old. They lived in Wiedenbrueck, Westphalia, in the British zone of occupation. Agnes had heard from them about a year ago; she was reasonably certain they were alive.

A trip to the British zone was added to my future agenda as was my promise to come back to Sindlingen as soon as possible. When we said goodbye to Agnes and her family, I had no idea that within a few weeks I would be assigned to Oberursel, north of Frankfurt, just a half-hour drive from Sindlingen. We would see each other often and with most surprising developments.

Back in Mondorf, the "gains" and "losses" in Ashcan were beginning to stabilize as we settled into a daily work routine. But much to our frustration, a lot of our time was being wasted, too. A major problem in our interrogation process was caused by our own limited knowledge of Nazi party organization and the function of different branches of government in the Third Reich. Sometimes questionnaires from our agencies dealt with hearsay and misinformation. We would often spend hours unraveling an item. Wrong names and titles plagued us.

For instance, take the case of a Dr. "Moreno" in Flensburg, Germany, who claimed that he was Hitler's doctor. We were asked to track this down. One of our internees was Dr. Karl Brandt, Reichskommisar for Health. He had also been one of Hitler's doctors. He was obviously the man who could answer the questions from SHAEF. But Brandt said he never heard of a Dr. Moreno. After a lot of backing and filling, we discovered that Dr. "Moreno" was supposed to be Dr. "Morell." They had sent us the wrong name. Hitler's personal physician was Morell. Brandt then finally gave us the lowdown. He said Morell was a charlatan, a quack of the highest order, who had ingratiated himself with Martin Bormann, director of the party Chancellery and Hitler's secretary. Morell had become most powerful in Hitler's inside circle. But medically, he was "totally incompetent," said Brandt. He was treating Hitler with antigas pills—"little black pills"—which turned out to be strychnine and atropine. They would have killed Hitler if wiser heads hadn't finally intervened. Hitler had jaundice, and suffered from severe attacks of indigestion. "Morell was really responsible for many ailments that plagued Hitler, some real, others imaginary," Brandt told us.

SHAEF questioned us about PW Alfred Rosenberg and a visit to Argentina which Rosenberg reportedly made in 1944. He was supposed to have family and important connections there. None of these so-called facts were confirmed; they were at complete variance with the prisoner's statements.

Field Marshal Keitel received a letter from an American woman in Connecticut who recalled "with pleasure" the grand visit he had made to her home in that state. It turned out Keitel had never been in the

United States. The questioning in pursuing such false leads and rumored information often made us look silly. We wasted time and effort.

We were deep into a promising interrogation project when we were ordered to prepare medical profiles on each of the internees. It took two days out of our intelligence-gathering routine. This particular interrogation project was never resumed after that long interruption. Other matters intervened. Our paper work was mammoth. Military government forms dealing with registration of personal property, securities, and negotiable wealth took a week to complete. I felt like an IRS agent after that one.

Each of us took turns being "duty officer." This involved standing by in the dining room during meal hours. It meant manning the intelligence office when arriving or departing prisoners were processed. It also meant participating in inspections of the prison rooms and other facilities. All of this Mickey Mouse activity prevented us from meeting the reporting deadlines put on us by the War Crimes Commission. We plodded on.

Under the guise of welfare officer I was free to go from room to room and to make small talk with the occupants. No interrogation or interview was involved. This gave me a chance to become acquainted with a larger number of our "guests" than would otherwise have been possible. If my contacts had been strictly limited to formal interrogations, I might not have met more than a dozen or so of all the Nazi prisoners in the months I spent in Ashcan and Nuremberg. I wouldn't have had the opportunity to observe the renewal of old rivalries; to witness their jockeying for position; their efforts to curry favor with their conquerors. I had a chance to meet some of their families, and that created emotional episodes I would just as soon have avoided.

On the other hand, I got to know several of the prisoners extremely well and was able to learn about the rise of National Socialism firsthand.

I Knew the Top Nazis

IN CINCINNATI, in the spring of 1947, I addressed the Exchange Club luncheon on the topic: "I Knew the Top Nazis." My recollections were to reassure my listeners that it could never happen here. Now I'm not so sure. Looking back on the daily association with the Nazi leaders, I've decided that under circumstances similar to those in Germany, any nation might produce a gaggle of unscrupulous opportunists, power-hungry leaders and followers, propagandists and rabble-rousers. Creatures of their environment, and—alas—makers of their environment.

The first top Nazi I interrogated was Walter Buch, the chief "justice" of the Nazi courts. These courts dealt only with Nazis who had committed offenses against other Nazis. Officially, this organization was known as the Reich Investigation and Arbitration Committee.

As we began talking, Buch was quick to point out that he had little contact with the political leaders of the Third Reich, especially the Fuehrer. He prided himself on always having judged matters according to purely juridical viewpoints. Buch was often "interfered with" by people such as Goebbels, the Nazi Propaganda minister. This was especially true if one of Hitler's pets was brought before the committee, or if the "court" came up with a decision with which Hitler, Bormann, or Goebbels disagreed. In such cases the judges were simply overruled.

Buch had a very low opinion of Martin Bormann, who was his son-in-law. His daughter, Gerda Buch, had married Bormann when he was on the staff of the Supreme Command of the SA, the Brown Shirts, in 1929. She herself was an ardent National Socialist. Like Bormann she detested Christianity in all its forms. She was anti-Semitic and subscribed to the most radical tenets of Nazism. Buch insisted that "Bormann made a monster out of my daughter." But Gerda must not have had any doubts about her husband. She bore him ten children. The first was named Adolf, for his godfather.

Buch lamented that Gerda had encouraged Bormann to have a child by his mistress, a famous actress, when she herself was pregnant. She had a reason for this magnanimous gesture. The Fuehrer would be getting *two* children "of priceless German stock" instead of just *one.*

Buch accused Bormann of being loyal only to Hitler, and then only because it would help him personally in his search for unlimited power. He blamed Bormann for many of the decisions made toward the end of the war when Hitler was no longer able to function, physically and mentally. It was Bormann who gave the orders to eliminate all evidence of concentration camps by killing the inmates and destroying the barracks. It would be claimed that Allied bombings were to blame.

Buch confided that his son-in-law actually had deformed thigh bones, abnormally short and "out of proportion to the rest of his bone structure." It explains why Bormann seldom appeared in photographs.

Probably the most notorious case brought before Buch's courts was a squabble between Goering and Julius Streicher. In 1940 Goering had hauled Streicher before the Nazi party Arbitration and Investigation Committee when an issue of *Der Stuermer* appeared with a story that Goering's only child, Edda, was conceived by means of artificial insemination. Goering was furious and demanded that the editor be kicked out of the party and deprived of all his titles and perquisites. It wasn't the first case against Streicher brought to Buch by unhappy Nazis, but this time, said Buch, "we were ready to stop that sick mind once and for all." Streicher's personal life and his shady business transactions had been thoroughly investigated before he was found guilty. But Hitler intervened. The sentence was altered. Streicher was stripped of his Gauleiter rank and other Nazi honors and "exiled" to his farm, the Pleikershof, near Nuremberg. But he was permitted to continue publishing his pornographic, anti-Semitic newspaper, *Der Stuermer*. While Hitler no longer welcomed him in the inner circle, Streicher was able to rationalize his punishment and remained ever-loyal to his Fuehrer.

I had probably heard more about Julius Streicher than about any other of the Nazis and was curious and eager to meet him when he was assigned to my "sphere of influence." Military government forms needed to be prepared on him; a good excuse to start the study. He was brought to my room for a short interview, but our initial meeting stretched into two full hours. Streicher wanted to talk. And talk he did. He was addicted to talking.

First of all he wanted to explain the bandages on his wrists. And the sores on his scalp. He traced these wounds to the time he was taken prisoner with his wife Adele. They had just been married. She had been his faithful secretary for a long time. They planned to die together in the "defense of Nuremberg" as U.S. forces appeared. Instead they changed their minds and decided to commit suicide. A joint grave was dug in preparation. But then, instead of dying, they decided to go into hiding, to continue their fight against international Jewry as soon as it became feasible again. So he grew a beard, put a black patch over one eye, and disguised himself further by dressing in Tyrolean costume. They went into hiding in Austria's mountains. Oddly enough, they were discovered by a Jewish American officer who saw through the disguise.

Streicher and his wife were brought to an interrogation/processing center in Augsburg. He claimed he was manacled so tightly that his wrists became sore; the wounds festered. He unbuttoned his shirt and bared his chest. It was covered with sores, small wounds caused by burning cigarettes. He charged that he was badly mistreated by his American guards. They were an engineer battalion, all black, and commanded by a Jewish officer, not black. Every morning Streicher and his wife were required to strip naked and walk up and down before the black soldiers in formation. He said he was told that he was "reviewing the troops."

He spoke of an incident in which he was stripped and then a GI overcoat was draped over his shoulders. A "crown" of barbed wire was forced on his head. (This would explain the sores on his scalp.) His private parts were exposed from under the coat, and a sign, "Julius Streicher, King of the Jews" was placed at his feet. Then he was photographed while onlookers jeered. Furthermore, "I was given potato peelings on a newspaper for food. I was made to drink the water out of the urinal in my prison cell," he said.

It was some story. I faithfully wrote it all down and made it part of my interrogation report. It came to light months later in the course of the trials in Nuremberg.

I attended three sessions of the Nuremberg Trials, and this, the hearing for Streicher, was one of them. At first we thought I might even be summoned to the witness stand to testify my having seen and reported the sores and his general condition at Mondorf. Fortunately, that didn't happen. Those sores *were* from cigarette burns, and his scars *were* real.

Streicher's defense attorney brought up the tortures to which his client had been subjected. The testimony was struck from the record on motion made by Justice Jackson, the prosecutor for the United States. The court was not in a position to conduct an investigation. The matter was really irrelevant and added nothing to Streicher's defense. When Streicher got on the stand he launched into a raucous propaganda tirade.

He had a loud argument with his attorney. The president of the court had to silence him and threatened to send him back to his cell. Justice Jackson asked that Streicher be cited for contempt of court. But the questioning continued without any more problems.

It would have been interesting if Streicher had been permitted to finish his story in court. When he told me of his mistreatment he said that the torture was ended by a Jewish American officer who came to visit him in his prison cell and brought him hot chocolate to drink. Streicher claimed to have been "touched so deeply" by this humane gesture from a Jew that he burst into tears.

Whenever I talked with Streicher, he lectured me. It was impossible to stop the flow once he started one of his harangues. He had been an elementary school teacher, was fired by his superiors who were "obviously influenced by Jews." He had also been a soldier in World War I, and was decorated with the Iron Cross. His political career began soon after the war ended. He was a member of the Socialist party for a while and then let his anti-Semitic views guide him into a labor union which specialized in blaming the Jews, as a symbol of capitalism, for the troubles of the German workers. In 1920, Streicher founded his own party, strictly anti-Semitic. He became a notorious rabble-rouser who told his students "exciting stories about the crimes of the Jews." He wrote anti-Semitic plays for the children and developed an endless supply of hate-filled anecdotes about the Jewish people.

This crude racist (he said himself that he was a "Rassenfanatiker") would tell me about his exploits with eyes sparkling. He would get so excited bragging about his accomplishments and influence that he started shouting his stock phrases. On several occasions I had to tell him to calm down. He considered himself the perfect anti-Semite. One of his major peeves was having been denied an active role in the formation of the infamous "Nuremberg Laws." After all, he had inspired the concept. "But Frick and others made the law and took all the credit."

Streicher's convictions about the baseness and wickedness of the Jews more than matched those of Hitler and Goebbels. "I am the most knowledgeable expert on Jewry in all Germany," he boasted. "The Jew is a mutation, a different kind of creature, a humanoid sub-species." I found it hard to resist tipping over the chair he sat in while delivering this claptrap.

He never changed his views. He endured the snubs of his former colleagues and seemed almost proud of being reviled and ignored. One time he pointed out that he was closer to Hitler than anyone else in the party. He was extremely proud of being one of a very few whom Hitler addressed with the familiar "Du."

As leader of his little band of fellow Jew-haters, Streicher heard of this man Hitler, who was the spokesman for a German Workers party in Munich. Streicher decided to go to Munich to hear Hitler speak. With a faraway look in his eyes, he described his first meeting with Hitler to me:

> It was on a winter day in the year 1922. I sat unknown in a public assembly in the large hall of the "Buergerbräuhaus" on the Rosenheimer Strasse in Munich. Suspense was in the air. Everyone seemed tense with excitement, with anticipation.
>
> Then suddenly a shout. "Hitler is coming!" Thousands of men and women jumped to their feet as if propelled by a mysterious power. Their right arms were raised as in a blessing, and over and over they shouted, "Heil Hitler! Heil Hitler!" With difficulty his companions led Herr Hitler through the welcoming mass of people.
>
> And then he stood on the podium. His face bathed with joy. Then I knew that in this Adolf Hitler was someone extraordinary. Stillness descended. Now he spoke. First slowly, almost inaudibly, then ever stronger, bolder, and, finally, reaching a crescendo. Here was a voice like that of God. Here was one who could wrest out of the German spirit and the German heart the power to break the chains of slavery.
>
> Yes! Yes! This man spoke as a messenger from heaven at a time when the gates of hell were opening to pull down everything. And when he finally finished, and while the crowd raised the roof with the singing of the "Deutschland" song, I rushed to the stage.
>
> "Herr Hitler! I am Julius Streicher! I know now that I can only be a *helper*. But you are the *Fuehrer*. I offer you herewith my entire organization in Franken."
>
> Hesitantly at first, he looked at me through the deep blue of his eyes. It seemed like an eternity. Then he took my hand in greatest warmth. "Streicher, I thank you." (Streicher, ich danke Dir.)
>
> Thus Fate summoned me to the greatest task of my life.

That's the story of Streicher's first meeting with Hitler. I decided I should have more. I had just met one of Hitler's staunchest adherents— and the one who was the least admired by his colleagues. Though Streicher's talents were primarily vocal, Hitler had rewarded him with positions and honors far beyond his ability. In spite of defeat, imprisonment, the revulsion of humanity, and even the scorn of his jailmates, Streicher remained a rabble-rouser to the end.

Streicher, lounging on his prison cot, dressed in cast-off GI work clothes, hardly looked like someone who once held thousands of sensible Germans spellbound. He fascinated me, not because he was an entertaining conversationalist, but because he was a man who lived and succeeded exclusively by emotion.

"Hansi"—John E. Dolibois at age twenty months.

The fifth schoolyear in Neipperg School, Luxembourg-Gare. John Dolibois, at far right in the second row, shares the bench with Jean Kayser; Rene Kelsen is in front of John.

The city of Luxembourg, atop honeycombed cliffs. At center is St. Michael's Church, where John Dolibois served as altar boy. Photo taken in 1945.

Cowboy in Luxembourg. John's sister Marie
sent this cowboy outfit from the U.S. in
1930.

Papa and John (in cap at center) arrive in Akron, Ohio.

In Akron, 1931. John's sister Marie and her daughter Madeline, Papa, and John in front of their house on Spalding Street.

Helping brother-in-law Albert Felton deliver milk.

Miami students Winnie and John.

Brothers reunited in the Saar after the war—Heinrich, John, and Kasi.

With Lt. Malcolm Hilty in Luxembourg.

Newly promoted Captain Dolibois of U.S. Military Intelligence.

The Palace Hotel and Casino in Mondorf, known as "Ashcan" while it was being used to imprison top Nazis after the war.

Reichsmarschall Hermann Goering. Note that photo is signed to "John Gillen," the name used by John Dolibois as interrogator.

Dr. Robert Ley, Reichsleiter, German Labor Front.

Julius Streicher, the "Jew-baiter."

Grand Admiral Karl Doenitz.

One day he approached me with an offer to write his "Bekenntniss"— his "creed." He said he could best explain his devotion to Hitler, Nazism, and his own fanatic anti-Semitism, by putting it all down on paper. It seemed a good idea to me. I could probe into his psyche without having to listen to his speeches and I wouldn't have to write myself memos and decipher my notes after a session with him. We discussed it at a staff meeting, and my colleagues concurred.

We located a beat-up old typewriter, and even found a typist. He was Franz Schwarz, son of the Nazi party treasurer, who had accompanied his father to Ashcan. The younger Schwarz was president of the German breweries and also an "SS Brigadefuehrer." The latter position explains why he was arrested, but his presence in Ashcan was primarily due to his accompanying his ailing father. Nobody was interested in interrogating Schwarz. He had time on his hands. He could type. So I arranged for Streicher to dictate his credo—his testament—to Schwarz. The document was finished August 3. Streicher handed it to me ceremoniously, pointing out, "This is my last work, my last message to the world." Several days later he brought me a final page of his "work." It was a pencil sketch of the veranda, the guard tower, and a corner of the Palace Hotel. He titled it "Im Haus der Internierten," "in the House of the Interned." It was signed STREICHER, in old German script, which he insisted on using whenever he wrote in longhand. The sketch by Streicher is interesting. He was an indifferent watercolorist, by hobby.

The first chapter of his creed was titled "The Call of Fate." It starts with an explanation:

> I was a peasant boy of five when I heard the word "Jew" for the first time. It came from the mouth of my mother. From a traveling salesman, a city slicker, she had ordered material for a suit for my father. She selected the cloth from the samples, and paid for it in advance. When the shipment arrived, the cloth was not the color and the quality my mother had selected. She felt herself cheated, and we children cried with her.
>
> Then, when I started to school and heard the story of the suffering Christ from the parish pastor, I was horrified to learn that the Jews showed no sympathy for the bloodied Saviour; that they were not satisfied with the torture He had already endured, and that they demanded his crucifixion from the Roman Pontius Pilate. *In that initial hour of religious instruction I realized for the first time in my life that the character of the Jew was abominable and detestable.*

You can guess that the rest of his "Bekenntniss" dealt with his big obsession in detail: a rehash of all his rantings of more than two decades; distortions of the Bible, and references to other anti-Semitic writings. He lifted statements out of context to prove the existence of a Jewish "race." I found it strangely amusing to note the similarity in sound of the two words in the German language: *Rasse*, meaning race, and *hasse*, the verb for hate. Streicher made the most of either word. Here was the supreme rabble-rouser, in the flesh. A relatively stupid, lusty man, with the lowest IQ (106) of the twenty-two major Nazi criminals tried in Nuremberg.

In this same writing, Streicher explained how he started *Der Stuermer*, the pornographic anti-Semitic weekly newspaper. He attributed the early success of the venture to the Jews themselves. He claimed that he deliberately exaggerated his stories and charges, his filthy descriptions, to such an extent that Jews "flocked" to the newsstands to buy up each edition. Thus they hoped to keep *Der Stuermer* out of circulation. "But that's exactly what built up the circulation," Streicher gloated. "Thanks to the Jews, we sold thousands and thousands of issues."

His writings offended even some of the supportive German racists. His speech was blunt, tactless, and at times, uncouth. He took great pride in his strength and sexual vigor. He boastfully admitted that he had been a great fornicator. Even then, at age sixty-one, he contended that the only true test of his physical health would be to make a woman available to him.

I was present when a psychiatric commission consisting of a Russian, a French, and an American doctor examined Streicher. This commission was to determine whether Streicher's anti-Semitic obsession sprang from a diseased mind. When the doctors asked him to undress for a physical examination, the female Russian interpreter for Dr. Krasnushkin started to leave the room. Streicher leered at her and said, "What's the matter? Are you afraid of seeing something nice?" The doctors decided that while he suffered from a neurotic obsession, he was not insane.

Streicher maintained an elaborate library which came chiefly from Jewish sources. Whenever the SA or the SS burned synagogues, schools, libraries, or confiscated the homes of prominent Jews, they were ordered to preserve the best samples of Jewish books, manuscripts, documents. Whenever Nazi fanatics vandalized public buildings in the countries they conquered, there were always Streicher henchmen on the lookout for the best of Jewish literature. Eventually, Streicher collected, at *Der Stuermer* offices, the best samples of Jewish writings from all over Europe. He read these materials voraciously and acquired considerable knowledge about Jewish history, culture, religion, and customs. In his own writings and speeches he distorted his findings to make points for his anti-Semitism.

Streicher bragged about his collection, the "Stuermer Bibliothek." When he was taken to Nuremberg and questioned about it, Streicher directed his questioners to its hiding place. His collection had survived the bombings and destruction of Nuremberg. I had the opportunity to visit it several times after it was discovered in the basement of a warehouse. It's difficult to describe how it felt to see this valuable collection of works written by Jews, about Jews, and for Jews, assembled from all over Germany and Europe. Undoubtedly, it was the most valuable private collection in the world.

It occurred to me that Streicher, a man who reveled in the title "Jew-Baiter Number One," a man who had literally given his life to wiping out Jewish culture in Germany and Europe, became the one person who had preserved for posterity that aspect of Jewish culture. The Stuermer library was taken around the world after the war. It was exhibited widely, and then, as many of these works as possible were returned to their rightful owners and institutions.

Streicher operated a publishing house, too. In 1938, Peter Deeg wrote *Hofjuden*—an "exposé" of the House of Rothschild, an anti-Semitic tome of more than five hundred pages. Julius Streicher is listed on the flyleaf as the publisher, and Adolf Hitler wrote a dedication. Several copies of this book, along with other Nazi literature, were on the shelves of the prison library in Nuremberg. We all agreed they didn't belong there. I confiscated several of the Nazi books for myself. Streicher autographed *Hofjuden* for me on October 10, 1945: "To Mr. First Leutnant Gillen, in remembrance of the days in Nuremberg!"

I have another Nazi book in my possession, *Wir Alle Helfen Dem Fuehrer* by Dr. Robert Ley. He signed it for me on October 18, exactly one week before he committed suicide in his cell at Nuremberg. I was on duty the night he ended his confused life.

The first time I met with Ley was in Ashcan at Mondorf on June 23. I was doing an interrogation for a Major Penfold and a Major Stroud from the War Department. They had given me a list of questions about the "Reichsarbeitsdienst"—the German Labor Front—which Ley directed.

Prisoner Ley was brought to my room. As he came in, he smiled broadly, bowing over and over as he approached my table. Short in stature, he resembled Streicher in physique: thick-set, balding, dressed in GI fatigues. He held out his hand in greeting. Of course, I had to ignore this friendly gesture. Shaking hands with prisoners was verboten. His smile faded rapidly. I asked him to sit down, and then, in prescribed fashion, asked the first question. "Wie heissen Sie?"

He rolled a long "R-R-R-R-Robert Ley." Then "R-R-R-Reichsleiter." His stammering caught me by surprise. I had heard many of his rabble-rousing speeches on the radio. I'd seen and heard him on the movie screen and had noted his ability to rouse mob spirit with his words.

So I decided he was playing a game and challenged him. His smile reappeared. Ingratiatingly, he explained. He had been a flight officer in the German Air Force in World War I. His plane was shot down over Arras, his pilot killed, and he received severe burns and a head injury. He was unconscious for a long time and was unable to speak after regaining consciousness. He was taken prisoner by the French. Eventually he spoke again, but always with a stammer—unless, and then came that simpering smile again—he could have a little sip of that good American whiskey. Indeed, he always overcame his speech defect with a good slug or two before appearing in public. It explained everything. This vocal Nazi, who had been the surrogate speaker for Hitler on many occasions, able to rally Germany's work force to the Fuehrer's cause, was half-drunk when he delivered those forceful speeches. The "inner voice" which forced him into his work had alcoholic content. I realized I had an unstable type of personality before me, but at this point I needed information.

Ley was the seventh of eleven children. His father was a small farmer. Ley worked his way through high school and college and was close to a doctor's degree in chemistry when the First World War started. He finished his studies in 1920 and became a teacher at a university in Westphalia.

Ley divorced his first wife. His second wife committed suicide in 1942 (tears in his eyes). After that he lived with a young girl from Estonia, whom he never married (twinkle in his eyes).

Ley couldn't carry on much of a sensible conversation. He talked with both hands, waved his arms. He jumped off his chair and paced up and down the room, shouting, his stammering getting worse. When I asked him to sit down again, he smiled, obediently took to his chair, and heaved a big, relaxed sigh. This scene occurred three or four times during each session.

The leader of the Labor Front had organized some thirty million workers. You couldn't get a job in the Third Reich without a membership card in the "Arbeitsdienst." Ley was able to inspire workers for Hitler and the Reich. He displayed a fantastic imagination. He was full of ideas, and he definitely looked at the world through rose-colored glasses. Here was an uninhibited optimist, and the original visionary. In Nazi circles Ley was a social outcast. This didn't bother him because he was unable to hold a grudge. He gave the impression of being intellectually gifted, vital, tough. But he really was just a bullshitter of the highest order. The sad part of it was that he believed in his ability to deliver. The prison psychiatrists at Nuremberg later explained that Ley actually had a damaged brain; he had no judgment, only spontaneous emotional responses. "The inhibitory centers of his brain had ceased to function," said Dr. Douglas M. Kelly.

Ley was directly responsible for my being sent to Nuremberg and becoming involved during the early months of the trial. I have mixed emotions about that. In September 1945 I was resentful and annoyed. Now, looking back on it, I could kick myself for not staying longer, getting more involved, making history. But more of that later.

After our first session, Ley started following me around like a puppy. He came knocking at my door under all kinds of pretexts. On October 18, in Nuremberg, he wrote inside the cover of his book, "To Mr. First Lieutenant Gillen, in sincere gratitude for his extremely noble and humane behavior in the time of my greatest suffering."

I felt like a hypocrite. The role I played as "welfare officer" shouldn't have fooled anyone. As part of his orientation each prisoner in Ashcan at Mondorf was told that he was being held for the purpose of getting information, that everything he said would be a matter of record and could be held against him. They should have known as early as 1943 that the Allied nations would hold them responsible for the war crimes and the crimes against humanity that were being committed. But I suppose they couldn't believe Germany might ever be defeated. In Mondorf they still couldn't believe they would be tried for their crimes. Whatever motivated them, many were responsive to and grateful for a kind word and a sympathetic ear from any one of us among the victors. And if they thought they were outsmarting us with tricky answers to our questions, their colleagues would quickly come along with contradictions and talebearing to set the record straight. Or to present another viewpoint.

They came down the hall together, a young sergeant and a private. They were making the regular morning inspection. I'd heard about this pair, and decided to watch the show, because a show it was. Irony. The sergeant was from Brooklyn, Jewish, dressed in his best class-A uniform. He sported quite a few decorations, most of which he had earned. There were a few extras. He wore a fouragière of the First World War, although he was only about twenty-five years old. But he looked impressive. The private opened the door to a prisoner's room and yelled "Achtung!" Inside, the prisoner came to rigid attention. Sergeant Alfred Friedel entered. He checked the bed to see if it was made up properly. He checked the shoes or boots under the bed to see if they were shined. He stepped to the windowsill to check for dust, and then inspected the prisoner's personal appearance. (Of course they all had five o'clock shadow since the prison barber shaved them every other day.)

If the prisoner did not meet the sergeant's standards, Friedel would step back and read the riot act in definite Yiddish German, making the

Nazi feel right at home. The prisoner who got chewed out the most was none other than Joachim von Ribbentrop. I had to appreciate the irony of this. The ex-foreign minister, former ambassador to the Court of St. James, had the best image of the Nazis. The propaganda ministry had pictured him as the finest of pure Aryan Germans, best-dressed man for nine consecutive years. He was 100 percent Germanic, impeccable, the super diplomat. Now he was being restricted to his room by a young Jew from Brooklyn for not keeping himself, or his room, in proper order.

I never interrogated von Ribbentrop. Visits to his room were among my courtesy calls, passing the time of day, making small talk. My contacts with General Jodl and Admiral Raeder were along the same line. But I did get to know Admiral Doenitz and Field Marshal Keitel quite well.

Doenitz began our relationship with a request to help him improve his English. He wanted to know what books to read. I ended up spending about a half hour each day giving him English lessons.

Doenitz had an imperious attitude. He was constantly in competition with Goering. The latter insisted he was the senior commander of all internees, as Reichsmarschall and the one-time successor-designate of Hitler. But Hitler had specified in his last will and testament that Doenitz was to be president of Germany and commander in chief of all military forces. In reality, the other internees paid no attention to either of the two. It was a case of every man for himself. For our part they were all of equal rank—prisoners. Colonel Andrus certainly made that clear on many occasions.

I translated one letter which Doenitz wrote to General Eisenhower. In it he registered his complaints and his request for "quarters suitable for a man of my rank, and treatment that does not dishonor my unbesmirched standing as a soldier."

He was arrogant, a master of sarcasm. His biting comments about his colleagues juiced up many of our interrogation reports. He was particularly harsh in his judgment of those who had a vial of potassium cyanide on their persons when taken prisoner. In his opinion these were cowards. If they intended to avoid being taken prisoner, they should have used the poison then and there. But carrying it around afterwards "like nasty little boys hiding forbidden sweets in secret pockets" was "unmanly nonsense."

Doenitz showed a lot of class. If he was not in complete control of himself, he put up a damn good front. One day I asked him how he could afford to be so calm and assured under the circumstances. He replied that he had written a set of guidelines for himself, and whenever he felt depressed or discouraged he would read those guidelines and gain new strength. He seemed pleased with my question and surprised me by asking if I would like a copy of these guidelines. He wrote them out for me. Here is what Doenitz was telling himself, over and over:

1. Never lose the self-assurance about your unblemished life.
2. Recognize the one-time greatness of the hour. Your whole life will be judged by your present conduct.
3. Therefore, you must never do anything that is weak or small. The German people, who love you and believe in you, expect that you conduct yourself now as you did always, as their Grand Admiral.
4. Therefore, something bad, that is, shameful, can happen to you only through your own fault.
5. Either way, your fate is sealed with honor. You can face the future with cheer and in peace, because:
6. If justice rules, which I must assume it will, you will be acquitted. In that case, even the enemy will have acknowledged your impeccable character.
7. If politics plays a role, and you are found guilty for expediency's sake—the now silent people of Germany will never forget you—you will go into immortality, and thus render your people your last service, by being sentenced.
8. One way or the other, it can only end up for the good.
9. Therefore, endure all present indignity with good cheer. It can take nothing from you and really makes no difference.

There you have the "nine commandments" of Grand Admiral Doenitz. He gave them to me signed "DOENITZ, Grossadmiral, To Lt. Gillen in friendly remembrance."

One morning I dropped in on Field Marshal Keitel and found him sitting on the edge of his cot. He hadn't slept all night and was in agony. A large inflamed carbuncle on his neck caused tremendous discomfort. He couldn't lie down. When I asked him why he hadn't reported this to a guard, he just looked at me. I got the message. The old Prussian wasn't about to complain to an ordinary soldier.

Our Doctor Miller performed minor surgery in the infirmary, and Keitel was given extra pillows so he could lie down and rest. When I checked on him the next day he was in an unusually talkative mood. He showed me pictures of his family, and, pointing to a photo of his sons, said, "When my sons and I walked down the Kurfuerstendamm, people would stop and heads would turn. Ja, we were a family! We were something to look at."

I believed it. Keitel was the perfect image of the Prussian general. His high throat-choker collar with red and gold trim and the red stripe down the side of his trousers made him stand out in a crowd, especially the crowd he was with now. As Hitler's chief of the OKW, the Armed Forces High Command, Keitel was nothing more than a "yes man." The real workhorse in the OKW was Jodl. But Keitel had been the top dog among the generals. His conditioning to unquestioned obedience was absolute. He never would dare to disagree with Hitler. In fact, he considered Hitler the greatest military strategist, a "military genius." He also pointed out that Hitler always had someone take notes when he conferred with generals, and thus made it clear that any disagreement would be a matter of record. That's all the warning Keitel needed. "It's hard for you Americans to understand the Prussian code of dicipline," he said to me.

Keitel's aloofness didn't fool anyone. He lost one son in Russia. He didn't know where his other sons were. This depressed him; made him gloomy. On the other hand Keitel could behave like a teenager. The summer sun had been particularly strong for several days, and he had spent most of his time sunbathing. He was proud as punch of his tan, frequently eyeing himself in the mirror in the entrance hall of the Palace Hotel, the only mirror available to prisoners. Thinking he was not observed, he posed and postured.

I decided it would be fun to have the autograph of the man who signed the surrender on the Eastern front, ending World War II in Europe. The prisoner obliged, signing "KEITEL" on a three-by-five card, on July 6, 1945, just as it appears on the surrender documents. Then I decided to go for a pair. Jodl signed the unconditional surrender in Rheims, ending the war on the Western front. So I got his autograph, too—"JODL."

One of the most notable among the early Nazis was Wilhelm Frick. I had a request for detailed information on his early background since our intelligence records showed little about him. This is not surprising. Frick had done most of his dirty work so unobtrusively that one seldom read about him in the press.

He wore his hair in what we used to call a "short butch." He was dressed in a wool shirt and khaki GI jacket. He was soft-spoken, very correct, a cooperative subject. He had been a police official in Munich when Hitler attempted his ill-fated "putsch" in November 1923. His cooperation with Hitler forces landed Frick in jail. If the revolt had been successful, he would have become police president of Munich. Alas! It failed. He was unemployed after serving his prison sentence. He said he didn't join the party until 1925. He firmly believed in Hitler because Hitler was fighting communism, which Frick hated. He pointed out that his superiors and many government officials in Bavaria had been tolerant of the upstart Nazis because most of the officials were rightists who feared communism. They were willing to look the other way when the Nazis got out of hand.

"I'm of sound, healthy peasant stock," Frick described himself to me. He earned his law degree at Heidelberg University, but preferred to be known as a regular fellow. He impressed me as a somewhat colorless bureaucrat who dotted all the i's and crossed all the t's. Methodical, scheming, he never lost his powerful attraction for Hitler.

Frick served in the Reichstag—the Parliament—and became a steady, though stodgy, echo of Hitler's words. When Hitler became chancellor of Germany, under President Paul von Hindenburg, Frick was named minister of the Interior. As a fanatical technician, he moved in on his task with cold fervor. He formulated one law after another, each one giving Hitler more power. An enabling act in March 1933 allowed Hitler the legal right to promulgate laws without approval of Parliament. Frick dissolved the Communist party and confiscated its property. He dissolved trade unions, eliminated the Social Democratic organization, and forbade the forming of any new political parties. His laws abolished civil rights, free assembly, the privacy of the mails and telephones, and permitted the search of houses without warrants. All of these "laws" were built upon the emergency legislation justified by the Reichstag fire in 1933. They were "for the elimination of the misery of the people and the Reich."

Frick played an active role in the anti-Semitic program as well. Marriages between Jews and Germans were forbidden. Jews were not considered Germans. They were not even permitted to display the German flag. It was Frick who determined who was a Jew. "Anyone descended from three Jewish grandparents or from two, if he practiced the Jewish religion."

As we discussed all of his accomplishments—of which he seemed rather proud—Frick assured me that he had functioned only "under orders from the Fuehrer and Goering." He was a "pillar" of the Party-State. He described his own anti-Semitism as "correct, legal, and orderly." Emphasis on legal.

He appeared rather bitter about Himmler, whom Hitler had appointed chief of the German police. He said Himmler ignored him from that time on. And Goering treated him as if he were a little boy, "inconsequential." Frick reaffirmed his support of Nazi party principles. He couldn't understand why he was arrested. He was a public servant. The laws he had promulgated were for the public well-being. The concentration camps had only been under his "nominal" control. It was Himmler who took them over, and when Frick learned of some of the excesses, he registered his disapproval. But he was told it was none of his business.

I saw Frick only once after the indictment was served in Nuremberg on October 21. He left me with the feeling that he wouldn't put up much of a fight at the trial. He expected to be found guilty. When the tribunal sentenced him to death by hanging fourteen months later, I could only say "Amen."

Some of our prisoners were never called by visiting teams. I think they felt neglected. Sometimes they even pouted. Why were they brought to this interrogation center if they weren't going to be questioned? I had to agree with this viewpoint at times, especially in those cases where the internee was rather insignificant in the whole scheme of things. One example of this was Prince Philip von Hesse, the nephew of the Kaiser and a grandson of Queen Victoria. He had been persuaded to join the Nazi party by the Kaiser's young son, August Wilhelm. Prince Philip told me that he'd allowed himself to be persuaded only because he feared the spread of communism.

Von Hesse had performed only minor service to the government of the Third Reich. He was a special envoy to Rome, and he recalled that he was once chosen to carry a message from Hitler to Mussolini. He said he undertook that task because he had to go to Rome anyhow to take some plants there for his villa garden. He didn't even know that the letter from Hitler to Il Duce was the announcement of the forthcoming "Anschluss"—the annexation of Austria; Hitler was reassuring the Italian dictator that he had nothing to fear from the move.

Only after he had delivered Hitler's message did von Hesse realize the importance of it. He was to telephone Hitler with Mussolini's response. "He took the news very well," was Hesse's opinion.

Philip von Hesse had a title, "Oberpraesident" of the province of Hesse/Nassau, an administrator. I don't know what became of him after we put the lid on Ashcan, but I thought of him often in the months that followed.

In the vicinity of Oberursel in the Taunus Mountains stands a fabulous Schloss Hotel Kronberg. This castle had been built by Empress Frederika, daughter of Queen Victoria, and wife of the German emperor who served just a few short years at the turn of the century. Prince Philip von Hesse was the owner of the castle at the time he became a prisoner in Mondorf. The property was confiscated—as was all Nazi property—and General Eisenhower used the handsome facility as an officers club after the war. I spent many pleasant weekends at Kronberg when I was stationed at Camp Sibert, the Military Intelligence Service Center for USFET, in Oberursel.

Eventually the property was turned over to the German government, which in turn sold it to a prominent hotel chain. It is now a luxurious resort hotel. Several times during our travels to Europe betwen 1965 and 1979, Winnie and I stayed at Kronberg, "for old times' sake." On one such occasion our youngest son Brian, at age seven, was with us. I vividly recall Brian's summoning us one evening to the little tower room he was occupying. He couldn't sleep. He was worried about that big oil painting hanging over his head. "It might fall off and hit me on the head," he said.

"Oh Brian, that's foolish," I told him, "that portrait has been hanging on that wall for more than a hundred years."

"On the same wire?" asked Brian.

We moved the bed away from the wall and tiptoed out of the room.

During our embassy years, Brian visited us in Luxembourg. We decided to spend a long weekend at Schloss Hotel Kronberg, taking Brian back to the scene of his astute observation. The tower room in which he had slept in 1965 is now an office. The oil portrait is no longer on the wall. But the magnificent trees, the splendid English gardens, and attractive stables brought back memories of earlier times when the place was an oasis in a Germany that lay in ruins and disgrace. I thought of Philip von Hesse. He had certainly been out of place in the PW enclosure in Mondorf.

Another person who seemed to have been sent us by mistake was Franz Xaver Schwarz. He was the father of the president of the German breweries who typed Streicher's credo for me.

When Hitler was released from prison in 1925 and was banned from speaking in public, he utilized his time to establish a solid party apparatus. He gathered around him a group of gullible functionaries who could be relied upon to help build a sound foundation. One of these was an efficient accountant at the Munich City Hall, Franz X. Schwarz. With a sharp pencil and the spirit of a skinflint he became indispensable to the Nazi party as the party treasurer.

He collected the monthly dues and kept a meticulous account of every pfennig. No big money ever came his way as the contributions from wealthy supporters were channeled into other treasuries. So was the income from property, investments, and the confiscated wealth the Nazis acquired. Schwarz was a likable old Bavarian who had lent respectability to the organization of street brawlers and bullies that rallied around Adolf Hitler. By 1926 Schwarz had meticulously recorded dues from fifty thousand members of the Nazi party. Now in Ashcan, the old man was ailing, bedridden, and the German doctor, Pfluecker, was concerned about his heart. In our staff meeting it was decided I should look in on Schwarz to determine of what use he might be.

When I opened the door to his room and saw Schwarz lying on his cot, I stopped dead in my tracks. Ye Gods, it was my Papa. The resemblance was amazing—the same build, round face, white hair, and the unmistakable mustache. I recovered. "Good morning, Herr Schwarz, I'm Leutnant Gillen of the prison staff."

The old boy had seen the look on my face when I came in and said outright, "May I ask why the Herr Leutnant looked so shocked when he saw me here?"

I explained. "You look exactly like my own father, Herr Schwarz." I took a snapshot out of my billfold and showed it to him. He saw the resemblance, too. It had a tremendous effect on him. "It was meant to be so," he said with a tremble in his voice. "I will die here, and God has sent you to give me comfort."

"Well, why not," I thought to myself. The old man looked harmless. Nothing in our reference material on him was significant. Obviously he was here only because of his imposing title, "Nazi Party Treasurer." It soon became clear that he had played a minor role in the machinations and conspiracies of the regime, but he became useful to us now in our gathering of information.

One by one, the other Nazis called on harmless old Papa Schwarz. They apparently needed his shoulder to cry on. He was not going to play a significant part in what lay ahead. Many of them took Schwarz into their confidence. In turn, I visited him daily and answered his questions honestly. I showed him documents and photos of concentration camps and proof of other atrocities. He was horrified, indignant. He had been kept in the dark about all this activity. He said he had been used, his own plodding integrity exploited and compromised. If he was aware of the excesses of the Nazi regime, he played a good role of innocence. More likely, I think, he was one of many with their heads in the sand.

He was now eager to share confidences and to tell us what he knew about his colleagues. He reported faithfully on conversations he was having with those who came to chat with him. He didn't hesitate to ask searching questions; he relayed their answers to me. In our interrogation process, he was very useful. And within a few weeks he was able to get out of bed and move around the compound. Schwarz was not tried in Nuremberg. In fact, we shipped him home several weeks before we ended operations in Mondorf. I don't know what became of him.

I was duty officer on a day Hermann Goering received his comeuppance at the hands of one of our PW labor cadre. The former hotel salon was the dining room for the internees of Ashcan. The food was served by the German PW. Heavy porcelain dishes were used, and the food was eaten with spoons only. No knives or forks were permitted. The prisoners sat at heavy tables in their usual cliques. Streicher and Ley were together at one end of a table. Goering sat alone at another. I was standing near him when a German PW, a corporal, brought a plate of stew and set it before his former Reichsmarschall. Goering looked at the plate in front of him, then disdainfully waved his hand.

"You can take that slop away," he said to the corporal. "I fed my dog much better than that back home."

The former German soldier took the plate in both hands, drew to attention, clicked his heels, and said: "Ach ja, Herr Reichsmarschall, in that case your dog ate much better than we German soldiers did."

With that he made an about-face and took Goering's plate back to the kitchen. Irony. Six months earlier that soldier would have been shot for his impudence. The tables had turned. Goering was declassified.

I met that German PW again, nearly forty years later. On June 28, 1983 I was awarded Honorary Citizenship of the city of Mondorf-les-Bains, in reference to my "most important special mission and activities in Mondorf from May to August 1945, and by unanimous decision of the town council."

With the mayor and other dignitaries welcoming us was a man who looked vaguely familiar. In time he introduced himself as Rudolf Diebenbush of Koblenz, Germany. Of course, I wouldn't remember him, he explained. He had been a PW at the Palace Hotel when it was the Central Continental Prisoner of War Enclosure for the high-ranking Nazis. As a member of the PW work cadre, his job was to keep the lobby and the stairways clean and proper. And at mealtimes he helped serve the food to the internees.

This was the corporal who had been ordered by Goering to remove the stew. He confirmed my recollection. He had been told that a former American officer, one of the interrogators at Ashcan, was being honored by the city. His Luxembourg friends invited him to the ceremony. He didn't know me by name, but "Lt. Gillen" he recognized immediately.

Diebenbush accompanied the official entourage the rest of the day. We toured the Palace Hotel which had changed considerably since 1945. It was restored to its more glamorous status as a health spa, offering baths, massages, and treatments for all kinds of ailments. It was razed and replaced by a more modern facility in the spring of 1988. (I thought it should be preserved as a monument to victory over totalitarianism.)

While visiting the attractive park, the Palace Hotel, and a fancy new Casino in Mondorf, Rudolf Diebenbush and I had occasional opportunities to swap recollections. He reminded me of the time one of his "Kameraden," named Franz Schmuz, was working in the bath facilities. He entered one of the bathrooms unexpectedly one day and surprised Dr. Robert Ley in the bathtub, masturbating. "Why do you look at me so stupidly? I'm only human!" Ley roared at him.

Prisoner Schmuz had other unpleasasnt encounters with the Nazi "Bonzen." General Ritter von Epp narrowly missed hitting Schmuz in the head with a riding boot one day when the hapless bathmaster tried to hurry him along. One must appreciate the gallows humor of the person who placed a man named "Schmuz" in charge of the bathrooms. Schmutz means dirt in German.

Listening to Diebenbush share his impressions of his unusual assignment made me appreciate the wide gap that existed between the top Nazis of the Third Reich and the common people of Germany. Obviously, the prisoners of war in the labor cadre relished the status to which their shining leaders had been relegated. Diebenbush told me how fortunate he considered himself to have been in Mondorf in 1945.

"As an ordinary, common German, I witnessed the 'Goetterdaemmerung'—the twilight of the Gods—of the Third Reich, and I played a direct role in the fall of those Gods," he told me. "If you kept your eyes and ears open you quickly got to know the character and being of this Masterclique; their strengths and the weaknesses, their vices, and their shabbiness."

What shocked him most of all was the realization that his country had been governed by these "power-hungry rivals, using cut-throat tactics to get ahead of each other at the expense of the German people."

Then he added, "And we were stupid enough to fall for all that crap."

11

From Luxembourg to Oberursel

THE EASIEST NAZI to interrogate was Hermann Goering. He's been described as everything from the devil incarnate to a silly fat eunuch. I concluded early in the game that Goering was nobody's fool. He was an able, shrewd manager, brilliant and brave, ruthless and grasping. At times he turned on his charm and it was almost a pleasure to be with him. At other times he was simply a pain in the ass. But every hour spent with him was interesting. His varied activities in the Nazi regime provided endless discussion on many topics. He was Hitler's designated successor. He was president of the Reichstag; the Reichminister of Aviation; commander in chief of the Luftwaffe, in charge of the defense of the Reich; he was the Forestry and Hunting Master; a member of numerous councils. He was the marshal of the Reich. There was none higher, except Hitler, who had just one title, "Fuehrer." And Goering loved to talk.

The Luftwaffe commander said he was unable to stop the ruthless bombing of Rotterdam in which tens of thousands were killed. He claimed he was unaware of Holland's surrender until it was too late to call off the bombers.

He took credit for Hitler's decision not to invade Great Britain, yet he justified the vicious air raids on England as "necessary."

"Bormann, Goebbels, and Ribbentrop influenced Hitler against me toward the end," he said time and time again; "they envied me, they didn't trust me."

"To understand anti-Semitism," he lectured, "you must distinguish between the Eastern European Jew and the German Jew." Goering considered the former inferior and their elimination justified. "I befriended and protected many German Jews."

I asked about one of his immediate subordinates, an ace of his entourage in the Luftwaffe, Field Marshal Erhard Milch. "Isn't he a Jew?"

Goering explained, "No, he was born a *bastard*. His biological father was a Jew, but his legal father was a Christian." In this case, as in others, the law could be stretched if it was convenient to do so. "In Germany, a Jew is whoever I say is a Jew," said Goering.

He was critical of Hitler in private; publicly, during the trials, he continually expressed his devotion and loyalty. Occasionally in our conversations he would complain about Hitler's turning against him, as in 1944, when Goering suffered from severe tonsilitis. Hitler didn't even send a get-well message to him at the hospital.

When the subject turned to atrocities, Goering always went on the attack. "How about the Russians' massacre of the Polish officers in the Katyn Forest?" he demanded. "The Soviets have been the executioners of millions of their own people, including officers of their own pre-World War II army." I'm afraid I never rose to the occasion in such instances. Of course, Goering was right. The Russians were hardly in a position to charge "crimes against humanity." I changed the subject.

When Goering learned of our dropping the atom bomb on Hiroshima on August 6, 1945, he gloated, "Aha, now who are the war criminals?" I liked it better when I asked the questions.

Goering and several other military leaders predicted the "Cold War," that within a year the Soviets and the United States would be in total disagreement about almost everything. I didn't tell them that this was already the case in the summer of 1945. Their predictions of things to come gave us food for thought.

What really made Goering an interesting subject for interrogation—although an unpredictable one—was his willingness, almost eagerness, to accept responsibility. He was one of the few Nazis who did not deny his part in the conspiracy. He admitted his complicity in the use of slave labor. "They served to help in the economic war. We used this labor for security reasons. So they could not be active in their own country and work against us." He admitted using inmates of concentration camps in his underground aircraft factories. He was proud of having been Hitler's active agent and one of the prime leaders of the Nazi movement. In all this it seemed almost as if he would admit to anything so as not to lose his place in the limelight.

Shortly before we ended our operations in Luxembourg, Goering urged me to visit his wife and daughter. He gave me a photograph of himself with both of them, and wrote on the back of it, "Lt. Gillen has my full confidence and gratitude." Signed, Hermann Goering. I was to use this photo as identification if a visit to his family became possible.

The Nazi prisoners seemed to get information about our operations before we did. One afternoon in early August I was approached by four different inmates wanting to verify a rumor. They had heard they were going to be moved out. Was it true? When?

Sure enough, a few days later the breakup of the Central Continental Prisoner of War Enclosure number 32 was announced in staff meeting. No time was wasted after that. Only one prisoner needed to be told the news. Within ten minutes the whole bunch knew. When I made my usual rounds on August 9, most of the PW were sure I was coming to say goodbye.

Apparently Keitel and Jodl had mentioned my request for their autographs to the other prisoners. When I came into von Ribbentrop's room he sheepishly handed me a strip of three-by-five card with his name "Joachim von Ribbentrop" written on it. I was surprised. It was a friendly gesture I hadn't expected from the cold, self-serving foreign minister.

Since I had little contact with von Ribbentrop, I learned most about him from the other prisoners. He was considered an arrogant, demanding administrator. His public behavior clearly showed his lack of diplomacy. When he was ambassador to Great Britain he attended a formal reception of the diplomatic corps and greeted the king with outstretched arm and the Nazi salute, "Heil Hitler." He told me at first that Hitler had ordered him to do this. Later, in a conversation in Nuremberg, he claimed he had intended it as an honor to the British monarch. Also at Nuremberg, his secretary, Margaret Blanke, told me that he often kept visiting ambassadors waiting a half hour or more in his outer office. Frequently he cancelled meetings at the last minute and made visitors, regardless of rank, reschedule appointments two or three times. Blanke told me that von Ribbentrop's wife really made the decisions. "She was an aggressive, pushy bitch."

As a declassified prisoner, von Ribbentrop was a frightened nonperson. His colleagues had turned against him. He blamed himself for many failures. "I made so many mistakes," he lamented. But he then quickly added that the military made even more, and that's why everything had become so hopeless. More than all else, he was deeply hurt by being left out of Hitler's last will and testament, the listing of successors and new government officials the Fuehrer "appointed" before his suicide.

Von Ribbentrop joined the Nazi party in 1932 and was made foreign policy adviser to Hitler a year later. Actually, Hitler didn't need a for-

eign minister, just someone to run errands and confirm his judgments, a
function the incompetent, boastful Ribbentrop was well suited for. He
had no training for the position of foreign minister. In earlier years he
had lived for a short time in Switzerland, in France, and in England.
While he lacked a formal education, he had an ear for languages, and
could handle French and English with reasonable proficiency.

He was an opportunist of the highest order; he married the rich
daughter of the Henkell champagne firm for which he worked as a
salesman. He acquired the "von" for his name from an aunt whose husband was knighted in 1884 and who adopted Joachim Ribbentrop when
he was thirty-two years old. Thus he became *von* Ribbentrop.

Hitler was impressed with the title, the fancy von Ribbentrop house,
and the presumed knowledge of foreign countries and languages. Indeed, he needed a flunky of that type, an amateur diplomat who simply
performed exactly as he thought Hitler wanted. While he later claimed
to have worked for peace, the record and the testimony of witnesses made
it clear that he played an active part in the conspiracy to make war. The
attacks on Poland, Norway, and Denmark and the attack on the Low
Countries were all carried out with Ribbentrop's knowledge and
consent.

In one discussion with me he admitted to having participated in a
meeting at which it was decided civilian populations should lynch Allied
aviators taken prisoner. But he claimed that Hitler made such decisions.
He only acquiesced because he admired the Fuehrer and was a faithful
follower. During the trials it was proven that his diplomatic efforts were
closely connected with war. He definitely took part in the administration of territories illegally invaded by the Germans. He assisted in carrying out criminal policies, particularly those involving the extermination
of the Jews. He was in total sympathy with all aspects of the Nazi creed.
In short, von Ribbentrop would certainly be in the top rank of those
charged with crimes against the peace and crimes against humanity.

As word spread about the closing of the Mondorf operation, other
prisoners, one by one, became ever more friendly. Alfred Rosenberg
brought me his autograph. Streicher, Seyss-Inquart, Darré, and Count
Schwerin von Krosigk did the same. I found it amusing that my "collecting autographs" was discussed among the inmates, and how eagerly they
wanted to get into the act. Goering topped them all by bringing me a
large, formal photograph of himself in gala uniform. He took his pen in
hand to sign it, and then, with an impish look on his face, said: "Herr
Leutnant, shall I inscribe this to your real name or shall I just write John
Gillen?" The old fox studied my reaction. What the hell! I shrugged it

off. Two can be as mischievous as one. "Oh, John Gillen will be just right," I said. He wrote: "To John Gillen with best wishes and sincere gratitude, Hermann Goering." No title, no rank. Thus he wanted me to know we were pals, in his opinion.

My reputation as an autograph collector made the rounds, even though I had originally sought only the signatures of Jodl and Keitel as signators to the surrenders. I would get a special assignment in Nuremberg because of this.

Things moved fast now. By order of Colonel Andrus a "Letter of Authority" was issued August 10, 1945. It directed the movement of thirty-three internees of Ashcan to the vicinity of Frankfurt, Germany. A convoy of six ambulances, a command car, a jeep and trailer, and a 2½-ton truck with baggage was organized. It was under the direction of Lt. Col. R. W. Owens, the deputy to Colonel Andrus. Owens was to continue on to Nuremberg with another officer and two enlisted men. The rest of the convoy would proceed to Wiesbaden and then to Oberursel, Germany.

Five or six prisoners were assigned to each ambulance. I was in ambulance number one, with a driver and a guard. My prisoners were Admiral Doenitz, Minister Schwerin von Krosigk, Field Marshal Kesselring, Admirals Leopold Buerker and Gerhard Wagener, and General Warlimont. As the convoy moved from Luxembourg across the Moselle into Germany, near Trier, the nervous chatter of my passengers came to an abrupt end. Through the rear window of the ambulance they could see what their glorious Third Reich now looked like. A large portion of Trier lay in total ruin. In some areas rubble hadn't been cleared off the streets. Our vehicles snaked through passages just wide enough for one at a time.

For the high-ranking Nazis in our ambulances this was the first look at the condition of their country, the destruction that was the aftermath of Hitler's determination to "fight to the last man." They were shocked, speechless; one sobbed unashamedly. The rest of the journey went on in silence.

When we delivered the prisoners in the first two ambulances to our intelligence installation in Wiesbaden, I said goodbye to Doenitz and the others, expecting never to see them again. It now occurred to Doenitz that he was no longer in the company of Goering, Streicher, von Ribbentrop, Ley, and others. He convinced himself he would not be tried as a war criminal. His attitude immediately became one of confidence, even arrogance and smugness. His guidelines had served him well. The enemy was "acknowledging [his] impeccable character."

But Doenitz was jumping the gun. He was one of the twenty-two major Nazi war criminals indicted and tried at Nuremberg. Wiesbaden was just a small detour. We would meet again.

We took the rest of our charges in the remaining four ambulances to Oberursel the same day. I got my first look at the Military Intelligence Service Center, United States Forces, European Theater (MISC-USFET), but I didn't know yet that I would be spending the major portion of the next year there. It was a former DULAG—*Durchgangslager*—a German prisoner of war processing center. The prison barracks, housing for officers and enlisted men, office buildings, and other facilities were already in place. American forces had simply driven the Germans out and taken over the camp as a PW interrogation center for our side. Very convenient.

We turned our charges over to the guard detail at MISC, and started the return journey to Luxembourg. As the designated convoy commander for the return trip of the six empty ambulances and the other vehicles, I took the lead in the jeep.

We had traveled less than an hour when we came upon a row of five 2½-ton GI trucks, halted along the side of the road. As we passed them, a noncom stepped into the road and signalled us to stop. I ordered a halt for my vehicles and climbed out of my jeep. The sergeant saluted and took me to his captain, who was carrying on an animated conversation on his two-way radio. Then it hit me. A powerful stench, sickeningly sweet, nauseating. Several of my men in our own convoy had gotten out of their vehicles and were vomiting by the side of the road.

"What's that horrible smell, Captain? What in God's name are you hauling?" I asked him as soon as he stopped talking on the radio.

He looked at me oddly, climbed out of his jeep and motioned me to the back of the first truck behind his lead vehicle. He hadn't said a word to me yet. With a quick motion he untied the knot of a rope and flipped back a corner of the canvas cover. I stared at a load of rotting corpses, stacked like cordwood. Putrefied. Most were naked. Some still wore the pajama-like striped pants, the concentration camp uniforms, now just rotting rags. It was the most horrible sight I had ever seen.

"There are thousands of them, five truck loads," the captain finally said. He motioned with a wide sweep of his hand at the row of trucks behind us. Each was covered with a tarpaulin. Their drivers were sitting numbly in each cab behind the steering wheel, staring straight ahead as if in a trance, oblivious of the foul odor.

The captain spoke again in a flat, laconic tone. "We're hauling them from one mass grave to another. Don't ask me why."

His jeep had broken down. That's why their grim procession had come to a halt. He had radioed his command post. They were to be met by another escort about twenty miles down the road. The important thing was to keep his gruesome load moving. And I came along at just the right time.

Within minutes I found myself leading a bizarre caravan: six empty ambulances, an empty weapons carrier, followed by five 2½-ton trucks loaded with the obscenity of the Nazi final solution. Thousands of once warm human beings, exterminated and dumped into a vast pit. They were now being taken to a more suitable burial spot. I led the parade.

The Holocaust was real. If I'd ever had any doubts, they would have been erased the moment I saw the consequences of barbarism stacked on that truck bed. I can still smell that foul odor of death. It rises in my nostrils whenever I think of that chance meeting along a highway in Germany. Nor will I ever forget my convoy command, which was gratefully short. I was relieved of it a few miles down the road when a new escort met us and took those five trucks with their appalling cargo to another destination.

My own caravan continued in the direction of Luxembourg, back to Ashcan, where the individuals directly responsible for that ghastly transport were awaiting their own end of the road. I wondered if I would be able to face the Jew-baiter Streicher, or the racial supremacist Rosenberg, the next morning. Would I be able to behave in the correct manner demanded of us?

I didn't have much time to reflect on the experience of that long, long day. Just before plopping dead-tired into bed, I was informed by a grumpy Colonel Andrus that we would be moving the remaining fifteen internees to Nuremberg early the next morning. He had been given only twenty-four hours notice. He was annoyed.

The following day, before the sun had properly risen in the sky, we had loaded our charges into the ambulance transport and were heading for the airport near Luxembourg City. Two C-47s had been sent from Metz for a passenger airlift. Not even the pilots knew the nature of their cargo. You can imagine the astonished look on their faces when the Nazis climbed out of the GI ambulances and lined up to board the planes.

This wasn't a luxury flight by a long shot. The "passengers" were seated lengthwise along the tube. A small honey-bucket toilet at the rear of the plane, a urinal hanging on a door. No fancy seats, no carpeting. The doors and escape hatches were closed, but not locked.

Colonel Andrus was nervously checking out the arrangements with security foremost on his mind. Something was cooking. Aha! He had it. Kaltenbrunner! Here was the most dangerous of the fifteen. He was the former head of the RSHA—Reich Security Headquarters—in the top echelon of the SS. Dr. Ernst Kaltenbrunner was the successor to the "Hangman" Heydrich who had been assassinated in the village of Lidice, Czechoslovakia. In reprisal the entire village was razed by the Nazi SS and all males in the community (nearly two hundred) were executed.

Kaltenbrunner was a giant of a man, heavyset, large head, with a deep scar which ran from his nose to his left ear. He was missing some teeth. Definitely not someone you want to meet in a dark alley, even in broad daylight. He was a specialist in police work; held a doctor of law degree, although he was considered rather stupid. A heavy drinker and a chain-smoker, Kaltenbrunner was among the chief exterminators; a genuine gangster. So Colonel Andrus figured if anyone among the fifteen could cause trouble on this air trip to Nuremberg it would be Kaltenbrunner.

Special precautions needed to be taken. Andrus spotted me. The prisoner was handcuffed to my left wrist. Then Andrus told me sternly not to take any chances. "If he starts to run or goes for the door, shoot!" This was said loud enough for Kaltenbrunner to hear; clear enough for him to understand.

But it didn't help my state of mind. If that six-foot-four-inch, 182-pound mass of muscle and bone went for the unlocked door to the wild blue yonder, I'd go right with him. Every time he raised his handcuffed hand to scratch his head I was lifted up off my seat. I've never been more scared in my whole life. As for Colonel Andrus, he rode on the other plane.

But fortunately Kaltenbrunner decided to die a more glorious death at the hangman's noose. I survived the trip. Actually, his manner was quite docile, belying his appearance. He was soft-spoken, almost frightened. He wanted to talk, and I let him. He felt the need to explain his feelings about the Jews. Admittedly, he hated them, but he said that he had not been involved in their treatment in concentration camps. In fact, he claimed to have remonstrated with Hitler on the treatment of the Jews. But, after all, "I am a soldier and I only obeyed orders."

I didn't argue with him. I just listened. I knew that he and Adolf Eichmann had been boyhood friends in Linz, Austria. And even if Kaltenbrunner personally had never killed a Jew or anyone else, he was responsible for sending countless thousands to their death. The concentration camps were under his supervision. For instance, there was plenty of proof that he had given orders to poison the inmates of Dachau. He had also requested the bombing of several other camps by the Luftwaffe. He had tried to wipe out all evidence of the camps' existence before the Allied armies could get to them.

Kaltenbrunner suffered a cerebral hemorrhage at the start of the trials at Nuremberg. He attended only a few sessions during the early months.

Later, in the courtroom, he showed no signs of mental deterioration and continued to bluster and lie throughout. The Tribunal ruled him guilty of crimes against humanity and war crimes. Nobody could argue with that verdict.

Kaltenbrunner was a ruthless killer, determined to save his own skin. His soft talk didn't change my mind about him, but it helped pass the time. I felt very much relieved when the pilot put the old "Gooney Bird" down. The C-47 tends to bounce upon landing, and a few of the Nazis turned pale before we rolled to a complete stop in Nuremberg. So did I.

Transports were waiting at the runway. The prisoners were quickly unloaded. I said goodbye to Colonel Andrus who seemed genuinely sorry to have our association come to an end. I liked the dapper old gent, but I was glad to get away from the people in his charge, away from the depressing gloom and doom which constantly hovered over them. Without looking back, I scurried on to the plane. In just minutes we were in the air, bound for Luxembourg. I sat alone in the twenty-eight-passenger compartment, wondering what would come next.

The following day I went to my office in the Palace Hotel. Except for the few officers and men of the 391st AA Bn and the German PW work cadre, the CCPWE was deserted, a part of history. The infamous internees were all gone.

At the HQ in the Hotel Schleck, Captain Sensenig was busy boxing the records and documents accumulated during our three-month work period. He told me we were transferring our operation to the Military Intelligence Service Center in Oberursel, "as soon as possible." This meant I could go the next day too, if I could get a ride or a flight to Frankfurt. Sensenig and Hilty were leaving that afternoon. The customary army red tape had become unwound during the summer of 1945. Travel orders and authorizations were on "self-serve."

I walked back to my quarters in the Pension Wellkomm to gather my belongings. Tramping along the road adjoining the hotel grounds, I came upon a strange spectacle. By the fence stood a middle-aged Luxembourger, hands in pockets, beret at a jaunty angle on his greying head. He was shouting in the direction of the Palace Hotel. "Hallo Meier! Hallo Meier! Wie geht's in Berlin?" over and over.

At first I was puzzled. Then I remembered that Hermann Goering had often boasted to the German people early in the war: "If the British and the Americans ever bomb Berlin, my name is Meier."

The Luxembourger was rubbing it in, assuming Goering was within earshot. The man was enjoying himself so much I didn't have the heart to tell him that Goering and his Nazi colleagues weren't there to hear his taunts. They had made their final journey to Nuremberg where judgment awaited them. The quality of respect for the *Obrigkeit* (the authorities) has never existed in Luxembourg, where people think pretty much as we Americans do—the Bronx cheer, the cynical suspicion that any leader is likely to have clay in both his feet and in his head.

I lucked out the next morning. I hitched a ride on a flight to Frankfurt at the Luxembourg airport and made connections with the mail truck from the Frankfurt-Main Air Base to MISC/USFET in Oberursel.

The first order of business was to report to my new commanding officer, Colonel William R. Philp, an unusually sympathetic, first-rate, genial person whom I liked at once. He suggested I get settled in my billet, and then take a few days leave. The MISC was just getting organized and until our function was clearly spelled out by HQ USFET, there wasn't anything for an interrogator to do. In other words, get lost!

I told Colonel Philp about my sister in Wiedenbrueck, Westphalia, and asked if I might go to find her. I lucked out again. Military Intelligence was releasing a prisoner of war to British Intelligence. He was General Graf von Schwerin, apparently related to Graf Lutz Schwerin-von Krosigk whom I had delivered to Wiesbaden just a few days earlier. He was to be taken to an estate, "Moorman," near Werne in the British zone of occupation. I was authorized a jeep, and issued travel orders to the British zone with the understanding I could continue on to Westphalia after delivering the prisoner.

But first I got located in my new quarters. The camp in Oberursel included a group of small houses, actually model homes, initially constructed by the German Public Housing Administration. We now used the neat facilities for officers' quarters. They were ideal. Mal Hilty and I shared a delightful cottage right near the officers' mess. He had the downstairs, with a small living room, bedroom, and kitchen. I had the upstairs, a bedroom and bath. If he let me use the kitchen, I'd let him use the bathroom. Fair deal! We lived happily in this setup from late August until the following June. We each went our own way, but enjoyed each other's company whenever we wished. The best part for me was hearing Mal sing his operatic arias in the shower. He had a magnificent tenor and the shower had perfect acoustics.

On Friday, August 17, my prisoner, General von Schwerin, and I started our journey north. In just two hours we entered the Gut Moorman. It was a charming stone castle, surrounded by a moat and some of the most magnificent trees I had ever seen. I signed the general over to the British officer of the day, and continued on to Wiedenbrueck.

Locating Liesel's house was easy. When I rang the doorbell I braced myself for another emotional welcome. She certainly had no idea I was coming; that I was even in Europe. She would get the surprise of her life. But it did not turn out that way. Her husband came to the door instead. I had known Flory Krenzer in Luxembourg before we left in 1931. He was a professional woodcarver, specialized in wood figures and church ornaments—the carvings on pulpits, pews, and altars. He was a Social Democrat, had actively opposed the Nazi regime and spent six months in a concentration camp. He had an artificial leg, a permanent reminder of Nazi brutality.

But my reunion with my sister Liesel would have to be postponed. As luck would have it, she and her little daughter Inge had been able to get a ride on a truck going south. Impatient about the status of our sister Agnes, and hoping to get news of the rest of the family, Liesel had gone to Sindlingen. There she would certainly learn about my presence in Germany. I wouldn't be able to surprise her after all.

My brother-in-law Flory had some good news. They had received a postcard from our brother Heinrich. He was a prisoner of war in a British PW camp near Flensburg, far north in Germany.

When the Germans occupied Luxembourg in 1940, Heinrich was living and working in a small suburb of the city, Reckenthal. He was among the first to be rounded up by the SS and forced into the German army, on a punitive basis. He had been born in the Saar. As a native German he should have volunteered. He had betrayed the Fatherland by not doing so. Heinrich was picked up at six o'clock one morning and rushed off into training as a medic. His wife and daughter, Henny, did not hear from him for three years. During that time he went through the entire Russian campaign. He had also become a guinea pig in innoculation experiments to control black fever. His health would suffer for the rest of his life. But in 1945 it was great to learn that he was safe as a PW of the British.

There was no mail service between the British and the American zones of occupation, so I decided to write to Heinrich from Wiedenbrueck. I also wrote a letter to the commandant of the PW camp. I explained my situation and requested permission to visit my brother. The British Military Government office in Wiedenbrueck graciously accepted my letters for posting, and I fervently hoped to hear from the commandant soon. I would find a way to get to Flensburg.

I cut short my visit with Flory, eager to return to Oberursel by way of Sindlingen, and still catch Liesel and Inge at my sister's. It worked. At Agnes's home, in high spirits, we celebrated being together again.

Now I could report fantastic progress to Papa and Marie back in Akron. I had found two sisters, and knew that Heinrich was safe in a

PW camp. Now if I could find our brother Kasi, my personal mission in Europe would be fulfilled. It was almost too much to hope for, but I hoped.

Back in Oberursel on August 20, I found Mal Hilty in the midst of packing. He was getting ready to visit Salzburg, to attend the famous Mozart Music Festival. "Come along, Dolly!" was all the invitation I needed. In no time at all, my overnight bag was packed again. My orders for personal leave did not expire until the end of the month. Mal had commandeered a jeep, and we were zooming down the Autobahn a short two hours later.

I can't begin to describe the Salzburg festival. One thing the Nazis did not ruin during their regime was the cultural life for which Germany and Austria are noted although the works of many composers had been verboten. Hitler's own taste for Wagner and other heavies had dampened musical spirits, but the works of Mozart, in his own birthplace, were to be enjoyed to the fullest in August 1945. Mal Hilty and I entered into it with gusto.

We saw and heard the Vienna Boys' Choir; I was thrilled by the voice of Esther Rethy. Felix Prohoska was conducting the Mozarteum Orchestra. We attended every performance during our four-day stay.

We also had a chance to visit Berchtesgaden. It was an exciting experience. We drove up a treacherous mountain road to the Kehlstein, atop of which was Hitler's hideout, the *Adlerhorst*, the Eagle's Nest. We drove as far as the tunnel, where the road ended about two hundred feet from the summit. We walked through the tunnel to the elevator which rose right through the rock into the lobby of the picturesque structure. In this setting the Fuehrer had entertained, bullied, and harangued the likes of Mussolini, the Austrian Chancellor Schuschnigg, and other important personages. The view from the terrace on top of the Kehlstein was breathtaking. Hitler had chosen an ideal spot for his aerie.

On the way to the Eagle's Nest we passed over the Obersalzberg, a foothill, on which Hitler had built his Bavarian home, the Hofberg. His mistress Eva Braun had been principal hostess in the house which is so prominently mentioned in every Hitler biography. This was the home in which he had been most comfortable. Surrounded by the plush residences of his followers, the Hofberg was the focus of top Nazi leaders' social life. Everything revolved around this meeting place, the hub of much crucial Nazi activity.

The Hofberg was set afire by the SS shortly before the surrender. It was destroyed further by American forces. Only the ruins remained, a symbol of the death of Nazism. I stood in the empty frame of what had once been the famous picture window of the house. I imagined Hitler standing on the same spot, looking out over the valley and the town of Berchtesgaden, plotting and dreaming. What would he say now if he could stand in the ruin of his most beloved dwelling and reflect on the state of his Thousand Year Reich? I was glad when Mal Hilty shook me out of my reveries and proposed a drive around the spectacular Salz-kammergut region.

Our peaceful drive made us forget all about the horrors of war, the shattering of men's dreams. It was hard to believe that just a few months earlier this beautiful Germany had been at war—a world war which ended in suicides and the unconditional surrender of its leaders.

The trip to Salzburg and Berchtesgaden was inspiring. I was ready for work again when we arrived back in Oberursel.

CHAPTER

12

The German General Staff

THE MILITARY INTELLIGENCE CENTER in Oberursel held all kinds of
PW, most of them generals and admirals, members of the German General Staff. While Mal Hilty and I were vacationing in Salzburg, a project
plan had been developed by Operational Intelligence. Captain Sensenig
was in charge. The project was a study of the German General Staff, a
study divided into three parts. Part one was the early history through
World War I. It was to determine the principle and purpose of the GS.
This part would also include a study of the General Staff in the 100,000-
man army following the First World War, when the GS was formally
banned by the Treaty of Versailles, and its responsibilities were distributed among a number of officers.

The second part of our study involved the GS and National Socialism.
The third section dealt with the General Staff in World War II.

It was an ambitious project, of considerable importance to military
historians. A detailed outline of each part of the study was prepared by
the interrogators. Questionnaires were made up, and different questions
were presented to the PW best qualified to answer them. A study of
personal opinion and reaction would be combined into the replies to
questions.

We picked General of the Artillery Walter Warlimont to be leader of
the project among the prisoners. He would collect the data from the
others and arrange it into proper order. I was director of the project with
the title "Chief of Section and Chief Interrogator."

Thus, I plunged right into a busy schedule within hours after our
return from Salzburg. Field Marshal Kesselring, General Warlimont,
and General Blaskowitz were sitting in my interrogation room when I

came to work. It was "old home week," but quite different from operations in Mondorf. The prisoners had considerable freedom of movement within the compound. They were "blue ribbon" inmates, which meant they were housed in one of the individual homes—codenamed "Florida"—in reasonable comfort. They were excited about having something to do.

During the late thirties and early forties, General Warlimont was second in command of Armed Forces Operation, directly under Jodl. His rank compared to that of a four-star U.S. general. He played a vital role in the current history of the German General Staff Corps, the GSC.

On July 20, 1944, Warlimont was standing near Hitler in the Fuehrer's headquarters on the Eastern front. You'll remember this is the date on which an attempt was made to assassinate Hitler. The assassin, Lieutenant Colonel Claus Schenck von Stauffenberg, had propped a briefcase holding a bomb against the leg of a table at which Hitler and his staff were working.

When the bomb exploded, Hitler was practically lying on top of the table, in the process of pointing out a position on the large situation map. This probably saved his life as the force of the explosion went sideways and through the floorboards. Warlimont was one of the most seriously wounded in the assassination attempt. In fact, his head injury was so bad that he was given a medical discharge. He retired to his home in Gmund on the Tegernsee, a lovely lake in Bavaria. If he had remained active until the end of the war, he might well have been high on the arrest list and possibly charged with crimes of which some of his colleagues were found guilty.

When the American army reached his community in early May 1945, Warlimont voluntarily surrendered and was brought to Ashcan in Mondorf as a former member of the German General Staff. He immediately turned into a "cooperative witness for the prosecution." He supplied a lot of information. I would say almost too much. Mal Hilty had interrogated him in Luxembourg, and often complained about the volume of work a Warlimont interrogation generated. Now I was coordinating his contributions. Like Hilty, I, too, never caught up with the amount of material assembled.

My first interview with Warlimont concentrated on Hitler's decision to violate the nonaggression pact with the Soviet Union. Jodl, as chief of the Armed Forces Operations staff, journeyed to Bad Reichenhall for a meeting with the OKW (Armed Forces High Command) staff officers. Warlimont was a colonel then, chief of the planning session. They met on July 29, 1940 in Jodl's railroad car. Warlimont said he thought the unusual gathering was for the purpose of receiving a decoration or pro-

motion. Instead, he learned that he and his senior officers were to prepare plans for a surprise attack on the Soviet Union. The Fuehrer had
decided it must be done as soon as possible, within a year at the most.

Warlimont claimed he was "shocked." England wasn't defeated yet.
Hitler himself had written in *Mein Kampf* that Germany must never
again fight a war on two fronts. That's why Germany lost the First
World War. The officers protested. They thought Stalin had kept his
promise and lived up to the terms of the Moscow Pact. But their objec-
tions fell on deaf ears. Jodl said it was better to attack now while German
forces were at full strength. Sooner or later Bolshevism would have to be
defeated. "No further discussion! The Fuehrer has decided," said Jodl.
Warlimont was ordered to prepare the planning papers. "That was the
beginning of my doubts about German leadership," he said in recounting the incident.

Warlimont seemed always to be on hand when the surprises came. He
told me Jodl telephoned him on December 11, 1941 to announce that
"the Fuehrer has just declared war on America." It, too, came as a
shock—the second in his career as chief of planning. Warlimont told me
he had never even considered a war against the United States. Now he
was to develop a plan to counter whatever action the Americans might
take.

Warlimont had a low opinion of Keitel as commander in chief of the
OKW. He was "a man who held a position for which he was magnifi-
cently unqualified." When the North African campaign bogged down,
Keitel relieved Warlimont of his post. Later he rescinded the action in
"typical Keitel fashion—wishy-washy."

At first, our GS project was a hit-and-miss affair. We weren't sure
what direction it should take. Then one day Warlimont came into my
office. He gave me a lengthy report entitled "The Political Attitude of
the German General Staff since 1920." I glanced at it briefly, not sure
how I would use it. Warlimont was fidgeting. I could tell he had something else on his mind. I suggested he come out with it. He did. He
wanted to visit his wife and his three children in Gmund, Bavaria.
Would I take him there?

I reminded him that he was a prisoner of war. We could not just arbi-
trarily arrange a home visit for him. But he was very persuasive. I heard
him out. Warlimont's wife was of American descent. Her mother was
somehow related to the Anheuser family—of Budweiser beer fame. She
had married a German opera singer, the Baron von Kleydorff, in 1903,
when he was on a U.S. tour. General Warlimont and his wife, Anita, had
three children, two daughters, sixteen and seventeen, and a son, eleven.
He was distraught about being away from his family. There had been no

mail, no news. He just wanted to see them once more to make sure they were all right.

I considered his plan so farfetched that it became intriguing. Why not try it and see what happens? So on August 31 I sent the following message to my CO:

SUBJECT: Documents for GSC Project (General Staff Corps)
TO: OI Chief

1. In the course of an interrogation, PW Walter WARLIMONT revealed that a number of books and documents of great intelligence value are hidden in his own home and vicinity. Their exact location is known only to PW.
2. These books and documents could be of great value in the study of the German General Staff Corps, and of the "OKW in the Domestic Power-politics of 1935-1945." They may also contain information which WARLIMONT considers important for the war criminal trials in Nuremberg.
3. A list of these books and documents, their contents, and general location, as prepared by PW WARLIMONT, is attached hereto.
4. Permission is requested for undersigned officer to accompany PW WARLIMONT to GMUND and TEGERNSEE vicinity for the purpose of securing the above-mentioned material. The trip would require approximately 3 to 4 days.

JOHN E. DOLIBOIS
1st Lt. CAV
GSC Project Section

I enclosed a list of the principal books and documents to be secured. The material and reports we would collect on this "mission impossible" were located in Warlimont's own home, in the private library of a Count von Luxburg, in Rottach, and in the home of Professor Herbert Kraus who resided in the hamlet of Unterstein, near Berchtesgaden. We would be collecting books and personal reminiscences of General Hans von Seeckt (commander of the post-World War I, 100,000-man army.) We would find schemes and organization charts of the OKW, manuscripts on "General Jodl as Officer and Personality," and "The Moral Attitude of the German Officer Corps." All this and more.

The matter deserved a letter, at least. I started it through channels, and forgot all about it within the hour. But not Warlimont. He started to pray, and hope beyond hope.

Meanwhile, another development which would have an effect on my work was taking shape in Nuremberg. Dr. Robert Ley wrote the following letter on August 27:

Mr. 1st Lt. Gillen
Officer of the American Army
Most Honored Mr. Lieutenant!
    Please visit me. I have important, perhaps decisive information to reveal. It might be of greatest significance to all further proceedings. I have confidence in you, therefore I turn to you.
With greatest respect

DR. ROBERT LEY

This pencilled note was intercepted by Colonel Andrus, now commanding the Internal Security Detachment under the Office of the Chief U.S. Council. Good old reliable Andrus wrote to Col. John H. Amen, a deputy to Supreme Court Justice Robert Jackson:

SUBJECT: Attached Communication
TO: Col. Amen

1. The attached note was written by PW Robert LEY, and is addressed to a Lt. GILLEN, an interrogator at ASHCAN. This officer is in reality 1st Lt. JOHN E. DOLIBOIS, now stationed at the USFET Interrogation Center, APO 757.
2. It is suggested that Lt. DOLIBOIS be requested for temporary duty with this Headquarters, in order to obtain the information held by PW LEY.
3. If at all possible, every effort should be made to have Lt. DOLIBOIS permanently assigned to this office. His work at ASHCAN was superior; his interrogation ability is outstanding. He would undoubtedly be a valuable addition to your staff.

B. C. ANDRUS
Colonel, CAV.
Commanding

On September 5 I was on my way to Nuremberg "on temporary duty for a period of approximately six (6) days, for the purpose of carrying out the instructions of the Theater Commander. . . ."

I felt trapped. I knew that Colonel Andrus was unhappy with the way things were going in Nuremberg. Some of his superiors were not particularly in sympathy with the proposed Nuremberg Trials. He wasn't getting the material and personnel support he thought he needed. In his opinion the prison which he now commanded should have top manpower priority. Almost all of his Luxembourg staff had been rotated or sent home and he was left with what he called "cast-offs" and "very mediocre officers." Andrus wanted some familiar faces around him. I would have to be alert or I'd be stuck in Nuremberg for the duration.

As I drove my jeep through the shells of buildings and heaps of rubble that was Nuremberg, I could see families living in second-story rooms which had been cut in half by the bombing. People in ragged clothing were cooking their food at open fires. Every cellar of bombed-out buildings was occupied. At one point I was shocked to see several grown men scramble for one cigarette butt thrown into the street by a passing American soldier. As I halted at a stop sign, four young children came up to my jeep begging for food and "chew gum." Cigarettes were most in demand, not necessarily for smoking, but for trading.

The Nuremberg prison compound had been badly damaged by the devastating Allied bombing and gunfire. The foundations of all the huge buildings were shaky. Outside walls were propped up with timbers while repair work was going on. I saw hundreds of German PW working on the buildings. Ironically, many of them were still wearing the Waffen SS insignia on their uniforms. Inside those walls were their former officers awaiting trial. It was almost too much irony to absorb.

I could appreciate why Colonel Andrus was apprehensive. The PW workers far outnumbered the one battery of guards policing the prison and the work crews.

The Palace of Justice loomed large in front of the prison buildings which were in the same compound. Hastily erected wood tunnels connected the prison with the courthouse in which the trial would be held. The offices of the prosecuting staffs of the four major powers were also in the Palace of Justice. Of first priority was the restoration of the courtroom and the adjoining facilities. The time schedule was ridiculously tight. I was glad my duty here was temporary. The hectic pace, the frantic atmosphere, were overpowering.

Colonel Andrus welcomed me cordially, genuinely glad to see me. Within a few minutes he led me on a tour of the jail, formerly the state prison of the State of Franken (Franconia). German civilian criminals occupied two wings of the jail. A third wing was referred to as the "witness wing," where more than fifty political and military leaders were interned. They were the lesser known Nazi "Bonzen"—witnesses for the prosecution and possibly the defense. Some of them would be tried in later sessions of the Nuremberg Tribunal. A number of our internees from Ashcan were held in this wing.

The last stop on our prison tour was the "war criminals wing." Just before we entered it through strict security, Andrus presented me with an ID card—my personal pass—to the "Area of the Palace of Justice." It was blue, with the number 1208. I turned it over. On the back was a special imprint: "The bearer is authorized to enter the WAR CRIMINALS WING, NUERNBERG PRISON by order of Col. Andrus."

My name was already inscribed on it. It looked very "permanent." Andrus read the expression on my face. "There are only twenty of those issued, Johnny. That's a very special privilege. Use it from now on to come and go as you please."

In Ashcan, at Mondorf, I thought life was pretty grim and rigid for the declassified Nazi leaders. But that was luxury compared to the war criminals wing in Nuremberg. The twenty-two major defendants to be tried in the first session of the trials were in solitary confinement. There was no communication between them. Once a day, for two prisoners at a time, a fifteen-minute walk was permitted in the prison yard, which was about a block square. A high stone wall surrounded the prison yard. One prisoner walked up and down one side of the wall, a second prisoner on the other. No talking was permitted.

The prison wing they occupied was three stories high, although all were housed on the ground floor. A wide corridor ran the full length of the building, with cells nine-by-thirteen feet on each side. A heavy wooden door opened to the corridor from each cell. One high, barred window was on the opposite wall. It faced on the prison yard.

In the center of the wooden cell door was a small opening through which food and drink were passed. The guard—one to every four cells—used it to observe the prisoner.

A metal cot was fastened to the wall in each cell. A flimsy table and a straight chair were the only other furnishings. A lavatory bowl and a small toilet were at the wall opposite the cot. The toilet was set in a niche, which provided some privacy for the prisoner when he used that facility. Even then, his feet could still be seen by the guard.

Prisoners were allowed family photographs, tobacco, writing material, and toilet articles which they kept on the table. Extra clothing and other personal possessions were kept on the floor next to the bed. The cells were lighted by one electric bulb in a reflector fastened to the door. The light was dimmed at night, but was still bright enough to read by. Once a week the prisoners were individually marched to the shower room where they bathed under supervision.

The waiters who brought the food were not permitted to speak to the prisoners. The guards could speak to them only when giving directions or correcting them for a breach of discipline. In spite of all these precautions and the rigid routine, two of the major Nazis were able to commit suicide. That paragon of discipline, that master of perfectionism in security, my friend Colonel Andrus, could never forgive Ley and Goering for outsmarting him.

In the weeks ahead I would become thoroughly familiar with the prison layout and the daily routine in the war criminals and the witness wings. But on this first visit to Nuremberg my assignment was to find out what valuable information Dr. Ley was willing to give to me only.

First I got acquainted with Colonel Amen. Then Ley was summoned. He would be interrogated by the two of us. I could have told Colonel Amen this wouldn't work. Ley acted as if I were a total stranger. He was polite, formal, and stammered more than ever. We made small talk. He was dismissed. I assured the colonel that Ley was willing to talk but reluctant to speak to both of us at the same time. Obviously he considered his information confidential; he would share it only with someone he trusted completely. If Ley considered me just the interpreter, rather than the confidant he expected, he would not talk. Amen agreed that I would see Ley alone.

Later that day I visited him in his cell. I had guessed right. I got a totally different reception; it was as if he hadn't already seen me that morning. He was effusive. "Finally, you have come to see me," he burbled, "you are sent from heaven."

But within minutes he was in deep despair. "There is no reason for living, all is lost," he wailed. It took me a while to cheer him up. Soon he was his ebullient self again; the rose-colored glasses were back on. We finally got around to his urgent note, and I started prodding him for the "decisive information" he wanted to give to me alone. For a moment I thought he had forgotten all about it. But suddenly he became enthusiastic. "Yes, of course," he had so much to tell me. He needed to organize his thoughts. He needed to write it all down. There was so much involved and he wanted to get his facts straight. So he needed lots of paper and pencils.

By now I became suspicious of his whole scheme. But upon consultation with Colonels Amen and Andrus it was agreed to humor him. I visited him again the next day and delivered several pads of paper and a fistful of pencils. To Colonel Andrus this meant just one thing. I would have to come back to Nuremberg to get the information Ley was preparing for me. I was beginning to think Andrus and Ley were in cahoots. Looking back on it, however, I now realize that my eagerness to get away from the entire Nuremberg procedure was foolish. Here I was involved in making history. All I could think of was getting home.

Thanks to the delay in getting Ley's "revelation" I didn't have to stay in Nuremberg any longer. I was tempted to visit Streicher, Goering, and some of the others in the war criminals wing, but decided against it. The goodbyes had been said a few weeks earlier. I let it be.

But I did have a long session with Major Kelley, the prison psychiatrist. He conducted medical and psychiatric examinations, testing the internees. He specialized in the Rorschach Test, the well-known and highly useful method of personality study. Kelley could not speak German and had to rely on interpreters to assist him in interviews of prisoners who didn't know English.

When he learned that I had majored in psychology at Miami University, he got all excited. I would be familiar with terms and procedures. He urged me to stay on at the prison and work with him, but I was still determined to get out of Nuremberg as soon as possible. And stay away, if I could help it. On the other hand, his suggestion was challenging, even though he was overestimating my scientific capacity.

Back in Oberursel, General Warlimont was still counting on our making a trip to Tegernsee to see his family. I wasn't able to convince him it would never be allowed.

And then it happened. Colonel Philp sent for me and offered the opinion that Warlimont's proposal was mighty interesting. He had decided not to route it through channels, knowing full well that G-2 USFET would never allow me to drive off with a four-star German general—a prisoner of war—on a document hunt in Bavaria. So he was willing to accept full responsibility for the hare-brained venture. He would authorize the mission. He grinned broadly, peered over his spectacles. "You're on your own, Dolly," he said.

Soon I had my orders. ". . . to proceed to Tegernsee and Berchtesgaden, Germany, by military motor transportation for a period not to exceed five (5) days to carry out the instructions specified by the commanding officer. . . ." The second paragraph read: "In the performance of this duty, the above named officer is authorized to transport and return to this station the German PW Walter Warlimont. By order of Col. Philp."

We were on our way, General Warlimont in civilian clothes, posing as my German interpreter. I was the driver, slightly nervous, and not particularly comforted by the .45 strapped to my belt. I don't know how I would ever have explained my shooting of a four-star German general trying to escape. Faith prevailed. My prisoner was anxious to see his family. He had voluntarily come into captivity. Why would he want to run away? The trip turned into a rare adventure.

There were some tricky moments, too. We stopped at a U.S. military installation in Augsburg for lunch. Of course, I was entitled to eat in the officers' mess, but my German "civilian" interpreter was not. In fact, they weren't even going to feed him. I persuaded a reluctant mess sergeant to give us a break and let Warlimont have some food in the kitchen. I couldn't help overhearing the instructions the sergeant gave my travel companion as he took him to the cookery: "Hey Heinie, chow down at the table over there, and be sure to rinse those dishes in the sink when you're finished." That was a general he was talking to. But I wasn't about to tell him. Neither was Warlimont.

The two lovely Bavarian-style houses overlooked the beautiful Tegernsee. One was the home of my prisoner; the other, next door, belonged to his in-laws, the Baron and Baroness von Kleydorff. I discreetly admired the scenery while Warlimont was greeted by his overwhelmed wife and children. Mrs. Warlimont and her children didn't know what had happened to the general during the five months of his absence from them. There had been no exchange of letters or any news. And I couldn't help feeling somewhat self-righteous, being able to do a good turn. I guess there was room for a humane gesture in this hate-filled, war-torn Germany.

I was a welcome guest of the two families. The atmosphere was warmed even more when I unpacked the supply of coffee, sugar, C-rations, cheese and crackers, chocolate, and cigarettes.

I spent four restful days on the shore of the Tegernsee, in the home of the baron and his American-born wife. Warlimont was with his family next door. On one day we undertook the mission which had made the trip possible. We located and packed the books and documents. The rest of the time, he relaxed with his family, and I enjoyed the peaceful lakeside.

Warlimont had pointed out the home of Field Marshal Kesselring and that of the Reichsminister for Labor and Social Policy, Franz Seldte, both a short distance from his house. I decided to do another good turn, and to call on their wives. They welcomed me gratefully as I was able to reassure them about their husbands' health and whereabouts. I also learned a little more about these men now in the witness wing of the Nuremberg prison. I felt my visit to the two ladies was a small step toward improving relations between Germany and the United States. Hostilities had ended. The time had come, in my opinion, to develop greater understanding.

Mrs. Seldte invited me to tea—after I had given her several packets of tea and sugar. I also provided a small tin of cookies. In the course of amiable conversation I bragged about my son, Johnny-Mike. My hostess jumped up excitedly and rushed out of the room. Soon she returned with a handsome pair of Lederhosen—brand new, just right for a little boy's preschool years. It was the genuine article, real leather, beautifully made. They would last forever.

And so they have. Johnny-Mike wore them. Then our son Bob. Years later our third son Brian romped around in the same leather shorts. Most recently our grandson Ryan outgrew them. They still look neat, especially with that patina good leather acquires with age.

The visit on the Tegernsee ended when my travel orders were about to expire. Warlimont had to leave his family again, but this time under much more promising circumstances. I was fairly certain that he would not be accused of any crimes and would not be brought to trial. His cooperation and his service to our side would assure eventual release. But first, there was more to do at the interrogation center in Oberursel.

On our way back from his home in Gmund am Tegernsee, Warlimont and I had an unusual encounter just a few miles outside of Bad Toelz in Bavaria. We were traveling along a narrow country road when I heard a siren and saw some military vehicles approaching. I pulled over to the side of the road and stopped. In seconds a jeep, going about seventy miles per hour, zoomed by, the siren and a large horn mounted on its hood. Close behind came a staff car with four stars prominent on a front license plate. In the back seat sat none other than General George S. Patton, Jr. Next to him perched a white dog, scowling as fiercely as its master. They passed in a flash. I saluted smartly, and my salute was acknowledge with a dip of the swagger stick the general raised in my direction. Before I could collect my wits the speeding two-car caravan was out of sight.

I cast back my thoughts. Two years earlier General Patton had handed me my commission at Fort Knox, Kentucky. Now he passed me on an obscure country road in Bavaria where he was now the military governor. The war was over. Victory was ours, no small thanks to General Patton.

And in my jeep by the side of the road sat a declassified four-star German general who had masterminded some of the operations which Patton and his Third Army had so successfully smashed. What would Patton have done if he had known that he just passed Walter Warlimont, General of Artillery, of the Germany High Command? Doggone! I wish there had been some way I could have flagged down that staff car. But then I might have had a bushel of trouble explaining what I was up to riding around the countryside with a PW of that magnitude.

Warlimont was at a loss for words when I told him who had just sped past. "Unglaublich! Unglaublich!" he said over and over. Yes, incredible indeed!

On this same trip from Bavaria to Oberursel the true identity of Lieutenant Gillen was made known to the enemy. My sister Agnes had given me the address of Maria and Henny, the wife and daughter of my brother Heinrich. They had been evacuated during the heavy fighting in the Saar in February. They were living temporarily on a farm not far from Stuttgart. Since this was on the route we were traveling, I decided to make a small detour and to surprise my sister-in-law and niece. I would be able to bring them the great news that Heinrich was alive, and that I would try to see him if the British authorities allowed. They had no idea where Heinrich might be, if he was even alive. I would be the bearer of joyful tidings—the kid brother from the United States. It would be another exciting experience.

So I told General Warlimont that I had a personal errand to perform. I had no trouble locating the farm where Maria and Henny were staying. As we approached the house, an old man hobbled toward us, full of curiosity. Before I could say anything, he announced that the whole family was out in the field, digging potatoes. He gave me directions, and I continued driving on a wagon track some five hundred yards beyond the house. A dozen or more people were digging in the field. I jumped out of the jeep and walked toward them, having already decided I didn't want Warlimont to hear me ask about my family—which wasn't named Gillen.

Work stopped completely as I approached. I must have scared the hell out of them as I strode forward in an American officer's uniform with a .45 on my hip. They all laid down their hoes and rakes; there would be no resistance. I quickly identified myself and stated the purpose of my being there. I could feel their sense of relief.

But much to my disappointment I learned that my sister-in-law and my niece had gone back to the Saar to check on their house. They would be back in two or three days if they could get a ride. Again, as in the case of my sister Liesel, I was denied the pleasure of a big surprise. I told the farm family who I was and gave them the news about my brother and told them they should pass it along to his wife and daughter when they came back. With that, I returned to my jeep and cranked up, ready to drive off.

Across the field, running after me, came the farmer's wife. "Herr Dolibois! Herr Dolibois!" she called out. I had forgotten to tell them where my sister-in-law might find me.

So much for "Lt. Gillen" and his nom-de-guerre. I looked at my prisoner. He had heard all right. A mischievous smile, and then reassurance. "Don't worry, Herr Leutnant Gillen, your secret is safe with me."

It didn't make much difference anyway. And it was rather pleasant to be able to talk with him about my family.

In turn, Warlimont shared with me some of his early background. As a lieutenant colonel he was the military representative at General Francisco Franco's headquarters in Spain in 1936. The Spanish Civil War was just beginning and Hitler felt it was his duty, as a National Socialist, to support Franco. Warlimont had been sent to Spain to observe the situation firsthand and to make recommendations. His nom-de-guerre was "Guido."

I was intrigued by the stories which Warlimont told me. We agreed to prepare a formal interrogation report upon our return to Oberursel. It would be an interesting adjunct to our reports on the German General Staff.

During his months in Luxembourg, Oberursel, and then Nuremberg, General Warlimont kept an abbreviated personal diary. He made daily entries, accounting for each day's happenings and impressions. Most daily entries were no longer than a sentence or two.

When I saw him for the last time in December 1945, in the jail in Nuremberg, he begged me to take this journal—actually a stack of loose notes—to his wife. There was no way I could assure him of being able to return to Tegernsee area, but he insisted on my taking it.

The daily entries in his journal had no intelligence value, it being just a personal account. Only his family would find it interesting. I put it with my own personal papers and mementos, and forgot all about it.

In February 1977, thirty years after my return from Germany, I met Professor Harold C. Deutsch, of the Army War College, who had come to lecture at Miami University. He told me that he had interviewed General Warlimont two years earlier for a book he was writing. He gave me Warlimont's address.

I immediately wrote to my former prisoner and travel companion. By return mail came a letter from his wife:

Thank you very much for your letter to my husband, the photo of "Lt. Gillen" (which I return as you may like to have it back).

I am sorry to inform you that my husband died last October shortly after his 82nd birthday. He suffered from cancer for 7 years, not knowing the cause of his illness; but he kept up hope, an upright appearance, his marvelous good looks and bright intelligence to the last moment.

It is a pity you found our address so late. I am sure he would have enjoyed seeing you again and remembered your "special arrangement" in 1945. I would very much appreciate if you would send me the "diary." I am very grateful to you for having kept it for us all these years.

Fancy you remembering our having a son and two daughters. Our oldest daughter is married to an American and lives in New Hampshire. Our second in Germany, and our son near Munich, which is lucky for me. He was a great help to me when my husband died. I have five grandchildren; one beautiful girl of 24 years studying law in New Hampshire, two in Kassel, and my son has a sweet girl of 10 and a darling little boy of three. I can well understand how proud you and your wife are of your grandchildren.

I wonder if you see Prof. Deutsch? Could you give me his address since he evidently doesn't know my husband is dead.

I would enjoy very much meeting you and Mrs. Dolibois some day when you are again in Europe and I'm looking forward to hearing from you and receiving the diary and photos. Thank you very much in advance.

My very best wishes for you and your family,

Yours,
Anita Warlimont

I sent the yellowing journal notes. I enclosed some photos I took in 1945 when my prisoner and I visited his family. On May 1, 1977, I heard from Mrs. Warlimont again:

Let me thank you most sincerely for sending me my husband's diary which means so much to me and my family though it brings back memories of very hard times. It is to be regretted that politicians create war and hatred between nations, when there could be good feelings and personal friendship when occasion is given. Your help and cooperation were of greatest value to my husband and myself and we were ever grateful to you.

Maybe you will remember that my mother, having stayed at her house, was American. My brother is living in Philadephia with his American wife—my eldest daughter in New Hampshire with her American husband. So I am very much connected with your wonderful country.

It would be wonderful if we could meet in spring or coming fall on occasion of your youngest son studying in Luxembourg. I will let you know my new address in Munich as soon as possible, since I am going to live with my son and his family in a new home.

I do hope you and your family are well and happy. Please accept my heartiest thanks for your kindly keeping and sending me the diary.

With very best greetings,
Anita Warlimont

I didn't hear from the lady again, so I never received her new address. A pity. It would have been interesting to look her up and to chat with her about the happenings of many years ago.

Wednesday, September 17, 1945 was a red-letter day. We drew our liquor ration for the month, a bottle of scotch, one of bourbon, and three bottles of Fundador (Spanish) brandy. The latter was plentiful for some reason. On the spur of the moment that evening I decided to requisition a jeep and drive to Sindlingen to see my sister Agnes and her family. Her husband Gusty was a big smoker. He could have my cigarette ration. I would let him have the booze, too.

I arrived in Sindlingen, halted my jeep in front of the "Gasthaus zum Stern," and braced myself for the tumultuous welcome my two nieces

Ilse and Marianne always gave me. But this time, nobody came running outside to greet me. With some misgiving I walked in the door and got the surprise of my life. There, at the kitchen table sat my brother Kasi and his wife Klaerchen. Everyone in the room was grinning from ear to ear. They had waited all week for this moment.

When the war began with the German invasion of Poland in 1939, Kasi and his wife were living in Beckingen, in the Saar region. They had left Luxembourg even before Papa and I came to the United States. Beckingen was his wife's home town.

Eventually, Kasi was drafted into the German army and served in North Africa. The German campaign there ended in failure, and Kasi was transferred to an outfit in France. The American liberation of France had begun with the big invasion on the beaches of Normandy and Britanny.

The Nazis were struck another blow on August 15, 1944, when a landing, code-named *Dragoon*, took place in Southern France, between Cannes and Toulon. A fleet of over a thousand ships, including nine aircraft carriers, arrived off the Riviera. This invasion met with minimum resistance. Lt. General Alexander Patch commanded the American Seventh Army, General Jean de Lattre de Tassigny the French First Army. They were helped by French Maquis and resistance agents. The Germans retreated toward the Rhine, and my brother Kasi was taken prisoner by the French. The war was over for him.

He spent more than a year in a French PW camp south of Strassbourg. In early September 1945 he decided to go for broke. Escaping from his guards on a work detail, he managed to get across the Rhine and eventually turned himself in to an American unit at the edge of the U.S. zone of occupation. He was interrogated by an intelligence officer, and in the course of interrogation produced the last letter he had received from our Papa back in 1938. Kasi had carried that letter with him throughout his army service.

When the American interrogator saw the letter, he decided a German PW with a father in the USA couldn't be all bad. Furthermore, who needed one more PW at this stage of the game? Kasi was released. Armed with an ID and documentation from the American army, he found his way back to Beckingen where his wife lived with her parents. Kasi and Klaerchen (little Clara) managed to find transportation to Sindlingen where our sister Agnes would surely have news about the rest of the family.

Thus they found out that his kid brother was an American officer and would probably drop in unannounced, as was customary, any time.

They relaxed and waited. Sure enough, I showed up a few days later with booze, cigarettes, and other goodies scrounged from the mess in Oberursel. Another fantastic reunion. But that isn't the end of my incredible story. It reached its climax on the following weekend.

We had agreed I would come back on Saturday afternoon, when we would celebrate in style. When I arrived at my sister's inn that afternoon, I saw a hollow-cheeked, obviously wearied older man, sitting on the front doorstep. He wore a faded German army jacket, baggy trousers, and a vaguely familiar look. It was my oldest brother Heinrich. I almost walked past him before I recognized him. He had been waiting patiently for me. I'll never forget the joy of his greeting, the warmth of his embrace. Heinrich had suffered immensely, and had aged almost beyond recognition. The Russian campaign and the pain of illness he had endured had taken their toll.

The rest of the family was assembled inside. I met niece number four, Henny (Henrietta), age nine, and got a big hug from my sister-in-law Maria. And then I had to get the story of this unbelievable roundup.

Remember I had driven to Wiedenbrueck in August and learned that Heinrich was a PW in a British camp. I had written the commandant. When he received my letter he sent for my brother. They gave him a knapsack, a slab of bacon, two bedsheets, a can of beans, and his release. "Go home and good luck!" was the order.

Heinrich rode a freight train, hitchhiked, and walked. Four days later he arrived in the village to which his wife and daughter had been evacuated. Liesel had written to him after my visit and told him of their whereabouts. He had not heard from them or vice versa while he was at the Russian front for nearly three years. On getting to the farm near Stuttgart, Heinrich walked up the same lane I had driven with General Warlimont just two days before. He was dead tired. Though anxious and eager to see his family, he decided to sit in the grass under a tree by the lane and rest a bit. He fell asleep.

A short while later a woman and a young girl came walking up the same lane. Maria and Henny were returning from the Saar, coming home to the farm where they had lived as evacuees since early February. Maria saw a man sleeping in the shade, a knapsack at his side. The stencilled name on the knapsack read "H. Dolibois." Imagine *that* reunion!

It was only later, upon getting to the farmhouse, that they learned of my visit there two days earlier. They wasted no time in getting to the Gasthaus zum Stern in Sindlingen. Picture their happy surprise to find Kasi and Klaerchen there, and to learn that I would be coming on Saturday—the next day, in fact.

We sat up all night. The storytelling never stopped. I had to account for fourteen years in the United States, and I wondered how I could ever crowd the description of this reunion into one letter to my family back in Akron, Ohio. Would they even believe this unreal course of events?

13

When Hess and Goering Met Again

PW KESSELRING AND I had worked on an outline on his role as commander of the German troops in Italy. When the interview ended I decided to walk him back to the house "Florida" in which he and Warlimont were interned. Ordinarily, one of the guards escorted a prisoner between the detention area and our interrogation rooms. This time I took on the responsibility.

We sat on the small terrace on the side of the little house. Our conversation turned to nonmilitary matters, particularly my visit to his home and his wife. We spoke of his family and his long career. "What do you consider the most important lesson you have learned in life?" I asked the old soldier.

I expected a philosophical reply. He was inclined to get wordy on occasion. This time he surprised me. "Let me think about that, Herr Oberleutnant," he said. "That is a question deserving a thoughtful answer."

The next day he gave it to me, in writing. In his stiff, up-and-down script, with last name and full military title in the upper left-hand corner, he had written on a sheet of paper:

The experience of two world wars and two revolutions in the highest leadership position, and as a declassified prisoner of war, has convinced me more than ever that
Character is to be valued more highly
than Knowledge and Ability,

and that therefore the development of character
is to be preferred above all.

KESSELRING

In the left-hand corner he wrote "To First Lieutenant Gillen in grateful understanding of his soldierly duty and comradely demeanor."

The War Department Historical Section began to notice our output. Before long several of their prominent historians came to visit us in Oberursel on a regular basis. Among them was Dr. George Shuster, who soon after the war became president of Hunter College in New York. My Miami friend, Professor Harry Howard, came to the interrogation center, and with him several others whose writings have since become valuable additions to the history of World War II.

One day in early October we received word that Warlimont and Kesselring were being transferred to Nuremberg. Apparently the prosecutors were eager to interview them, too. I complained to the OI chief in an interoffice memo: "In view of the manner in which the entire GS project was planned and prepared, the loss of these two prisoners seriously affects the project." Would we just halt our work or what?

"Don't worry about it," said my commanding officer. "We'll continue the project by long distance." I would be assigned a brand new jeep to commute between Oberursel and Nuremberg whenever it became necessary to involve the two generals or anyone else participating in the study. Col. Philp also promised that I would not be assigned full time to the Nuremberg establishment. He understood my "PW fatigue." Meanwhile, Warlimont and Kesselring were readied for the move to Nuremberg. They both were deeply depressed and worried.

I was due for another side trip myself. I had promised to drive my brother Kasi to the Saar. I had my own jeep. The men in the motor pool stencilled Johnny-Mike's name on the windshield panel in handsome script. The vehicle was at my disposal for the rest of my time in Europe. It was a pretty good deal.

On Saturday morning, I tossed my overnight bag in the jeep and picked up Kasi at Agnes's house. In no time at all we were on the road to the Saar Basin, the region in which my family had its beginning. It turned out to be a sad journey.

The Saar was badly destroyed when the invasion of Germany began in earnest. Fighting was fierce in the area. In March, Patton's Third Army roared across the French border at Lorraine and raced eastward. In their path, not much was left standing intact. As we drove into Saarlouis, Kasi pointed out the church in which Papa and my mother were married.

Only one wall and part of the old belltower remained. We drove to the house in which my parents lived when they were first married. It was a total ruin.

I steered my jeep through the rubble on the main throughfare. We came upon two women clothed in black threadbare dresses and aprons. They called to us, but I drove on, knowing that, like many other Germans I passed in the streets, they were begging for cigarettes, food, anything. American GIs were noted for their generosity. Kasi put his hand on my arm. "Stop John!" he directed. I braked the jeep, he jumped out and embraced each of the two ladies who had run up to the vehicle when we halted. Then he pointed to me. He could say no more than, "This is Hansi!" They were speechless. So was I.

The two women were my mother's sisters, our Aunt Lena and Aunt "Bibi." Of course I remembered them from my boyhood days. Papa and I had last visited them and their families before we came to America in 1931.

They insisted we come to their home, the cellar of what I remembered as a magnificent house. My Uncle Johann had been the schoolmaster of the town before his death. The Maas family was one of the most prominent.

Our two aunts and my cousin Anna, ten years older than I, were living in the ruins of their once proud home. A few pieces of furniture had survived the bombing and the fires. A potbelly stove stood in one corner of the drafty cellar. The smoke from its fire was directed out of a shattered basement window. Potatoes were roasting in the fire. It was their dinner time. They insisted we eat with them. The menu was potatoes, salt, and pepper.

You should have seen the joy on their faces when I produced a can of Spam, some powdered milk, hard biscuits, and coffee. Coffee! You'd have thought I was bringing pure gold. We ate a feast I will long remember.

Both of my aunts died a few years after the war, but Winnie and I visited my cousin Anna in 1965. The lovely old house had been rebuilt. Twenty years after my first dramatic appearance life was back to normal for Anna. She too had not fotgotten our banquet in the cellar in October 1945.

With Kasi's guidance I visited several more cousins and uncles. Some lived in houses that had been spared severe damage. Others were crowded together in makeshift arrangements "until better times." Kasi and Klaerchen were forced to live with her parents. But he was full of hope. He owned a small plot of land on a hillside near the edge of town and being a builder, he would soon have his own house again.

I drove to Wallerfangen where Heinrich, Maria, and Henny were temporarily housed with relatives. Their own home, actually that of Maria's parents, was occupied by French soldiers. It had been requisitioned by the French Army of Occupation.

I was determined to help my brother and his family get into their own house. On the following Monday morning I told Colonel Philp about my visit to the Saar. I've already mentioned that he was a sympathetic, compassionate man. In no time at all, I had "orders" from the commanding officer, supplementing standing travel orders with the magic name "Eisenhower." Colonel Philp let me have his staff car and driver. I returned to the Saar Basin within hours, in style.

The French military governor for the district, which included Wallerfangen, was headquartered in Dillingen, the county seat. At midafternoon the colonel's staff car, with me in the back seat, pulled up in front of the French "governor's" building. My driver held open the door and saluted smartly as I climbed out of the car. The French sentry at the entrance to the building nearly dropped his rifle as he drew to attention.

I stomped officiously into the reception area and demanded to see the officer in charge. I was immediately ushered into his office. He was a lieutenant. I was wearing Herb Sensenig's captain bars. I outranked him. Ball one for our side. An American captain speaking French was ball two. The orders with the name Eisenhower and the USFET stamp clinched it. An easy walk!

I came right to the point. The house at 14, Elizabeth Strasse in Wallerfangen was my family property. It was to be vacated at once and would be the home of my brother "Henri Dolibois" and his family. (For once, my French name made an impact). Furthermore, my brother was in the construction business. He would certainly be needed in a community which required much repair. "How soon can my house be ready for his occupancy?"

The French lieutenant was on his toes. "Mon Capitaine, pas de problème. Please give me two hours. I'm sorry. We did not know." I could afford to be forgiving. "Thank you, mon Lieutenant. Do you smoke?" A carton of Chesterfields appeared from my attaché case. I could have had the whole town after that. We shook hands, saluted. The entire visit had taken five minutes.

The drive from Dillingen to Wallerfangen took fifteen minutes. When I passed through the Elizabethstrasse, a French motorcar stood in front of house number 14. Two noncoms were piling their gear into the car.

The house itself was in good condition. By evening, three soldiers had even cleaned it to perfection. On the front door was a yellow placard. The dwelling was "off limits" to Frenchmen—defense d'entrer.

This was Heinrich's home until his death in 1975. His wife Maria died during our embassy years in 1984 and their daughter Henny sold the house shortly thereafter. She lives with her husband and children in another village not far away.

My good turn had been done. I was back in Oberursel by midnight. I could report to Papa that all of his children, but one, Charles, had survived the war. All were safely settled in their homes in postwar Germany.

In Oberursel our work on the GSC continued in routine fashion. Some prisoners were gradually released. They were sent to other countries for interrogation or possible trials; some were moved to Nuremberg for further investigation and court appearances. Many were sent home, their usefulness to us ended.

"GOERING, HESS CRIME LISTING GETS WORLD OK." This was the headline of a story released in London to the world press. It read in part:

> Announcement last night of the list of 24 Nazi arch-Criminals destined for quick trial at Nuremberg created immense satisfaction throughout the United Nations, reports today indicated. The names of the 24 military, political and ideological leaders of the Nazi regime, all but one of whom are in Allied hands, were released by the prosecution committee of the international tribunal representing the U.S., Great Britain, Russia, and France.
>
> The list is headed by Hermann Goering. Rudolf Hess, Hitler's ex-deputy, who has been in a British prison since 1941, is number two man on the list. . . .

Martin Bormann, deputy to Hitler in the closing months of the war, was the only one on the list not in an Allied prison. At the time he was supposedly still at large. Gustav Krupp von Bohlen und Halbach, the big munitions czar, was not in the Nuremberg prison either. His health was so poor that he was kept under surveillance elsewhere. He never appeared for the trials.

"There are no small fry on this first list," commented the official Soviet newspaper *Pravda*. "These criminals were not mere officials of a cannibal fascist regime. They were the masters themselves, the commanders and inspirers who directed Hitler's hordes and instructed the butchers."

On October 11, I received orders for "detached service for a period of sixty (60) days to Nuremberg, Germany." After the sixty days detached service I could handle the Nuremberg connection by commuting, as necessary. I told Mal Hilty to save the upstairs in our little house for me. "I'm coming back."

I took the long way to Nuremberg. Word had reached me that Col. William W. Dawson, the national president of Beta Theta Pi fraternity, was the military governor of Baden-Wuertemberg with headquarters in Stuttgart. I decided to call on him to see if he still remembered me.

It was mid-afternoon when I parked my jeep in front of an imposing edifice that housed the offices of the American Military Government. I walked into a vast waiting room filled with people. They were all Germans, filing claims, seeking housing, trying to locate families, and making hundreds of other demands on the persons representing the occupation powers in their state. I figured I'd have a long wait if I expected to see the busy colonel.

This was confirmed by the harried receptionist in the outer office. So I just gave her my name and asked her to tell Colonel Dawson I said hello. With that I sauntered back to my jeep. Just as I started to drive off, I heard my name called. It was Bill Dawson himself, running down the steps toward me. His big smile and warm greeting were like manna from heaven. Of course he remembered me. I was a breath of fresh air for him too.

"You're staying overnight," he insisted. "We'll have a nice dinner together. We have a lot to catch up on." It was settled. All of his appointments were cancelled for the rest of the day. I followed his car, weaving in and out of the mostly military traffic of Stuttgart. Soon we were climbing a steep hill and approaching a splendid villa, the residence of the military governor.

A breathtaking view of the city below, a drink, great conversation, and an outstanding dinner made for a highlight evening. A good night's rest, and I was on my way to Nuremberg early the next morning.

Colonel Dawson died just a few months after this signal visit. I didn't see Stuttgart again until 1982, thirty-seven years later. The headquarters of the U.S. European Command is located in that city now. I was invited by General William Y. Smith to a briefing and a tour of his command. It was a VIP visit; the general's twin-engine jet flew Winnie and me from Luxembourg to Stuttgart. His official car met us at the U.S. Air Force Base and drove us to his headquarters. Winnie spent the day sightseeing and shopping with Mrs. Smith. I was shown charts, slides, graphs, and movies. I got an informative look at the operations and facilities of the U.S. European Command. At the end of the busy, heady day of meetings and briefings, I was taken to General Smith's home. Winnie was already there.

We dressed formally for a splendid dinner with other generals, two

U.S. admirals, and several prominent Stuttgart city officials and citizens. When all the guests had left, and we were bedding down for the night in our comfortable guest room, I had a strange sensation of déjà vu. I had been here before.

I was sure of it the next morning, when Winnie and I joined the Smiths for a delightful breakfast on a pleasant closed-in porch. We admired the scene below us in daylight. This was the house in which I had spent the night as Colonel Dawson's guest in 1945. When I mentioned it to General Smith, he led me to the entrance way and pointed to a bronze plaque I hadn't noticed the night before. On it were inscribed the names of all the American occupants of this villa: military governors, civilian administrators, commanding generals. At the top of the list was the name of the first occupant, Col. W. W. Dawson.

At the time of my trip in October 1945, the road to Nuremberg was lined with trees in autumn glory. The drive took me through vineyards and along orchards. Apple and pear trees were loaded with fruit. The countryside was peaceful and inspiring. But as I approached the city of Furth, touching on Nuremberg, the scenery changed drastically. Ruins on top of ruins. The smell of rot and misery was in the air.

I decided to make the best of this temporary assignment. In addition to working with Warlimont and Kesselring on the unfinished GSC project, I looked forward to interpreting for the prison psychiatrist, Major Kelley. Furthermore, Colonel Philp had given me a special, personal assignment. He wanted to put together a scrapbook of autographs and photos of the high-ranking Nazis. It was to be a distinctive gift for General Eisenhower. My reputation as an autograph collector had caught up with me. However, this particular assignment would be more difficult than I thought. Picture taking at Nuremberg was forbidden and by now some of the top Nazis might be less inclined to give out autographs. How would I manage to do this favor for my CO?

I was on detached service with the Internal Security Detachment. Comfortable billets were now available, much better than those of my first visit. When I checked into quarters, most of the officers were sitting in the clubroom drinking brandy. You guessed it, the Fundador Spanish kind. Colonel Andrus explained my assignment.

I was one of five Americans with ready, daily access to all prisoners. There were two chaplains, Catholic and Protestant, Father Sixtus O'Connor and Reverend Henry Gerecke. Dr. Juchli, a lieutenant colonel, was charged with the prisoners' physical well-being. Dr. Douglas M. Kelley looked after their mental welfare. I would be responsible for their morale. "Keep 'em in a good mood. Cheer them up." But at the same time I would be alert for intelligence and information and act as interpreter for Dr. Kelley, testing I.Q.s and personalities. The GSC project would be squeezed in between these other duties.

Colonel Andrus expected a full-time replacement for me "soon." And when this new officer arrived, I would be released from the Internal Security Detachment and could concentrate on my German General Staff Corps enterprise. Fair enough!

Early next morning, Major Kelley and I breakfasted together and then made the rounds. Streicher's cell was the first stop. He seemed pleased to see me again. I detected no change in his attitude. His conversation was as anti-Semitic as ever, his arrogance no less. He did plead with me to visit his wife, Adele, at nearby Pleikershof, his farm.

Ley rubbed his hands together in glee when he saw me again. He was almost finished with his important writing. He assured me it would make me very happy, and it would even "help" my career because I would be the overseer of his grand scheme. I wondered what he was up to.

Goering grabbed my arm, actually pinched it hard. "My dear, dear Gillen!" He was pleased to see Kelley and me together. The major had visited his wife, and now he hoped I would do the same. Goering was particularly proud of having completely overcome his drug habit.

I took note of his appearance. The shabby Luftwaffe uniform, minus all decorations, hung in folds about his now diminished form. His face had color. His blue eyes were alert. His voice was steady and strong. One could almost say that his imprisonment had been good for his health.

Goering said he had concluded that he still had a duty to perform. He was ready for the trial, ready to defend Germany and tell the "gentlemen on the winning side certain truths." I listened without comment. When Goering was in one of his expansive moods there was no use arguing or commenting. He had some rough months ahead of him; plenty of argument too.

He spoke of Hess. He wanted to know if I had met the Fuehrer's former deputy. He seemed perturbed about his mental state (amnesia) and offered Dr. Kelley his assistance in helping Hess remember. "Of course," he pointed out, "we knew all along that Hess wasn't really normal. His flight to England made that very obvious." It disturbed Goering that Hess did not know him and remembered absolutely nothing of "the glories of the Third Reich." I think he figured that Hess's loss of memory might also have some effect on his own defense. Would he have to fight the battle alone?

In the afternoon I volunteered to take over the OD (officer of the day) duty for a friend, Capt. Calvin Curtis. This gave me a chance to move freely around the witness wing and to check on some of the inmates who had been with us in Luxembourg.

Warlimont almost cried when I walked into his cell. He really hadn't expected to see me again. His situation had deteriorated, especially the living conditions. So he was tremendously cheered to learn that my primary purpose for being in Nuremberg was to continue the GSC project we had begun in Oberursel. I gave him the photos I had taken on our visit to his family. He choked up then, and no longer tried to control his emotions.

I talked with Franz Seldte, the minister whose wife I had visited in Tegernsee. He couldn't thank me enough for the news I brought him. He was delighted when I mentioned the gift of the Lederhosen from his wife. He insisted on making a sketch of the suspenders I "must find" for the leather shorts. They had to be authentic.

Prior to the visit, I had not talked much with Seldte. His attitude impressed me. He was confident that he would not be tried for any crimes. He was a civil servant, really nonpolitical. He was prepared to help in every way as a witness. Seldte said he was almost glad to have this prison "experience." It would make a better man of him. He had no complaints, no protests. As far as I know, Seldte was never brought to trial.

I was shocked to see the old Nazi party treasurer, Franz X. Schwarz again. He had been rearrested and brought to Nuremberg as a witness. The old man was sitting in a social room with Kesselring and General Boetticher, the prewar military attaché at the German embassy in Washington. The witness wing of the prison allowed more freedom for the internees than the war criminals wing. Cell doors were left open. The prisoners could circulate and visit each other.

Schwarz praised the Catholic chaplain effusively. In my subsequent talks with Father O'Connor I found him to be a sympathetic, understanding person. He was conscientious. He worried about those prisoners who wanted to become Catholics. How genuine was their wish? He was most interested in Streicher, regarding that one as a real challenge. I assured him Streicher was one soul he would not win over.

Sex reared its head on my watch that afternoon. A guard brought me a note which had been intercepted. PW General Karl Wolff had written to a woman prisoner named Guyon-Witschel. Wolff was one of Himmler's top adjutants in the SS. He was involved in some scheme for the surrender of German troops in Italy, behind Hitler's back. There was a lot of such activity toward the end of the war. I guess you would call it a part of the P.Y.A. operations of every government in crisis—protect your ass.

Guyon-Witschel was a notorious woman spy. She was held on the special women's floor of the prison. One of the guards had been bribed to take the note from Wolff to her. It read, "Don't worry, the Americans will never release a pretty woman to the Russians." I was curious. I climbed the steps to the upper floor. The doors to the women's cells were kept locked. Apparently this had something to do with the rumor that one of the women prisoners had become pregnant by one of our own guards.

I wanted to talk to Madame Guyon-Witschel about the exchange of notes. It apparently had been going on for some time. As I unlocked her cell door and entered, I came upon a very handsome woman in her early thirties. She wore a long robe and high-heeled shoes. She literally towered over me when she stood up. I asked her to sit down. I get nervous when I talk to such tall women.

I showed her the note which had been intercepted. She glanced at it and smiled. It wasn't a coded message, no hidden meanings. Just reassurance. I asked how this exchange of notes was possible. She shrugged. "The guards like me," she said. She reached for a cigarette from a small pile of them on a tin plate. They were American, not PW ration. I asked where she got them. She answered my question with a short tug at the belt of her robe. The robe fell open. The gorgeous wench was stark naked under her mantle. She grinned wickedly at my being taken off guard. I'm not sure I displayed much savoir faire. To act indignant would make me look even sillier. So I just nodded knowingly and said, "Let me see if I have this figured out right, Fräulein; whenever you want to add to your supply of smokes you expose yourself to one of the guards on duty, and he tosses in a cigarette in appreciation?"

That was it. She had lots of friends on guard duty. They liked being kind to her. They would even carry notes from one cell to another.

I had nothing more to say to the blasé damsel. When I came out of her cell, the guard, standing just a few feet away, snapped to rigid attention, more so than necessary. His ears were red as beets. I stepped up to him and stared hard in his face—trying to keep from laughing. "If you don't tell, I won't either," I said, and walked away. His reply came an instant later: "YES SIR!!" It sounded relief all over. I waited two days and then wrote a suggestion in the day book. We needed some Women's Army Corps personnel for the women prisoners.

Weeks later I mentioned the incident informally to Colonel Andrus. By then it was too late to track down the guards on duty during my discovery. Meanwhile action had already been taken in regard to handling the women's floor of the prison. Captain Grace Auer headed a small team of WACs, and an army nurse, Lieutenant Mears, arrived. My comment to the sentry outside Guyon-Witschel's cell had gotten around. The men on guard duty were extra courteous to me whenever I came through the prison corridors.

The funniest part of that episode took place some time later. We were at a small gathering of officers, a sort of "thank-God-it's-Friday" affair. Colonel Andrus recounted the story of the notorious woman spy who put on a peep show for the GI guards. He screwed up the story. He identified the seductress as Margaret Blanke, not Guyon-Witschel. Poor Margaret Blanke, another female prisoner, was a mousy old lady who had been von Ribbentrop's secretary. I didn't correct the boss' story. He was too proud of his ability as raconteur.

I often went to work with Colonel Andrus, arriving at 0830 sharp every morning. On the trip from our billets to the prison and the courthouse I listened to his corny jokes over and over. "Hell, I was fourteen years old before I learned that God's last name wasn't Damn," was one of his favorites. It was repeated every time we had a new passenger in his car.

I visited Emmy Sonneman Goering and little daughter Edda at Burg Veldenstein in Neuhaus. The old woman who answered the door took one look at my uniform and announced that "the Gnaedige Frau is not receiving visitors." So I gave her the photo of Goering with his wife and Edda, and showed her the message he had written on the back. She took the picture and disappeared without a word, closing the door firmly in my face. In a few minutes she was back. Frau Goering would see me.

Mrs. Goering was a handsome woman. She looked every bit the wife of the Reichsmarschall of the Third Reich. She received me graciously, told me of the visit from Major Kelley and thanked me for my courtesy. I was able to tell her that her husband was in good health. I relayed his greeting, and expressed the hope that the strict rule forbidding visitors would eventually be relaxed so that she would be able to see him in prison.

Little Edda was a beautiful child, the image of her father. Bright and perky, polite and well trained. I gave her some chewing gum and chocolate. When she voluntarily kissed me on the cheek saying goodbye, I nearly broke up. I remembered that a child's embrace has to be earned.

I came for a second visit a month later. Mrs. Goering had been arrested, charged with conspiracy in the confiscation of art works. Edda was in a children's home in nearby Postheim. I went to see her, this time with a letter from her father which her mother was supposed to read to her. Under the circumstances I ended up with the child on my lap, reading her the heart-rending letter from her "Pappy." Her questions left me limp. How could I explain to this five-year-old why her father was in prison? When would he come home? And where was her mother?

Streicher's farm wasn't far from the prison in Nuremberg. I told him I would go visit his wife Adele. He wrote a letter in which he admonished her to "visit the sick" and "help the poor." He also gave me a pipe she should keep as a souvenir. It was given to him by a Jewish American officer sometime during his captivity. It had a special meaning for him; and he had nothing else to offer her. He explained to me why he was urging his wife to help the poor. He said he was always concerned about the downtrodden and the helpless. Then he must have noticed the doubtful look on my face. So he told another of his stories.

Each year at Christmas time, he used his influence to release twenty to forty political prisoners—Communists and Social Democrats of Nuremberg—from Dachau concentration camp. But "no Jews were released by me," he added. As Gauleiter, he planned an elaborate Christmas party for those whom he had arranged to be freed, and for their families. The prisoners didn't know they would see their families until Streicher personally threw open the doors and allowed them to enter and greet their loved ones. Surprise!

Later he helped these returnees from Dachau in getting good jobs. He admitted that in doing so he won many followers for the party, and that he arranged their release for this reason. But his action also proved that he cared for those who suffered, except Jews. So much for compassion.

Streicher, the man who incited to murder and annihilation, wrote in February, 1944: "If the danger of the reproduction of the curse of God in the Jewish blood is finally to come to an end, then there is only one way—the extermination of that people whose father is the devil."

In his prison cell in Nuremberg in October 1945, that same man suddenly put his hand on my arm and held it there for a long moment. Then he said to me: "Please, Herr Oberleutnant, when you see Adele, tell her to put her hand on the same place. In that way we can be close to each other for an instant."

I spent a couple of hours one day in the prison library looking through banned books. I took several for souvenirs and gave a copy of *Mythus des 20. Jahrhunderts* to Major Kelley. Shortly thereafter, we conducted the Rorschach Psychodiagnostic test on the Nazi philosopher Alfred Rosenberg, author of the *Mythus*.

The Rorschach is a projective test of personality. The subject is asked to interpret ten standard abstract designs—"ink blots." His interpretation is then analyzed as a measure of emotional and intellectual functioning and integration. Dr. Kelley showed Rosenberg the design and asked what it represented to him, "What do you see here?" I was the translator. The doctor timed the response, observed facial expressions, bodily movements, and analyzed the answer or answers. A lot can be discovered by use of this method.

Rosenberg made a bad showing. He was dull, frightfully confused. Obviously he was unaware of his intellectual limitations. This contributed to his befuddlement. He was rated low-average intelligence.

Rosenberg had enjoyed some influence on the Nazi party only because of his close contact with Hitler, not because of great intellect. He was born in Estonia of a German father and a Latvian mother. His father was an executive in a German trading company. Young Rosenberg received a diploma in architecture in Moscow in 1918. He witnessed the Bolshevik revolution and ended up hating everything Russian and Bolshevistic. His violent anti-Semitism sprang from his dual hatred. Rosenberg's contributions to *Mein Kampf* helped to strengthen Hitler's attitude and that of other Nazis. Rosenberg became a propagandist. He tried to become a diplomat in a brief stint as ambassador to Great Britain. But he failed. Finally, Hitler made him "Deputy to the Fuehrer for the Spiritual and Ideological Training and Education of the National Socialist Party." This title gave Rosenberg the authority to implant his anti-Semitic, anti-Communist beliefs. He was editor of the newspaper *Voelkischer Beobachter* and other publications. Folk studies, the labor movement, education, Strength-through-Joy (Kraft durch Freude), and ideology occupied his time.

Kelley and I spent several hours with him, engaging in stupid discussion on "race problems." We wanted some clarification of his views. He never completed a sentence. He jumped from one confusing thought to another.

I had his book *Mythus des 20. Jahrhunderts* with me. I asked him to autograph it for me. He took it out of my hand, held it behind his back, and said he didn't want me to have anything to do with his book.

Startled, I asked why. He explained. "You are working for your country, you are a good soldier and a Christian, and I don't wish to change your way of life. If you were to ever read this book, you would renounce the church and your Christian beliefs immediately."

That's what I call a firm belief in the power of your writings. I promised not to read his book; I just wanted it for a souvenir. So he acquiesced and signed his name on the flyleaf. And I kept my promise.

I recalled that one of the Nazis in Mondorf had told me that no one in the party had ever read Rosenberg's famous book even if every Nazi leader, regardless of rank, had a copy. They had to buy it. "Rosenberg should go down in history as the man who sold more copies of a book no one ever read than any other writer."

In my daily rounds I ran across some weird characters. A Dr. Pfann-mueller from Munich demanded to be executed at once. On his prison wall was a picture of Hitler, under which he had scribbled "Der Moer-derer." Some of my colleagues decided that was his way of trying to get in good with the Americans. The truth is he wouldn't have been allowed a picture of Hitler in his cell. With the inscription "murderer" under it, the violation of the rule was ignored. Pfannmueller had really out-smarted someone.

A character named Ka jun-Chan, a Moslem, demanded a German-speaking Mohammedan priest. I couldn't help him.

In another cell sat a man named Roepert. As I recall he had been Himmler's chauffeur. He complained about the noise level in the prison which prevented him from enjoying his radio. I was puzzled. Radios were not allowed. When I checked his cell, he was sitting on his cot with his ear against the wall, selecting his stations on an imaginary dial. I promised to do something about the noise—and stayed away from his cell.

What were all these people doing here? I wondered. There were in-mates such as Freyend, Salman, Wagener, and Luebbe who had been military aides and secretaries, truly insignificant figures. Nobody inter-rogated them in Mondorf and they were equally neglected in Nurem-berg. It appeared they were arrested because they happened to be with one of the major Nazis when arrests were made. We were feeding and lodging minor political figures, Nazi party functionaries, and junior of-ficers. I suppose in the long run they considered themselves better off in prison than to be hungry and homeless on the outside. Their country-men probably envied them.

Among the prisoners was SS Colonel Otto Skorzeny, the "superman" who had rescued Mussolini in September 1943 when the Italian dictator was held prisoner in a castello on top of Gran Sasso in the Appenine Mountains. Skorzeny engineered the dramatic rescue using gliders to reach the Mussolini prison and a small private plane to take him away. The colonel, a superspy, was leader of an SS commando unit. His acts of sabotage were legendary. He was suspected of an attempt to kidnap Ei-senhower. He was behind the deception and disguises used by Waffen SS during the Battle of the Bulge.

When I walked into his cell, he was doing one-arm pushups, reaching number forty-seven when I interrupted him. When I commented on his ability to perform this difficult feat, he showed me one better. He did a handstand on the seat of his chair, raising and lowering his body in a balanced vertical position.

A Viennese, Skorzeny stood six-foot-four, an imposing figure. He had at least a dozen scars on his face, honor marks of duels he fought as a student. I wonder why no one has made a movie of his derring-do?

Major Kelley decided to give Rudolf Hess the Rorschach test, which provided the first opportunity for me to come face to face with Hitler's former deputy. Hess had been brought from England on October 10, 1945. He had been held by the British since his spectacular flight on May 10, 1941.

When Kelley and I came into his cell, Hess jumped off his cot, clicked his heels, and drew to attention, stiff as a poker. Dressed in a well-worn Luftwaffe uniform without insignia, and soft leather flight boots, he still looked more military than any of the Nazis I had met to date. While his demeanor was strictly formal, polite, he still spooked me. The deep-set eyes, the bushy eyebrows, the faraway look on his face set him apart as someone not quite normal. I recalled from "Triumph des Willens" his fanatic, almost mystical appearance as he presented Hitler to the adoring multitudes. He stepped up to the Swastika-embellished podium. "Der Fuehrer spricht!" he shouted in introducing the object of his worship.

Like Rosenberg, Hess was born in a foreign country, in Alexandria, Egypt. He never saw Germany until he went there to study at age fifteen. As a student he came under the influence of the famous professor of geopolitical science, Albrecht Haushofer, who served as a father figure to Hess and influenced much of his political outlook.

At Haushofer's urging, Hess joined the Nazi party in Munich. He became one of its principal brawlers. He was injured in a number of street fights and received a serious gunshot wound in the leg during the "putsch" in November 1923. Although he fought in the same regiment as Hitler during World War I, the two never met until they became active in Munich. Hess was sentenced to prison in Landsberg, and there served as Hitler's secretary and coordinator in the writing of *Mein Kampf*. By then he was totally wrapped up in everything Hitler believed and said. Hitler was his God. Hess became the deputy Fuehrer of the Third Reich. He was Hitler's staunchest supporter.

Hess and Goering were always in competition, especially in matters pertaining to the air force. Hess had finished his pilot training shortly before World War I ended. He fancied himself an authority, but always came in second to Goering. In fact he was always second in everything. He loved parades, spectacles, ceremonies. His juvenile personality needed someone to dominate him, and Hitler was it. Hess was completely satisfied, preferring his party activities even to his wife and children, whom he largely ignored.

In dealing with others, Hess always managed to withdraw into himself in case of dispute. He swallowed his anger, buried every annoyance. Yet he harbored intense suspicion of almost everyone except his beloved Fuehrer.

Now in his prison cell, he sat down on his bed between Dr. Kelley and me. He spoke perfect English, but the psychiatrist decided I should sit through the test just in case an interpreter was needed. Hess was quite cooperative. Kelley had explained the procedure, and his subject was curious. He took his time studying each card and telling us what he thought it was. He could give as many responses as he wished, but the doctor was interested primarily in how he behaved during the test, not so much in what he saw.

After the test, Kelley explained to me that Hess revealed an introverted personality, shy and withdrawn. He had a strongly suspicious nature. The latter emphasized a paranoid element. The doctor officially diagnosed Hess as "suffering from a true psychoneurosis, engrafted on a basic paranoid and schizoid personality, with an amnesia, partly genuine and partly faked."

I had already diagnosed Rudolf as a flaky jerk. I had read about his hypochondria. I knew that he had turned to astrologers, nature healers, and quacks, when none of the many physicians he consulted through his lifetime could cure his imaginary illnesses.

Our intelligence reports told us that in prison in England Hess had feigned loss of memory most effectively. "I don't remember" was his stock answer to intensive questioning over four and one-half years. Eventually, he had talked himself into a genuine amnesia. When he arrived in Nuremberg, he was deep into it again. He remembered nothing about his past, his associations, his actions. I thought he was putting on one helluva good act.

Two months later, in court, he suddenly announced: "My memory is again in order. I simulated loss of memory for tactical reasons."

In subsequent conversations with me, Dr. Kelley said this confirmed his original opinions. Hess's action was typically hysterical. The refusal to admit that anything had been wrong with their minds is common with people who have been insane.

But during those October days in 1945, all attention was focused on Hess's condition. Kelley had proposed hypnosis, but Justice Jackson refused permission. He held that if Hess should have a fall, or something else went wrong while he was in an hypnotic state, we'd have all kinds of trouble.

Next, Kelley proposed to Hess that he could give him "shots" which would bring back his memory. Hess pretended to be pleased. Two days later because Kelley wanted to test his emotions, we told Hess that Justice Jackson wasn't in favor of such shots. Hess hit the roof. "Who's the defendant, he or I? It's unfair!"

Meanwhile, Goering had offered his help, but to no avail. Goering was upset because he wanted all Nazis to be supermen, without weaknesses. On the other hand, he had never considered Hess particularly strong. He told me that Hess's amnesia was due to excessive masturbation. "Hess always was an odd one," he said, "he couldn't satisfy his wife either." This was "in strictest confidence." Goering's conversation reminded me of Streicher's gossip about Goering, for which the Jew-baiter was kicked out of the party.

In making my rounds to "boost morale," I restricted my visits in each cell to just a few minutes. Whenever I came to Hess he greeted me formally, always submissive, correct. When I asked him how he felt, he would recite all his ills, starting with severe stomach cramps which plagued him constantly. He was always moody, depressed, not really interested in making conversation. In all the time I talked to him, he never remembered anything.

I wanted to know more about his flight to England. What I had heard from other Nazis was too sketchy. Even today, I wonder about the complete, true story. Was Hitler really unaware of Hess's mission? Had Hess "flipped his lid" in taking off for the British Isles? How did he get past the radar, the strict surveillance?

On May 10, 1941, Hess responded to what one of his astrologers had read in the stars. He, Hess, "was ordained to bring about peace." Six weeks before Hitler's invasion of Russia in violation of the Moscow Pact, Hess flew to Scotland. He parachuted from a height of twenty thousand feet and landed on the estate of the Duke of Hamilton, who was reputed to be sympathetic to Germany. One heard of the Clivedon set, Sir Oswald Mosely, sympathizers and appeasers in Great Britain. If these influential people could persuade the British government to let Hitler defeat Russia, what course history then?

When Hess touched down in an open field, a farmer with a pitch fork thought the invasion had begun. Instead of being taken to the duke of Hamilton, Hess ended up in the local constabulary.

In 1984, Winnie and I were the guests of Major General John H. Mitchell, commandant of the Berlin Brigade. Among our various special activities was a helicopter flight over Berlin. I saw the Spandau prison on the edge of the Berlin Wall. From an oblique angle I spotted a single, lone figure walking slowly along a path in the prison garden. This was Rudolf Hess, no longer the military icon I remembered. Stooped, he shuffled along slowly.

At age ninety-one, he was still tending his little garden; he answered no questions. He refused to see his family, received no visitors. A contingent of Russian, French, British, and Americans guarded him on a rotating basis.

On Monday, August 17, 1987, radio and television stations across the United States broadcast in their evening news the terse story that Rudolf Hess, ninety-three, the former deputy of Adolf Hitler, and the last remaining major leader of the Third Reich, had died. No cause of death was given. The three Western powers announced on the next morning that Hess's death had been a suicide.

In retrospect, I regard Rudolf Hess a tragic figure. Alone at Spandau, he served as a grim reminder of Nazism and Nuremberg. His carefully prepared role of eccentric had served no useful purpose. After a full medical examination back in 1945, the Tribunal had ruled that "there is no suggestion that Hess was not completely sane when the acts charged against him were committed." He was found guilty of conspiracy and crimes against the peace; and not guilty of war crimes and crimes against humanity. The Russian judges filed a dissenting opinion in which they insisted that Hess was indeed guilty of crimes against humanity and should be given the death penalty.

I remember that in the fall of 1945, I took part in several confusing bull sessions on the trials and the defendants. In an effort to shed some light on the subject, Justice Robert Jackson conducted a seminar at the Grand Hotel for American officers. It was a nippy evening in late October. A cold wind, warning of winter, whistled through the cracks in the plywood boards that covered holes not yet repaired. Jackson was explaining the objectives of the International War Crimes Tribunal. He outlined the organization and the process to be followed. I jotted down some of his comments:

"These trials are an extension of U.S. Foreign Policy; they are a laboratory to test our ability to get along with allied nations."

"Aggressive warfare is wrong in spite of just or unjust grievances."

"We've purchased our rights to ex-post facto laws with the lives of thousands of young Americans. Society progresses at the expense of individuals."

"The reputation of American justice is in our keeping."

I decided historians would have their fun with these quotes and others in the years to come. Some mighty big holes have been punched in Justice Jackson's theories since that October night in the Nazi city of Nuremberg.

My own spirits were in conflict. I was proud to be a part of such a vital undertaking. But I was also weary of prisons and prisoners and the misery all around me. I just wanted to go home to my family.

Nuremberg Journal

DR. ROBERT LEY was elated, bubbling with enthusiasm. His writing was finished. With great flourish he presented a stack of handwritten notes. This was the vital revelation which would alter the proceedings. Here was the "decisive information" he had promised.

Major Kelley and I had given him the Rorschach test a few days earlier. The psychiatrist had already drawn conclusions about the "imperfect functioning of Ley's brain." We thought it useful for him to analyze Ley's information as a part of the personality study. I had the material typed and translated and gave Colonel Amen the original. Copies were made for Kelley and others.

Not surprisingly, the document was of no value. It was just another speech to the German people. It read like Dr. Ley sounded—disorganized, random, farfetched. He encouraged friendship between America and Germany. "America is the conqueror; you the conquered; consequently America will lead and you will follow," he admonished the people of Germany.

Between Germany and America there stands something like an evil spirit—anti-Semitism. Until the Jewish problem is resolved in Germany, I see no chance to gain the trust of Americans. Only when we seriously tackle this problem can we take the next step of bringing the German people under American protection and make them a member of the American commonwealth.

This step must be taken *with* Hitler, not *against* Hitler. Only then, will we have the necessary authority, leadership, discipline. The National Socialist idea—purged of anti-Semitism—joined with a reasonable democracy—is the most valuable thing that Germany can contribute. Only National Socialism works continually against Bolshevism. . . .

Something similar to the Party must be reorganized. The men are still around, and they are the best representatives of German leadership. The most respected and active citizens are those men who worked as Gauleiter, Kreisleiter, and Ortsgruppenleiter. They should be used for this noble purpose, effecting a reconciliation with America; they could accomplish miracles.

Ley proposed himself in charge of this reconciliation, this reconstruction of Germany. We would solicit help of Jews from all over the world. Invite them to come to Germany, to be a part of this great plan.

The head of this action, the leadership, should remain under the present form and appearance in Nuremberg. The American staff in the front office of the Palace of Justice, the German working staff in the internment wing of the prison . . . solitary confinement, of course, should be abolished. I do not ask for any other favors. It is clear that the technical assistance of propaganda be placed at the disposal of me and my staff. This procedure would guarantee a strict secrecy and would offer the American authorities evidence that we are acting in an honorable and fair manner.

I should only like to call attention to one more thing in the utmost clarity. If America does not take over, then Asia will! Germany is leaderless; if it wants to live at all . . . it must attach itself somewhere, either to America or Asia. Asia is on the march; America must act, and Germany must place itself without hesitation and with utmost trust under America's protection.

He concluded: "I have done my duty in expressing this courageously— even if it costs me my life. May God see that things happen for the best."

There were many pages in the same vein. A mishmash of nothing. This was the "revelation" which prompted him to write to me in September and resulted in my being transferred to Nuremberg.

I tried to prepare him for the official reaction, if there would even be one, but he wouldn't listen. He lectured instead: "Through history it has always been obvious that the party which was right was successful. In every war, victory came to the right side. Since we, the Germans, led by National Socialism, lost the war, it is obvious we must have been wrong. And since anti-Semitism was a vital part of our program, I know that anti-Semitism was our big mistake."

Colonel Amen advised that Ley be told outright that his plan was refused. Dr. Kelley, Pastor Gerecke, and I went to his cell to tell him. He took it very hard. He became violently disturbed. He stood against the wall with arms outstretched and begged to be shot. "You are the victors. I have nothing to live for. You will try me like a common criminal," he stammered, and then began to sob uncontrollably. It was decided to put a twenty-four-hour guard at Ley's door. He would be observed around the clock.

At about that same time a rumor spread that a group of young German airmen were going to storm the prison and rescue Goering. Colonel Andrus ordered security tightened. Goering was confined to his cell; no daily walks in the prison yard for him. The Reichsmarschall was furious. Andrus was picking on him, he complained. And while he was at it, he thought he should mention that the guards outside his cell were purposely noisy, singing, whistling, and talking loudly, obviously on Colonel Andrus's orders, "just to annoy me."

Dr. Leonardo Conti, a former minister of Health and one of Hitler's doctors, committed suicide. He hanged himself on the cell window bars, using the sleeve of his shirt. Chairs were now removed from each cell at night. Inspections, the search for poison capsules and other instruments of death, were now stepped up, from once a week to daily.

The grapevine was functioning beautifully. The air was thick with tension in the war criminals wing as rumors spread about the starting date of the trials. Complaints increased ten-fold. Prisoners summoned the chaplains, the doctors, or me on the slightest pretext. Invariably they asked: "Is it true the trial will begin soon?"

I wondered how they communicated with each other in solitary confinement. What was the signal system they used? It was a mystery.

In my morale-boosting rounds each day, I tried to see as many prisoners as possible, spending a few minutes with each. I was learning more and more about them, but one could hardly judge my visits of intelligence value. Seyss-Inquart complained of bleeding gums and wanted chewing gum to relieve the problem. Kaltenbrunner, the coldhearted, worried incessantly about his wife. Funk, the former president of the Reichsbank, looked as if he might collapse any moment. His health was very bad.

I looked in on Hjalmar Schacht, the brilliant finance and economics expert. His English was flawless. He was quite confident he had nothing to worry about. He assured me he was not involved in the planning of the specific wars of aggression. His participation in the occupation of Austria and the Sudetenland was of such a limited basis, he claimed, that it didn't amount to criminal activity. He had definitely not been one of Hitler's inner circle, the members of which regarded Schacht with undisguised hostility. Finally, his arrest had been ordered by Hitler in July 1944. "The Fuehrer's gang suspected me of complicity in the bomb plot," he said. Schacht was tried as one of the twenty-two major Nazi war criminals and was acquitted along with von Papen and Fritsche, the assistant minister of propaganda.

One day in October wives were permitted to come to prison. They could bring letters and even some clothing and toilet articles. They couldn't see their husbands, however. This meant one of the chaplains or I would act as go-between. Thus I met Mrs. Jodl, a sharp, intelligent woman. She brought flowers. I remember being surprised that her sourpuss Prussian might enjoy flowers. You never know.

Mrs. Jodl asked if she might be allowed to serve as witness for the general. She could prove that her husband, along with others in the military and civilian leadership, was quite willing to throw Hitler out—after the war. (Don't change horses in midstream.) She made some cogent points in distinguishing between the political and the military. It was the old argument: "A soldier simply obeys orders." I promised to relay her offer and her views to Justice Jackson's staff.

Mrs. Adele Streicher brought a letter and a package for her husband. She called him "mein Schlumps." I looked for the meaning of that pet name in the dictionary. I learned it was a synonym for "Schlamp"—a sloppy fellow, a slouch, a slovenly, unkempt slob. Streicher must have earned that sobriquet for his mind, not his body. He meticulously cared for the latter. Every morning in his cell he stripped to the waist and splashed cold water on his chest and back. He scrubbed himself to the pink. He spent a half hour doing calisthenics and flexing his muscles.

His wife brought him a clean shirt, a pipe and tobacco, and some apples. He was allowed only the shirt. In turn I gave her a letter from Streicher in which he expressed deep feelings and sentiment, especially for his two sons from a previous marriage, Lothar and Elmar. It was strange. In person he never showed much emotion about anything unless it was anti-Semitism. In his letters he was close to maudlin. One paragraph of his letter took the censor to the Bible to "decode" what might have been a secret message. It read: "The first 8 days? Read John, ch. 18, verses 19 and 20; and Matthew, ch. 27, verses 1, 2, 27, 28, 29 and 30. *The* day—20 November. I am proud."

With the Biblical reference Streicher was reminding his wife of their first eight days in captivity. The last sentence refers to the date on which the trial would begin. The indictments had been served on October 20, the day before he wrote his letter.

Mrs. Streicher told me the whole story of their mistreatment in Augsburg. I pretended not to have heard it before. She also complained of not being treated like the other prisoners' wives. She was paid no allotment and had nothing to live on. I'm afraid I couldn't be sympathetic. Thanks to her husband and his coworkers there were millions who had nothing to live on.

I also talked to Mrs. von Ribbentrop. According to my logbook, she impressed me as "a homely old bag." I can't remember anything else about her visit.

Back in Mondorf in the CCPWE, I had had no opportunity to talk to von Papen. He was kept in the annex behind the Palace Hotel. Now, in Nuremberg prison, I visited with him frequently and found him another interesting subject. He told me his version of how Hitler came to power and what life in Germany was like during those early Hitler years. I came to the conclusion that von Papen played a minor role in all of it, even though he tried to build up his importance in our conversations. I made a brief entry in my log: "Von P. is less significant than people around here think."

Von Papen helped Hitler form a coalition cabinet in 1933. He aided Hitler's appointment to chancellor on January 30. As vice-chancellor, he participated in the Nazi consolidation of control. Well over a year after Hitler became chancellor, von Papen made a speech denouncing the Nazi suppression of the free press and the church. "I protested the existence of a reign of terror. I spoke out against the '150% Nazis' who were mistaking brutality for vitality," von Papen told me. A few days later he was placed under house arrest by the SS. His associates, including the man who had helped him prepare the above speech, were murdered. Von Papen himself was released after a few days.

Nevertheless, he "remained loyal to Germany." He accepted an appointment as minister to Austria, was involved in Nazi political demonstrations and supported Nazi propaganda activities. Hitler recalled him shortly before the occupation of Austria in 1938 and sent him to Turkey as ambassador. In 1944 Turkey broke off diplomatic relations with Germany and von Papen returned to the Reich in August of that year.

The Tribunal found von Papen not guilty of crimes against the peace and the common plan of conspiracy. He was discharged in October 1946. At first he had some difficulty in finding a home. He was not wanted in the British zone; he owned property in Bavaria, but it had been requisitioned by the U.S. Army. He also owned a villa in Wallerfangen in the Saar. It was badly damaged. Von Papen employed my brother Heinrich to restore the building. He lived with a friend in Nuremberg while the repairs were being made.

Heinrich worked on von Papen's villa for more than six months in 1947. Of course, the ex-war criminal didn't know that Heinrich Dolibois was the brother of Lieutenant Gillen of the Nuremberg prison. In fact, my brother himself didn't know of my involvement with the Nazis until years later. I've always wondered if von Papen would have hired my brother if he had known.

"I'm a sailor, not a politician," said Fritz Sauckel on the one occasion I went to his cell. Here was a genuine nonentity. In a room with more than three people he would go unnoticed. Even his wispy mustache was immature. Small in stature, limited in intelligence, Sauckel went to sea on a merchant ship after attending grammar school for only five years. A month after World War I began, his ship was captured and he remained a prisoner of war in France for five years.

Upon returning home he became a factory worker, joined the union, got involved in strikes and politics. He also sired thirteen children. Naturally he ended up as one more worshipper of Adolf Hitler who rewarded him for his puppy love by naming him Gauleiter of Thuringia.

Sauckel did what the party told him to do. He was employed to obtain labor for Germany. That's all. The fact that more than five million foreign nationals were forced into slave labor to help Germany's war effort didn't bother him. The fact that countless thousands died under subhuman conditions didn't concern him. He was only the supplier, not the executioner. Blame Himmler. Blame Goebbels. They even corrupted the Fuehrer.

Sauckel firmly believed Germany was defending Europe from "international Jews" and the corrupt allies. So it was perfectly all right to uproot millions of workers from other European countries to help Germany win the war.

I think that pipsqueak actually felt honored to be listed as a war criminal in company with the major Nazis. His morale didn't need boosting by me. I never went to his cell again after the first visit.

Another person who had not been with us in Luxembourg was Baldur von Schirach, the Hitler Youth leader and Gauleiter of Vienna. I met him for the first time when I took a box of photos and books to him. It had been brought to the prison by his wife. He proudly showed me the pictures of his four children, beautiful kids. He boasted that his mother was American. He was thoroughly familiar with the Boy Scout movement in the United States, and explained at length that Germany would never have gone to war if the German youth had been similarly organized. "So why did you have the Hitler Jugend instead?" I asked.

"Ah that's a long story. You have to understand that I was very foolish. I believed everything I heard and saw about Hitler. I followed him blindly. Actually, there were two Hitlers. One—prior to 1934—human; the other—after 1934—superhuman."

Von Schirach, at age seventeen, admired Hitler. He genuinely disliked him toward the end. He claimed that he, von Schirach, was in danger himself. "We all are to blame," he said.

He told me of Hitler playing with his dog, "exactly thirty minutes, not one second longer." Hitler would go into a trance, "lasting exactly ten minutes. He was quite strange, almost frightening." But when he first met Hitler he was profoundly inspired by him. He could only think of serving Hitler and, through Hitler, Germany. Von Schirach was an ardent anti-Semite, stimulated by early negative readings about Jews. Nazism became his religion.

He organized the German youth movement almost all by himself. His insatiable appetite for work made him the ideal youth leader. He visited all the camps, every town and village. He checked on his subordinates personally; gave only oral orders. He admitted to the seizure of property of all other organizations in Germany under the authority granted him by Hitler himself. He married Henriette Hoffman, the young daughter of Hitler's personal friend and photographer. He maintained that he was not a homosexual as was rumored throughout the years of his leadership. "In fact," he said, "I was a strong foe of sexual aberrations, urged my aides to marry and have children to 'avoid' arousing suspicion."

Von Schirach sincerely regretted his role in the Nazi movement. He said he was sorry that he led the young people of Germany down the path of Nazi party ideals. Dr. Kelley classified him a true romantic. To me von Schirach indicated that he was willing to pay the price for his mistakes. The Tribunal took him up on that. He was sentenced to twenty years in Spandau prison and served the full term.

Von Schirach and I talked about the Lipizzaner horses and the Spanish Riding School. He gave himself credit for saving the school by allowing, and arranging for, the evacuation of the stallions in March 1945. I pointed out to him that he waited until the last minute, when it was almost too late. While we were speaking of evacuation his consience must have bothered him. He suddenly blurted out that he had approved the evacuation of Vienna's Jews, "but only at Hitler's suggestion." However, he never participated in actual atrocities. On the contrary, he claimed he argued with Hitler against the deportation of Jews. Hitler had become furious and ordered him out of the house. After that, said von Schirach, he was ignored at party functions; he had actually expected to be arrested.

The October days were dwindling fast. My daily, ever shorter, visits to the Nazis in both the witness and the war criminals wings, were getting more strenuous, and meaningless. I spent an hour or two with Warlimont and Kesselring on the GSC project. They coordinated information gathering with other members of the General Staff Corps in the prison. I was assigned a room in the Palace of Justice for this work, and could summon prisoners from the witness wing there. Thus I got to know General Heinz Guderian, the famous Panzer general, whose armored exploits in the invasion of Poland, France, and later Russia, changed combat tactics so radically. Trench warfare was out. Rapid striking mobile movement was in. Guderian admired and understood Patton. He knew more about him than any of us Americans ever did.

I still had to carry out the assignment Colonel Philp had given me, to get the autographs and photos of the high-ranking Nazis. Gathering the signatures was easy. I worked out a foolproof method. It was more dignified, too. I prepared a simple, one-sentence statement in English and German.

"This is to certify that the following is my proper signature."

"Ich bestätige hiermit dass dieses meine richtige Unterschrift ist."

Then I asked each prisoner to sign two of these statements, "for the record, and to protect yourself" in case documents needed to be verified.

I got every autograph I wanted. Later I simply cut off the statement part, saving only the signature. The photos presented a problem. Then one evening I headed for the "Panther Pit" in the Grand Hotel. That was the bar where American and British officers could gather after duty hours. I sat next to an American navy officer. I introduced myself and accepted his offer of a drink. I asked him about the naval presence in Nuremberg. "No oceans within a hundred miles." He explained that his assignment was with Naval Intelligence. He was working on documents and materials related to activities of the German navy officers imprisoned at Nuremberg.

"By the way, an interesting thing happened this morning," he said. "It had nothing to do with my purpose here, but I was available, and got the duty."

As he told me his story, I could hardly believe my ears. Hitler's personal photographer, Heinrich Hoffman, had been brought into the Navy Intelligence office. He carried with him a suitcase full of photographs of "everybody under the sun." The good Lord was smiling on me that night. I bought the next drink and told my companion why I was extremely glad to run into him. "No sweat! Stop by my office tomorrow and pick out what you want. We'll make copies for whatever you need."

It took just ten minutes to select pictures of the major Nazis. By late afternoon of the next day I had two prints of each. One for me, and one for Colonel Philp's scrapbook. I was elated. So was Colonel Philp when I turned the signatures and photos over to him. I've been told that a scrapbook with photos and signatures of the twenty-two major Nazis tried at Nuremberg is on display in the Eisenhower Museum in Salina, Kansas. I've never seen it, and I don't need to. I have a duplicate among my own mementos.

On August 8, 1945, the governments of the United States and of the United Kingdom of Great Britain and Northern Ireland, the provisional government of the French Republic, and the government of the Union of Soviet Socialist Republics signed an agreement establishing a Tribunal for the trial of the war criminals.

A charter annexed to the agreement defined the constitution, the jurisdiction, and the functions of this Tribunal. It was given the power to try and to punish persons who had committed crimes against the peace, war crimes, and crimes against humanity as defined in this charter.

On October 20, 1945 an indictment was lodged against the defendants as major war criminals. A copy in German was served upon each. The trial would open exactly thirty days later. Counsel for the defense could be chosen by the defendants, or, at their request, would be appointed by the Tribunal.

I walked into Goering's cell the morning of October 21. He was ranting: "The Russians accuse us of doing what they have been doing all along."

He was afraid he wouldn't have time to find a lawyer and prepare his defense. "There's only one small sentence on me," he sneered, "and all the charges for each 'criminal' read the same."

Streicher stood, legs apart, hands on hips, in the middle of his cell, when I came to him. "This so-called indictment is 'reine Wurst'—pure baloney—they must have their victims. I am suspicious of such international justice. International Jewry is a better description."

Rosenberg blamed the Russians for it all. "Are you on the judges' side?" he asked me inconsequently. "I'll never get a fair trial. My witnesses will never be allowed out of the Ukraine. Sure there were errors made. I kept all complaints in my files. Now the prosecution will use them as evidence against me."

Rosenberg claimed that "confiscation of art and literature" mentioned in the indictment against him was a farce. "The victorious Allies are doing the same thing right now," he said.

I was in no mood to argue with any of them. They would all have their day in court, an opportunity to defend themselves, which was much more than they ever gave the people they had in their power.

Keitel judged the indictment "hair-raising," the charges unfair. How could twenty-two criminals be prosecuted as a council which planned the war? How would such a council be possible in a dictatorship? "No one knew what the other's duties were," he said. "The Fuehrer principle was that each one was to mind his own business."

He thanked me for my visit. Then he surprised me by offering his hand. He had never done more than snap to attention when I entered or left his cell at other times.

Doenitz took the indictment better than any of them. "How typical of American humor! They list three charges against me, and none of them will stick."

He was reading *Big Rock Candy Mountain*. It was his third book in English and he was proud of how much he could read and understand. "It's more enjoyable than preparing a defense." On second thought he wanted my reaction to his asking for a U.S. Naval lawyer to defend him. He was sure there would be many eager to handle his case. This was a legal matter I couldn't advise him on.

Three days after the indictments were distributed I met a newcomer in the officers' mess, Lt. Gustav Gilbert, my long-awaited replacement. Gilbert was a psychologist by profession and could hardly wait to get to work on the Nazis. The two of us joined Colonel Andrus and Lieutenant Colonel Owens at lunch and there and then mapped out a plan for my "succession." It was agreed I would stay on a few days longer to get Gilbert acquainted. He would be officially designated as the prison psychologist. The intelligence phase of our operation would end. We also agreed my departure would be wise since the interrogation reports and personality studies I had prepared in Mondorf, and in Nuremberg, might well show up as part of the prosecution evidence when the trial took its course. Therefore, my continued contact with the defendants would have a negative effect.

Later in the afternoon I made the rounds with Lieutenant Gilbert and introduced him to the prisoners as my replacement. Those in the war criminals wing were told I was returning to the United States. Prisoners in the witness wing, such as Warlimont and Kesselring, would see me only in an office in the Palace of Justice when I came from Oberursel occasionally to continue work on the GSC project.

On the next evening I served my last round as officer of the day. All was quiet as I settled down in the cell we used as an office for the OD. I planned to read a while before stretching out on the cot for some shut-eye. I heard only the regular pacing of the prison guards, and the sporadic coughs and snores of the inmates, sounds to which I had become accustomed but still found unnerving.

Suddenly a guard burst into my cubicle. "Sir, there is something wrong with prisoner Ley in cell 11," he cried out excitedly. The sergeant of the guard was right behind him. The three of us rushed into Ley's cell. The lifeless body of the onetime leader of the *Reichsarbeitsdienst* sat on the small toilet seat, his legs stretched out rigidly, face beet-red, eyes bulging. His mouth was stuffed with some kind of rag. The doctor was on the scene in minutes. Dr. Robert Ley was pronounced dead by strangulation at around 8:30 P.M., October 25, 1945.

Ley desperately wanted to die. That much was obvious. He chose an extremely slow and painful method. He had torn a hem off a GI towel and tied it into a loop. This he hung over a water pipe, about two and a half feet above the toilet seat. The flush button was on top of that upright pipe. Ley put his head through the knotted loop he had improvised with the hem of the towel, then sat down on the toilet and strangled himself. He had torn up his underwear and stuffed the rags in his mouth to keep from making any noise. The guard at the door could only see his feet. If Ley had been a few inches taller this method of strangulation would have been impossible. He was the right size for the low toilet and the height of the water pipe.

While the medical officers and other officials finished their examinations, I walked out into the corridor to observe the action of the other prisoners. They were asleep or pretended to be asleep.

Two days later I had lunch with Dr. Juchli, who filled me in on the aftermath. Dr. Juchli had been the "undertaker." The postmortem examinations of Ley's brain revealed definite brain damage in the frontal lobe area. The body was wrapped in brown butcher paper and placed in an open box. A German mortician hauled it away to a cemetery whose location was kept secret. Juchli said a couple of old gravediggers tipped the open box letting the body fall into the grave. They kept the box for firewood, a sparse commodity. The nude corpse of the man who once directed the German Labor Front lay facedown in the gravel and mud. The gravediggers shoveled earth on top of him and then leveled the surface to conceal the grave. I guess this was a fitting end for a Nazi. I attended an opera that night, Mozart's *Magic Flute.*

Two days after the Ley "funeral" I left Nuremberg. I didn't return to the prison after that, although I made a half-dozen quick trips to Nuremberg in the months that followed. On three occasions I sat in the back row of the spectator's section of the courtroom and listened to the proceedings of the trial. Thus I saw the members of "the class of 1945" of Ashcan in Mondorf only from the far end of a crowded courtroom.

The trials which began on November 20, 1945 had to take place for political and psychological reasons. What the Nazis had done was not to be treated as propaganda, like the stories told during the First World War. War crimes had been committed. Murder on a shocking scale.

The German slaughter was carried out methodically; it was impersonal, organizationally efficient. The Gestapo, the SD, and the political bureaucracy organized pogroms, racial murders, and kept accurate records of the inhuman proceedings. The German people didn't take a direct part in the operation of the concentration camps, slave labor, and the killings. But they heard Hitler say again and again that in the event of war he would not like to be a Jew in the Third Reich.

The extermination of six million Jews is not an exaggeration. I saw and heard enough to suspect that the numbers might have been greater. Hundreds of books have been written describing the Nazi regime from beginning to end. Many writers criticize the International War Crimes Tribunal. It's true that British, American, and French forces weren't simon-pure in the conduct of the war. We bombed civilians, we organized hunger blockades. On occasion, the activities of our commando and OSS operations were as brutal and illegal as those of the German SS. And certainly the government of the Soviet Union has been the executioner of millions of its people, not to mention the crimes against humanity committed against other nationalities. Class and ethnic enemies have been exterminated ruthlessly by many nations throughout history. Where does it stop?

But still, the single-minded pursuit, on the part of men like Bormann, Eichmann, Heydrich, and Kaltenbrunner, of their goal of getting rid of Jews is unique. It was the mass slaughter, the crematories, the organized hatred which set the Nazi operation apart. It was the work of men like Himmler, Streicher, Sauckel, Rosenberg, and all the rest which resulted in what we recognize as the atrocities of the Nazi regime.

I happened to be in court when one witness gave testimony on the extermination of Jews in concentration camps, Rudolf Hoess, the commandant of Auschwitz from May 1, 1940 to December 1, 1943. He estimated that in his camp alone, in that time, 2,500,000 persons were exterminated, and that another 500,000 died from disease and starvation. Hoess described the screening for extermination by stating in evidence:

We had two SS doctors on duty at Auschwitz to examine the incoming transports of prisoners. The prisoners were marched by one of the doctors who would make spot decisions as they walked by. Those who were fit for work were sent into the camp. Others were immediately sent to the extermination plants. Children of tender years were invariably exterminated since by reason of their youth they were unable to work. Still another improvement we made over Treblinka was that at Treblinka the victims almost always knew they were to be exterminated. At Auschwitz we endeavored to fool the victims into thinking they were to go through a delousing process. Of course, frequently they realized our true intentions and we sometimes had riots and difficulties due to that fact. Very frequently women would hide their children under their clothes, but of course when we found them we would send the children in to be exterminated.

He described the actual killing by stating:

It took from 3 to 15 minutes to kill the people in the death chamber, depending on climatic conditions. We knew when the people were dead because their screaming stopped. We usually waited about one-half hour before we opened the doors and removed the bodies. After the bodies were removed our special commandos took off the rings and extracted the gold from the teeth of the corpses.

Hoess admitted that beating, starvation, torture, and killing were general.

Inmates were subjected to cruel experiments at Dachau in August, 1942; victims were immersed in cold water until their body temperatures were reduced to twenty-eight degrees centigrade, when they died immediately. I heard testimony about other "research" procedures, including high altitude experiments in pressure chambers, experiments to determine how long human beings could survive in freezing water, experiments with poison bullets, experiments with contagious diseases, and experiments dealing with sterilization of men and women by X-rays and other methods.

In another session I attended, evidence was given of the treatment of the inmates before and after their extermination. There was testimony that the hair of women victims was cut off before they were killed, and shipped to Germany to be used in the manufacture of mattresses. The clothes, money, and valuables of the inmates were also salvaged and sent to appropriate agencies for disposition. The gold teeth and fillings taken from heads of the corpses were sent to the Reichsbank. After cremation the ashes were used for fertilizer, and in some instances attempts were made to utilize the fat from the bodies of the victims in the commercial manufacture of soap. I have held a bar of soap of that kind in my own hands. I've seen a lampshade made from human skin, and the shrunken head used as the desk decor in the office of an SS official.

There are people who challenged our right to try the military leaders such as Keitel and Jodl. "They just did their soldierly duty," I've been told. On the subject of "Murder and Ill-treatment of Civilian Population" the leader of a special task force to deal with the population in militarily occupied territory testified:

When the German army invaded Russia, I was leader of Einsatzgruppe D, in the southern sector, and in the course of the year in which I was leader of the Einsatzgruppe D it liquidated approximately 90,000 men, women, and children. The majority of those liquidated were Jews, but there were also among them some communist functionaries.

I saw an order issued by Keitel in 1941, and drafted by Jodl. It stated that:

In view of the vast size of the occupied areas in the east, the forces available for establishing security in these areas will be sufficient only if all resistance is punished, not by legal prosecution of the guilty, but by the spreading of such terror by the armed forces as is alone appropriate to eradicate every inclination to resist among the population. . . . Commanders must find the means of keeping order by applying suitable draconian measures.

You can see why I was eager to get away from the men responsible for so much misery and horror. When I reported back to Oberursel, Colonel Philp greeted me by saying, "I'm glad I was able to get you out of that, son."

I settled down to a routine schedule again, attacking my GSC project with new enthusiasm. We still had several dozen members of the German General Staff in the camp, which was now named Camp Sibert for the G-2 general in charge of USFET military intelligence. We translated documents, interviewed prisoners, wrote reports. Every three or four weeks I drove to Nuremberg and turned over the fruits of our effort to General "Wild Bill" Donovan, who had taken charge of the GSC project. I saw Warlimont only twice during those trips. Gradually, I pulled away from personal contact with prisoners I knew from the summer months in Luxembourg.

Christmas 1945 was near. In a corner of the little house in which Mal Hilty and I were billeted rested row upon row of "Care" packages Winnie and my family in Akron had been sending me for several months. I counted twenty boxes containing clothing, canned foods, dolls and toys, and special gifts for my brothers and sisters and their families. I would be super-Santa Claus on Christmas Day. Only one item was missing, fresh meat. Food rationing in postwar Germany was in full force. Meat was the scarcest item.

I spoke of this to my friend one day. He came up with a brilliant idea, "Let's go hunting." We could shoot a wild boar. There's nothing like roast pork for Christmas.

Neither of us had ever hunted before, but one snowy December morning, a Saturday before the big holiday, we headed for the wooded Taunus Mountains. Armed with our carbines, sandwiches scrounged from the mess sergeant, and a canteen of hot coffee laced with that Spanish brandy, we were ready to remove at least one wild porker from the slopes of the Taunus.

It was a beautiful winter day. The pure white snow on the pine trees glistened in the morning sun. Our spirits were high in that winter wonderland. But all the wild boar had left town. Furthermore, we hadn't the faintest idea of how to go about hunting for them. We drove through the forest lanes in our trusty jeep. Then we parked the vehicle and wandered in wide circles through the woods. Not a boar in sight.

After several hours we gave up. We drove the jeep to the side of a creek, unloaded our food ration and ate lunch. I was sipping my coffee when Mal suddenly poked me and pointed across the creek. There, not more than forty feet from us, stood a young wild boar, giving us the eye. I guess the beast felt quite safe with the running water between it and us. So did we. Mal motioned to me. My shot. Slowly I raised my carbine, and he raised his. I aimed, fired. Mal fired a split second later. We had a wild boar!

The next challenge was to get to it. We found a place to ford about five hundred yards upstream. Once we got to the other side, and to the dead boar, we had to retrace our steps, lugging our game by his feet. It was a struggle, but we managed.

In the town of Oberursel we found a German butcher. For a carton of cigarettes and a bottle of Fundador brandy, he butchered and dressed our booty. I had enough roast, chops, and other cuts to feed a small army.

Our family Christmas was all I'd hoped for. Kasi, Heinrich, Liesel and their families all gathered at Agnes's home in Sindlingen. We lacked nothing; the wild boar clinched a most successful feast.

For me the holiday season was marred somewhat by news of the death of General Patton. I was determined to pay my last respects to the general and made a quick round trip to Luxembourg to witness his burial at the American Military Cemetery in Hamm. It was my first visit to the cemetery where some nine thousand GIs were buried. Most of them lost their lives in the Battle of the Bulge north of the city. The thousands of wooden crosses presented a sight I could never forget.

Today, the Military Cemetery in Luxembourg is a most beautiful and impressive shrine. The white crosses and Stars of David marking the final resting place of the 5,074 American men, and one woman, are now made of marble. General Patton's grave stands alone at the head of the many rows of markers. The chapel towering over the entire area, the monuments with maps of the campaign and the names of thousands missing in action and lying in unknown graves, leave each visitor with an image never to be forgotten.

I've mentioned Kronberg Castle, which was reserved as an officers' club and later became an outstanding resort hotel. The officers stationed at Camp Sibert often relaxed at Kronberg, and I have pleasant memories of dinners and dances in this luxurious environment. Beautiful tapestries, parquet floors, huge fireplaces, and a grand art collection added to the castle's Tudor charm. It made us forget the desolate, shabby German atmosphere outside.

Nurses from the American military hospitals nearby and WAC officers from USFET headquarters in Frankfurt provided feminine charm to the Kronberg surroundings. For special events officers of other nationalities working for the Americans in the vicinity were invited. On one such occasion someone pointed to an attractive young lady who worked for the U.S. Information Service in Bad Homburg. She was connected with Radio Luxembourg and hailed from Gasperich, a suburb of Luxembourg City. I approached her table, tapped her on the shoulder and spoke to her in Luxembourgish. She nearly fell off her chair. Her name was Anny Poncelet. Tall, slender, dressed in a special uniform for non-Americans in our employ, she appealed to all the guys looking for dance partners and good company. Since she was about a half foot taller than I, dancing was out. But our conversation in our native language and common interests made for good company. We became fast friends.

Like many youngsters who grew up in Luxembourg during the Nazi occupation, Anny Poncelet had exciting stories to tell. She had been active in the Luxembourg underground. Having been conscripted to work as a typist in the German Security office in Luxembourg, she risked her life by supplying copies of arrest lists prepared by the SS. Many potential victims of the Nazi occupiers thus were warned and helped to escape.

Anny married an American soldier in 1946 and came to live in Pennsylvania, where her son, Robert, was born. Some years later she was divorced and returned to Luxembourg, where she married an engineer, Metty Steimetz. They moved to the Belgian Congo, and our correspondence came to an end.

During the uprisings in the Congo in 1968, the Steimetzes returned to Luxembourg. Through my Neipperg School friends, Anny was able to get in touch with me. Later that year, she was hired by Miami University as executive secretary of the European Study Center we established in Luxembourg that same year.

During the ten years of her service to Miami, her son Robert graduated from the university. He remained in the states, became an American citizen, and is now a successful corporate executive in New York City.

For several years after she quit working for Miami, Anny and her husband lived in Spain and Florida, and just recently returned to Luxembourg to enjoy retirement in Remich on the Moselle. Miami students who attended the European Study Center in Luxembourg will not forget "Mom" Steimetz, who looked after them so well during her tenure. The Miami connection for Anny Poncelet Steimetz began back in the winter of 1945–46 when we met by chance at Kronberg Castle.

We finished our German General Staff Corps project by the time the big snows came to Oberursel that same winter. The old-timers who had arrived in Europe before me were going home one by one. Mal Hilty met a German girl whom he intended to marry. He signed up for an extended tour and would remain in Germany indefinitely. My own stay in Oberursel would last quite a while longer. I still didn't have enough points to return home.

Responsibilities were shifting. I began to worry about my next assignment, when Colonel Philp asked me, "How would you like to be the Post Transportation Officer?" This was a fancy name for being in charge of the motor pool. It would change my occupational specialty number from PW Interrogator (9316) to Motor Transport Officer (0600). I would continue to work on special operational intelligence assignments as they developed. And since I had another specialty—instructor—I would teach German one hour each day to officers and enlisted men eager to learn the language. This came under the army's official I&E program. My teaching time was increased to two hours per day when I added "Industrial Management" to the curriculum, thus refreshing my civilian skills for my eventual return to Procter & Gamble.

Teacher, motor pool officer, and counterintelligence specialist provided plenty of work for me. In January 1946 I was promoted to captain. My fourth wedding anniversary telegram to Winnie shared the good news of my promotion with her and my family.

The German Viewpoint

MY LEADERSHIP TALENTS were put to the test when I took on the motor pool assignment. I hadn't been in charge of troops since Camp Chaffee, Arkansas, and my first association with the personnel turned into a collision.

Our motor pool people had the highest venereal disease rate and the second highest AWOL record of any unit in the immediate vicinity. Without a doubt, the morale was the lowest of any outfit in the USFET.

About a half mile from the entrance to Camp Sibert was a German machine tool factory. A section of one building housed the motor pool. The vehicles—command cars, jeeps, trucks, and personnel carriers— were parked in a large area adjacent to the building. Repairs were made in the "shop" inside the building. The dispatcher and the motor pool officer were accommodated in offices at the corner of the factory building, right near the entrance to the area. Most of the vehicles now under my command were in dire need of repair. So was the relationship between the officers of MISC and the motor pool personnel.

I decided a diagnosis of the ailment was needed first. I called a meeting of my noncommissioned officers and the enlisted men, removed my insignia of rank, took a deep breath, and stepped into the middle of the assembled group. "I'm just a dumb bastard who got drafted into this man's army just like you guys did. I hate every damn bit of it, and I can hardly wait to get out. But until then I have a job to do. So hear me out." That's how I started. Then I took another deep breath. "All right now, I'm not wearing any bars and I'm not carrying a silly swagger stick. I want you to think of me as one of you guys." I urged them to level with me. Let it all hang out. I wanted to know what the hell was wrong with this outfit. And then I would ask them to help me set things straight. "Let's talk!"

There was a long silence. I waited. Finally, one of the sergeants spoke up. After that I was swamped. Why were they so demoralized? Why so much unhappiness above and beyond the normal gripes of all soldiers? Well, I found out.

An officer from "up at the camp" would call the motor pool and demand a jeep and driver, "pronto!" Then he would direct the driver to take him on a mission miles away, sometimes requiring an overnight stay. The driver would have no advance notice of where he was going and how long he should be prepared to stay. There was no chance to be prepared by bringing along a shaving kit or change of clothing, or even spending money for food and lodging. There were no copies of orders to facilitate eating or staying at U.S. or Allied army installations. The driver was completely on his own, unprepared.

When an officer "got the hots" and wanted to see his "Fräulein," he'd call the motor pool for a vehicle and a driver, any time, day or night. The driver would often sit in an open jeep in rain or cold weather for hours while the "Brass was having a bang" and a party with his girl-friend. There was seldom a thank-you or any other consideration of the soldier.

Frequently officers would insist on taking out a vehicle on their own. A lot of them couldn't drive properly. They'd bang up the jeep or command car and not report the damage. In case of a maintenance problem or malfunction, nothing was said when the vehicle was returned. The next driver would find himself stuck out in the country some place with a mechanical failure that could have been prevented with minor repairs back in the shop.

Each speaker was more bitter than the next. The complaints were legitimate; just getting them off their chests was therapeutic. After about two hours of this session, the sullen resentment was wearing off. We began to work on solutions. We made a deal, and a lot of promises. If I corrected the situation and eased their unfair burdens, they would stop the boozing during duty hours, stop the reckless driving and careless maintenance, and obey the regulations. We would work together to control the VD, and there would be no AWOLs. I asked for one month to put the program into effect.

The solutions were so simple it was almost ludicrous. We established a duty roster. No driver or mechanic would be on duty more than forty-four hours per week. Weekend duty or night assignments would be rotated with compensatory time off. A regular furlough routine and an R&R schedule were worked out. A personnel carrier was fixed up to make scheduled round trips to Heidelberg, Rheims, Paris, and other cities.

We "employed" two German workmen who washed the vehicles and even painted them when needed. Their wages were paid in food, candy, and cigarettes. We hired two German drivers who made regular rounds into Frankfurt during the day and evenings. Two German buses were fitted out for this purpose. Officers wanting to go into town for personal reasons had to travel on those buses. Only those with official travel orders would be assigned a driver and a vehicle. At least eight hours advance notice was required for booking transportation for an overnight journey. A set of travel orders for the enlisted personnel had to be made available. I assigned a vehicle to each driver, allowing him to paint the name of his choice on the windshield panel, and making him responsible for its appearance and maintenance.

In short, I entered one of the most satisfying experiences of my military career. The hardened combat GIs who worked in our motor pool began to take great pride in their unit. There were no AWOLs, not one case of VD, and the thirty-three men who made up our cadre would have killed anyone who so much as gave me a dirty look.

One of my men was Bon Dittman from Toledo. He retired from his job as driver for a dairy company in that city a few years ago. Bon and his wife Rena have corresponded with us faithfully ever since he and I came home.

Last winter, Winnie and I were vacationing in Naples, Florida when I received a call from Frank Marinelli, who had been the motor pool sergeant. He had seen my name in the local newspaper in connection with a speech I was making to the Naples Council of World Affairs. He tracked me down and we had a pleasant visit. He hails from Buffalo, New York. Just recently he sent me a package containing several of his well-executed paintings, including a street scene of Oberursel.

Quite a few of the men wrote to me after they returned home and were discharged. Some wrote enroute to the USA as did Corporal Calvin Giles, on April 19, 1946:

Dear Capt,

Just a few lines to let you know how things are going here in Belgium. It's really chicken here. They keep you on the old GI ball. But nothing a good soldier can't take. I didn't get to see you before I left. So I want to tell you goodbye and good luck. You was one of the best officers I have seen in the army and I'm dam proud to be working under you. You are a man who can feel proud to be an officer. I only wish there was more of them in the army. What you said went & whatever you promist the boys they got it & I'm proud of you

and believe me, you can go home feeling and knowing that every man liked
and respect you. I can't explain it in words but what I want to say you are one
hell of a good man and I want you to keep up the good work.

> Always a friend for ever
> one of the old boys
> CALVIN GILES

Good luck Sir. I give you a salute.

That is one of several accolades I have cherished all these years. Could
any man ever expect a more genuine tribute than such a GI letter? I'll
never forget Cal Giles, Bruce Godfrey, Calvin Byrd, Bon Dittman,
Frank Marinelli, Branko, Sutton, Seyzka, Cummings, Strilka and all
the rest of that bunch of genuine GI Joes of the MISC Motor Pool.

Nor will I ever forget the time their goodwill and friendship almost
landed me in the prison stockade. It happened the day I was promoted to
captain. I had gone to bed early. A knock on the door awakened me.
Three of my men stood in the hallway, their helmet liners in hand.
"Captain, the boys of the motor pool are all together celebrating your
promotion. We was wondering if you would come and have a drink with
us?"

How could I resist such an invitation? I was dressed and ready in no
time, and the welcome I received was exuberant, and somewhat lubri-
cated. Drinking with enlisted men at that time was enough to get me in
trouble, but what happened after a series of well-placed toasts put me on
the path to sure destruction.

"Hey Captain, have you ever gone frog hunting?" Of course I hadn't.
That led to the next summons: "All right guys, let's take the Captain on
a frog hunt!"

It was an unusually balmy night for January. Almost like an evening
in April. A dozen or so of my stalwart command boosted me into the GI
truck. They were all carrying carbines. I wasn't armed. I was coming
along to observe. I was mystified, however, by how frogs were hunted
with carbines.

The truck headed west in the direction of the Rhine River, toward
Mainz. Apparently the driver had driven this route before. When he
turned off the main road toward the river, he doused his lights. On the
truck, the conversation dropped to whispers. Apparently this was necessary so as not to alert the frogs to our coming. The truck stopped and we
silently dismounted. In total darkness we crept to the edge of the river.
Each of my men tok a position a few feet apart from each other, facing
the water. I was deeply puzzled by these maneuvers.

Then I made out a glimmer of light across the river, a burning cigarette. I spotted two or three more, and then was jarred out of my puzzlement by the crackle of gunfire all around me. This was immediately followed by screams and curses—in French—on the other side of the Rhine. Now at last, it dawned on me. My boys were shooting at French soldiers and their female companions "making out" on the French side of the Rhine. The "frog hunt" was their way of protesting U.S. nonfraternization rules which French soldiers didn't have to obey. Firing carbines over the heads of the lovers was one way of signalling envious displeasure.

By the time all this occurred to me, we were on the run back to our truck, doubling over with laughter. Within minutes the frog hunting expedition was on the way back to the barracks in Oberursel. My boys were so pleased with themselves I simply couldn't lecture them about the dangers inherent in this adventure. It would have ruined the evening. In truth, I was greatly relieved when I was safely back in my own bed. At least ten army regulations had been broken that night, and this officer, derelict in his duties, would have paid the price. I thought it best to keep the secret and never discuss our "Watch on the Rhine" with anyone.

In the summer of 1945 Germany's condition was desperate. There was no central or state government; county and city administrations had ceased to exist. There was no mail service. Transportation had broken down. Destroyed bridges had halted railway and highway transport. Navigable rivers were choked with sunken barges, ships, and wrecked bridges. Millions of people from Nazi-occupied countries, now freed from forced labor, needed to be returned to their home countries. They were the DPs, displaced persons. German refugees from the East were streaming into Germany. In the bombed cities shelter was at a premium. Famine was close on the heels of the population. As occupation authorities, we were hard pressed to keep the German people from starving.

In the first months after the end of fighting, military governments had to round up and intern war criminals. Nazi officials by the thousands had to be identified and tagged as ineligible for public office or anything other than manual labor. Schools were closed while textbooks were being revised and teachers retrained. School buildings left standing served as temporary shelter for the homeless or as makeshift offices.

From the moment of their entrance into Germany in the last months of the war, the Soviets had been working at cross purposes with their Western Allies. In the towns and cities along our ways of advance, American and British military officials sought out Germans who had resisted Nazism and appointed them to administrative posts, pending elections. On the other hand, the Soviets, on their triumphal advance, were accompanied by Moscow-trained German Communists whom they appointed to key administrative posts. We wanted a self-supporting Germany. The Soviets were bent on exploiting German industry, agriculture, and labor for the benefit of the USSR. Our interrogation group in the MIS Center at Camp Sibert decided we needed to be brought up to date and to thoroughly familiarize ourselves with current thought and conditions in this new Germany.

Colonel Philp ordered the development of a project to get the German viewpoint. He picked several operational and counterintelligence officers to interview German civilians. I was assigned to the project. Our mission was to travel around in the American zone of occupation, to talk to clergymen, educators, public officials, farmers and landowners, refugees, ex-soldiers, skilled and unskilled workers, writers and newspapermen, publishers, doctors, businessmen, craftsmen, politicians, nobility and plain people, young and old. In many cases the people we interviewed didn't know we were Americans. We often dressed in the uniform of German soldiers, supposedly returning from PW camps, on the way to their homes. (My Saar dialect helped tremendously when I played that role.) At the end of our interview tours, we compiled a view seen through German eyes: *Ordinary* Germans were hard hit by the Allied declaration that the whole German nation was responsible for the Nazi evils and the war. In 1945–46 they were suffering from a defense complex. The stock phrases were well known:

"We never expected Nazism to turn out the way it did."

"We were *forced* into everything."

"We never knew about the concentration camps until the Allied troops liberated them."

A step beyond sheer defense was the common justification and glorification of many Nazi measures. Hitler's method of ending unemployment and his restoration of the sense of national pride came in for great praise. Few people defended the way in which the Jews were treated, but most felt that it was good to break Jewish power. The view was gaining ground that perhaps concentration camps were politically necessary. I should add here that, at the time, the findings and evidence submitted at the International War Crimes Trials in Nuremberg had not yet been made public.

Most people I talked to were sorry Germany did not win the war. "If only we had not attacked Russia. . . ." "I don't see what business the Americans have over here." Many people claimed that they did not want the war, but once they were in it, they wanted to win.

To many of the *nobility*, the twentieth of July 1944 was the day of catastrophe, not the eighth of May 1945. Hitler hated the aristocracy, they said. He and Himmler deliberately ordered the sacrifice of elite divisions and purged officers who came of noble families; they feared and despised the old order. The twelve years before 1945 showed a fatal "rule by the inferiors" (Herrschaft der Minderwertigen) when the best elements and the best traditions of Germany were stamped out.

The aristocracy vigorously defended its own tradition. Authoritarian education, where the father guides every step of the son, was still esteemed. Prussianism in its pure eighteenth century form was a dignified, high-minded social order. The rulers had a strong sense of justice, and a keen concept of personal responsibility for their subjects. They were loved and respected. The later distortions of Prussianism misrepresented the true great tradition of the German aristocracy.

I left them proud of their past, and tragically depressed about the catastrophe of July 1944 when the attempted assassination of Hitler failed. Unconditional surrender on May 8, 1945 was inevitable when men like Hitler were at the helm.

In order to get some *pro-Nazi* opinions I interviewed identified sympathizers. A wealthy, middle-class woman, forty-five years old, educated, still a devoted servant of Hitler, deemed his rise to power the beginning of a new world. While not a party member because "it was not fitting for a woman to do so," she was very active in the NSFV, the Nazi Women's Association. She "loved" being able to help other people, "loved" rendering social services. I asked her about the persecution of the Jews. She didn't see much of that, and then, the present American reports were surely exaggerated. However, the Jews had all the jobs. It was unpleasant, to be sure, but those were revolutionary times.

Germany's nonaggression pact with Russia was a diplomatic maneuver to gain time. What about the sanctity of treaties? "I don't know about those things, I am a woman."

She didn't listen to foreign broadcasts, because they only confused her. She believed that America declared war on Germany first. The Fuehrer wanted the best, and he was deserted by people at home. She believed in victory until the very end.

According to *intellectuals* the Nazis had no global view, no understanding of international affairs. In France, all throughout the first year of German occupation, the Nazis had a glorious opportunity to win the French over to full collaboration. They failed to seize the chance.

Was there something in the whole people that made Nazism rise and fall? A clergyman said that the Germans unquestionably wanted and were prepared for the very form of Nazism that they got. Another man, a psychologist, felt that the good and the bad of the Germans came out in the regime—the great ideals and plans, and the inflexibility and the narrowness that prevented the proper translation of ideals into reality.

Germans could not believe they were a brutal people. "You Americans should constantly pound it into us that we had men like Streicher," one man said. "Perhaps that will make us search deeper into ourselves and our past, to find the flaw in our character that made the concentration camps and the Jewish purges possible."

In 1945, Germans quietly watched every move and every man of the U.S. occupation army, and tended to look for American intentions in even the smallest individual action or attitude. The destruction of leftover food by U.S. troops was criticized frequently and was considered the sign of a basically hostile attitude.

Every one of the interviewed Germans from all walks of life was upset about the law dealing with Nazis, Law Number Eight. It denied professional positions and even employment to members of the Nazi party.

The law was considered unjust because it hit many people who were only passive party members for opportunistic reasons. Many people were not allowed to join the NSDAP for one reason or another. These people then became "150% Nazis" in order to remain in good standing. Law Number Eight let *them* go unscathed. The law was impractical because it took too many persons from those positions where they were needed for reconstruction. Law Number Eight was unwise, because it threw an added large number of people onto the street, into hopelessness, and "into the hands of communism."

Many Germans doubted that the four-zone system would endure. A retired high official compared Germany to an oil drop floating in the water. "You can separate the drop," he said, "but it will tend to flow back together." German unity is a force too strong to overcome.

A noted economist and sociology professor exclaimed: "This division of Germany into four occupation zones is strictly arbitrary; Germany is one economic unity. None of these zones can live without the others for any length of time."

The reaction to nonfraternization ran the gamut from indifference through deep, sympathetic concern, to outraged protest.

For many *women* I interviewed, the end of their Hitler dreams had tumbled them into chaos with which they couldn't cope. One middle-aged woman, a convinced Nazi, harked back in a long, misty reverie to the beautiful world of the Fuehrer. Others still sighed for the sharp, stiff elegance of the Wehrmacht. One young ex-soldier said to me that German women would go wild with delight "if a company of German soldiers would today march down the street."

Germans generally were dismayed at the blacklisting of prominent artists like the pianists Walter Gieseking and Hans Knappertsbusch.

The genius of these men lay in their art. If they became party members or played for the Nazis, they did it because they believed that their art came first, no matter who listened to it.

On all levels—public schools, universities, and adult education—a great vacuum existed in Germany. This was keenly felt everywhere. The demand was high for books, lectures, information, and schools. People felt cut off from knowledge. They felt that they had for years been cheated of information and deprived of facts. They wanted to make up the loss.

For the Germans, the arrival of American troops meant the end of air raids, tension, and privation. They expected the Americans to cut the red tape which the bureaucratic system of planned economy had instituted. They expected the Americans to show them how democracy works and how democratic people live and act. But they didn't think we were doing it fast enough. "We don't expect too much after the short period of six months and we realize that, in a way, all Germans have a certain responsibility for this war," explained a teacher, an admirer of America. "But life goes on, and even the most modest ones among us need a little encouragement, a ray of hope."

"After all, we never really hated the Americans as we hated our French and Russian enemies. We realized that Goebbel's propaganda always lied to us, also about the Americans," another remarked. "I can't tell you what we expected, but most of us expect something positive from these generous Americans."

These are just a few of the opinions elicited from Germans I interviewed. I don't know if our complete report of seventy-two pages ever reached higher authority. I'm not even sure our own intelligence community was made totally aware of it.

But in the years that followed the tragic state of affairs of 1945–46, things began to change in postwar Germany. Punishment, retribution, and dismemberment were exchanged for a more far-reaching and human program of reconstruction. Our long-range policy for Germany began to pay dividends of friendship and trust. The Marshall Plan, instituted in 1947, marked the beginning of a new attitude.

The German Federal Republic under the able leadership of Chancellor Konrad Adenauer came into being in 1949. Within four years the people on the streets of Germany were healthy looking, alert, and well dressed. It was a brisk and prosperous Germany. Vast reconstruction projects, aided by the Marshall Plan, were rapidly restoring the war-blasted cities. The majority of the people now freely admitted German responsibility for World War II. There was no longer any hedging on that point. At the same time they rejected the past. They faced the future. American guidance and leadership, coupled with intelligent economic assistance must share substantially in the credit for this miraculous regeneration.

In the spring of 1946, my own life in a Germany on the road to recovery was almost pleasant except for the fact that I longed for my wife and son back home in Akron. I taught my German and Industrial Management classes on a regular basis. More and more of my time was spent on motor pool activity. My men and I had decided to make ours the best and safest transportation unit in USFET. We even won a prize for the best safety slogan submitted: "DEATH is so Permanent. Drive Carefully."

At every opportunity I traveled to various parts of Europe, combining business with pleasure. The business end dealt with visiting supply depots to negotiate for automotive parts and equipment. We needed newer vehicles to replace our well-worn combat machines. My recreational travel included journeys to Paris, Luxembourg, Heidelberg, Salzburg, and to the homes of my brothers and sisters. I was less and less involved in intelligence exercises. In that connection, operations now focused on counterintelligence and gathering information about Soviet political activity. A new line of "specialties" was being developed in Camp Sibert.

Thus, time sped by. My long-awaited orders to return home finally materialized in late May. I was ready. My goodbyes to my family, and to friends in Luxembourg and at Camp Sibert, were short and sweet.

After the usual red tape delays and snafus, I was finally put aboard a very rusty Liberty ship, the SS *George Weems*, in Antwerp, Belgium. This was the same port from which my father and I had sailed for the U.S. in 1931.

My travel companions were Capt. Alois Schneider, a Camp Ritchie alumnus; Sgt. Wilbur Harris, and T.Sgt. George Poppin. Our final military assignment was to serve as official escort for boxes and boxes of documents, classified and unclassified, stowed in the hold of the ship. On deck of the weary old cargo ship were a number of tanks and armored cars, lashed together, for shipment to the scrap heap back home. I didn't think we'd make it across the waters with that clumsy load.

The seventeen day crossing of the Atlantic was anything but smooth. We endured one of the worst storms in history and I was violently seasick for days. My ardent prayers for delivery from misery, wretchedness, and martyrdom went unheard. At last the sea calmed. The sun came out. I was reborn. Two days later we sighted America. Our ship dropped anchor just a few hundred yards from the Statue of Liberty, almost in the same area in which the SS *Lapland* moored on July 4, 1931.

But impatience to set foot on firm United States soil had to be curbed.

The U.S. Merchant Marine, manning the worn-out *George Weems*, went on strike for some reason or other. They left us with a skeleton crew, and abandoned ship. We howled and complained to no avail. But this was the land of equal opportunity. So we soon figured out how to hoist a "taxi flag." In short time a small motor launch pulled up alongside our floating junk pile, and for a price brought us to terra firma.

I reported to the port commander, New York Port of Debarkation, and was referred to an officer representing NYPE, Camp Kilmer, New Brunswick, New Jersey. This time everything clicked. My orders were on file. I officially surrendered the documents we had escorted. In turn I learned that I was to report to Camp Ritchie, Maryland, for five days of temporary duty, and then proceed by rail to Camp Atterbury, Indiana, for "disposition under the War Department Readjustment Regulations 1-1 and 1-5 cs." In other words, get out of the army.

I was able to persuade the officer in charge to "correct" my orders. He prescribed for me to go directly by rail to Camp Atterbury, bypassing Camp Ritchie. I was authorized five-days delay enroute. I collected eight hundred dollars advance on back pay and per diem. Then I called Winnie in Akron. She would make plans to leave for New York at once. Meanwhile I would arrange for hotel accommodations and call her back on where we would meet.

Now frustration set in. Arranging for a reunion and second honeymoon in New York City in June 1946 wasn't as easy as I thought it would be. It took twelve telephone calls for me to conclude that all hotels in NYC were booked solid. In desperation I consulted my travel companion, Captain Schneider. He made a brilliant suggestion. "Don't you remember Sgt. Walter Schnyder from Section Five at Camp Ritchie?" he asked. Of course I did. Well, Sergeant Schnyder was now assistant manager of the Waldorf-Astoria. "So what are you waiting for?"

I dialed the number of that world-famous rooming house. Got through to Mr. Schnyder immediately. "Certainly," he remembered me. A room? No problem!

I called Winnie with the good news. She was leaving Akron on the train that evening, and would arrive in the Big Apple the next afternoon. We would meet at the luxurious Waldorf-Astoria. I was on pins and needles. Now all I had to do was make final preparations for Winnie's first visit to New York City.

Would you believe that for twenty-five dollars Xavier Cugat and his celebrated orchestra played our song—"Begin the Beguine"—when Winnie and I walked into the ballroom, the Starlight Roof? Would you believe a gala luncheon at the Hotel Astor, and a wonderful dinner and show at the Copacabana? And to maintain the proper balance, we even took a ferry boat ride to Staten Island, past the Statue of Liberty and the SS *George Weems*, still creaking and clanking in the harbor.

It was a weekend we would never forget, especially our reunion at the Waldorf. Sergeant Schnyder had given us the bridal suite. The cost? Nine dollars per night.

I was waiting for Winnie in the lobby. I spotted her coming in, looking like a million bucks; one would have thought she had always stayed at the Waldorf. I held back, watched her advance to the desk, get the room number, and then stride to the elevator. I couldn't wait any longer and caught up with her just before the bellhop closed the door. We were together again. My European adventure had ended. I vowed never to leave the good old USA again.

The Road Ahead:
An Enlarging Future

PROCTER & GAMBLE had held my job for me in Cincinnati. I was assigned to the Fatty Acid Division—an all-chemical manufacturing operation, producing the ingredients for detergent soaps and cleaners. Immediately I was lost. Chemistry was never one of my strong points. Writing job descriptions, rating performances, and making procedure studies could be hazardous.

We bought a house under construction in Valleydale, not far from where I worked. While waiting for our home to be finished, we became house-sitters for one of my coworkers who was traveling out West. I mowed the extensive lawn, trimmed hedges, and handled the care and feeding of some twenty-five chickens. These were kept in a large coop on the edge of a wooded area at the back of the property. I had my first encounter with the impishness of my son. Among his capers one day, Johnny-Mike decided to free the feathered captives under my charge. He opened the door to the coop and the fowl took off. I spent a long evening and the better part of a night rounding up chickens from all over the neighborhood. This was a far cry from rounding up prisoners of war and high-ranking Nazis.

That fall the Nuremberg trials came to an end. The news headlines around the world screamed the verdicts. "Guilty and sentenced to death by hanging: Goering, Streicher, Ribbentrop, Frick, Keitel, Jodl, Kaltenbrunner, Frank, Sauckel, Rosenberg, and Seyss-Inquart."

Grand Admiral Raeder, Rudolf Hess, and Minister Funk of the Reichsbank were given life imprisonment; von Schirach and Speer were sentenced to twenty years; Von Neurath, fifteen; and Grand Admiral Doenitz, ten. The Tribunal sentenced Martin Bormann, who was tried in absentia, to death by hanging. Schacht, von Papen, and Fritzsche walked out of prison as free men.

As I read of the sentences meted out, I remembered the many times Goering had assured me that he would never be hanged. I had misunderstood his certitude. He didn't mean that he would be judged innocent or less guilty than the others. He meant he would cheat the hangman. He produced a capsule of potassium cyanide an hour before the noose was to be fastened around his neck. In his suicide note, addressed to Colonel Andrus, Goering emphasized that none of the persons charged with inspecting his cell and his person throughout his captivity should be held responsible. He maintained it was "practically impossible to find the capsule. It would have been pure accident."

On October 11, 1946, Goering, upon hearing his sentence, wrote to the Allied Control Council as follows:

> I would have allowed myself to be executed by a firing squad. But the German Reichsmarschall should not die on the gallows. I simply cannot allow that for the sake of Germany. Furthermore, I have no moral obligation to submit myself to the punishment fixed by my enemies. Therefore I choose the manner of death of the great Hannibal.
>
> I was aware from the beginning that I would be sentenced to death, because I viewed the entire trial as a political stunt of the victors. I was willing to endure the trial for the sake of my people, and I expected that I would be granted the right to die like a soldier. Before God, my people and my conscience, I consider myself not guilty of the crimes of which an enemy court has convicted me.
>
> Hermann Goering

I felt no compassion upon reading the reports on the verdicts and the executions. I was totally detached. The whole thing was far, far away.

On our peaceful, pleasant Banbury Street we scraped and painted, scrubbed and polished. We laid sod, built a fence, hung drapes and curtains. We celebrated Thanksgiving in our own home at last.

But a certain restlessness began to set in. I couldn't quite muster the confidence needed to handle my job at P&G. It's a great company, a generous employer, and I had never met a nicer bunch of people to work with.

The problem was my insecurity about the chemistry of it all. As a student in high school and college I concentrated on learning English. I carefully avoided the sciences with technical terminology, difficult language. My interest was in personnel management, working with people. But there were no openings at P&G in that field. I was promoted and received a salary increase. Still I had my doubts. I had nightmares about mixing fatty acid with fatty alcohol, or whatever, and blowing up all of Ivorydale.

In that frame of mind I was chatting with my friend Ed Brown at a Beta alumni dinner one evening. Ed was an officer in the General Fraternity. He was also interested in Miami University affairs and had just come from a visit to Oxford.

"Are you married to Procter & Gamble?" Ed Brown asked me. I explained, eager to unload my feelings of uncertainty, of being a square peg in a round hole.

"Well then, how would you like to work for Miami University; live in Oxford?" The university was in the process of establishing a full-time alumni program. They were looking for an alumni secretary.

I thought of our cozy little house that Winnie had spent many hours fixing up. She was expecting our second child in about four months. She was entitled to sit back untroubled, to enjoy the comforts of our haven. But she also knew that I was ill at ease with my responsibilities at work. If she had any doubts, regrets, or concerns about the move she didn't voice them. Meanwhile, Ed Brown tossed my hat in the ring at Old Miami.

A number of interested and influential alumni wanted to look us over. Next we met with members of the board of trustees. Both Winnie and I felt we were running a gauntlet. We were told that one person had the final vote or veto. This was J. Paul McNamara, president of the alumni association and member of the board of trustees. If he weren't impressed, I'd stay with the fatty acid tanks at Ivorydale.

By the time I got to this final interview, I wanted the Miami job. I wanted it for all the good reasons in the world. It soon became obvious that McNamara knew what he wanted. He fired a dozen questions at me, and when the interview came to an end I found myself relaxing. I think he liked me. I liked him. I got the job.

That was forty years ago at this writing. In all those years, through ups and downs, J. Paul McNamara was the most loyal, steadfast supporter any man could have. His love and devotion for Miami University inspired me through all the years as alumni secretary, director of Development, and vice president for University Relations. I owe a lot to him, and to the many friends he rallied in support of my efforts. One alumni association president, Ken Gambee, had brought me to Miami as a student in 1938; another made possible my return as a staff member in 1947. Both worked ardently for the establishment of a full-time alumni program at their beloved alma mater. I had to succeed.

So, on May 1, 1947, I became the first full-time alumni secretary of the university in its 138-year history. I left Procter & Gamble for a much smaller salary, but with the comforting assurance that I could come back if I ever changed my mind. I must confess there were occasions when I was both tempted, and forced, to consider this possibility.

I started commuting from Cincinnati to Oxford every day. A month later we found a house to rent in Oxford. It was an enormous house, four bedrooms, three sitting rooms, dining room, and a fuel bill to give any household budget the jitters. It was partially furnished, otherwise we would have rambled in empty rooms, our voices echoing in reminder of the comfort and conveniences we had enjoyed in the modern house we sold in Cincinnati. What a test of Winnie's loyalty and support this venture proved to be, especially when our second son, Robert Joseph, was born on August 26 of that year.

Where does an alumni secretary work? Office space was at a premium. But there was a faculty lounge in Ogden Hall, a student residence. There was a men's rest room adjacent to that lounge. I got the rest room, pipes and all. The fixtures were removed. I also got an old desk, a chair, and an antique wood filing cabinet. The adjacent lounge, the "front office," was equipped with two working tables, another desk, some folding chairs, and an old Elliott addressing machine. I inherited a Woodstock typewriter of uncertain vintage. Other assorted equipment was scrounged from places where it was no longer wanted. It was an inauspicious beginning for a program that was expected to instill immense pride and unwavering support, and set new records in philanthropic giving.

What does an alumni secretary do? One answer to that question was offered by Jack B. Fullen, for forty years the alumni secretary at Ohio State University: "The function of the alumni secretary is to develop interest where none exists, and to make it useful to the institution where it does."

How does one accomplish this? R. W. "Tubby" Sailor, alumni secretary at Cornell University, explained that the alumni secretary "is expected to be able to speak convincingly at schools; to talk cleverly at club banquets; to organize new groups diplomatically and intelligently; to raise money successfully; to write convincingly, cleverly, and without monotony for the magazine; to manage the office skillfully so that it runs perfectly while he is on the road; and to be strong and rugged enough to take the punishment that comes from one-night stands, banquets, irregular hours, and indiscreet entertainment."

This proved an accurate description. I would learn, eventually, to add a few words of my own, such as "he also needs a superwoman for a wife and partner."

The first Miami Homecoming after the war brought vast numbers of alumni back to Oxford. Most of our personal friends were veterans. Many gathered in our large house—which had become the focal point for alumni get-togethers. But the food and liquor bill was staggering. I needed to talk to Wallace P. Roudebush, vice-president for Business Affairs.

"W. P." is a Miami legend. He graduated from the university in 1911 and immediately took over the business management as secretary to the president. The Miami campus is a monument to his devoted, talented services. His farsightedness and imaginative planning made possible a campus which today is among the most beautiful and spacious of any around the country. Mr. Roudebush gave his all to Miami University from 1911 until his death in 1956. If a furnace needed stoking, he was there to do it. He insisted on signing every check personally. Consequently, bills weren't always paid on time. But they were paid eventually. He never did anything impulsively. He thought things through. If you wanted your office painted, he would want to deliberate on that a while. You might change your mind and select another color, and if the painting had been done right away, it would be too late to accommodate the change later. Wouldn't it? As it turned out, everything eventually was always painted in what became known as "Roudebush tan."

I served with Mr. Roudebush on the athletic advisory board for many years. I recall the members of that board at one time expressing concern about parking on football days. The university would have to arrange something for the thousands of fans who came to Oxford for Saturday afternoon games. Mr. Roudebush said he himself would look into it.

At the meeting of the athletic board after the next home football game, the vice president for Business Affairs reported his findings. He said he had waited until the end of the first quarter of the game. Then he went all around Miami Field and all the way through town. He found that everyone was parked. Nobody was driving around looking for a space. Never mind the fact that some game-goers were parked as far away as College Avenue on the west end of town, and walked a mile to the stadium. They were parked, weren't they? There was no parking problem.

But back to my own personal budget deficit. One never found W. P. Roudebush in his office during regular hours. He was always somewhere on campus, tending to business. But he was a creature of habit. He regularly came to Coffee Pete's, an uptown coffee shop, at ten o'clock each morning. That's where I cornered him.

Mr. Roudebush always spoke in questions. "Wouldn't it be better to paint this room a nice tan color?"

When I sat down next to him at Coffee Pete's he wanted to know how this—"What do you call it? Alumni Program?"—was doing. I told him.

I mentioned our substantial bill at Hornung's Market. And I asked how one goes about being reimbursed for travel to alumni club meetings.

He was not sympathetic. He wondered if it was really necessary to travel to all those clubs. For instance, how many people come to an alumni meeting in St. Louis? Is it worth spending $150 round trip to meet with thirty alumni? That's five dollars per person, isn't it? That's about what the average alumnus contributes each year, isn't it? Not much profit in that, is there? Wouldn't it be better to encourage the alumni to come to Oxford instead?

"Mr. Roudebush, when they come to Oxford I have to entertain them, like at homecoming. So I need a representational allowance to buy the food and drink."

Mr. Roudebush wasn't convinced. "I don't see why they should expect *you* to entertain them, do you? I don't recollect that we've ever had that problem before. If I recall correctly, and tell me if I'm wrong, isn't Miami University 138 years old now? How do you suppose we got along all these years without somebody providing free food and drink for alumni coming back to Oxford?"

No money for travel and entertainment. You're on your own! I couldn't get angry with the man. He was so damned nice, even when he said no, you almost wanted to shake his hand and thank him.

So my financial burdens had to be met in some other way. Paul McNamara persuaded members of the board and prominent alumni to contribute to a fund that would help underwrite travel and entertainment until such time the annual fund could assume those costs. A second solution to my problem? My "Recollections of an Interrogator" and "I Knew the top Nazis." I went on the speaking circuit. The honoraria were paid directly into the fund.

But I wasn't over the hump yet. The first threat to my job security came just three years after I had launched my new career.

One day, I was passing the open door to the office of Dr. C. W. Kreger, vice president for Academic Affairs. "Dolibois, I want to see you," he hollered at the top of his voice.

"What kind of arrangement was made with you about your salary when you were hired?" He came right to the point. I gulped. I couldn't recall any "arrangement." I just understood I was an employee of Miami University.

That's not the way *he* understood the situation. He was of the opinion that Miami would pay my salary for three years, after which my compensation would be paid out of the annual fund I was directing. Furthermore, the alumni association was to become independent of the university; it was to assume full financial responsibility for its operation, including my salary and that of any other staff members. This arrangement was to go into effect May 1, 1950. To Dr. Kreger it was a fait accompli. He dismissed me with a wave of the hand. What the vice president for Academic Affairs was assuming would mean that nearly all alumni donations would be used to pay salaries and operating costs. There would be no gift funds for scholarships, student aid, faculty research, the library. Furthermore, I had no intention of asking my friends to contribute so my family could eat. If I were going to raise money for university programs, I must be able to do so without shame and apology.

I was fuming, and stormed back to my office. I wrote my letter of resignation, addressed to President Ernest H. Hahne. Unless assured in writing, by noon Monday, that Miami University was continuing me on the payroll, I was quitting. Down deep inside I hoped Proctor & Gamble was serious about that standing offer to return. Meanwhile, Winnie and I spent an anxious weekend.

On Monday morning I started to clean out my desk. No word had come from the president. At 11:15 the phone rang. Marie Marshall, the president's secretary, advised that Dr. Hahne had just returned from out of town. He had dictated a reply to my letter. I would have it within the hour. Dr. Hahne wrote: "I believe that it is wise for the University budget to carry your salary. Inasmuch as this is the practice used by other state-supported universities, I see no reason why it should not continue here at Miami."

The crisis had ended. Miami was now recognizing its financial obligations to maintaining sound alumni relations. Eventually, Dr. Kreger became not only a staunch supporter but also a close personal friend.

The alumni association I inherited could boast of a long past but little accomplishment. It was founded in 1832 when Miami had just sixty-nine graduates. Through more than a century, the association met only once a year. Its function was purely social and nostalgic.

The best way to develop alumni interest and build financial support is through personal contact. This meant organizing and maintaining chapters around the country. Speaking engagements on the War Crimes Trials led to meeting alumni. Our program was gaining strength. But I was a new man in town. I met with an identity crisis. How do you spell Dolibois? How do you pronounce it? Where did you get that accent? Luxembourg? Is that a town in Germany?

Patiently, diplomatically, I spelled, pronounced, explained. After overcoming those stumbling blocks, I faced another. Miami University is *not* in Florida.

I remember my first trip to New York City. The alumni wanted to see a football film. I obliged. After getting off the train at Grand Central I hailed a taxi, suitcase in one hand, film case in the other. The taxi driver looked at me quizzically.

"What have you got there buddy, a stag film?"

"No," I answered, "it's a football film."

"Oh yeah? Who looks at a football film in March?"

I continued to explain. "The alumni of my university, Miami University."

"Oh yeah? How's the weather down there?"

"No, it isn't in Florida. It's in Oxford, Ohio."

"Oxford is in England."

A moment of silence. A quick examination in the rearview mirror.

"Who are ya playin' in this game?"

"Ohio University."

"Oh yeah? Where ya playin', in Columbus or in Miami?"

"This isn't Ohio State we're playing. It's Ohio University, in Athens, Ohio."

"Oh yeah? Athens is in Greece, buddy."

We'd arrived at my hotel. I paid my fare to the skeptical driver and firmly resolved never to bring another film to New York City. I kept my pledge for twenty years, and then Miami, the little giant killer, beat mighty Purdue University. The New York alumni wanted to see the game film. I obliged.

After arriving at LaGuardia airport, I stepped into a taxi, suitcase in one hand, film case in the other. It wasn't the same driver or the same cab. But I did get a funny look. "What you got there, buddy, one of those porno films?"

I was twenty years older and wiser. "Yes!" I said. "I'm going to show it to a bunch of octogenarians at the Waldorf-Astoria tonight."

We rode into the city without further conversation. Now and then I caught him eyeing me suspiciously in the rearview mirror. I thought he looked a little hurt. Just before we arrived at my hotel, I decided to level with him. "Hey, I was just kidding, driver. This is really a football film."

"Oh yeah? Who looks at a football film in March?"

I braced myself. "The alumni of my university, Miami University."

"Say, that's the outfit in Ohio that beat Purdue, right?"

Right! Nothing succeeds like success. The identity crisis was gradually abating.

Another experience that stands out in my memory is that of working with the "GI students" who helped swell college enrollments dramatically in the postwar years, and played a significant role in changing the campus scene.

Following the treacherous attack on Pearl Harbor on December 7, 1941, a patriotic fervor had swept over the campus. Within the first week, hundreds of Miami men and women abruptly quit their classes and volunteered for military or public service. Most thought the war would last only a few months, or, at best, a year, after which they would return to their studies. They were simply interrupting their college careers for a short period.

But volunteers and draftees were in for the duration. It did not end until after the devastation of Hiroshima and Nagasaki in 1945. Would they ever come back to Miami? Many of them did.

The federal Congress had passed Law Number 346, the Serviceman's Readjustment Act of 1944, popularly known as the "GI Bill of Rights." It made possible a college education for anyone under twenty-six who had served in the armed forces of the United States since September 1940. Of course, this included those whose education had been interrupted by such service. The GI Bill provided tuition, fees, books, and a monthly allowance of fifty dollars for room and board. If the ex-serviceman had dependents, the subsistence allowance was seventy-five dollars per month.

At Miami, GI enrollment swelled dramatically with the opening of the school year in September 1946. While Winnie and I were preparing our home in Cincinnati for occupancy, hundreds of our former Miami classmates and friends were returning to Oxford to finish their studies. GI students from all over the United States, and from every branch of service, now walked down old Slant Walk on their way to classes, the library, or their dorms. Among the forty-one hundred students enrolled at Miami were two thousand veterans. They swapped stories about Guadalcanal, Midway Island, and the beaches of Luzon. They reminisced about tank battles in Normandy, bridgeheads on the Rhine, and air raids on Berlin.

I came to Oxford one weekend just to see their temporary quarters in Withrow Court gymnasium. They were sleeping in double-deck bunks; they were using footlockers, and clothes racks made of steel bars. This was the military all over again. But they took it in stride, determined to begin a new life.

By Thanksgiving 1946, they were moved to a veterans community south of the main campus where they were housed in genuine army barracks, brought to Oxford from Fort Knox and Camp Breckenridge in Kentucky. Officially, the rows of barracks were designated "Miami Lodges." The ex-GIs had their own names for them.

The Miami Lodges were set up near another postwar development which accommodated veterans with families. Prefabricated duplex dwellings and house trailers were arranged in a huge cluster. This was Veterans Village, Miami's first facility for married students. Nearly two hundred families lived in "Vetville." The strollers and baby buggies parked at the doors of many of these tiny units gave a new look to the Miami scene.

The facilities were cramped and crowded, but that didn't faze the young man studying with a book before him and a baby on his lap. He was now the resolute collegian, earnestly striving for success, determined to reach his goal. His wife probably went to classes with him, taking turns at baby-sitting with the next door neighbor. Other GI wives worked in Oxford business establishments or enrolled in noncredit courses in sewing, cooking, nursing, and interior decoration. Vetville was a happy, self-governed community.

Classroom space at Miami University was another scarce item. Twelve makeshift buildings were brought from military bases to the university campus. These temporary facilities were all filled to capacity when I arrived on campus in May 1947. That's why the first alumni office was a former restroom and faculty lounge in Ogden Hall. At least it was more permanent than the "temporary" army barracks, some of which served Miami for more than two decades. Before the present Shriver Center was constructed, a temporary Student Union, the "Redskin Reservation," served a steady stream of students taking coffee breaks at all hours of the day. The "Res" was also a makeshift facility, consisting of two army recreation halls thrown together to form a useful, popular social center.

The exodus from the lodges began in 1953 when three new residence halls were completed in the Fisher Hall area of the Miami campus. Vetville was gradually replaced when the university constructed permanent apartment buildings for married students. In time, Oxford became inundated with married student housing, as well as apartments for single students not interested in the more restrictive university dormitories.

The veterans were a far cry from the typical students I had known before the war. To begin with, they were, and looked, older. There was less bounce in their walk. A slower, more deliberate, step revealed a maturity not noticeable in a college sophomore rushing off to the "libe" or the "lab." You could pick out the veteran among those sitting in the Purity or other student hangouts. He drank his beer more slowly, deliberately. His conversation was generally more subdued, seldom punctuated by raucus laughter or carefree shouts. It focused more often on his studies, his plans for the future. Only on certain occasions, and when in the company of other veterans, would he talk about his war experiences.

And usually, it was the one who had never seen combat who boasted most of his exploits.

In the classroom the GI student was the one who kept the teacher honest. The professor was challenged, his theories were questioned. It was not unusual to see an older student get up and walk out of a class in which the lecturer was obviously not prepared. In short, the veterans had wasted enough of their time. They were serious about this business of education.

I was chapter counselor and adviser to the Betas during those postwar years. In some cases, the Beta students I was advising were a year or two older than I. At first I was surprised to find veterans in the fraternity, until I realized that for some, the close comradeship of fraternity life was just what they needed. For them, the word "brotherhood" had a deeper meaning than it had for the nonveterans, the younger members. GI students joined fraternities, or returned to them, for other reasons. Eating and sleeping in a fraternity house with just a few, was preferred to living in large residence halls or dormitories with several hundred.

The veteran tolerated the song fests, the serenades, or the sometimes juvenile pursuits of the younger "kids" in the house. They would even participate on occasion, in a sort of good-humored way. But generally they frowned on the "hell week" initiation activities and similar programs. These were judged puerile time-wasters.

Not everything I say here applied to all GI students. There were exceptions. When an ex-serviceman-turned-student got in trouble, it was big trouble. When veterans drank to get drunk, they went at it with a vengeance, and the consequences could be devastating. When they got into a fight, it became a battle.

A GI who could shack up with a Fräulein in Germany or a mademoiselle in France just by offering a candy bar or cigarette, had to learn new techniques in courting a college coed.

Younger students at Miami, those who had not seen military service, looked up to veterans. They respected, even admired, the men and women who had served their country and won the war. They regarded them as heroes. There was relatively little friction or animosity. All of this contributed substantially to the ease with which GI students fitted into the college scene. Such ready adaptation and acceptance wouldn't have been possible if the students on the GI Bill in 1947 had been met with the antipathy, resentment, and official indifference that confronted Vietnam veterans a generation later.

After the Second World War, men and women in all walks of life were given a chance at getting a college education. Persons who never dreamed of going to college were now able to join the chosen few, the elite of earlier years. Real democracy was at work in the academic life of the United States. It had far-reaching and positive results.

Academic courses were changed to accommodate the needs and interests of the GI students. More emphasis was placed on such subjects as automotive engineering, and engineering sciences. Paper technology, systems analysis, aeronautics, and other new courses were developed. The School of Applied Science emerged; and the School of Business Administration expanded classes in international finance and world banking. Freshmen students were writing themes about North Africa, New Guinea, and the Solomon Islands as veterans shared experiences from around the world.

The impact of veterans on intercollegiate athletics and recreational sports was strengthened by experience on military service teams. Many later distinguished themselves as national sports figures in professional athletics and coaching. Miami's Athletic Hall of Fame boasts a number of outstanding personalities who played at Miami as GI students.

What kind of alumni were those veterans? Top-notch! From where I sit, the graduates of Miami, whose college career had been interrupted, or made possible, by military service, stand out as loyal, supportive alumni. I look at the figures for annual and capital giving and I look at the list of leaders in alumni and development affairs over a period of years. The names of an overwhelming number of former GI students stand out as successful, ardent supporters of the institution. They are ever-grateful, appreciative of the opportunities given them, glad to have survived both a global war and the struggle for that GI degree.

Excellence and distinction do not grow of themselves. They must be nurtured and ultimately paid for. The Alumni Loyalty Fund was started in 1918 by President Raymond M. Hughes. Its purpose was to solicit an annual contribution from alumni to underwrite those programs for which tax money could not be used, i.e., scholarships, special library collections, faculty travel, emergencies. Each year the president's office would mail a postcard to alumni urging them to send a dollar to the Alumni Loyalty Fund. By 1947, when the alumni association took over the responsibility for soliciting such gifts, the Loyalty Fund was raising around $6,000. By 1961 the annual support had grown to more than $100,000. The half-million dollar mark was passed six years later. Now the annual fund brings in more than $5,000,000 annually in cash and gifts-in-kind.

We changed the name Loyalty Fund to "Miami University Fund," making it clear that not only alumni but all friends of the university could contribute. Miami became a leader in alumni support among all public universities in the country.

How did that happen? First of all, fund-raising is most successful through personal solicitation, people persuading people to give. But Miami alumni, parents and friends are scattered all over the United States. It was difficult to organize class agents and local fund committees. We had to rely almost exclusively on direct mail.

Then one day one of my fund-raising letters was returned by an alumnus who knew something about direct-mail solicitation. He helpfully had used a blue pencil to show me how my letters could be improved. The writer was John Yeck, class of 1934, who had been one of the senior leaders at Camp Manatoc when I was there as a Scout. After graduation from Miami he became a professional Scout executive in Dayton, Ohio. Later he resigned to go into business with his brother Bill, who had been my director in the Concord Camp at Manatoc. "Yeck and Yeck" handled direct mail advertising and related activities and, as the "Yeck Brothers Group," became nationally known.

John was an expert letter writer. He offered to critique my efforts. We asked him to serve on our development advisory council so that we could benefit from his expertise on a regular basis. In time, there evolved a formal business relationship. John Yeck's firm not only helped us design appealing letters but also printed and mailed them from their Dayton office.

Our Miami University Fund letters became known as "Happy Letters That Work." We received awards from the Direct Mail Advertisers Association, the Fund Raising Institute, the American Alumni Council, and the Council for Advancement and Support of Education. Our letters were low-key. We made the donors feel good about giving. We felt that our alumni responded because they wanted to; they had a friendly and pleasant feeling about the university. All our letters kept this in mind.

Our mailings were informal and personal, always signed by me, making each letter appear to be a direct line from me to the individual constituent. We mixed humor with seriousness, alternating our styles from letter to letter—nostalgia, common sense, pride, challenge, and humor were all ideas worked into a year's campaign. The letters were reproduced simply, never elaborate or costly. They worked.

But our letters alone weren't responsible for the remarkable success of our development and alumni program. I had an excellent staff. Over the years our activity expanded and more personnel was added. My first coworker was Helen Jo Scott Mann, who eventually became university editor and was responsible for the monthly magazine, *The Miami Alum-*

nus. My first full-time secretary was Ethelwyn Fox, a bright sixteen-year-old graduate of College Corner High School, five miles from Oxford. She was just what I needed at the time—loyal, efficient, capable, and full of the pioneer spirit. She could never keep shoes on her feet. A bare foot peeking out from under the typewriter table was an office fixture. A few years later Ethelwyn married a Miami graduate and moved to Marengo, Illinois, where her husband, Don Martello, is a high school teacher. She runs a Writer's Service, typing manuscripts for aspiring and established authors. Young Miss Fox was the first of a long string of dedicated pros in our program. Ours *was* a pioneer effort.

But we lacked specific direction. To provide some guidelines, Paul McNamara appointed a Long Range Program Committee to make a survey of alumni opinions, and to develop a master plan for us to follow. The chairman of this committee was Dr. Charles R. Wilson, class of 1926, and head of the history department at Colgate University. He organized a year-long study which concentrated on admissions and scholarships, student life, faculty and curricula, intercollegiate athletics, and public relations. Fifty prominent alumni took part in the survey, meeting with Miamians, using questionnaires to get their views. The result was a master plan which pointed the way for the alumni program for years to come.

I think one of our most significant accomplishments was the Miami University scholarship program. In postwar years, so-called "scholarships" were awarded only to students who demonstrated financial need. This didn't seem quite right to me and my alumni colleagues. There were athletic scholarships for students who excelled in sports. But the youngsters who excelled in academics could be rewarded only if their parents were willing to submit themselves to an intense bureaucratic examination of their economic status.

We decided to "test the market" in 1961 after many alumni parents complained about this unfair procedure. With a speech entitled "Scholarships: Do They Deserve Them or Need Them?" I appeared before service clubs and PTAs. There was vast support for the concept of the old-time merit scholarship programs. People were ready to make a distinction between awards for merit and grants for need.

At the behest of the alumni association, Miami's President John D. Millett took such a plan to the board of trustees which unanimously authorized it. Thus Miami University became one of the first institutions in the country to again give out scholarships on the basis of academic achievement, leadership, ambition, and special talent. At the same time we established a student grant-in-aid program for those who needed financial help. This included a tailor-made plan for assistance to minority students.

Today our merit scholarship policy is funded with a multi-million dollar endowment built up in the past twenty-five years, every cent from contributions. Recognition for academic achievement is an excellent recruiting device, attracting top-notch students to the university. Many other colleges and universities have gone back to awarding merit scholarships, as was done before World War II. Those who objected so strongly to the Miami system now point with pride at the high caliber students on campus, students attracted by those scholarships.

I think what motivated me the most was being in position to give to a new generation the kind of assistance and encouragement that made possible my own education at Miami. I had earned my scholarship in 1938, and now I was glad Miami saw fit once more to encourage deserving youngsters by providing incentive and reward.

One day in 1965 I received a letter from a high school senior in Marietta, Ohio. She was coming to Miami as a freshman. She had applied for a scholarship and been turned down, not because she wasn't qualified, but because there just weren't enough awards to go around. In her cordial letter she thanked me for the opportunity of applying for a merit scholarship. She was grateful for our consideration, and she complimented us for having a program that made students feel appreciated and wanted.

This letter was so well written and sincere, that we decided to create a special scholarship for this young lady. The local newspaper ran a story about Susan Lallathin from Marietta who earned a scholarship for being sensitive and thoughtful, in addition to being an outstanding student.

I met Susan Lallathin for the first time seven years later at a Miami alumni dinner in Washington. Her unusual name attracted my attention. We both recalled our earlier exchange of letters. She had since graduated from Miami and was working at the White House. Our son Bob was a lieutenant in the navy, serving in Washington, and at the same alumni dinner he met Susan. They had been classmates but didn't know each other on campus. Today, Susan Lallathin Dolibois is the mother of our two grandchildren, Ryan and Sara. Bob is in association management in Washington, D.C. Susan works part-time for Mrs. George Bush.

Our son Mike, no longer called Johnny-Mike, completed his residency in orthopedic surgery and established his practice in nearby Hamilton. Mike married Alison Hodgson, whom he met in his senior year at Miami. Our first grandchild, Kristen, was born in Columbus, and three years later her sister Lauren arrived. Watching our two granddaughters grow into lovely young ladies added substantially to the pleasure of living in Oxford. Dr. Dolibois has made Oxford home for his family.

Our third son Brian Charles was born eleven years after we thought our family was complete. Brian, like his two brothers, graduated from Miami University, and is now working as a computer programmer in Denver, Colorado.

While the boys were growing up, I began to feel the first pull toward Europe in 1963. After a seventeen-year absence, I wanted to see my old stamping grounds again. By then many colleges and universities were conducting alumni tours to Europe. I decided to try it, too. With thirty-five Miamians, and sixteen-year-old son Bob as assistant tour host, I arrived in Luxembourg. Little evidence of the war remained. The Marshall Plan had performed economic miracles in Luxembourg. Sightseeing in the Grand Duchy was a delight. Locating old friends added a special flavor. I had no relatives in Luxembourg. Brother Charles's widow, Rose, had died. There was no trace of my niece Renée, their adopted daughter. Rose had never written to us in the States.

Bob and I did manage a quick side trip to the Saar, where I could introduce him to my brothers Kasi and Heinrich and their families. Liesel joined us from Wiedenbruck for a family reunion of sorts. My sister Agnes and her two daughters, Ilse and Marianne, had immigrated to Chicago after her husband Gusty died. Our Papa never saw any of his European family again. He died in 1948.

This first postwar trip to Europe whetted my appetite for more. Two years later I persuaded Winnie to join me on another, a private trip. We took seven-year-old Brian with us. That was in 1965, when we were treated so royally at the Spanish Riding School in Vienna. This second visit also strengthened my ties to my native Luxembourg.

When Dr. Kreger died in 1961, President Millett brought Ray Wilson from Colgate as provost of Miami University. Dr. Wilson soon thereafter added a course in international studies to the curriculum. An optional feature of this course was a semester or year of study abroad. One of his Miami classmates of 1926 was Koishi Hasegawa, a professor at Waseda University in Japan, and they engineered a student exchange program between the two institutions. But their plans died aborning when Professor Hasegawa suffered a fatal heart attack. The study-year abroad plan went back to square one.

Dr. Wilson would not be discouraged. One day he and I chatted about the possibility of linking with an educational institution in Europe. I started thinking. There was no college or university in Luxembourg. Perhaps Miami could establish a branch in the Grand Duchy, staffed by our own faculty. Additional teachers could be recruited on a part-time basis from Luxembourg's educational system, which includes university-level instruction. A Miami branch in Luxembourg could offer courses in European history, political science, economics, and European literature. And of course, French and German. Luxembourg's central location would facilitate cultural trips to museums, concert halls, and government institutions in Western Europe. Brussels, Paris, Bonn, and The Hague all could be reached within hours. It was ideal.

Ray Wilson shared my enthusiasm, but that's as far as it went. Our colleagues were not persuaded. Where in God's name is Luxembourg? What kind of French do they speak? (This is from French teachers who had never been to Europe.) Modern transportation? Indoor plumbing? I exaggerate, but you get the idea. The point was that nobody got excited. The roadblocks were in place. The obstacle course had to be run.

At about this time in 1967, I was organizing another alumni tour to Europe. Luxembourg was again on the itinerary. Tour participants included Warren "Bud" Nelson, Ohio's director of highway safety, a member of the governor's cabinet. Governor James Rhodes had just established an office of economic development for Ohio in Brussels and I decided it ought to be easy to convince the governor that an educational relationship with the Benelux area might also be beneficial. At a cocktail party at Nelson's home in Lebanon, Bud steered me to the governor and encouraged me to make my pitch. Jim Rhodes was enthusiastic. He appointed a commission made up of several trustees, alumni, and the dean of fine arts. I was named chairman.

In Luxembourg my tour companions enjoyed the physical charms of my native country. Our itinerary included a formal dinner with select Luxembourg officials as our guests. The guest of honor was the Honorable Patricia Roberts Harris, U.S. ambassador to the Grand Duchy. Luxembourg's Ministry of Education was represented. Others attending were the director of the American School; Dr. Carlo Putz, president of the American Luxembourg Society; and a few prominent businessmen from American and Luxembourg firms.

The purpose of the dinner was to find out if there was any interest in our establishing a Miami University European Study Center in Luxembourg. The response was overwhelmingly positive.

We particularly needed faculty interest and support. Professor Warren Mason of our Department of Political Science was traveling in Italy with his wife Bonnie. I persuaded them to join us in Luxembourg to help sell the idea.

The governor's commission returned to Ohio with a positive report. But there was still a lot of doubt. Why Luxembourg? Why not Aix-en-

Provence in France or Basel in Switzerland? How about Copenhagen, or Vienna? We kept open minds. I kept my fingers crossed.

Correspondence from Luxembourg officials expressed much interest on their part. Miami's President Phillip Shriver heard all viewpoints patiently. He was willing to go along with the idea, but it had to be done right. It needed everyone's cooperation. Former President Millett, now chancellor of the Ohio Board of Regents, cleared the way for state support.

A four-man committee, chaired by Dr. Mason, traveled to Europe to inspect other possibilities. Serving on the committee were Professor Dwight Smith of the Department of History, Vice President for Student Affairs Robert F. Etheridge, and I. We made a round of visits to different places. We gave Luxembourg close scrutiny. We talked to educators, government officials, and interested citizens in every country and city being considered. Miami graduate Dr. Leslie S. Brady, Cultural Affairs officer in the American embassy in Paris, was extremely helpful.

After our "inspection trip" the committee unanimously agreed on Luxembourg. Its minister of Education, Jean Dupong, was willing to provide classroom space. They would also let us use the Luxembourg National Library and other educational facilities. The American Luxembourg Society would find housing for Miami students as paying guests in private homes. The American embassy gave its blessing.

A consultation committee worked out details: the course of study, credit, finances, staffing, etc. Every Tuesday evening we met in my home throughout the winter and spring months. Warren Mason was the mover and shaker, keeping the committee active and alert. My job was to round up financial support. Until we started to collect student fees, only gift money could be used for travel, purchase of equipment, scholarships, and miscellaneous start-up costs. Many Miami alumni, interested in international education, responded with generous contributions. We established several good-sized endowments for lasting support.

United States Senator Mark Hatfield of Oregon gave the commencement address at Miami University in the spring of 1968. On our way to Oxford from the airport we discussed my dream about a Miami branch in Luxembourg. "That's a capital idea," he said. "You ought to involve Perle Mesta."

That, too, was a capital idea. Madame Perle Mesta, appointed the first minister to the Grand Duchy of Luxembourg by President Truman in 1949, was the famous "hostess with the mostest." She had inspired the fantastically successful Broadway hit "Call Me Madam," and was a legend in the Grand Duchy. Senator Hatfield arranged a luncheon in the

Senate Dining Room in Washington where I had a chance to meet the famous lady.

I'll never forget the occasion. Mrs. Mesta was a dynamo, even in her retirement years. Dressed in pink from head to toe, she arrived in an immense black Cadillac at the senators' entrance to the Capitol building. At lunch our conversation was frequently interrupted as senator after senator came to our table to kiss her hand and pay homage. She loved talking about Luxembourg. She agreed to serve as honorary chairlady of the Consultation Committee and was delighted when I suggested we name one of our student scholarships for her in appreciation of her interest. She promised to do her best to attend the opening ceremony if her health and schedule permitted.

We were interrupted by a telephone call. As the phone was brought to our table, I couldn't help but overhear the conversation. It seemed she was late for an appointment with Vice President Hubert Humphrey. "Hubert," she cooed into the phone, "I'm sorry I've kept you waiting. I've been engrossed in talk about Luxembourg and lost all track of time. Now you wait right there and I'll be over in twenty minutes."

Thus ended my memorable visit with the famous Perle Mesta. I'm sure that having her name connected with the Miami University European Center contributed to the ready acceptance of our program in Luxembourg.

On October 10, 1968, the opening convocation of the center, with Dr. Warren Mason as its first director, was held in the Municipal Theater. Their Royal Highnesses, the Grand Duke and Grand Duchess, honored us with their presence, as did a number of government officials and prominent citizens. Ambassador George Feldman entertained the Miami officials, including President and Mrs. Shriver, at a luncheon. Winnie and I sat for the first time at table in what was to become our own dining room in 1981.

When Richard Nixon was elected president of the United States, some of my Ohio friends in Congress persuaded him to appoint me to the Board of Foreign Scholarships which administers the well-known, highly respected Fulbright Program, the Cultural and Educational Exchange Act. During my tenure, the program was directed through the offices of the assistant secretary of state for Educational and Cultural Affairs. I was excited about working at this level of our national government. I hoped I could be useful.

Bimonthly meetings of the board were productive, busy sessions lasting two or three days. The Board of Foreign Scholarships takes part in the selection of thousands of Fulbright grantees, those coming to the

United States and those going abroad. When I asked what happened to the grantees following their return from abroad, I learned that there was no continued contact. "Why not have a Fulbright Alumni Association?" I suggested. Its members would become a powerful voice in lobbying Congress. Organized on a geographical basis, they could interview candidates for grants, and promote educational and cultural exchange. The possibilities were endless. My proposal struck a responsive chord. I prepared a working paper.

During the thirtieth anniversary year of the BFS a Fulbright Alumni Association was organized. But alumni themselves finally did the job, not the BFS or the State Department. President Jimmy Carter's administration transferred the BFS to the jurisdiction of the U.S. Information Agency. State was no longer involved. My own membership on the board ended in 1977. After eight years in this challenging assignment I missed being a part of the Washington scene, missed hobnobbing with diplomats and foreign dignitaries. I found that sort of life could easily become habit-forming.

During my thirty-four years in university advancement, my colleagues and a large number of alumni volunteers engaged in all kinds of endeavors of benefit to Miami and the community. We organized support for educational bond issues. We sponsored lecture series and public concerts. We established endowments to support these projects in perpetuity. Young artists were enabled to exhibit their works under alumni sponsorship. A Young Artists Guild arranged concerts for promising musicians. We promoted books on the history of Miami University, including *The Miami Years* and *Men of Old Miami* by Walter Havighurst; we published a biography of Raymond M. Hughes, *A Leader of Men*, written by Arthur C. Wickenden. Ophia Smith, wife of one of our former history professors, published *Old Oxford Houses* with our assistance. Contributions to the Miami University Fund made all such projects possible.

National recognition came to the Miami University Alumni Association when the American Alumni Council presented us with its Alumni Administration Award in 1966. This honor was repeated six years later. Our program ranked in the top 1 percent of all public and private institutions of higher education. This was a tribute to the thousands of Miami alumni whose volunteer efforts made possible these achievements.

Fund-raiser or Builder?

UPON OCCUPYING my first alumni office in the faculty lounge and former men's rest room of Ogden Hall in 1947, I had voiced a solemn vow to some day have an alumni building of our own. This dream didn't begin to materialize until July 1, 1965 when Dr. Phillip R. Shriver became Miami's seventeenth president. Among other things he named a cabinet of four vice presidents, and I was one of them. I would continue my responsibilities in development and alumni affairs and would now officially represent a vital area of the university community.

Miami University owned an attractive piece of land on the southern edge of town, overlooking an abandoned cornfield in a broad valley below. This site was originally acquired to provide a new residence for Miami presidents. But the plans were abandoned because Dr. Shriver and his family preferred the traditional old Lewis Place which had served as home to Miami presidents for several generations. So the lot on top of the hill at the edge of town was made available to the alumni association. All we needed was the money to build on it.

Miami had a good friend in William Murstein of Hamilton, Ohio, founder and owner of Wilmur's department store. He was civic-minded, involved in national and international philanthropic projects. He had already contributed a valuable collection of etchings by the twentieth century master Georges Rouault to the university and had established a merit scholarship endowment in memory of his brothers. I had good reason to believe Bill Murstein might be interested in funding a future alumni headquarters. The board of trustees, always supportive of our development efforts, would surely name it the Murstein Alumni Center.

Mr. Murstein agreed to contribute half of the total cost of the building if we could match his gift with contributions from alumni. In amazingly short time, a number of generous donors materialized. In 1968, we were able to dedicate the new Alumni Center. Unfortunately, Bill Murstein died shortly before the dedication. He never saw the finished building of which he would have been immensely proud.

At about that same time, another major donor came to the fore, Fred W. Climer, class of 1917. Like so many Miamians he had married a classmate. Fred and his wife Irene were from Akron where he was vice president of the Goodyear Tire and Rubber Company. It was Fred who had presented me to P. W. Litchfield, twenty years after that gentleman had awarded me my Eagle Scout badge. Mr. Climer was active in the alumni club in Akron with Ken Gambee and others who sold me on Miami University. Later he was instrumental in the establishment of the Goodyear plant in Luxembourg. Fred proposed a capital gift to the university for an addition to a student residence hall. This would be a wing with guest rooms for trustees and official guests of the university.

I made a counterproposal. Since we were building the Murstein Alumni Center, why not add a guest wing to it? We would call it the Climer Guest Lodge. It would have nine guest rooms, one for each trustee. It would also have a small social lounge and a kitchenette for breakfasts and snack service. The adjacent Alumni Center would be handy for board meetings and social gatherings. Mr. and Mrs. Climer were delighted. In 1969 we dedicated the Climer Guest Lodge, a beautiful addition to our alumni headquarters and hospitality center.

Other gifts made possible seminar rooms, faculty lounges, or library sections in tribute to former faculty members. Almost every academic building on the campus has one or more such memorial rooms. They add much to the campus atmosphere and the learning environment. They are reminders of a "Miami Family" whose members are never forgotten.

While the new university library was under construction, I was asked to be on the lookout for a donor who might furnish an area housing rare books and artifacts, manuscripts and documents. Then one day the morning mail brought me a "personal" letter from Santa Fe, New Mexico. When I opened it a check for fifty thousand dollars fell out. The letter was from Ken Grubb, a former student of Walter Havighurst. His check was a contribution to the Miami University Fund and was earmarked for whatever purpose might best serve as a tribute to his beloved teacher. I moved fast. I suggested the special collections library room as a splendid way to honor Professor Havighurst. Ken Grubb agreed enthusiastically, and added substantially to his initial gift because he wanted to do it right. His contribution made possible an exquisitely designed reading room and an adjoining stack holding Miami's rare collections, including the many books written by Walter and Marion Havighurst.

I shall never forget the rewarding day on which I took the decorator's plan to Walter and Marion and surprised them with the news of Ken Grubb's generous gesture. It was one of the highlights of my career as a development officer.

Another good friend of the university was Fred C. Yager, who had graduated from Miami in 1914. Fred was a successful broker. In time he became one of my favorite people. His wife had died shortly before I met him. He had no children, no other family. He took a liking to me, and I, in turn, to him. I enjoyed the excitement and challenge of his friendship. He spoke his mind whenever he was so inclined. His sense of humor was refreshing. He entertained lavishly, and Miami's Athletic Director John Brickels was one of his favored guests. Fred enjoyed "Stub" Brickels's company, as did so many. It naturally followed that he would ask Brickels's opinion on how the Yager fortune might eventually benefit Miami University—that is, if he, Fred, "should feel inclined to make a generous provision." Brickels had the answer: "a new stadium." Fred posed the same question to President Millett who agreed. Miami Field, which had been in service since 1918, was located on a site better suited for an academic building. It was the smallest of all the stadia in the Mid-American Conference.

Fred Yager became known as a super football fan, whose name would probably be on a future stadium. The cultivation process was under way. Fred loved it. When Phillip R. Shriver became president, he too endorsed the proposal. He regularly invited Fred Yager and his friends to home football games. On several occasions through the years, the game ball was presented to Mr. Yager after a significant victory. He was guest of honor at athletic banquets and a regular attendant at pregame luncheons and postgame receptions.

Yet, I think I'm the only person in whom Fred confided that he really didn't "give a good Goddamn for football." He'd never seen a game until after he'd agreed to consider giving part of his estate to a stadium project. It was our private joke.

Fred's nephew had graduated from Miami in 1929. The young man was killed in a tragic auto accident shortly thereafter. He had been close to his uncle, and when Yager became an active participant in Miami affairs, the uncle decided to honor his nephew's memory. He wanted to finance a memorial gate to the university. I was urged to find a good place to put it.

Now frankly, Miami needed another entrance gate like I needed smallpox, but I wasn't about to discourage the donor. Especially not one like

Fred Yager who had a mind of his own. So where could we put another gate?

The window of my office in the new Murstein Alumni Center looked out over the valley of Bull Run Creek, also known as Collins Run. The valley once held a lush cornfield, but now was overgrown with ragweed, slewgrass and burdock. I envisioned a neat park and playground, eighty acres of green belt around that portion of Oxford, an attractive approach to the city. I took Fred Yager to the top of the hill. I invited him to visualize a handsome shelter with cooking grills, benches, and tables for picnics; a softball diamond, a nature trail, and of course, "entrance gates." This all could become Maurice Peffer Memorial Park. Fred reached for his checkbook. He was elated. He more than tripled the size of the gift he had originally intended.

Within a year that wasteland was transformed into a first-rate "village green." In time we added a fountain, toilet facilities, a handsome patio, and a walk leading to the park area from Murstein Alumni Center. Stone benches provided a resting place for those going up or down the walk. A sundial spelled out a bronze message: "We live in deeds, not years." From my office window I could watch Cub Scouts having a picnic, kids flying their kites, fraternities playing ball, and families having outings. Peffer Park was the place for Alumni Weekend parties and outdoor class reunions. I began to understand the definition of development as "alertness to opportunity." There were many opportunities not to be missed in the planning of programs and facilities that added to Miami stature and charm. Professionally and personally I felt challenged.

Ever since we decided on the Sesquicentennial Chapel as our first major capital project, I was convinced that anything was possible if all segments of the university family worked together. Alumni and students, faculty and staff agreed to commemorate the 150th anniversary with an all-faith chapel. President Millett said it best:

> There can be no finer gift to the future. As laboratory facilities and technical books become obsolete and are replaced, and become again obsolete, this Chapel will stand firm for the enduring inspiration of the spirit.

Gifts of all sizes began pouring in when the chapel project was first announced. Some gave Chapel Shares of one thousand dollars or more; others contributed Progress Shares of three hundred to one thousand dollars. There were opportunities for named or memorial gifts: the pipe organ, choir loft, the portico, chimes, the chancel, windows, pews, pulpit, altar, and baptismal font.

The chapel stands today, an oasis of quiet in a campus that has grown larger and more hurried. It is used for student and alumni weddings, baptisms, and memorial services; organ recitals, lectures, and religious services or observances by campus organizations of whatever faith. It is a sanctuary for meditation.

In the process of building the chapel, we also had learned how to conduct future campaigns for capital projects. I had long been convinced that we needed an art museum at Miami. Over the years we had acquired a number of valuable art objects, gifts in kind contributed by alumni and friends of the university. I saw the human enlightenment of an art museum in balance to library resources and laboratory instruments. A museum would attract further gifts, bringing increasing enrichment in the years ahead. But I came up against inertia, indifference, even outright obstruction and hostility. I was told over and over there were adequate museums in Cincinnati and Dayton, and galleries in Middletown and Hamilton. In fact, we had a small gallery in our own fine arts building. I would need a lot of support if this particular dream was ever to materialize.

Miss Orpha Webster, professor of art emeritus, was loved and respected by one and all. In looking back on her many years of teaching at Miami, she recalled with much affection one of her favorite students, Walter Farmer, a noted interior decorator in Cincinnati. Walter was also a prominent collector of art and was courted by several large museums wanting to inherit his valuable collection. In Miss Webster's opinion, Walter Farmer's acquisitions should come to Miami University. She took Winnie and me to Farmer's home where we saw an immense collection of the finest ancient Roman artifacts, pre-Columbian glass, statuary, Luristan bronzes, paintings, etchings, tapestries, and antique furnishings. We were impressed with his catholicity of taste, his knowledgeable presentation of the works he cherished.

In time I got to know Walter Farmer well enough to ask him about his plans for the future. Would he consider giving his collection to Miami? He was very blunt in his reply. He'd love to give his collection to Miami, but only if we had some place to display it. He wasn't about to have his precious treasure stored in boxes in some basement or warehouse. It was meant to be seen and appreciated. So, if Miami wanted it, Miami would have to build an art museum.

Orpha Webster became a loyal supporter. She had influential friends. She was instrumental in our getting a few other valuable items, particularly the Elma Pratt International Folk Art Collection, named for the donor.

But officially, we got a cool reception. Miami's provost, David Brown, said it all in a letter to President Shriver: "My strong and basic conviction is that museum-like activities have only indirect and rather small spill-over benefits to the classroom and to our major enterprise of educating students. The museums that populate so many university campuses are prestige monuments, tone-setters—not educational laboratories. We must not divert dollars. . . ."

Dr. Brown pretty much spoke for many of his colleagues in the academic division, especially the art department itself. He advocated authorizing the museum project only with "the specific and clear assurance that the capital and operating costs be covered by gift dollars not available to the university for higher priority needs."

He went on: "Thus the crucial question is, 'could the dollars that would be spent on a museum be in fact spent elsewhere?' My guess is that because of the nature of alumni giving, the depth of John's enthusiasm for the museum project and the special desires of several major donors now in the pipeline, there are many dollars that would be used on this project that would not otherwise be available. . . . If you agree with my belief that museums are not of direct educational value in terms of the academic program of the University, then it would seem logical to assign the responsibility for operating the museum to public relations and thereby to John Dolibois."

In other words, if Dolibois wants it, he'll have to get the money to build it; and then operate it afterwards. The president and the board of trustees encouraged me to proceed on that basis. In short time we had an art museum advisory committee hard at work in promoting interest and financial backing. Several major donors bequeathed substantial sums to Miami for the art museum project.

In our home one evening the phone rang at eleven o'clock. My good friend Fred Yager was on the line. He was upset. "Can you come and see me right away, John? Goddamn it, I can't sleep. I have to talk to you."

I dressed and drove the fifty miles to Dayton, arriving at his apartment long after midnight. Fred was pacing the floor. "Why didn't you tell me you were planning to build an art museum? Didn't you know that my wife was an artist? Hell, I'd rather give my money to Miami for an art museum than a football stadium." He fumed on for at least ten minutes. I just listened. Suddenly he announced he'd made up his mind. He would see his attorney first thing in the morning and change his will. He would leave his money for the art museum project.

I broke into a cold sweat. My museum project was not enjoying one tenth as much interest as a new football stadium. If Fred Yager changed his will, everyone would accuse me of having persuaded him to do so. I'd really be in hot water.

I talked fast, reminding Fred that everyone associated with Miami was aware of his commitment to the football stadium. It would be very embarrassing to change things, especially since architectural plans had already been drawn. The board had already consented to name the stadium for him. Furthermore, I would be tarred and feathered and run out of town if he changed his will in favor of the museum.

Eventually, we had a calm discussion of what could be worked out. He still insisted on having a role in the development of the art museum. But if I could assure him that Miami would indeed construct a football stadium that was reasonably priced and not too ostentatious—in short, *possible*—he would stick to his original intent. The sun was coming up when I said goodbye to Fred Yager and started out for home.

He did change his will that same morning. He provided generously for a bequest to a hospital in memory of his mother. He spelled out a generous gift to Miami University for the art museum. The bulk of his estate was earmarked for the Fred C. Yager Memorial Stadium at Miami University.

In due course, a magnificent art museum was built. It was designed by Walter Netsch of Skidmore, Owings and Merrill. It is of modern design, on which Walter Farmer insisted. It is a great asset to Miami University. And shortly after its opening it came under the jurisdiction of the academic division of the university—much to my relief, I should add. I was hardly qualified to supervise a nationally accredited art museum.

While I was involved in development projects, another movement was taking place. The student unrest which swept over the entire nation in the 1960s also embraced Miami Univeristy. A determined minority of restless college students forced us to examine, and even change, institutions, rules, and values which were once considered inviolate. All of a sudden we were dealing with activist, alienated students. They were articulate, irreverent, humorless, and relentless in their contempt for what they viewed as adult hypocrisy. Among them were sensitive and perceptive individuals. They were highly intelligent. It didn't matter that a great majority, a "silent majority," remained largely content, conservative, and apathetic. It was a well-organized minority that called the shots.

One evening Winnie and I returned from a movie in Hamilton. On turning into the campus on our way home, we were shocked to be confronted with police cars and barriers. We smelled tear gas and saw students being threatened by police dogs. The student rebellion had begun at Miami. I felt that something very precious was being destroyed, but the "revolution" had to run its course. The university was in crisis. As a member of the president's cabinet, I wanted to restore order. I believed in cracking down. If this meant mass expulsions and mass firings, so be it.

President Shriver heard me out, and listened to many others of the same opinion. And then he did what he thought was right. He made concessions. He closed down the university on demand of the radicals and in response to their threats of violence. He listened to all sides. He talked to radical faculty and students, when most of us felt he should ignore them, turn a deaf ear towards them. Along with many others, I gnashed my teeth in anguish, and decided our president lacked guts; he was allowing himself to be used. And I frankly told him so.

I was wrong. Phil Shriver saved the university. He endured abuse, stress, and strain, and almost single-handedly re-established a sense of unity on the campus. Miami University is deeply in debt to him. Besides that, he has been a personal friend to me through all the years since. Having that friendship is one of the rewards for service to Miami which I cherish most. By example, he taught me patience, tolerance, and greatness of heart. When it was all over he wrote to me: "I am most appreciative of the role you have played in helping to keep us afloat in spite of these stresses, and for this I am most grateful." I accepted that accolade somewhat shamefacedly, not sure that I deserved it.

The odd aspect of the entire student unrest affair was that I actually sympathized with the students in their views of the Vietnam War and the need to restructure the governance of our colleges and universities. I simply disagreed with their methods. I failed to see how being unkempt and filthy could help them sell their views. And I couldn't see how the war in Vietnam could be ended by holding sit-ins at the library or burning down ROTC buildings.

While we were coping with student unrest in Oxford—and across the nation—our son Bob was on a destroyer in the Gulf of Tonkin. Bob had graduated from Miami in 1969. He was enrolled in the NROTC and commissioned an ensign at commencement time. His first duty was on the USS *Eversole;* his first combat was on February 15, 1970 when his ship bombarded a Vietnam base camp on the Mekong Delta.

This was a devastating experience for Bob, and I will never forget the long letter he wrote the same day expressing his horror and concerns. He wasn't sure the fight was "fair": ". . . not so much as a scratch sustained by an *Eversole* sailor." Bob was worried because he just felt numb afterwards instead of being elated or, on the other hand, nauseated. He questioned this "Pyrrhic victory."

No, our son didn't take kindly to the war in Vietnam. But he did his duty and we were mighty proud of him. Our concerns for his safety and well-being were intermingled with the resentment we felt toward the "protestors" safely doing their thing here at home. It was all very confusing.

The tragic shooting at Kent State University brought an end to this disturbing period on university campuses. One by one, colleges and universities which had been closed reopened; schedules were resumed. Sanity was restored. Some necessary reforms were made. And in our development effort we had to do some healing too. Miami alumni, parents, and friends had recoiled in horror and reacted instinctively. And they split. Some were angry at students for revolting; others were angry at the administration either for standing firm or giving in.

In June 1970 I wrote a long letter to all alumni, bluntly addressing the issue. I asked our constituents to let me know what they think, how they feel. Helpfully. Constructively. Miami needed their advice. Their responses would be made available to the trustees, to the students, to all in between who were interested.

I admitted that the Miami University Fund had suffered; mailings had been delayed; prepared appeals scrapped; attention distracted. The fate of the fund and all the services performed through it was in their hands.

At alumni club functions, and in subsequent mailings, we stressed the fact that "there *are* fine students at Miami who receive and should receive assistance; that there are books to buy, trees and ideals to plant; men to remember and fine projects to encourage." The response to this fence-mending was most heartening. Miami contributors reacted positively to a potentially negative situation.

Within another year, Miami was being recognized nationally for the successful growth of our program. I was invited to many institutions as consultant, to explain how we did it. It was easy. At Miami we had the wholehearted support of the president, the board of trustees, a vast majority of faculty and students, and, of course, thousands of alumni. I can't recall ever having an Alumni or Development Council proposition turned down. There was never lack of encouragement or support. It stands to reason such a team effort would lead to success.

I was checking off my thirtieth year at Miami when talk about a major gifts campaign first started. A feeble effort to raise a million dollars had been made back in the early twenties; it had failed for the obvious reason that no groundwork had been laid. This time, we were ready. Feasibility studies, organization, and implementation began in 1976-77.

Our goal was set at fourteen million dollars. The campaign was dubbed "Goals for Enrichment." The first five million dollars we expected to raise was earmarked for academic enrichment: faculty grants, library support, research, scholarships, and laboratory resources. The art museum, a conference center, and "relocation, enlargement and modernization of the football stadium" were the three major capital projects to be funded with gifts pledged to Goals for Enrichment. The slogan "larger usefulness awaits" appeared on all promotional literature.

Our dear friend Fred Yager died during the campaign. As promised, his estate provided a good base for the stadium project, with additional financing coming from the state of Ohio. Fred C. Yager Stadium is a handsome addition to the Miami campus. The boldly modern art museum was under construction when we launched the major gift program. By then enough gift funds had been committed to enable us to start the building itself. The Fred Yager Lecture Hall is a striking feature of the art museum. So is the Orpha Webster Gallery.

Joe and Sarah Marcum, from Hamilton, Ohio, contributed generously to the cost of the Timothy Marcum Conference Center in memory of their son, who had been killed in an auto accident. The Marcum Center now stands on the site of romantic old Fisher Hall which had been razed when it was beyond reclaiming. The three-story brick center is modeled upon the Wren Building of William and Mary College in Virginia, the oldest academic structure in the nation. In addition to the guest rooms, and conference and meeting facilities, the Marcum Center includes a Memorial Room which contains the memorabilia of four-star General John Edwin Hull, class of 1915. The room is in honor of all Miamians who have given their lives in defense of our country.

Goals for Enrichment was chaired by Charles Mechem, CEO of the Taft Broadcasting Company, a Miami grad who subsequently became a member of the board of trustees. Charlie was assisted by a cabinet of twenty-two dedicated men and women. Their efforts were greatly advanced by the gifts from Fred Yager, the Marcums, and Walter Farmer. And when the job was done, we could announce that more than fifteen million dollars had been raised.

When the campaign was officially launched, I told myself it would be the climax of my Miami career. If it met with success I would take early retirement in 1982, ending thirty-five years of affiliation with the university. I wanted to share my experiences with others aspiring to a career in university advancement. I would become a lecturer and consultant on university relations. I would emphasize in my speechmaking that enthusiasm and eagerness, a strong excitement about the opportunity to serve, were essential to success in development work; that it requires a willingness to accept an entry-level position, to learn about the profession from the bottom up. Among other qualities I would list a kind of self-reliance that leads to the pursuit of excellence. Development workers would need to show compassion and a liking for people, a willingness to serve them all, rich or poor. And finally, I would list two elements which helped me enormously in wending my way through the Dolibois years at Miami: first, a scrupulous sense of fair play, respect for the rights of my fellow man; and second, a sense of humor, the ability to laugh at the frequent absurdity of the human condition, and most important, the frequent absurdity of my *own* condition. I wasn't always successful at living up to this "code of the profession" but I tried, I really tried.

When our son Bob returned from his three years in Vietnam, he was considering signing up for a second tour in the navy. "And after that, what will you do?" asked his mother. Bob had always talked about becoming a lawyer. Now he was no longer sure of that course. When pressed by Winnie, he announced his decision. "I want to follow in Dad's footsteps," he said.

Winnie was astonished. "You want to be a fund-raiser?" Bob's reply will always loom large in my memories.

"Dad's not a fund-raiser," he answered, "he's a builder. When he goes to the office in the morning he passes the Sesquicentennial Chapel, one of the first projects for which he raised money. His office is in Murstein Alumni Center, next to Climer Guest Lodge, both of which his efforts made possible. From his office window he looks down on Peffer Park. It is there because Dad had the vision to develop it."

He continued: "Across the street is the art museum for which Dad struggled against all odds. In every section of the campus is a building with seminar rooms, lounges, or libraries which Dad and his colleagues brought into being. One out of every twenty students he meets on campus has a scholarship, a loan, or grant, for which Dad's activities are responsible. He's building a better university, not just raising money."

Needless to say, when Winnie repeated that conversation to me, with tears in her eyes, I walked tall. I've walked tall ever since.

My tenure at Miami didn't quite reach thirty-five years. In the summer of 1981, the goal of our major gift campaign was in sight. By the end of the year it was surpassed. On October 1, I thanked the alumni who made my thirty-four years at Miami a rewarding and satisfying career. Leaving Miami after so many years was a wrenching experience. At the same time, of course, I was ecstatic. You'll have to excuse that. I had never been appointed an ambassador before. It would take a little time to get adjusted.

Upstairs at the Embassy

SWITCHING FROM VICE PRESIDENT for University Relations to Ambassador Extraordinary and Plenipotentiary was heady stuff. The swearing-in ceremony at the State Department and meeting with the president at the White House were enough to inflate anyone's ego. But then came the VIP flight to Paris and a glamorous party and overnight stay at the American embassy. By the time our driver Claude delivered us to our own embassy in Luxembourg on the evening of October 11, 1981, I was all primed for what was obviously going to be a fantastic experience.

At 11:15 the next morning we were ready to present my credentials to His Royal Highness, Grand Duke Jean. I had made one trip to the palace earlier that morning to meet with Christian Calmes, the marshal of the court, who would steer us through the presentation ceremonies.

I was pleased to learn that the Grand Duke would receive us informally. Usually this solemn function calls for several new ambassadors to appear at the same time. In that case, "grande tenue"—white tie and tails and decorations—is required. The entire affair, although colorful, could be somewhat stiff and impersonal. I decided the less formal presentation was a good omen.

Since ours was an informal ceremony, the accredited members of our embassy staff had also been invited and were already waiting for us at the palace. Marshal Calmes ushered all of us into the elegant ballroom for a short wait. Suddenly there was a flurry of activity. A door opened, and the marshal led me into what is known as the Kings' Room, where the Grand Duke and the Grand Duchess greeted me. I presented my credentials, a formal letter from President Reagan, attesting to my status and authority. I had prepared a short formal speech, but the Grand Duke graciously waved the protocol aside, and motioned for the marshal to bring in Winnie.

I spent the rest of that memorable day making courtesy calls on the foreign minister and a few other government officials. The Luxembourg protocol officer briefed me on the procedure for the weeks ahead. I would visit the prime minister and all the other ministers of state. I was expected to call on the bishop of Luxembourg and the grand rabbi; then pay my respects to the mayor of the city, the chief of the European Court of Justice, the president of the Chamber of Deputies, and the president of the Council of State.

Calls on every ambassador of every nation represented in Luxembourg were required. Winnie was to visit their wives. After that, each of the ambassadors and their wives would make return calls at our embassy. Eventually I should visit major industries, get acquainted with business leaders, bankers, and the president of the labor unions. The next few weeks would be busy ones.

Luxembourg is a constitutional monarchy, ruled by the Grand Duke. The diplomatic atmosphere is sprinkled with glamour. Protocol is strictly observed. I love pomp and ceremony, so all of this activity added to the charm and the challenge of adapting to our new lifestyle. I could hardly wait to take on my first chore as the American ambassador to Luxembourg. It came sooner than I expected, and with it came the realization that I was just a simple public servant after all.

On the morning of our second day, we were scheduled to welcome a group of traveling Americans, members of the Los Angeles Council of World Affairs. The meeting, at nine o'clock sharp, was to be an embassy briefing, with coffee and croissants. In anticipation of all ahead of me, and after the exhilarating encounters so far enjoyed, I was all charged up, dressed and ready a half hour before the visitors were due. It was a good thing. They arrived fifteen minutes early. Winnie was still upstairs dressing. Dominique, the butler, was setting the dining room table for the twenty-five guests.

I saw the bus pull up in front of the embassy, watched the U.S. Marine security guard open the gate. I rushed to the front door to greet our guests. The door opened, and the first, a woman, entered. I put on my best smile, held out my hand. "Welcome to the American embassy," I said. She handed me her raincoat and sailed past me into the dining room. Dumbfounded, I didn't even know where the coatroom was. But I found it quickly, and while I was hanging up the lady's coat, another dozen or more of our visitors filed in. So much for my initial attempt at being ambassador extraordinary. I learned my first lesson. The *butler* commands the front door.

It appeared that other commitments had been made before our arrival. One of them was a concession to the American Women's Club. Winnie was the honorary president of this prestigious organization, whose principal activity is raising money for the annual international charity bazaar. The 1981 fund-raising project was a one-act play, "Don't Drink the Water." The setting of this comedy is an American embassy, and the use of our residence had been promised the Women's Club before our arrival.

Now the fun started. For the next entire week, we were confined to the upstairs; restricted to our bedroom and a small study. Dominique served our meals on trays. Downstairs was reserved for rehearsals and the actual performances. Seating for the audience was in the main parlors and dining room. The stage was in an alcove of the music corner. The library served as dressing room. For seven days we were treated to the sounds of stage construction, the moving of furniture, the voices in rehearsal, and the coaching of the director.

"Don't Drink the Water" was a hilarious success. Our part in it was to greet the theater-goers on arrival, and to host a champagne reception afterwards. It turned out to be the first of many charities we were expected to support. I was beginning to understand why so many ambassadors are millionaires.

Besides the many courtesy calls I had to make, a host of other official functions occupied our time. In just ten days we welcomed members of the Chicago Navy League, a People-to-People tennis group, and the faculty and students of the Miami University European Center in Luxembourg. I became an honorary member of Luxembourg Rotary, spoke to the American Business Men's Club, attended a MUEC convocation, and was interviewed for one hour on a RTL television show. Somewhere in that ten-day period we managed to be entertained at three dinners and two luncheons. The pace never slowed.

We celebrated our first Thanksgiving at a dinner with members of the American Luxembourg Society. On the Sunday before that, I read President Reagan's proclamation in the English-speaking church where I had joined the British ambassador two weeks earlier in placing a poppy wreath to commemorate Armistice Day. On Thanksgiving Day itself, we enjoyed our turkey dinner with the American members of our staff who had no families of their own. All of the embassy staff came to the residence for a surprise birthday party on December 4. I was celebrating my sixty-third, just a short distance from my birthplace in Bonnevoie.

Our third month in Luxembourg ended with a Christmas party for the entire staff and their families. Winnie had spent several weeks shopping for presents for each of the twenty-one children. We imported a genuine American Santa Claus from the nearby U.S. air base in Bitburg. A fifteen-foot Christmas tree adorned the large lobby of our house, and provided a perfect backdrop for the party. It also added to the spirit of the "Christmas Drink" several days later. This event, repeated annually, became a highlight of our social calendar. We invited all members of the diplomatic corps, government officials, prominent Luxembourg and American businessmen and their spouses. With Christmas music in the background and a generous banquette of food and drink, the yuletide spirit prevailed. I was particuarly pleased to have the Soviet and Bulgarian ambassadors attend every one of our Christmas Drink affairs. Meanwhile, Winnie was making her mark as a popular hostess.

Another popular hostess, Perle Mesta, was often mentioned by our Luxembourg friends. As the first resident envoy extraordinary and minister plenipotentiary, she had made a lasting impression, and not just for being the first. Her "open-house" generosity was appreciated no end by Luxembourgers who had endured four years of hardship under German occupation. The many GIs in and out of Luxembourg were always welcome at the residence on boulevard Emmanuel Servais. Stories about her legendary personality were still making the rounds when we arrived.

Mrs. Mesta's entry to Luxembourg in September 1949 was not as smooth as mine in 1981. She, too, came from Paris by automobile. A special welcome had been arranged for her. After all, she was the first American chief of mission named to Luxembourg. She should be welcomed in style. So high-ranking government officials were at the French-Luxembourg border with flowers, music, and enthusiasm.

But her chauffeur took the wrong road. She completely missed the welcoming party at the border, arriving in Luxembourg City by another route, unheralded.

In time, the persistent town fathers caught up with her. Flowers were presented. The band played. Speeches were made. Mrs. Mesta was overwhelmed. She was a woman of few words. She called for an interpreter to help her respond to all this warmth.

"I'm so happy to be here," she said.

"Ech sin esou glécklech hei ze sin," translated a Luxembourg linguist.

"I like you all very much."

"Ech hun Iech alleguer ganz gär."

"And I hope you will like me too."

"An ech hoffen Dir Kënnt mech och gär hun."

A titter ran through the crowd. The Luxembourg language has some double meanings, too. "Dir Kënnt mech gär hun" is also the expression used to tell someone to "go jump in the lake."

Having a woman minister was a new experience for the Luxembourgers. "What shall we call you?" one of them asked Mrs. Mesta. "Call me Madame," she answered. The rest is legend.

So is the title "hostess with the mostest." Luxembourgers told us about one memorable party given by Perle Mesta that touched the hearts of every citizen. She invited all the mayors of the country to her house for hot dogs and cokes. It was a gesture which appealed to Luxembourgers. They considered it a gracious salute to themselves.

Well, Winnie and I heard that party mentioned so often that we finally took it as a hint. We decided to try to match it. We invited not only the mayors. We included their wives, too. Our chef Christian prepared a batch of his fabulous canapés. We put a lot of champagne on ice. But the pièce de résistance was a surprise concert by the Miami University Men's Glee Club, which was on a European tour at the time. And when the glee club, distinguished in blue blazers and red ties, lined up on the curving stairway of the lobby, our eminent guests really perked up. When those marvelous young voices burst into song, history was made. The 114 mayors of the current Luxembourg generation won't forget our party, either.

The American embassy in Luxembourg was built as a private villa in 1925 and was sold to the German government for its legation in 1934. During the occupation, the building became one of the most notorious edifices in town as it served as the residence of the Nazi Gauleiter, Gustav Simon.

After the liberation, U.S. Air Force officers and VIP officials used it as their quarters. Our government purchased the property soon thereafter, and American envoys have made the mansion their private residence ever since.

Flanking the stately embassy residence is a second building, the chancellery, the official place of business. My office was upstairs, on the second floor.

The fenced-in compound is entered through a gate opening onto a wide circular drive which fronts the chancellery and the residence. The American flag flies on a tall pole in the center of the landscaped circle. A broad terrace and beautiful rose gardens complete the attractive decor. I thrilled each time I entered the gate. This was American territory, more than 3,500 miles from home.

A magnificent copper beech stood next to the chancellery. Its branches framed a spectacular view from my office window of the deep valley below and the hilltop beyond. The ancient suburb of Pfaffental

Top, J. Paul McNamara and his wife Mary with Winnie during a visit to Luxembourg, July 4, 1984. McNamara was Miami trustee and alumni president who hired John in 1947. *Bottom*, Senator Fulbright discusses his program with John, who served on its Board of Foreign Scholarships for eight years.

The Dolibois family gathers at the State Department for the swearing-in of John Dolibois as U.S. Ambassador to Luxembourg. Left to right: Susan Lallathin Dolibois, Robert J. Dolibois, Sara Elizabeth, Winnie and John, Brian C. Dolibois, John Michael Dolibois, and Alison Hodgson Dolibois. Front row: Lauren, Kristen, and Ryan Jeffrey.

Top, Winnie holds the Bible given John by Kathy Young Wiley, his administrative assistant at Miami, while he is sworn in. Administering the oath is Ambassador Lenore Annenberg, Chief of Protocol. *Bottom*, last minute instructions from President Reagan.

A vin d'honneur. The mayor of Eschweiler speaks.

His Royal Highness Grand Duke Jean of Luxembourg receives Miami University honorary degree from President Phillip R. Shriver.

Grand Duke Jean and Grand Duchess Josephine-Charlotte arriving with Winnie and John at the American Military Cemetery on a rainy Memorial Day.

Neipperg schoolfriends Jean Kayser (left) and Marcel Homan with John.

Sister Georgina Patton visits her famous grandfather's grave for the first time. Accompanied by Emile Weitzel, president of the American Luxembourg Society, and the Honorable Lydie Wurth-Polfer, mayor of Luxembourg City.

Top, John presents Grand Duke Jean to American veterans on the fortieth anniversary pilgrimage to Luxembourg. *Bottom*, at American Military Cemetery with Jewish leaders for memorial service. Right to left: Grand Rabbi of Luxembourg Dr. Emmanuel Bulz; Luxembourg Cantor Bernard Wolf; Rabbi Marvin Heir of the Simon Wiesenthal Center; and Alphonse Osch, president of the Union of Resistance Movements.

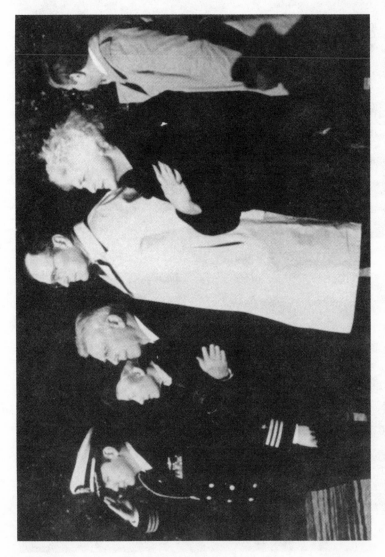

Vice President and Mrs. Bush, John and Winnie, and the vice president's navy aide during playing of the national anthem at the American Military Cemetery in Luxembourg. For security reasons, the vice president wore a bullet-proof vest during public appearances.

Vice President and Mrs. Bush arrive at Chateau Senningen for official dinner with Prime Minister Pierre Werner and Foreign Minister Colette Flesch.

Top, John Dolibois and Barbara Bush listen while the vice president speaks to American staff members at the embassy. *Bottom*, Their Royal Highnesses and Winnie and John receive the salute in the Palace of the Legion of Honor in San Francisco during the State Visit.

The embassy staff gives Winnie a surprise birthday party. Left to right: Dominique, the butler; Winnie; Claude, the chauffeur; Christian, the cook; and Aurora, the maid. Seated is Claude's wife Jeanny, Winnie's hairdresser.

Jean Calmes, president of the American Luxembourg Society, with Winnie and John at their farewell dinner given by the society.

The Dolibois' last visit with Grand Duke Jean at Chateau Berg.

Hiking through the Ardennes, Winnie and John savor their time in their second country.

hunkers down in this valley. On the hilltop sit the modern buildings of the European Center.

Every visitor appreciates the splendid setting of our embassy, but for me, its location held a special attraction. My Neipperg school friend, Jean Kayser, lived in an apartment across the street. Winnie and I could walk over there any time for a relaxing visit with Jean and his wife Malou. On pleasant summer evenings they often wandered over to our place. We'd enjoy a glass of wine or beer on our terrace and watch the evening lights come on in the valley below. We'd reminisce about our boyhood days, and relive the trials and tribulations of the war that had stirred both our lives.

Shortly after our arrival in Luxembourg, we invited all of my Neipperg schoolmates to dinner. Imagine the thoughts running through each of our minds as we all sat around the grandiose dining table. Here were friends with whom I had roamed the Petrusse Valley and explored the casemates under the city fifty years ago. We had hurtled down the valley slopes on makeshift sleds. We played soccer, mumblety-peg, and marble games together. Now we were dining elegantly in an American embassy, remembering.

Across the table sat Marcel Homan. He and I had knelt side-by-side as altar boys on many Sundays and holy days in the church of the Redemptorist Fathers. Next to him sat René Kelsen and his wife Runnes. In our school days, in Maitre Welfring's classroom, René had occupied the desk directly in front of me and Jean Kayser.

That initial dinner set the stage for other gatherings with my playmates of long ago. We met often, singly or in groups, for lunch or dinner; for promenades in the "Bambësch"; in a bowling alley; and even at a sauerkraut feast. These get-togethers were a relaxing contrast to the formal events that were part of our life in the embassy.

Luxembourg is known as an exotic tourist haven. But there is more to it than natural beauty. It's also a major center for "offshore" banks, 122 of them, employing more than eleven thousand persons. Furthermore, the little Duchy has a remarkably high profile on the international stage. France and Belgium may disagree, but Luxembourg *is* the alternative "capital" of the European Community. Some ten thousand EC employees work in the various offices of the European Court of Justice, Euratom, and the Court of Auditors. The European Parliament and the European Commission have staffs there, too. Twenty-six percent of the Luxembourg population is made up of foreigners.

At dinners in our embassy one could hear as many as six different languages spoken, a confusion of international words and sounds. You had to concentrate on just one or two persons, often switching from

French to German or English to Luxembourgish. If the person across from you or next to you spoke Spanish, Greek, or Italian, another linguist had to come to your assistance as interpreter.

Even the domestic staff was a mixture of nationalities. Dominique Molinari, our major domo, supervised the serving staff, recruiting outside help when necessary. He spoke French and Italian fluently. He also handled some German and English, even understood Luxembourgish.

Our live-in maid, Aurore Abreu, was Portuguese, but spoke French, too. Christian Duchambon, the cook, spoke only French. I often marveled at Winnie's ability to get all these people to keep house and to prepare and serve elegant dinners so efficiently, in spite of the language barriers.

As a rule, Luxembourgers are determined to cling to their own language. Despite its German base, it's sufficiently different to defeat most foreigners. I was grateful I could still speak it reasonably well, because that impressed the natives, especially those Winnie and I visited in more remote towns and villages.

Making "official visits" to various communities was one of our favorite activities. I had my chance to express our thanks, in Luxembourgish; to speak my piece for friendship and mutual understanding. Winnie and I took immense pleasure in these visits, but were thankful not all of the 114 mayors of the country were able to work us into their schedule. I was fighting my private "battle of the bulge." The delightful country restaurants and generous kitchens of Luxembourg were filled with temptation.

On November 11, 1981, we were eating lunch when the stillness was broken by the boom of cannons. At first I thought the Luxembourgers were celebrating the anniversary of the end of the First World War. Then I remembered news reports that the Crown Princess of Luxembourg was expecting a baby. The happy event was apparently at hand. Twenty-one blasts of the cannon would signal the birth of a girl. When the bursts continued beyond twenty-one, I knew the baby was a boy. Boys rate 101 shots. We counted. Sure enough, the firstborn was a boy, a crown prince, a future Grand Duke of Luxembourg. Church bells began to ring all over the city. Automobile horns were blaring. It was a momentous occasion.

The newborn prince was named Guillaume. In 1984 we had the pleasure of meeting him personally when he gave his first "audience." Winnie and I played a major part in it.

Icelandair was inaugurating a direct flight from Luxembourg to Orlando, Florida. To kick off the new schedule, Disneyworld characters Mickey Mouse, Minnie Mouse, and Pluto were brought to Luxembourg. This public relations stunt enabled us to invite the first-graders of the American school to the embassy to meet the representatives from Epcot and Disneyworld.

Would it be possible to bring Mickey Mouse and friends to the palace? Of course! And so, Prince Guillaume "received" his first official visitors, the Disney characters. The TV cameras and the press photographers who witnessed and recorded this historic event didn't faze him one bit. He looked and acted every inch a prince.

I wore my striped trousers and morning coat for the first time at the royal wedding of Princess Marie-Astrid to the Archduke of Austria, grandson of the last Austrian emperor. Six weeks later, we attended a second royal wedding, that of Princess Margaretha to Prince Nicolas of Liechtenstein. On both festive occasions the cathedral was filled to capacity. The royal processions were spectacular. We saw kings and queens, princes, dukes, counts, and barons, representatives of royal houses and governments. At the receptions after the ceremonies, we were literally rubbing elbows with these resplendent personages.

The much-beloved Grand Duchess Charlotte, mother of Grand Duke Jean, died on July 9, 1985. She had ruled Luxembourg from 1919 until her abdication in favor of her son in 1964. Even after that, her personal magnetism, her charisma, never let the people forget her presence.

I look back with pride on having been the official representative of the United States at the Pontifical Mass for the Dead. During the solemn rite my thoughts wandered back to my boyhood days, the only time I ever came face to face with that great lady. It was when I accidentally stepped on her toes. In remembering, I couldn't help shed a silent tear myself as thousands of Luxembourgers wept openly at the loss of the Mother of their country.

When we were not involved with official duties, hiking became our favorite exercise and recreation. It also gave us an opportunity to meet Luxembourgers unofficially. We were introduced to this pasttime in a singular way. A group of former Boy Scouts, "Les Anciens Scouts," just a few years younger than I, invited us to join them on one of their semi-annual outings. They had learned about my Scouting activities and decided we had something in common. We accepted the invitation.

We met the group, about thirty-five husbands and wives, at a rustic country restaurant in Scheidgen. It was a beautiful winter day. A six-inch layer of fresh snow—rather rare in Luxembourg—covered the ground and everything on it. A winter wonderland, a white blanket spread over a picturesque landscape. By 10:00 A.M. we were on the trail, and after tramping an invigorating twelve kilometers, we came back to the restaurant for a hearty meal. By then all of these strangers had be-

come good friends. It was a great experience in international understanding and friendship. We resolved to meet again for the next excursion, and we did.

That is how we were introduced to the "Circuits Auto Pédeste" for
which Luxembourg is noted. It is a network of 142 well-marked and
well-maintained trails that covers the whole country. The trails lead over
hills and through valleys; around lakes and across streams; through orchards and vineyards; open fields and into dense forests. Almost every
community in the country prides itself on having one or more of these
hiking circuits. They consist of a combination of roads, footpaths,
wagon trails, bridle paths, and logging roads. Each loop begins at a
designated parking area. It may be as short as three kilometers or as long
as twenty-six. It ends back at your car. In our four years we hiked 1,087
miles. We completed 103 of the 142 trails of the circuits.

These hikes gave us a good look at life in the Grand Duchy. Talking
with farmers in their fields, or vintners in their vineyards, helped me
understand how the average Europeans view Americans. We chatted
with workers on the roads, with foresters felling trees or planting seed-
lings in an enlightened forestry program. And we met other hikers.
Some wouldn't believe they were talking to the American ambassador.

Emmanuel "Manu" Tesch, chief executive of ARBED, Europe's
fourth largest steel producer, was the first person I met who had hiked
every one of the 142 trails in the Circuits Auto Pédeste. He gave us a
looseleaf booklet with individual maps of each trail. Thus, we had directions for exploring fascinating landmarks such as the Gorge of Wolves,
the Den of Robbers, the Devil's Bridge, the Coal Hole, and the
Cuckoo's Lair. The reliable blue trailmarkers led us into enchanting
forests with spittle-bug names such as the Laangeboesch, the Mier-
scherboesch, and the Haemeschterboesch. More strenuous wanderings
took us over the Leschpelterknapp, near Héischtergronn, not far from
the Schéimelzerboeschkaul. Just trying to pronounce the names dotting
each map was strenuous enough to maintain physical fitness.

Besides hiking, we enjoyed other aspects of life in Luxembourg. One
was the Octave, a centuries-old tradition in which thousands of pilgrims
flood the city to pay homage to the Virgin Mary, "Protectoress" of Luxembourg. The marketplace is crowded with booths selling food specialties of the Grand Duchy and neighboring countries. Villagers from
miles around take part in processions, street masses, and prayer gatherings. The city is abuzz with visitors day and night for two weeks.

Sitting in a food-stall, Winnie and I munched our metts and sauerkraut, and particularly enjoyed the Gromperenkichelcher (potato pan-
cakes). I recalled the last time I had spent a day at the Octave. It was in

May 1931. For doing so, I got my ears boxed by the Dechant Erasmy who accused me of having induced a classmate to pilfer the family cash register.

Life in a Luxembourg more than 1,025 years old has many charms because of its rich traditions. The "Buurgbrennen" is one of them. Winnie and I came upon it at the end of one of our hikes through a typical Ardennes village. On its outskirts, villagers, young and old, were erecting an enormous wooden cross. At the base of it they piled old tires and straw. Obviously, this cross was for burning. My first thought was of the Klan, but then we got the full story.

A cross-burning was taking place in every community of the hill country. The custom dates back some six hundred years and has something to do with the rites of spring. The next couple to be married have the privilege of lighting the fire. All the people gather around the blazing cross to sing and dance, and, of course, to eat and drink. The evil spirits and the cold of winter are driven out; spring is getting a rousing welcome. It is the occasion of a witches Sabbath, a form of Walpurgis Night. The simultaneous burning of crosses on hillsides for miles around presents a fantastic sight.

Another rite of spring is "Bretzel Sunday"—the equivalent of our Valentine's Day. On this Sunday a young man makes a great show of presenting a huge sugar pretzel to the girl of his choice. In leap years the girls give the pretzels to the boys.

On Easter Monday, thousands of Luxembourgers and tourists flock to the old marketplace in the city or to the village of Nospelt. It's the festival called "Emaischen." At this traditional event you buy "Peckvillecher," brightly colored ceramic bird whistles, available only once a year. They are made in Nospelt, and they're collectors' items. You have to fight for the opportunity to buy. Winnie soon learned to push her way into the throng along with the biggest "Grand Rue Marchers"—her name for aggressive shoppers.

Springtime usually brings floods to Luxembourg. In 1983 the rivers overflowed their banks three times, setting new records. All the villages along the Moselle were under water, some inundated to the second story. We viewed this as tragic, but Luxembourgers took it all in stride. Their sense of humor always prevails; witness, April Fool's Day.

On April first, the morning newspaper featured imminent plans for the development of a hydroelectric reservoir in the deep valley of Pfaffental, just below our embassy. There was even a photo of the construction of the dam which would result in a beautiful lake. Another photo showed an architect's rendering of how the old city's skyline would look after the lake was filled in. Winnie was furious at such stupidity and wondered what idiot was responsible for this hare-brained idea, the plans to ruin that ancient valley (and our view). April Fool!

Another newspaper reproduced a front-page photo of hundreds of Chinese bicycles parked in front of the Luxembourg town hall. The news item reported that hundreds of Chinese on their bikes had arrived in Luxembourg, a stop on a worldwide tour. They were all inside being received by the mayor. The superimposed photo of the bicycles in front of the town hall attracted many gullible Luxembourgers, eager to see the Chinese visitors who had pedaled all the way from China. April Fool!

On the morning radio broadcast, a great mimic of the voice of the Belgian prime minister announced that effective May first, all Flemish-speaking Belgians would need a passport to enter the French-speaking areas of Belgium, and vice versa. April Fool!

We had a traffic jam at the fairgrounds not far from our embassy on April 1, because a radio announcer reported that the city police were auctioning slot machines and pinball machines they had confiscated earlier in a raid on a number of establishments. Hundreds of potential buyers flocked to the fairgrounds to bid on the loot. April Fool!

Luxembourgers have a chance to play the fool during the Mardi Gras which precedes the Lenten season. Young and old go to work in costumes. Can you imagine a bank teller in a clown suit? A disguised grocery clerk? Of course, every town and village holds a Mardi Gras Ball or parade. The village band leads the masqueraded revellers and the floats. The emphasis is on humor, which the Luxembourgers are always ready to poke at themselves.

The annual gorse festival in Wiltz, the centuries-old dancing procession in Echternach, and all kinds of seasonal celebrations the year around, add zest to community spirit. We participated in cherry festivals, strawberry feasts, pork roasts, nut fests, and dozens of wine-tastings and harvests. Music festivals vie with each other. In the fall there is a "Kirmes" in almost every community. These street carnivals signal the beginning or end of the harvest season. They culminate in the Schueberfoér, the fair to end all fairs. It was started more than five hundred years ago by John the Blind, King of Bohemia and Duke of Luxembourg. It has been held annually ever since. It is set up on the vast fairgrounds near the American embassy, and lasts about three weeks. All day and every evening we could hear the oompa-pah bands, the barkers summoning fair-goers to the various attractions, and the musical cacophony of the Merry-Go-Round, the Whip, and a dozen other amusements. When the breeze blew right, we could even get a whiff of pommes frites, Belgian waffles, sausages, and popcorn.

We were delighted to take part in these celebrations and customs. Besides our own enjoyment, as American representatives our participation in Luxembourg traditions was important for relations between our countries.

The Chinese and the Soviet embassies are in the suburbs Dommeldange and Beggen, about a kilometer apart. They're impressive facilities, former chateaus. Showplaces. It's part of image-making. Our allies are supposed to be impressed by all that opulence, and can't help but make comparisons. Propagandists instruct them daily that the United States is crime-ridden, racist, warmongering, inflicted by poverty, unemployment, and discontent.

By contrast, here are the smiling and generous Communists. Champagne flows freely. Their tables sag with food. They are open-hearted and generous, while the Americans are hiding behind sturdy fences, marine guards, spotlights, and electronic security, constantly in fear of terrorists.

Yes, we were operating at a disadvantage. But that's what made it all the more challenging. U.S. ambassadors don't have unlimited representational budgets that allow lavish entertaining. Congress is rather stingy in its support of Foreign Affairs and embassies abroad, but we managed to put on a good show when necessary, even if we had to dip into our own pockets.

Our Fourth of July celebration is a case in point. When the first one rolled around, Winnie and I were immediately confronted with a problem: How to accommodate the crowd, especially if it rained. We had over one thousand names on the invitation list. In previous years the reception was handled in shifts, the first from 11:30 A.M. to 1:00 P.M., the second from 1:00 to 2:30 P.M., and I'd already heard gripes about second-class citizens—those who were on a less important shift.

My thirty-four-year experience with alumni reunions at Miami came in handy. We could put a tent on the terrace and then everyone could come at the same time. It's impossible, I was told. It's never been done before. Well, I'd heard that at Miami, too. The difficult will be done immediately, the impossible takes a little longer.

Our administrative officer was Francine Bowman, who prided herself on being of Polish descent. "Poles can do anything once they set their mind to it," Francine said. On Independence Day, a large blue and white striped tent miraculously appeared on the main terrace. A smaller tent was set up just off the dining room door, which led to a side terrace. At nine o'clock in the morning, a large van appeared at the residence. In just twenty minutes the furniture from the downstairs public rooms was loaded on the van. The van pulled out of the compound and parked on a side street around the block.

Tables with canapés and refreshments were strategically placed in the tents and in the house. A one-man orchestra, "Fausti," played a piano-organ, accordion, and drums, and sang anything on request. You could dance to his music, too.

More than a thousand guests passed through the receiving line. By mid-afternoon, when the last one was gone, the moving van reappeared. Within the hour you wouldn't believe we'd had a party. The only strenuous aspect of our Fourth of July event was shaking all those hands, coming and going.

We didn't attend official celebrations in the Soviet embassy between 1981 and 1985. The Cold War atmosphere prevailed. Washington usually advised me to pass them up, to send a lower-ranking representative. This doesn't mean we never got inside the Russian embassy. Actually, we were there for a number of private parties and more formal diplomatic dinners. I was to stay away only from those Soviet functions which held propaganda tones.

I made the required protocol visit to their embassy when Chairman Brezhnev died. Chernenko and Andropov also died during our four years in Luxembourg. Each time, I called on Ambassador Kamo Oudoumian, and signed the Book of Condolence. We enjoyed a good relationship with the Soviet ambassador, who liked to demonstrate this fact publicly. A bear hug and a loud, "Ah, my friend John!" was always designed to get media attention. It did.

We faithfully celebrated respective national days at every other embassy. Luxembourg's National Day is the highlight of the year's social calendar, a two-day commemoration, and honors the Grand Duke's birthday. The mayor and the city council invite all diplomats and leading citizens to a reception at the Villa Vauban. When night falls, a torchlight parade leads people to the palace where the Grand Ducal family appears on the balcony and is cheered by the throng. The evening ends with spectacular fireworks, shot off the large Adolphe Bridge which spans the Petrusse Valley.

The Te Deum Solonelle, a festive mass, is the first formal event on the next morning. Held in the cathedral, and attended by everybody who is anybody, the ritual calls for "grande tenue"—white tie and tails or formal native costume, and decorations. It is a most elegant scene.

A gala luncheon in honor of the diplomats from both Luxembourg and Belgium follows the religious service. The dress for this affair is "jacquette"—morning coat and striped trousers.

The afternoon is devoted to all kinds of festivities, such as folk dancing, outdoor concerts, and jubilant parades. And in the evening, diplomats, ministers, and special guests climb back into grande tenue for the colorful formal reception and buffet in the palace. The royal family greets each of the hundreds of guests personally. When it's over you pinch yourself to make sure this wasn't all a dream of fairy tales and life in medieval times.

When we arrived in Luxembourg in October 1981, the deputy chief of mission (DCM) was driving a new Plymouth sedan. The car assigned to me, as the "official car," was a partially armored 1973 Chrysler New Yorker. It had seen better days long before I inherited it. Its only claim to distinction was a stale cigar odor, and five miles to the gallon.

Eventually I confiscated the new Plymouth, and let the DCM have the unglamorous battle cruiser. He wasn't too happy about it, and pouted for several days. As it turned out the Plymouth wasn't much better. It didn't have regulation armor "for the ambassador's safety." And when the required two-way radio was installed, the Plymouth's battery died a sudden death at the slightest provocation. Much to my chagrin, its first demise occurred in the entrance to the Grand Ducal Palace.

I was leaving a traditional New Year event at which the royal family receives the members of the diplomatic corps. My driver Claude turned the ignition key. Nothing! He got out and kicked the tires, then raised the hood—much to the amusement of the crowd that usually gathers in front of the palace when something is going on. Behind us, ambassadors of other countries patiently waited for us to get out of the way. I sank down in the rear seat. Finally, several palace guards and a footman pushed us to the side where we could wait to be rescued.

I reported this embarrassing incident, but got no sympathy. Our embassy wasn't programmed for a new car for at least two more years. Money crunch.

Then along came JUBICA '82, an international jamboree for Boy Scouts and Girl Scouts from all over the world. Twelve American Scouts were participating, and I was proud to "inspect" their campsite and welcome them to Luxembourg. The encampment was at the Domaine Betzdorf, the estate on which Grand Duke Jean was born, and where he lived until he ascended the throne in 1964. The Grand Duke is the Chief Scout of Luxembourg. Along with other top-ranking officials, he, too, came to visit JUBICA '82. So did several thousand Luxembourgers. There were demonstrations of Scouting skills, exhibits, and competitions.

When the Sunday afternoon program ended, the Grand Duke's motorcade departed to the strains of "Wilhelmus," the Luxembourg equivalent of "Hail to the Chief." I was to leave next. The band struck up our national anthem, the Scouts and visitors applauded, and I proudly stepped into my car. Claude turned the ignition key. Phhtt! Nothing. I had cured him of kicking the tires, but he did raise the hood and a number of well-meaning spectators peered into the engine compartment with him. But we already knew what was wrong. Dead battery again.

There was nothing to do but sit. Meanwhile, other dignitaries departed, the crowd dispersed, and finally, someone arrived with cables. We jump-started our Plymouth, aptly named Fury, and headed for home.

I shared this adventure with Charlie Price, the U.S. ambassador to Belgium and later to the United Kingdom. He was a sympathetic and influential friend. I don't know how he did it, but within a month we were assigned a new car, a stretch Ford Granada, built in Europe, properly equipped and armored according to specification. I was indebted to Ambassador Price and to the Boy Scouts. The JUBICA event helped bring our transportation problem to a head, and to a solution.

The calm of early summer in 1983 was shattered by an unusual "crisis." It was brought on by the seventy-fifth anniversary of the Luxembourg Football (soccer) Federation. A match between two of Europe's most powerful and attractive teams—West Germany and Yugoslavia— was to be played in Luxembourg, a fitting way to commemorate a football anniversary. I was asked to get the U.S. Air Force Band, the famous "Ambassadors," to provide the music for this festive event. This took some doing. As a rule, the U.S. military bands in Europe performed only at official American functions. My good relations with the U.S. Air Force in Europe paid off. The band came to Luxembourg.

The match was scheduled for the Luxembourg Municipal Stadium on June 7, Winnie's birthday. I asked our political officer, Peter Holt, to represent me at the game. In the midst of Winnie's birthday dinner that evening, I was summoned to the telephone, an "emergency." The caller was Peter Holt.

"We have a problem here, Mr. Ambassador," said Peter. The Air Force Band had played the West German national anthem beautifully. Then came the Yugoslav hymn. But here they goofed. They played the wrong anthem, a royalist version, dating back to 1943 when Yugoslavia was Nazi-occupied, and the monarchy was to a lesser or greater extent collaborating with the invaders. This in contrast to the Communist partisans who eventually took over when the Germans were expelled. The playing of the tune couldn't have been more provocative under the circumstances—given that the opponents were West Germany.

The Yugoslav players were offended. They walked off the field, and refused to play. The game, being televised live to millions all over Europe, had already been held up fifteen minutes. The horrified officials were in a quandary. The U.S. band couldn't play the correct version; they didn't have the music.

Peter Holt put Mr. Dracho Popovic, president of the Yugoslav Football Federation, on the line. Fortunately for me, the man spoke German. I assured him that this was an honest mistake. The United States was not making a political statement. I apologized profusely. But he was unyielding. He had to protest strongly. His players would not come on the field until the right anthem was played.

Miraculous help came from a taxi driver of Yugoslav descent who lived, of all places, in my native Bonnevoie. Dragan Svetkovic had intended to watch the game on German television. Hearing of the problem during the broadcast, he took a record of the current Yugoslav national anthem from his collection and rushed it to the stadium. At last, the sound of "Ye Sloveni" came over the public address system. The ruffled feelings of Yugoslav players were soothed. The match began, a half hour late. Spectators, who had become increasingly restive, were delighted. And the Yugoslavs eventually lost the game, 4-2.

But I still had my work cut out for me the next day. First, I wrote a most sincere, heartfelt thank-you letter to the Yugoslav-Luxembourg taxi driver in Bonnevoie. Then I talked to the Yugoslav ambassador in Brussels. He suggested we also contact the Foreign Ministry in Belgrade. The commandant of the U.S. Air Force expressed his regrets. I reported at length to Washington. All of this just because someone accidentally took the wrong music out of the files.

Deep in the Heart
of Europe

On New Year's Day in 1983, I received a long letter from Jean Bartlett, my former high school teacher. It ended with the beautiful thought that "life is a canvas stretched upon the frame of character and supported by the easel of time." Miss Bartlett wished us a "1983 canvas filled with landscapes, cloudless skies, few shadows, and maybe even some rainbows." Among other holiday greetings was an attractive card from the Chinese embassy, with a unique, meaningful message: "I wish you a fresh New Year!"

In that spirit I tackled the challenges 1983 held in store for me. In my second year as ambassador I was gaining confidence. I was no longer at the tail-end of Diplomatic Corps lineups, no longer the wide-eyed newcomer. Grudgingly, even my DCM, the senior Foreign Service member on my staff, stopped acting as if I were the village idiot.

The State Department is an exclusive private club, its spaces reserved for "members only." Each time you enter its office building on C Street in Washington, you are profoundly impressed. You feel exceptionally proud when you visit the seventh floor with its elegant office suites and rich diplomatic reception rooms. But even with the rank of ambassador, you "belong" only if you are a career foreign service officer.

The career bureaucracy of the department will block the appointment of noncareer persons as ambassadors whenever possible. In spite of this, at least 30 to 40 percent of U.S. ambassadors in service are politically selected, appointed by the president. All this aside, the key people conducting the day-to-day operations at any embassy are the Foreign Service Officers. The noncareer ambassador then has to adapt to the system; cope with the power and influence of his FSO staff.

I was a political appointee. Unlike others I know, I was lucky. With two or three exceptions, the people assigned to "AmEmbassy Luxembourg" were intelligent and hard-working. They respected my inevitable presence and resigned themselves to coping with an "outsider." They served with loyalty and dedication, but they knew, as I did, that in some respects I would have to defer to their judgments. The attitude was, "we professionals know better." I acted accordingly.

The deputy chief of mission (DCM) is in the best position to stick it to an ambassador unfamiliar with State Department procedure. My "initiation"—we used to call it "hell-week" in the fraternity—had come off during my first few days in the embassy. On my desk sat a stack of telegrams a foot high. They dated back to early August and up to the day of my arrival. The DCM informed me that I should read and initial them. Then he walked out of my office. I started in. The reading was interrupted frequently by other commitments. But I always got back to it, determined to reduce the size of that pile. It never shrank. As fast as I read and initialed them a new batch appeared. The cable traffic ran continuously.

Janet Wilmink, my personally selected secretary, came to the rescue. Janet hailed from Milford, Ohio, and had attended the University of Cincinnati. I brought her to Luxembourg from the State Department pool of secretaries. I wanted some "home-state" support. Janet was a professional. She had been a secretary to a U.S. ambassador to Sweden, and knew the ropes. She was loyal all the way.

"Mr. Ambassador, why are you ruining your eyes?" she said when she saw me rubbing my bloodshot orbs. "You aren't expected to read every telegram that comes to this embassy. You're just supposed to see them." Janet suggested the right procedure. "You read *everything* pertaining to Luxembourg. You read the *summaries* of the cables dealing with NATO, the EC, or BENELUX countries. If you feel you should read more, go ahead. As for the rest of the traffic, you read only the *titles* to see if the subject matter is relevant or interesting. Forget those more than two days old. Your staff is supposed to read them and brief you later."

Dear Janet. She kept me from going blind the first week. And she kept me out of trouble for the rest of my tour. Blessedly, she stayed with me in Luxembourg all four years.

The senior career officers who served as my deputies were cut from a different mold. With them, career and institutional interests got the highest priorities. They hardly arrived at the post before they began scheming and planning their next assignment and promotion, worrying about efficiency reports and evaluations. Ambassadors can't order a bonus or promotion, nor can they overrule either the supervisor or the

FSO-controlled promotion board. The Foreign Service has substantial control over assignment of its members to posts abroad. The old-boy network of senior officers looks out for its own. They take care of each other.

My deputies were capable, hardworking. They knew the ins and outs of the State Department. I could depend on them to do their job, but they tended to be patronizing in their personal relationship with me. I never heard a compliment of a speech or debate or even a good dinner party. The attitude seemed to be, "So you want to be an ambassador? Go ahead! I won't stop you."

I learned to do it my way; wrote my own speeches, worked out my own social schedule. From them, I expected nothing except competent performance. And that, they gave me. It turned out to be a satisfactory arrangement, especially since all the other American personnel on the country team and the non-American employees gave strong support. They patiently steered me into the complex State Department procedures; helped me with acronyms and abbreviations which at first appeared to be insurmountable humps.

The "country team" is made up of the American members of the embassy staff and the heads of U.S. government agencies in the host country. In our case it also included the persons living in Brussels who were assigned or accredited to U.S. Embassy Luxembourg: my military attaché; the representative of the Office of Defense Cooperation for Belgium/Luxembourg; the agricultural agent; the drug enforcement agent; and the regional security officer. The American superintendent of the Military Cemetery in Luxembourg was also in this group.

The country team met in my office each month. The purpose of the meetings was to keep each officer and each agency abreast of what was going on; to coordinate assignments and activities. I was fortunate to have a great bunch of people on the country team.

One wintry evening in 1982 I gave a talk in Ettelbruck, the gateway city to the Ardennes. It's also known as Patton City as it was here that General Patton's troops made first contact with German forces in breaking up the Battle of the Bulge in December 1944.

Ettelbruck boasts a Patton Museum, a Patton Park, and a life-size statue of the general at a prominent intersection of the roads where American and German troops clashed. Every summer, a Remembrance Day is held in Ettelbruck in honor of the American liberators. The whole community takes part, as do units of the Luxembourg, French, Belgian, and U.S. armies.

In my speech I was trying to explain the position of the United States in INF deployment. I was stressing the importance of being able to negotiate from strength, that we wouldn't get the Soviets' attention until they recognized that we also wielded a big club.

When I finished, Edouard Juncker, the mayor of Ettelbruck, motioned me to follow him outside. He led me around the corner to a small public square in which stood a giant granite block, a monument erected by the city of Ettelbruck in honor of U.S. soldiers. The simple inscription read: "BECAUSE YOU WERE STRONG, WE LIVE IN FREEDOM."

Almost every village in the hilly countryside of the Ardennes and other regions of Luxembourg has erected a token of remembrance. At each such monument, without exception, flies the American flag.

The Ettelbruck episode, and my appreciation of a Luxembourg determined not to forget, helped tremendously in meeting the first item on my agenda—to get Washington more interested in the Grand Duchy.

The last member of a U.S. president's cabinet to make a bilateral visit to Luxembourg was then Vice President Lyndon B. Johnson. President Kennedy invited Grand Duchess Charlotte to Washington for a State Visit in 1963. The present Grand Duke had reigned for nearly twenty years without an official visit to the United States. I was determined to do something about it.

The opportunity presented itself when Luxembourg's Minister of Public Force Emile Krieps called on me. At meetings of the NATO Defense Ministers he had extended an invitation to Secretary of Defense Caspar Weinberger to come to Luxembourg. He solicited my help. In answer to my telegram on this matter to the Pentagon, I received an invitation to meet with the secretary of defense the next time I was in Washington.

My annual consultation was set for November 1982. A Pentagon appointment was arranged. When the clock struck ten on the morning of November 9, I walked into Mr. Weinberger's office. The secretary was delayed at the White House. At ten-thirty he was to receive West German Defense Minister Woerner at a full-blown official ceremony on the Pentagon parade ground—twenty-one-gun salute, troops in parade formation, the works. My chances of seeing Secretary Weinberger were nil. But I was told to wait.

At twenty minutes after ten I was rushed into his office. The secretary greeted me graciously, looked at his watch, and then said in a soft but urgent voice: "Mr. Ambassador, you have exactly ten minutes to tell me why I should come to Luxembourg." He motioned me to sit down. I started extolling Luxembourg's charter membership in NATO, its strong support of the United States. . . . "I know all that," he interrupted, again glancing at his watch. He wanted some special inducement, a justification.

So I told him the story of my speaking engagement in Ettelbruck. I quickly summarized my feelings about all the other memorials around the country. In telling, my emotions and my pride got hold of me. To my amazement, I noticed that Secretary Weinberger had tears in his eyes, too.

"I'll come to Luxembourg," he said. He stood up, took me by the arm, and led me out of the office with an invitation to come along to the welcoming ceremony for Minister Woerner. "Call me Cap, John," was the last thing he said to me at exactly 10:30 as he strode forward to shake hands with his guest of honor.

Cap Weinberger came to Luxembourg on December 1, 1982. He met with Luxembourg government officials, was received at the palace, and thoroughly enjoyed himself. In a major address to the Luxembourg Society for International Affairs, he began by saying that the American ambassador had told him of a visit to a small Luxembourg town on a cold wintry evening. Despite the late hour he had been taken to view a monument, a war memorial dedicated to the Americans who fought for the liberation of Luxembourg, with an inscription that read: "BECAUSE YOU WERE STRONG, WE LIVE IN FREEDOM."

"This was a very moving experience for Ambassador Dolibois," he said. "And the story was very moving to me in the re-telling."

The secretary went on to explain that in the towns and villages of America are similar memorials. Sometimes they are in the town square, sometimes in front of the courthouse, and at other times in city parks. But always they are erected in places that have a special reverence and meaning for the local citizens. And always the message is the same, whichever language it is written in. The message is that freedom is attained, and freedom is preserved, by strength and sacrifice.

"Those who erected these monuments," he continued, "learned the truth of that message by bitter experience. They knew the pain and anguish of war. They suffered, but they also knew they were fortunate—for they survived. But in surviving they incurred a solemn obligation to tell later generations of the lessons that they had to learn by experience and sorrow. That is why they built war memorials and why they put them in places where they will always be seen."

He told his audience that "the greatest memorial to freedom, built after World War II, was not erected of stone or marble, nor was it built by the victors alone." This monument is the NATO alliance. "It was built on a pact between nations united in common cause. That cause is peace." The Luxembourgers loved the speech and gave the secretary of defense a standing ovation.

I thought Mr. Weinberger's speech one of his best, and I told him so.

"Well, your story about visiting that monument in that little Luxembourg town on a cold wintry night inspired me," he said. "And now I can understand why you are so proud to serve as ambassador in this country."

Thus word got around Washington that Luxembourg was a great place for stopovers. Our list of VIP visitors started to grow.

When I first arrived in Luxembourg, we were deep into the Afghanistan problem. The Polish crisis reached its climax soon thereafter. The knottiest, most vexing point at issue was the deployment of INF missiles in Europe. Now add the Soviet gas pipeline, terrorism, and the difficulties in the Middle East, and you get the picture. There were even a few minor annoyances in our bilateral relations with Luxembourg. These, and other matters, called for frequent consultation with Luxembourg government officials.

On the whole, Luxembourg stayed the course with the United States. But it wasn't easy. One had to allow for political differences in Luxembourg, too. Washington couldn't, and shouldn't, take our friends in the little Grand Duchy for granted. Many present-day Luxembourg government officials were small children when U.S. forces liberated their country in 1944. Some weren't even born yet. So I didn't always find the same overwhelming sense of gratitude held by old-timers. Furthermore, Luxembourg attitudes, like those of other Western European nations, are influenced by their proximity to the Eastern bloc. Our allies are not so eager to be caught between the two superpowers.

I also found that Luxembourg has no political ambitions as far as influence on other nations is concerned, except to serve the European Community. Traditionally, the Luxembourgers seek compromise solutions to their problems. The government's reaction to American influence is dictated by the consensus of a coalition. Among Luxembourg politicians the interests of their country are well ahead of narrow political differences. In international affairs, Luxembourg policy is further influenced by its larger neighbors, particularly Belgium and Holland.

So I wasn't surprised the day demonstrators first appeared in front of our embassy. They were against our policy in Nicaragua. I decided to invite the young spokesmen for the protest group to meet with me for a face-to-face discussion. It was a friendly confrontation. As elsewhere in Europe, the outlook of young people in Luxembourg is influenced to a great extent by propaganda. The readiness of unfriendly media to ascribe bellicose intentions to the United States and its president, and to give the Soviets the benefit of the doubt, made it difficult to win support for our position.

During our discussion, a young Catholic priest, one of the leaders of the protest group, quoted Anthony Lewis of the *New York Times:* "The United States is the most dangerous and destructive power in the world." I was made aware that the fiercest denunciations of America are home-grown. I came to the conclusion that we do a good job of exporting anti-Americanism. Books by Norman Mailer, Noam Chomsky, and other writers of political fiction, and the exhortations of Jane Fonda, Susan Sontag, and Angela Davis, aren't lost on the youth of Europe.

When I was interviewed by Luxembourg reporters about Cuba and Nicaragua, my comments were treated with considerable skepticism. The younger newsmen weren't ready to accept the fact that Cuba is an instrument of Soviet policy. They were even more skeptical about the idea that the Sandinista regime in Nicaragua might perform a similar role at one further remove. Their opinions were certainly reinforced by the distrustful reports they received from our own country.

The deployment of the Pershing II and the cruise missiles was a major issue. Luxembourg was not directly involved, but we wanted its support. Again, we had to counteract the well-organized efforts of opponents of deployment.

The *International Herald Tribune* and other American print media in Europe devoted much space to what they dubbed the "peace crusade" which was "sweeping" the United States. Europeans were reading about massive protest marches. They read about hundreds of organizations in the U.S. advocating a nuclear freeze. A group called Physicians for Social Responsibility was spelling out the physical suffering their audiences would experience following a nuclear explosion. This body, and American church leaders, politicians, scientists, and other respected personalities protesting deployment, were getting tremendous coverage by the western media in Europe.

Insofar as they were influential, these disarmament movements, by their very nature, served to weaken Western defenses and to inhibit the willingness of western countries to project their forces beyond their borders. Furthermore, these movements were an obvious target for Soviet manipulation and penetration.

The Soviet Union promotes its foreign policy aims through what is called "active measures." Techniques include the use of disinformation, forgeries, front organizations, agents of influence, and the organization of mass demonstrations. Through these techniques the Soviets attempt to influence and manipulate foreign public opinion and the decisions of foreign governments. One of our functions in the American embassy was to counteract these efforts. We didn't get much help from some of our most influential reporters, commentators, and politicians.

Most of all, I objected to news articles quoting "knowledgeable officials." Quite often I found that an official call on a Luxembourg minister was made meaningless by a news story which contradicted the classified information I was discussing with him or her. Stories attributed to unidentified "administration officials" or "a White House source" or "a State Department official" could undermine any consulting effort. Washington is full of bureaucrats and politicians ready to give firsthand, inside (often classified) information to the press. Some of these people eagerly "leak" data to foreign embassy officials in an effort to curry favor, to be put on the embassy invitation list. These so-called leaks could ruin my day.

I was awakened one night by a call from my communications officer announcing the arrival of a NIACT—a night action telegram. The urgent communication directed me to deliver a classified message to the Luxembourg foreign minister "at the opening of business" that same morning. I already knew that Foreign Minister Colette Flesch was scheduled to leave for Strassbourg the same day. I also knew that she regularly jogged early every morning in the municipal park not far from our embassy. So the only way I could deliver this vitally important message was to catch her on the run before she left town. Madame Flesch was a personal friend; I hoped she wouldn't resent my diplomatic ambush.

I put on my running shoes and headed for the park while half of Luxembourg was still asleep. A morning mist hugged the ground. At exactly 6:10 A.M. I was waiting under the protective branch of a large chestnut tree at an intersection of pathways. I saw Colette coming around the bend. She spotted me. My early morning presence in the park surprised her, but she didn't slow down. I caught her stride and quickly delivered my spiel before I would run out of breath. I didn't think I could go the full distance with her. When I had done with my message, she stopped dead in her tracks. She put a gentle hand on my shoulder and looked at me kindly. "One thing I like about you, John, is that you never tell me something I don't already know," she said.

At the Chief of Missions Conference in London a few weeks later, I shared my park adventure with fellow ambassadors and Secretary of State Shultz. They got a good laugh out of my story, and we all agreed that there was no way of stopping the leaks or interfering with the "freedom" of the press, not in an open society like ours. Furthermore, our own government often leaks information deliberately to get reactions—trial balloons.

Winnie and I stole away for some mountain hiking in Austria during

the summer, and were fortunate to attend a concert by the Berlin Philharmonic Orchestra, directed by Herbert von Karajan, at the Salzburg
Music Festival. Our hosts were Hubert and Marietta Feichtlbauer of
Vienna, friends from Fulbright days. While listening to the glorious
music, my thoughts flew back to my first Salzburg Music Festival,
which I attended with Mal Hilty in 1945.

Those summer holidays and pleasant diversions prepared us for a
troublesome fall ahead. We anticipated problems in 1983, our apprehen-
sion fueled by media reports of forthcoming demonstrations and anti-
nuclear activities. It all had to do with the deployment of the Pershing II
and the GLCM missiles. If one writer suggested the peace movements
were losing their punch, nine others immediately responded with contradictions and detailed descriptions of the devastation to come. They
predicted bombings, burnings, and all kinds of violence on the part of
protesters. It almost looked as if they were rallying terrorists to the cause.
We hoped the doomsayers would be disappointed.

The Nicaragua situation was beginning to cause headaches. Congress
kept switching signals on us. At first, the U.S. would support the Con-
tras; then we wouldn't; and then we did again, in modified form; and
then we cut off all aid. How does one "represent" such a vacillating
position?

Meanwhile, the agitators from Cuba (and the USSR) managed to stir
up a handful of young Luxembourgers. A small group, the Association
of Solidarity of Luxembourg-Nicaragua (ASLN), stepped up protest
demonstrations in front of our embassy. These demonstrations were
more a nuisance than anything else.

The directional street sign at the top of boulevard Emmanual Servais
was covered with a crude hand-drawn pointer "To the Murder Embassy." One Saturday morning, protesters rolled barbed wire around the
embassy compound and padlocked two heavy chains on our gate. For
five minutes, until the marines removed the wire and cut the chains,
Winnie and I were "imprisoned." An American flag was burned in the
course of another manifestation. This gesture backfired on the demonstrators as hundreds of older Luxembourgers reacted adversely.

At first I tried to talk to these young people, but their minds were made
up. There was no room for discussion or enlightenment.

We received more threats, reports of ambassadors on hit lists. The
hostage situation reached crisis proportions. Increased security at American embassies in Europe was ordered. Consequently, a new, sturdier
fence was constructed around our compound. An "impregnable" gate
with barricades, a reinforced garage door, and electronic safeguards
were installed. A guardhouse was built at the entrance.

The Communist newspaper went berserk. I got so much publicity that some of my colleagues in the diplomatic corps were getting a little envious. Obviously, the Communists saw a propaganda advantage in this "security-complex" we were constructing. A full-page story with photos appeared in their newspaper, the *Zeitung*. It described the installation and erection of a "Fortress on Boulevard Emmanual Servais." "And why is U.S. Ambassador Dolibois, who has ordered all this restructuring, so frightened?" they asked. They answered their own question. It wasn't just because of terrorist threats incurred by the "Americans' dirty dealings in Lebanon" and "the American SS tactics in other helpless small countries like Grenada." No. "The Ambassador is really reinforcing his compound because he knows that when Reagan's gangsters and murderers invade Nicaragua, the whole population of Luxembourg will storm the 'Murder Embassy' in protest."

"And when will the Americans invade Nicaragua? It will be on the day the construction at 22 Boulevard Emmanual Servais is completed." All Luxembourgers were urged to watch progress on the work being done on the "Marine Guardhouse" and the rest of the "fortress"; and then to prepare themselves for the massive demonstration against the U.S. warmongers on the day it is completed, "the day on which the United States will attack Nicaragua."

From that issue on, the *Zeitung vum Létzeburger Vollek* reported daily, in print and picture, how the work was getting along. It urged its readers to "make a lot of noise around the U.S. Embassy and keep the Ambassador awake at night."

We didn't lose any sleep. The largest demonstration against U.S. policy in Central America rallied thirty-eight adults, four tiny children, and one dog. The Luxembourg Police Department sent eighteen officers to maintain order.

One day, after one of these protest manifestations, I was stopped on the Grand Rue—Luxembourg's pedestrian shopping zone—by a young girl. "Aren't you the American ambassador?" she asked. I acknowledged the compliment. "Well," she said, "I would like to know why you Americans are so concerned with Nicaragua?"

"May I answer your question with another, please?" I asked. She said yes. "Well, then, why are you *Luxembourgers* so concerned with Nicaragua?"

She thought for a moment. Then she smiled, nodded her head, and said, "Touché!" End of friendly confrontation. I looked for her at the next protest demonstration. She was not in the tiny crowd.

There were other anti-American incidents.

Stephen Hubai, superintendent of the American Military Cemetery in Luxembourg, arranged for Winnie and me to make an official visit to the cemetery in Normandy. On a pleasant spring morning, we drove to Bayeux, registered at the historic Lion d'Or Hotel, saw the famous Mathilde tapestry, and soaked up the atmosphere of the ancient city. Our visit to Omaha Beach and the Normandy cemetery was scheduled for the next day.

The sun was shining bright as we started our drive to the coast, but what started out to be a good day turned sour just as we came near the American cemetery. A lovely old Normandy farm had attracted my attention. Camera ready, I walked toward the handsome structure, and froze. On the high stone wall, surrounding the venerable farm buildings, was painted in large white letters, "AMI GO HOME!"

My temperature rose immediately. I thought of families who came to visit the graves of their loved ones, those "Amis" lying in the cemetery just a few yards ahead. How would they feel when they saw this unwelcome message? I fumed. Winnie urged me not to let just one more anti-American incident spoil our trip. But I couldn't get it out of my mind.

We were briefed by the superintendent of the Normandy American Military Cemetery, which is located on top of a cliff overlooking Omaha Beach, the scene of the greatest amphibious troop landing in history. The use of the site, 172 acres, was granted in perpetuity by the French government in gratitude of their liberation in World War II.

There are 9,386 American War Dead buried here. The remains of approximately 14,000 others originally interred in this region were returned home at the request of their families. In this cemetery are buried, side-by-side, a father and his son; and in thirty-three instances, two brothers rest side-by-side.

It was my honor to place a wreath at the base of the memorial, a semicircular colonnade with a loggia at each end. On a platform immediately west of the colonnade I saw a twenty-two-foot bronze statue, "The Spirit of American Youth," rising from the waves. Around its base is the inscription: "Mine Eyes Have Seen the Coming of the Lord."

What a beautiful, impressive place this is! I was sure it must go to the heart of every visitor, regardless of nationality. Like our military cemetery in Luxembourg, it is maintained by the American Battle Monuments Commission, an agency created by an Act of Congress in 1923. The landscaping contributes to the feeling of profound awe and respect. The Garden of the Missing affected me the most. Inscribed on its walls are the name, rank, organization and home state of 1,557 Americans.

On Omaha Beach there is still evidence of the German defences: rails or heavy angle irons and logs driven in the sand; concrete blockhouses and pillboxes remain. Barbed wire is still rusting along some areas. Along the brow of the vertical stone cliffs overlooking the beach run remnants of the trenches which held machine gun and mortar emplacements. The flat area at the base of the cliffs was heavily mined.

The first wave of troops had to disembark from their boats in water up to their waists, and wade ashore through these obstacles, under incredibly heavy fire. Against all odds, they went on to secure the beachheads, almost inch by inch.

After our tour, a committee of French citizens of nearby Colleville-sur-Mer invited us for coffee and cake. These friendly people did their best to make us feel welcome. When I was asked to say a few words, I told myself to be diplomatic, not to mention the disturbing message on the wall of the farm en route to the cemetery. But once I started to speak, I couldn't control what was in my heart. I simply had to tell these people how I felt about that graffiti.

"The 9,386 Amis buried in this cemetery *can't* go home," I said. "They made the ultimate sacrifice so that you and I could live in peace and freedom and prosperity."

There was deadly silence when I finished, but after the meeting broke up a few minutes later, each of our hosts came to me, solemnly shook my hand and said, "Merci!" Several of them had tears in their eyes. I put aside my regrets and made up my mind that from then on I would always speak up against anti-Americanism of any form.

On the following morning, Winnie and I continued on our journey to Mont St. Michel and then to the beautiful Quiberon peninsula and its Côte Sauvage in Brittany. Leaving Bayeux, we traveled the same highway, N-814, going south, past the same farm. The "Ami Go Home" message on its walls had been painted over, its unfriendly statement wiped out. For me, the sun was shining brighter on the lovely French countryside.

Not long after our trip to Normandy, another anti-American incident arose at a public lecture sponsored by the Miami Center in Luxembourg. The speaker was Ivor Richards, a member of the British Labor party and former British representative to the United Nations. He was having great sport ripping the Reagan administration apart. His remarks turned into a hard-ass anti-American lecture. I sat, squirming helplessly, in the audience. Then I remembered my resolve. I got up and walked out. My gesture was not lost on the audience. Jeremy Thomas, the British ambassador, called me later that evening to apologize. "Look here, old boy, that was rather boorish of old Ivor. . . ."

Back in the State Department they got wind of my stand. The next evaluation report on me from Washington referred to my being "outspoken." It noted that, "he is not reluctant to act when he thinks the U.S. is being unfairly criticized." I considered that a compliment.

Memorable Occasions

MAJOR TODD, our Office of Defense coordinator, escorted Winnie and me on our first official visit to HQ United States European Command (HQ USEUCOM) at Vaihingen-Stuttgart, and to HQ USAREUR, United States Army in Europe, Heidelberg.

A U.S. Air Force C-12 picked us up in Luxembourg, and after our two-day stay in Stuttgart took us to our next destination, a military airport I couldn't identify. There we were transferred to an army helicopter. Major Todd explained that this portion of the trip was to be a surprise.

Within minutes we were zooming over territory I did recognize—the city of Nuremberg. Someone knew about my experiences during the war. We touched down in the middle of the enormous arena in which thousands of uniformed Nazis of all ages had paid homage to Hitler and his cohorts at annual Nazi party rallies in the 1930s. The film "Triumph des Willens" was turned in this place. Now the arena was desolate, overgrown with weeds. The concrete ramps and stands were crumbling. I found it rather spooky on that gray, wintry day. We didn't linger.

Our helicopter landed at the headquarters of the Second Armored Cavalry Regiment, the same unit to which I had been assigned temporarily in May 1945. Colonel Reed was in command then; it was when we liberated the Lipizzaner horses. Now the commanding officer was Colonel David E. Maddox, who welcomed us and briefed us on his regiment's mission.

We lifted off again. Ten minutes later, we were back on the ground in the center of a small military base. It was Camp Hof. We enjoyed lunch with the troops and their officers, and received a Border Briefing. We were on the East German frontier, known as "Freedom's End." The mission of the mechanized cavalrymen stationed at Camp Hof was to patrol the border, a vast extension of the infamous Berlin Wall.

Winnie and I were given the grand border tour. Our helicopter traversed the miles and miles of meshed wire fence which separates East from West Germany. I was stunned. It wasn't just the wire fencing that was more shocking than the wall in Berlin. It was what went with it. A strip of freshly plowed land, sown with mines, ran along the fence. Next to it was a concrete pit about six feet wide and six feet deep. Then came a narrow road patrolled by an armored car and, at regular intervals, by trained dogs. Lookout towers were positioned about five hundred feet apart. Two guards armed with machine guns were stationed in each tower. With binoculars we were able to observe them observing us flying along their precious fence. They were obviously agitated. Were we about to attack? It was depressing, and yet, ridiculous enough to be amusing. All of this, to make sure their own people could not reach freedom.

I spotted activity below us and signaled the pilot to land. American soldiers in a jeep and on foot were patrolling the road on our side of the fence. We climbed out of our helicopter and walked toward them. These troopers had never met an ambassador. And this ambassador had never met young men assigned to such dismal duty in time of peace. In icy cold weather, young Americans walked and rode up and down this deserted country road, keeping their eyes on "the other side"—patrolling, prepared for—whatever? There was a small tarpaper shelter with a potbelly stove where from time to time they could go for warmth.

A short stretch down the road was a tiny village. Its name is Moerdlareuth, the men explained. It's also called "little Berlin" because the fence leading to it becomes a solid ten-foot wall, splitting the village in two. Before the wall was built, there were three hundred people in Moerdlareuth. Now there are just twenty living on the east side of the wall, and twenty-five on the free side.

We talked to the cavalry troopers. They belonged to the Second ACR; had been on duty for nearly three weeks. Their squad was rotated to the border camps for duty periods of thirty to forty days. I groped in my mind for something meaningful to say to these boys, all younger than our own three sons. But I decided speech making was unnecessary. They let us know that their spirits were boosted just by our being there.

When we walked back to the aircraft, one of the soldiers followed me. He was a nineteen-year-old American Samoan. "Excuse me, Mr. Ambassador," he said, "could I ask you a question?" Of course! "Do you get to see the President very often?"

"Not very often, son, why?"

"Well, I have a message for the President I'd like to give you."

"Okay. Let me have it," I said. "I'll do my best to see the President gets it."

"Sir, please tell the President that we're damn proud to be here, and we ain't afraid of nothing."

For some reason, I discovered a big lump in my throat. I quickly shook the young soldier's hand, said thank you, and boarded our helicopter.

Back in my office in Luxembourg, I wondered how I could get the young soldier's message to Ronald Reagan. I already knew that a telegram or letter through regular State Department channels would end up being intercepted by third-echelon bureaucrats. It would never reach the president himself.

My secretary Janet suggested I write directly to the president. So, I did. Not long thereafter, and much to my amazement, I received a personal letter on White House letterhead. It read:

Dear John:

Thanks very much for your letter and for telling me about your visit to the Second Armored Cavalry Regiment. Having been a cavalry officer, you can imagine my pride in reading your impression of them. Of course, I was *horse* cavalry, but evidently the spirit remains unchanged.

I'm particularly grateful for the message you passed on from the young trooper. I intend, at the first opportunity, to see that our people hear what he had to say. Americans need to know what kind of spirit motivates these young men in military service.

Thanks again for writing. Give my best to Winnie and, to both of you, a thank you for what you are doing.

Sincerely,
Ron

That should have been the end of the story. But three months later, President Reagan offered a patriotic address in honor of the nation's Thirty-third Armed Forces Day. He paid tribute to the soldiers, the sailors, the airmen, and the marines—in the United States and around the world—the ultimate guardians of our freedom to say what we think, go where we will, choose who we want for our leaders, and pray as we wish. He emphasized that we cannot afford to take our freedom for granted. It cannot survive without protection. "And for their role in protecting our freedoms, we honor the members of our volunteer armed forces today," he added.

Then Reagan said he got a letter from a U.S. ambassador in a European nation which passed along a message from a nineteen-year-old soldier. The president told my story, and quoted the message the young American Samoan had given me on that freezing winter day on the lonely road at Freedom's End.

The rest of the tale is unbelievable. That soldier happened to hear the president's talk on the Armed Forces Radio network. He nearly went berserk. He stormed into his commander's office. "The system works, the goddamn system works," he cried out. "I gave a message to an ambassador, he gave it to the President, and the President gave it to all the people!"

The CO called me from Germany to tell me all this. He said the morale of his entire troop was "sky-high" and that the soldier himself had reenlisted for another three years. "Thanks to you, Mr. Ambassador," he added.

It made my day. That experience is a major high point in my short career as a diplomat. And there were many. Today, on the wall of my study hangs a beautifully inscribed certificate, bearing the insignia of the Second Armored Cavalry Regiment:

TO WHOM IT MAY CONCERN: GREETINGS!
   Know ye that Ambassador John E. Dolibois has on this 10th day of February in the year of our Lord 1982 visited the Border of the Free World, guarded by this the oldest Cavalry Regiment on continuous active duty in the United States Army.
   Given under my hand and seal in the Federal Republic of Germany,

                              David M. Maddox
                              61st Colonel of the Regiment
                              Commanding

The last overnight stop on our unforgettable sojourn to Germany in 1982 was Heidelberg. Winnie and I were guests in the quarters of General and Mrs. Fritz Kroesen, the commander in chief, U.S. Army in Europe. Our genial hosts invited key staff members to a splendid dinner in our honor. The dinner table conversation focused on an attempt by a terrorist group in West Germany to assassinate General Kroesen just two weeks earlier. Thanks to this hair-raising experience, the Kroesens were forced to move from the elegant villa they had occupied on a wooded hillside overlooking Heidelberg Castle, and take up residence in more secure quarters on the base.

I was privileged to observe several army maneuvers in West Germany and particularly recall the "Carbine Fortress" training exercises in September 1982. Major units from European land-based U.S., German, and Canadian wartime forces took part, reinforced by elements from the Netherlands, Belgium, and Luxembourg.

My daytime base was a helicopter from which I was able to observe the mock battles by armored units, infantry, and helicopter fighters. At one point we touched down to get a firsthand look at a river-crossing of two armored battalions. While standing at the river's edge, I was approached by a small group of German officers. In their midst was the commander in chief of the German army, General Glanz. We shook hands and engaged in idle chatter while watching the troops slog through mud and water.

The irony of the situation struck me. Who would have thought in 1945, when the German enemy surrendered to us unconditionally, that forty years later we would be training side-by-side as friends and allies? It called to mind what Goering, Doenitz, and others had said to me in Mondorf: "Some day you will need Germany."

As I was talking to the general I couldn't help but wonder what he would say if I told him that after the war in 1945, I had interrogated some of his predecessors, particularly Field Marshals Keitel, von Blomberg, and Kesselring.

But even though we worked as friends and allies, diplomacy and tact were needed in dealing with memories of the war. The Bitburg affair soon brought home that point.

Ever since Kissinger days, everyone in the Department of State and in Washington fancies himself a roving ambassador-at-large. At the slightest sign of a problem, the bags are packed, and someone—from the secretary on down—is on the road as a troubleshooter even though in many instances an ambassador on the scene is better qualified to deal with the problem. He knows the language, the people, and the point at issue. But we insist on sending an "expert," with aides, assistants, note-takers, and, in some cases, secret service protection. We create added expense for the host country, while the troubleshooter plows in, rushes through a twenty minute briefing and a half-hour démarche, and then dashes off, leaving the details and the cleaning-up to the ambassador in residence and his staff.

The Bitburg fiasco is a splendid case in point. The Thirty-sixth Tactical Fighter Wing is based at Bitburg, Germany, just forty minutes by car from Luxembourg City. American personnel at our embassy were fortunate to be able to get medical attention and dental care at the fine clinics on the base. Each month, Winnie went to Bitburg to buy household supplies for our residence, and a few personal items. The air force people at Bitburg often included us in the social events and vice versa. Bitburg and Spengdahlem are two of the few U.S. installations in Germany where Americans are genuinely welcome, no protest demonstrations, no resentment, no ill-will. Thus I found out early on that President Reagan would be attending a summit meeting in West Germany, and might visit the friendly Bitburg Air Base.

Chancellor Helmut Kohl invited Reagan to extend his trip to the summit into an official State Visit to the Federal Republic. This would be particularly significant, in that May 1985 marked the fortieth anniversary of the end of World War II in Europe. A joint excursion to the German Military Cemetery in Bitburg was proposed as a symbolic gesture most appropriate to the mutual friendship of both nations.

But our intelligence hinted that we were heading for an international flapdoodle. Two thousand German soldiers are buried in the small German Military Cemetery in Bitburg. Forty-nine of them were members of the notorious Waffen SS. If the president of the United States went around laying wreaths in honor of SS soldiers, Jews and other victims of the Holocaust around the world would be offended. Why put the president in such a bind? Warning signals were sent to Washington. Look into this before all hell breaks loose!

But instead of letting our ambassador to West Germany, Arthur Burns, do his job and find a solution to the problem, Washington sent a special envoy, Michael Deaver, deputy chief of staff at the White House. Deaver was the man charged with the image-making of Ronald Reagan.

I guess Deaver was about five years old when the Waffen SS were butchering American prisoners of war during the Battle of the Bulge. I bet the Malmédy Massacre was never mentioned in his elementary school textbooks. Nor would he understand how millions of Jews might feel about the president visiting the graves of Waffen SS. It was reported that while in Germany, Deaver was busy buying BMWs at diplomatic discount for his friends in Washington.

He visited the Bitburg cemetery. There was snow on the ground, so he couldn't see the Waffen SS markers. The U.S. embassy in Bonn could have told him that every military cemetery has a register of names and ranks of all soldiers interred therein, snow or no snow. In fact, any kid on the street could have told him the same thing.

I called Ambassador Burns when we heard the first rumbles of discord about the president's itinerary. He shared my concern and encouraged me to follow through on an alternate program we discussed. I sent a telegram to Washington with a proposal: Let Reagan make his visit to the Bitburg Air Base. Let him speak to the Americans and the friendly Germans in Bitburg. After that, the president and Chancellor Kohl, and their retinues, could be airlifted by helicopters to the American Military

Cemetery in Luxembourg in fifteen minutes. They could land in the amply secure cemetery parking lot, and be welcomed by the Grand Duke of Luxembourg. Ronald Reagan would be the first president of the United States to set foot on Luxembourg soil in the history of both countries. All Luxembourgers would be delighted.

Then they could enter the cemetery, and place a wreath on the grave of General George S. Patton, Jr., in tribute to the 5,074 Americans lying under the white marble crosses and stars of David that stand in awesome serenity, row upon row, in that memorable setting. All American veterans would be delighted.

Just a short kilometer from the American Cemetery of Hamm is the German Military Cemetery of Sandweiler. Here lie some 10,000 German soldiers, most of whom died in the Battle of the Bulge, not an SS man among them. The president and the chancellor could place a wreath at the stone cross in the center of the scores of gravemarkers. This gesture of friendship and solidarity would delight all Germans. The entire journey and ceremonies would take no more than ninety minutes. The president would be spared the extensive negative criticism of a worldwide press. A lot of people would be happy.

My recommendation wasn't even considered. It got a half-assed reply from the State Department, with some lame explanation about protocol and timing. In short, "mind your own business!" Our great nation can put a man on the moon, but we couldn't move our president thirty miles from Bitburg to Luxembourg.

On Sunday morning, May 5, at the same hour that President Reagan was making the controversial visit to the German Military Cemetery in Bitburg, officials of the Simon Wiesenthal Center of Los Angeles and Luxembourg resistance leaders and concentration camp survivors of World War II joined members of the Grand Duchy's Jewish Community at the American Military Cemetery in Luxembourg. I was invited to attend. I accepted the invitation, much to everyone's surprise.

Initially ballyhooed as a protest rally, the ceremony was one of the most inspiring I have ever witnessed. I was proud to be a part of it. It was not filled with protest; it was deeply reverent and moving. Criticism of the president was inherent in the remarks that were made, but it wasn't vicious criticism. "We feel Reagan should have been here, not in Bitburg," said one person. Another pointed out that they came from the United States because a historic blunder had been made which needed to be challenged. "Let there be no confusion. Those interred here in the American Cemetery fought and died *for* the principle of Judeo-Christian civilization. Those buried at Bitburg fought to *end* it."

I took part in the laying of a wreath which bore the words, "To free us from tyranny was *their* cause. To remember them forever must be *our* cause." In my address I spoke of the need to remember the Nazi tyranny of forty years earlier, the responsibility to commemorate the liberation of the concentration camps, to honor those who fought to defeat Nazi Germany. I defended Reagan's wreath-laying at Bitburg, but emphasized that it was also important the ceremony in Luxembourg was taking place.

The press treated me kindly in covering the event. I know, however, there were others who criticized my taking part. The damage had been done. I still think Reagan should have come to Luxembourg. Only his personal charm and persuasive ability saved the rest of this controversial trip to Germany in 1985.

Winnie and I traveled to Bitburg that Sunday afternoon. We witnessed the dramatic landing of Air Force One, and heard President Reagan's speech to American and German military personnel and their families. I couldn't help feeling that with just a little effort and team work his entire journey could have been a tremendous success, without controversy and loss of face.

The conviction that Vice President George Bush should visit Luxembourg was deeply impressed upon me by Luxembourgers both in and out of government. Each time Mr. Bush came to Europe for meetings in Brussels, The Hague, Bonn, or elsewhere, I felt the needle. "Luxembourg is important too. Why doesn't he come to see us?"

I tried to bring it about. But my telegrams and messages through State Department channels never got beyond a deputy assistant secretary of state. In meetings where official visits were planned, the bureaucrats always opted for "more important" places. They took Luxembourg's friendship for granted. Cultivation of the little Grand Duchy wasn't necessary.

I began to see where the power was. Apparently George Bush had nothing to say about it. When it comes to diplomatic travel, the vice president, as well as the president, is a captive of State Department functionaries and his own advisory staff. On two private visits to the Vice President's House during the first two years of my tenure, Barbara Bush had expressed the hope that we would invite them. They had been in seventy-nine countries, but never in Luxembourg.

Then I lucked out. I was in Washington for consultations in October 1983. Faith Whittlesey, who had been named ambassador to Switzerland at the time I started my diplomatic career, was recalled to serve as assistant to the president for Public Liaison. I called on Ambassador Whittlesey at the White House. In the course of conversation I told her of my frustrations in getting through the State Department to arrange a Bush visit to Luxembourg.

"Oh, you're going at it all wrong," she said. "You must use the White House Signal, and talk directly to Bud McFarlane, the National Security Advisor. Do it while you're here, now."

"What's the White House Signal?" I asked. Of course, "they" hadn't told me about it. Political appointees don't get told everything they should know. The White House Signal is a special telephone number which gets you right into the top White House offices, including the president's.

Faith gave me the number, made me promise not to tell where I got it, and then suggested I go downstairs to the lobby and dial the magic digits. I did. "This is Ambassador Dolibois from Luxembourg," I said with a ring of authority. "Please connect me with Bud McFarlane's office." In just a moment I was hearing McFarlane's secretary. I explained that I was in the East Wing, and wondered if I could see Mr. McFarlane for just a few minutes. No problem. It was that simple. In no time at all, Peter Sommer, the National Security Council director for Europe, appeared and led me to the NSC office. But just as we entered, the "red phone" rang. The secretary held up her hand. "I'm so sorry," she said, "Mr. McFarlane has just been called to the Oval Office. The President is going to announce the invasion of Grenada." I gulped. I was undoubtedly the first U.S. ambassador in Europe to get *that* bit of news.

Still, my call was not in vain. Peter Sommer would talk to me and get my message to McFarlane. Sommer agreed that a visit to Luxembourg by a vice president was long overdue. He suggested I write a detailed letter to Admiral Daniel Murphy, the vice president's chief of staff. Meanwhile, Sommer would talk to Bud McFarlane who would surely support my request.

A month later I received a copy of a confidential memo from Charles Hill, executive secretary of the Department of State, to Donald Gregg, assistant to the vice president for National Security affairs:

Ambassador Dolibois may by now have been in touch with the Vice President, renewing his recommendation that Mr. Bush visit Luxembourg on his next trip to Europe.

During his tenure as Ambassador in Luxembourg, Dolibois has worked to allay Luxembourg's concern that its support of U.S. positions and interests might simply be taken for granted. To that end, he has, *inter alia*, encouraged visits by high-level U.S. officials. With regard to the Vice President, Dolibois reports that his hosts are sensitive to the fact that Mr. Bush has traveled to many European countries but has not yet had an opportunity to enjoy Luxembourg's hospitality.

Without presuming to judge the Vice President's schedule and other commitments, the Department believes that a brief stop in Luxembourg on one of his future trips would be a worthwhile goodwill gesture to one of our small, but very loyal, allies.

I had indeed talked to Mr. Bush. He wanted to make his visit to Luxembourg truly meaningful and asked how he might accomplish this. I earnestly suggested that he bring with him an invitation from President Reagan to the Grand Duke for a State Visit to the United States. I'd already learned that General Vessey and Secretary of Defense Weinberger had also proposed this to the president after their own visits to Luxembourg. In fact, General Vessey sent me a telegram after he "raised the visit" with the president. "The seed has been planted, but needs a little watering from Foggy Bottom," he informed me. Things looked good. That White House signal was a useful thing to have.

The "pre-advance team" to work out details of the visit by Vice President and Mrs. Bush arrived and stayed a week. They were followed by the "advance team," and now all hell broke loose. Installation of communication devices, telephones, including the "red phone"—a direct line to the White House—was of major importance.

One day Winnie was straightening the drapes next to the table holding the red instrument, and accidentally knocked the receiver off the hook. She said she heard the weirdest noises and was tempted to talk into the line to reassure Ronnie that "it's only me from over the sea." But she resisted the temptation. No emergency resulted. The busy work went on and on. And, finally, when we were all ready, the Lebanon crisis erupted. We got the word "they are not coming!" Imagine the wailing and gnashing of teeth. But soon came a reassuring follow-up: "They're coming," but two days later than originally planned. We started rescheduling and reshuffling. Then Andropov died (I think on purpose), and everything was up in the air again. Fortunately the funeral was a day later than expected, and we finally welcomed our official guests, the first vice president to visit Luxembourg since 1963.

At 6:35 P.M. on February 12, 1984, Air Force Two arrived at Luxembourg International Airport. Accompanied by the Luxembourg Chief of Protocol Paul Faber, I climbed the aircraft steps to welcome Vice President and Mrs. Bush. No sooner had we exchanged greetings when Mr. Bush reached into his coat pocket and pulled out a letter from the president to His Royal Highness. "We did it!" he said with obvious pleasure. I was elated!

Luxembourg's Prime Minister Pierre Werner and Winnie greeted our visitors when we came down the stairs from the plane. Hundreds of cameras clicked and flashbulbs popped. Reporters from France, Germany, and even Holland, had joined Luxembourg newsmen on the platform erected for the "photo opportunity."

The printed itinerary for the Bush visit was reduced to such detail that nothing could go wrong. The Luxembourgers went all out in making it a great occasion. Meetings with government officials and a formal dinner at Chateau Senningen topped off the evening. Early the next morning, after breakfast with Winnie and me, the Bushes participated in an "American Community Greeting" in our residence. Embassy staff and U.S. government officials of other agencies in Luxembourg, spouses, and children had a chance to meet and be photographed with our VIP visitors.

The Air Force Band from Bitburg was on hand at the American Military Cemetery for a formal wreath-laying ceremony. So were a bunch of Miami students. When I pointed them out to the vice president, he rushed into their midst, shook hands, and earned the Reagan-Bush ticket a lot of votes in one fell swoop. The Secret Service men were going out of their minds, but the young people were enthralled.

An impressive ritual at the Luxembourg Solidarity Monument, and then a "Press Availability"; in other words, a press conference. We raced from it to the palace for a private meeting and lunch with the royal family.

The whirlwind tour ended at 1:00 P.M., on the nose, with an official farewell at the airport. The Vice President had invited Foreign Minister Colette Flesch to fly to Moscow in Air Force Two for the Andropov funeral. Luxembourgers were impressed.

The State Visit was scheduled for November 13, 1984, just one week after the presidential elections. I'm sure Luxembourgers, along with me, hoped for a Reagan victory. If the State Visit should follow a defeat at the polls, it could be a crêpe-hanger. Meanwhile, other excitements were in store for us before we would wing our way to Washington.

The American Military Cemetery at Hamm is in a setting that touches the heart of every visitor regardless of nationality. Beautifully tended, meticulously groomed, the cemetery has thousands of visitors all year long. Nobody walks among those endless rows of white marble crosses and stars of David without a lump in the throat or tear in the eye. General Patton's lone marker at the head of his troops is in itself a picture one doesn't forget.

In 1984 and 1985, I visited the cemetery at least once or twice a week. These were the years marking the fortieth anniversary of the liberation of Luxembourg and the end of the Second World War. American veterans of the Battle of the Bulge, and the battles of the Moselle and the Rhine, came to Europe from all parts of the United States. Many brought their families on this tour of remembrance, the first in forty years, and, for many, the last. Those who made this pilgrimage in company with former buddies always requested a memorial service at the cemetery. As U.S. ambassador I was invited to welcome them and make a few remarks. I don't think I ever took part in such a ritual without feeling emotionally drained afterwards.

The "Amicale de Buchenwald" is an organization of former Luxembourg inmates of the notorious Buchenwald concentration camp. They were the ones lucky enough to have survived the ordeal, and they have not forgotten it.

In early April 1945, all talk among Buchenwald prisoners was focused on the advance of Allied troops, which were approaching Thuringen, the region in which Buchenwald was located. They heard the thunder of artillery and gunfire in the distance. The SS Kommandos tried to round up all the Jews, an exercise that turned into a cat-and-mouse game. Every time they managed to get several thousand into the camp square, there would be an air-alarm; the SS guards would scramble for the bomb shelters, and the Jewish inmates would run off to hiding places. When the all-clear sounded, the game would begin again. The Jews were to be "evacuated" (exterminated) before the arrival of the Americans. It was all part of the "final solution." Jewish and non-Jewish inmates collaborated in frustrating this process, hoping to gain time.

On April 8, the prisoners' "camp committee" sent an SOS signal to Allied troops on the illegal radio system they had rigged up: "Here is Concentration Camp Buchenwald. SOS-SOS-SOS. Please help! Camp is being evacuated. The SS will exterminate us!"

The evacuation had been ordered because the crematorium of Buchenwald had broken down. Mass graves for those already exterminated were being dug in great haste. But the frantic efforts of the German SS to conceal all traces of their crimes were constantly interrupted by air raids, rumors, and confusing orders.

Wednesday, April 11. Thousands of the prisoners had spent a sleepless night. Would they be annihilated by bombings? Would the SS make one last attempt to execute as many of their prisoners as possible?

At 11:30 A.M. the alarm siren came on again. Its meaning was clear. "Enemy tanks approaching!" Moments later, the PA system ordered all SS to leave camp immediately. They were to fight their last battle. Minutes later, the first Sherman tank crashed through the camp gates. Buchenwald was liberated. On the next day, the twenty-one thousand survivors held a memorial service for the fifty-two thousand who had died.

The Luxembourgers who survived Buchenwald have not forgotten. Every year since 1945, they meet at 11:30 A.M. on April 11 at the American Military Cemetery to commemorate their liberation and to give thanks.

Reverently, they assemble at the chapel, march silently past the memorial walls holding the names of the Americans "who sleep in unknown graves." They stand together at the cross marking that of General Patton, under whom served the Sixth Armored Division which liberated them and probably saved their lives.

At Patton's grave they hold a brief, but deeply moving, service. Johny Schmit, "Honorary Bugler of the Resistance," renders an inspiring "America the Beautiful," and then plays taps—the *Sonnerie des Morts.* Léon Bartimes, president of the Amicale and mayor of Beaufort, places a large wreath on General Patton's grave.

In 1984 more than a hundred veterans of the Sixth Armored Division, which on April 11, 1945 liberated Buchenwald, made a pilgrimage to Luxembourg. I thought it would be a great idea for them to have a joint service at General Patton's grave with the people whose lives they had saved forty years earlier. Colonel Edward F. Reed, who directed the Sixth Armored Division tour, eagerly concurred in my proposal. So did Mayor Bartimes.

But when I arrived at the cemetery that morning, I saw that something had developed far beyond my capacity to handle alone. On one side of Patton's grave stood thirty-five Luxembourg men and women, the members of the Amicale de Buchenwald. On the other side stood 124 American veterans. The people in both groups just looked at each other. The silence was deafening. Emotion had overcome them. As I wondered what I might say to relieve the tension, one of the Luxembourg ladies pointed to an American. "I think I remember you," she said. "Isn't your name Buddy?" With that, the two walked toward each other and embraced. Immediately, all the Luxembourgers and Americans came together, shaking hands, hugging each other, all of them crying. The ice was broken, the day was saved.

In the afternoon, the Sixth AD veterans moved on to Beaufort, and were welcomed by Mayor Bartimes at the historic, romantic Beaufort Castle ruin, a major tourist attraction.

"Wëllkomm a Merci!" said the mayor to his guests.

As Mayor of Beaufort and on behalf of the inhabitants of this town, I have the honor to welcome you men from America who, risking your own lives, helped in liberating our little home country forty years ago. I mean the veterans of the Sixth Armored Division. I would like to thank them for freeing us from Nazi terror. We remember the dreadful weather conditions of the 1944 winter under which you, as young soldiers, had to fight on our territory. I myself was out of the country. In 1942, I had already been arrested, and together with other Luxembourg resistance men, taken to the Buchenwald concentration camp. On April 11, 1945, your unit freed the 21,000 prisoners there.

As President of the Luxembourg prisoners, I am happy to receive you here in the castle of my home town, and to thank you for your liberation. The German SS were about to extinguish the rest of the camp when we saw the first American tanks approaching. Each year we commemorate the eleventh of April by laying a wreath at General Patton's grave, together with the honorable American Ambassador John E. Dolibois. As long as we live, we won't forget what you did for us; we owe you our life and our freedom.

With a specialty of the area, Cassis de Beaufort, we lifted our glasses to eternal friendship. The mayor urged everyone to "enjoy as many drinks as you like." Some of them did. It was a memorable occasion.

Far north, in the heart of the Luxembourg Ardennes, lies the village of Eschweiler, whose mayor, J. P. Strotz, invited us for a special visit. On a chilly afternoon in the fall, as we turned off the main road on approach to the village, our way was blocked by several hundred people of all ages. Apparently all of Eschweiler served as a welcoming committee. I was wondering why we were met on the open road, when the mayor led us a short distance into the adjoining woods. We came upon a small clearing in which stood a handsome monument. By its side rose a flagpole on which fluttered the Stars and Stripes in the breeze. It was a memorial to an American GI, George Mergenthaler.

Mayor Strotz invited me to join him in placing a wreath, and then led Winnie and me, and the rest of the people, a short distance into the village. We entered the parish church, and were greeted by the pastor and the retired schoolmaster, eighty-four-year-old Josef Harpes, who was also the village historian. Professor Harpes proudly recounted the story of George Mergenthaler.

When American troops roared into Luxembourg in September 1944, Eschweiler was liberated along with all the other outlying farm communities in the Ardennes region. A small task force was assigned to each village to help restore order and to assist the local administration. Among the handful of soldiers of the Twenty-eighth Infantry, the "Keystone" Division, was twenty-four-year-old George Mergenthaler, graduate of Princeton University, grandson of G. Ottmar Mergenthaler, a German immigrant and inventor of the linotype machine.

George Mergenthaler was billeted in the house of the village priest,

Pastor Anton Bodson. He soon became the "favorite son" of the whole community. A Roman Catholic, he attended mass faithfully every morning, even served as acolyte on occasion.

Eschweiler residents like to tell about the afternoon of December 16 when their young American friend came calling on them, house-to-house, to show off the sweater his mother had knitted and sent him for Christmas. They remember the exact date because on the following morning came the frightening news of a major German counterattack. It was the beginning of what became known as the Battle of the Bulge. The people of Eschweiler were directed to evacuate the village. Some of the heaviest fighting was to occur in their area. George Mergenthaler and a few members of his company were left behind to defend their position.

American troops recaptured Eschweiler on January 20, 1945. In the course of the attack and counterattack, thirty-six of the village's fifty-six houses were completely destroyed. The parish church received several direct hits. The roof, belltower, windows, and the interior were shattered. The Germans, in retreat, took with them all the horses, eighty-three head of cattle, more than a hundred pigs, not to mention the furnishings and other possessions of the villagers whose homes they had occupied and plundered.

Captured records revealed that twenty-eight American soldiers and their company commander, a captain, had been taken prisoners by the Germans. George Mergenthaler's name was not among them.

Eschweiler was a no-man's land for three days. Then evacuees returned, one by one. Liberating American soldiers were again welcomed enthusiastically. In their search for runaway farm animals and unexploded bombs and land mines in surrounding fields and forests, Eschweiler people came upon the body of an American soldier in a foxhole, in woods not far from the main road. They knew they had found George Mergenthaler by the sweater he was wearing. On March 26, the body was moved in reverent procession to the village cemetery and there interred. On the site where George's body was found, a monument was erected—the very monument we had just visited.

Ever since 1945, that memorial has been kept in good condition by the people of Eschweiler. The American flag is flown there proudly. On March 26 each year, a procession is held from the monument to the village church where a Mass of Remembrance is dedicated to George Mergenthaler.

In 1947, the Mergenthaler family came to Eschweiler to reclaim their son's remains. In appreciation of the people's kindness to their son, Alix and Herman Mergenthaler contributed substantially to the reconstruction of the parish church. In the narthex of that church, above a marble likeness of George Mergenthaler, is inscribed: "We gave our only son so that others could live in love and peace."

Above the main altar of the church is a colorful mural depicting the biblical scene of the loaves and fishes. Among the apostles, disciples, and followers gathered around Jesus, is portrayed a young man easily recognized as the American soldier, George Mergenthaler. Thousands of Americans have visited Eschweiler in the last forty years, and have shared the story and memory of the young soldier with the people of the community.

I was deeply moved in hearing and seeing all this. So much so, that I wrote a long letter to President Reagan to share this inspiring story. Two years later, in the course of the State Dinner at the White House in honor of the Grand Duke and Grand Duchess, President Reagan retold the story I had shared with him, exemplifying the bonds that hold our two nations together.

This had quite an impact on the royal family and the other Luxembourg guests, not to mention Winnie and me. But when the Reagan speech was rebroadcast in Luxembourg, the Eschweiler people were simply overwhelmed. The fact that the head of the most powerful nation in the world would deign to mention their cherished story, and their village, was just too much for the good people.

I stood tall as an American in Luxembourg at many other celebrations marking the fortieth anniversary of the liberation and the end of World War II. The return of U.S. veterans to Europe during this period of remembering gave me frequent opportunity to remind Europeans that these "Yankees" or "Amis" had been there before, had helped them immensely, and upon returning home took nothing from them. We basked in the warmth of the genuine affection the knowledgeable part of the population has for their friends from across the Atlantic.

CEBA stands for "Cercle d'Études sur la Bataille des Ardennes." It is indeed a "study circle"—Luxembourg men and women, who have banned together to make sure the sacrifices, the heroics, the lessons, and gratitude are not forgotten. All over the country, historic monuments, commemorations, museums, lectures, and reunions bear the stamp of CEBA. This organization gets involved in everything relating to the Battle of the Bulge. Their secretary, Tilly Kimmes, an enthusiastic, energetic stem-winder, has probably more friends and grateful admirers in the USA than any other living Luxembourger. Any former GI returning to the scenes of action of forty years ago is advised to contact CEBA for assistance. They have all the information on who fought where and when. CEBA can locate families in whose homes returning veterans were billeted as GIs. They have brought hundreds of the former and latter together for tearful and joyful reunions.

Camille Kohn, president of CEBA, is a walking encyclopedia on every weapon, order of battle, military advancement and retreat, associated with the Germans' last desperate effort to turn the war around. CEBA's proudest achievement was the erection of a "Monument to the GI" in Clervaux, an historic little town which suffered tremendously during the Ardennes Offensive.

The Monument du GI is a striking life-size bronze statue of an American soldier. The perfect reproduction of the familiar figure and characteristic stance, brings a tear to the eye of anyone who has ever seen the World War II soldier in action, rifle cradled in his arms or slung from his shoulder, confidently and proudly advancing along the road to the next village to be liberated.

Among the many events organized by CEBA which I attended, the dedication of a monument to the Ninth Armored Division in Medernach stands out. The Ninth celebrated a "return to Remagen" on March 7, 1985, forty years after they had miraculously captured the only remaining bridge providing a ready invasion route to Germany. This feat helped shorten the war immensely.

Before advancing into Germany, the Ninth AD was headquartered in Medernach, Luxembourg, so it was appropriate to erect a tribute to the division along the main highway into this little town. Crown Prince Henri of Luxembourg was invited to unveil the new monument. Top government officials and dignitaries were on hand. So were several hundred veterans of the famous division.

Prince Henri, assisted by the former division commander, pulled the cord which exposed the sturdy monument to view. At that point someone asked me if the Prince might like to meet the first American across the Remagen bridge. I checked with the Prince. He would be delighted. They brought the seventy-five-year-old sergeant to us. He was wearing a colorful jacket and snazzy baseball cap with the Ninth Division insignia. With special pride I turned to the young prince, who was dressed in an immaculately tailored suit and camel hair coat. "Your Royal Highness, may I present Sgt. Alex Dabrick, the first American across the Remagen bridge!"

The Prince held out his hand, Sergeant Dabrick grabbed it, pointed his left forefinger at the young man, and turning to me said: "Now who is this kid?" I nearly dropped my teeth. But the future Grand Duke took it right in stride and graciously pretended not to have noticed. Later, I saw him talking to his wife, obviously sharing the incident. Both were having a good laugh, and I decided to join in. I offered a mild apology, which they waved off, and then told me that they actually made a collection of these "amusing" incidents. The Princess told me that just a month earlier they were keeping an appointment with the mayor of a large American city. Their aide-de-camp announced them to the receptionist, a buxom young lady. She waddled into the mayor's office, and emerged a moment later, directing them in with a thumb-over-the-shoulder. "Okay, youse guys can go in now," she said.

Appreciating the humor, I shared these stories with an elderly American friend some time later. She wasn't amused. "Well, you know, we Americans don't go in for this royalty worship," she put me down. I diplomatically decided not to mention Michael Jackson, Johnny Carson, or Elvis Presley.

In the spring of 1984, a memorial tree was planted in front of the Villa Pauly in Luxembourg City. This was in tribute to the many who had suffered at the hands of the Gestapo which had used the villa as headquarters during the occupation. Our friend Emile Krieps, minister of Public Force and minister of Health, was one of those Luxembourgers who were badly mistreated by the Nazi gangsters. Ironically—willfully—Emile chose the very room in which he was severely beaten, as his personal office when he became minister of Health. Luxembourg wry humor!

In late March of that same year, the State Museum exhibited "Turner in Luxembourg," a wide collection of J. M. W. Turner's sketches and paintings of Luxembourg and the general area. A famous "copy" of a Luxembourg Turner by William Ward, authenticated and praised by John Ruskin, is owned by the Fogg Museum at Harvard. Luxembourg requested the loan of it for their big show, but the Fogg director, obviously thinking Luxembourg is a little city in Germany, turned them down cold. The State Museum director asked me to intervene.

Fortunately, we had a good friend in Brussels, Frank Boas, a Fulbright connection, who was on the Harvard Board of Overseers. Frank suggested I write directly to President Derek Bok of Harvard and explain the situation. I'm sure Mr. Boas added his two cents worth. The Ward copy was loaned to Luxembourg and became part of the Turner exhibit. Our embassy shared in the glory. The royal family and the Duke and Duchess of Gloucester attended the colorful opening of the Turner exhibit.

All this came about because Grand Duke Jean contributed an original Turner painting of Luxembourg to the State Museum—a valuable, significant gift. That prompted the museum director to organize the all-

Turner show. The project was three years in the making. It was a high-light cultural event of March.

But then—an exposé! A local newspaper came out with the front page story that the Turner which His Royal Highness had given the museum was a fake. At that very moment "a team of experts from five different museums from around the world was examining the work to get at the truth of it." Shocking! But then I got a funny feeling and looked at the date of the news account. *April first.* They had done it again.

That same winter was made memorable by a visit to Luxembourg from Sister Margaret Georgina Patton, the granddaughter of the famous general. The thirty-one-year-old Benedictine nun had been invited by the American Luxembourg Society as part of the celebration of the end of the Second World War. It was her first visit to the cemetery where her legendary grandfather was buried, and she captured the hearts of all.

Sister Georgina was born after General Patton's death. She converted to the Catholic faith in 1976 to join the order established by the Abbess of the Benedictine Convent of Jouarre, France, a convent that had been liberated by Patton's Third Army on August 27, 1944. The liberation inspired the founding of the Regina-Laudis convent in Connecticut in 1947.

When the young nun, dressed in the habit of her order, fell to her knees before Patton's grave and kissed the earth, I sensed the emotion gripping the people who had joined us at the cemetery. The small bit of drama enacted on a fog-shrouded December morning was another of so many moving experiences that enriched our lives in those embassy years.

End of the Journey

THE PRESIDENTIAL ELECTION of 1984 dominated the news in Luxembourg. Everyone talked about the future of the B-1 bomber, the MX missiles, nuclear freeze, and the ever-present dispute between the two superpowers. It all tied into our elections. Europeans felt themselves directly affected by what would happen in November. We did our best to explain the process, to calm fears.

My staff organized an election party at the Hotel Le Royal in Luxembourg City on November 6, 1984. Snacks, drinks, and the election returns. Prior to this party, I was featured on a one-and-one-half-hour TV interview, carried by RTL-Plus, the German channel. Viewers were encouraged to call into the studio to ask me questions. The whole thing was done in German, with many callers from the German side of the border. Trying to explain the American election process is difficult any time, but doing it in German poses new challenges. I earned my allowance that night.

On the day after the elections, Winnie and I crowded another official visit into an already tight schedule, this one to Wincrange, far up north. And then, two days later, our six suitcases were loaded into the car and we took off for Brussels; for us it was the first leg of the official State Visit by the Grand Duke and Grand Duchess of Luxembourg to the United States.

Arriving in Brussels just ten minutes before flight time, thanks to a traffic jam, we were relieved to be met by the Brussels Pan Am manager, a Mr. Berman. He presented Winnie with a bouquet of flowers and me with a box of chocolates, and gave both of us the assurance that the plane was still waiting. We'd never get treatment like that again, so we relaxed and enjoyed. It was a good beginning for what would be the climax of our ambassadorial career.

We registered into the Washington Vista International Hotel. All official guests were being lodged there while Blair House was being remodeled. The Luxembourg party of eighteen arrived in the afternoon on November 10. Paul Peters, the Grand Duchy's ambassador to Washington, his wife Renée, Winnie and I joined Ambassador Elwa "Lucky" Roosevelt, protocol chief of the State Department, at Baltimore-Washington airport. We were the official greeters welcoming Their Royal Highnesses and their retinue.

Thus began a tightly scheduled seven days of a fantastic tour. Imagine an entourage, which included a lady-in-waiting, butlers and maids, not to mention the American host team, the ambassadors, the aides, government officials, and all those needed for security. Traffic control, police escorts, sirens, signal lights, etc., all had to be coordinated in every city we visited. One minute tardiness could upset the whole routine. Amazingly, nobody was ever late, nobody got sick, there were no problems, ever. That took planning, and it was done efficiently, the American way. I was never prouder.

At nine o'clock sharp on the morning of November 13, I was whisked away to the White House and into the Oval Office for a meeting with President Reagan; Vice President Bush; Secretary Shultz; the principal staff: McFarlane, Meese, Baker, Deaver; and Richard Burt, assistant secretary of state for Europe. My job was to brief the president on what the Grand Duke was like, what he would probably raise in conversation with the president. I also provided some conversational items on Luxembourg. The half-hour session passed without mishap or misstep.

By now people had begun to assemble on the South Lawn, everyone getting into his or her toe-marked place for the ten o'clock ceremony. I spotted our Bob and Susie and our grandchildren in the "Gold Rope" area. Winnie was in place next to Ambassador Dobrynin of the Soviet Union, dean of the Washington Diplomatic Corps.

The welcoming ceremony defied description. Trumpets, drum and fife corps in colonial costumes, Marine Band, army, navy, air force, and marines on parade. Ruffles and flourishes! Pomp and circumstance! Reagan was in great form. The week after a landslide reelection, forty-nine states in his pocket, was a perfect time for him to welcome the Grand Duke and Grand Duchess of Luxembourg to the White House. The president had picked up several items I had mentioned in the briefing session and worked them into his welcoming speech.

When he repeated the George Mergenthaler story at dinner in the evening, my Luxembourg colleagues recognized the source again, and concluded I was really *in*.

A half-hour visit in the Oval Office with the president and the Grand Duke followed the lawn ceremony. Winnie and the ladies of the official party met with Nancy Reagan and the Grand Duchess in the Green Room for coffee.

At noon, a splendid luncheon was given by Secretary Shultz in the Thomas Jefferson Room of the State Department, and, while most members of our group afterwards toured the Freer Gallery and the Phillips Collection, I escorted Luxembourg's new Foreign Minister Jacques Poos to meetings with George Shultz, Cap Weinberger, and Trade Director Brock. By early evening, we were all back in the Vista Hotel, getting dressed for the gala black-tie dinner at the White House.

At seven o'clock, Winnie and I arrived at the White House for what turned out to be a great surprise for us. Our limo deposited us at the north portico, where we were escorted to the grand staircase. We walked up the red carpet, and were greeted by Vice President and Mrs. Bush, who led us into the Yellow Oval Room (family quarters) for a personal visit with President and Mrs. Reagan. Secretary and Mrs. Shultz, Ambassador and Mrs. Peters, and Foreign Minister and Mrs. Poos were also there. I was thrilled to be able to chat with the president personally, to share my impressions of Luxembourg, and to exchange a couple of humorous anecdotes with him. I pinched myself several times to make sure I wasn't dreaming.

In the course of our talk, the president told me I was doing a good job in Luxembourg, and he hoped I would "stay with" him through the next administration. "Mr. President, that's up to you and God," I said.

"Well, I can't speak for God," he answered with a twinkle in his eyes, "but as far as I'm concerned, I want you to stay on."

This brief, informal gathering was a personal highlight for Winnie and me. It left us with a warm glow that lasted a long, long time.

The State Dinner was glamorous. The Grand Duke responded eloquently to the president's toast. Spirits were high. After dinner, we were treated to a performance by the Twyla Tharp Dancers in the East Room which had been set up in cabaret style. The finale was an opportunity for the guests to dance to the music of the Marine Dance Band. The Reagans danced along with the rest of us until past midnight.

The Washington portion of the State Visit continued the next day with much pageantry at Arlington Cemetery. Then followed a luncheon in honor of Vice President and Mrs. Bush in the Luxembourg embassy, a tour of the Hirschhorn Museum, and afternoon tea at the Vice President's House.

The Mayflower Hotel Ballroom became a concert hall in the evening, when the Luxembourg RTL Orchestra performed grandly for a select audience which included Secretary and Mrs. Shultz and many Washington dignitaries. After the concert, some four hundred guests enjoyed a reception and buffet, along with an opportunity to chat with their royal hosts. We plopped into our beds both uplifted and exhausted. Our eventful journey had just begun. Baggage call was scheduled for 6:15 A.M.

Early on the third morning, our motorcade took us back to the Washington Monument and the Reflecting Pool, where official farewells were said. The helicoptors Marine One and Marine Two whirled us away to Andrews Air Force Base, where we boarded U.S. Presidential Aircraft (VC-137), a Boeing 707, which at one time had served Lyndon B. Johnson as Air Force One. It would be our plane for the rest of the State Visit. We took off for Colorado Springs.

At Peterson Air Force Base in Colorado we were met by the mayor of Colorado Springs and the commander in chief of NORAD. The first stop was the Air Force Academy. When our motorcade pulled up in front of the Academy Chapel, Winnie and I stepped out of our limousine into the arms of our son Brian. Some thoughtful organizer had arranged this surprise reunion. Brian was invited to all events and was a member of the official party for the rest of our time in the Rocky Mountains. This made our day.

We toured the Air Force Academy with General Winfield Scott, superintendent, and Brigadier General Marcus Anderson, commandant of cadets. We enjoyed lunch with some 4,300 cadets, all under one roof. Grand Duke Jean exercised his privilege as visiting head of state to grant amnesty and cancel all punishment. That announcement raised the roof.

We next visited Fort Carson, headquarters of the Fourth Infantry Division, which had protected Luxembourg City during the Battle of the Bulge. The Grand Duke conducted the review of the troops on parade—a dramatic show—which began when a cavalry officer on horseback galloped across Manhart Field, the parade ground, at top speed, drew up in front of the reviewing stand, and presented the Grand Duchess with a bouquet.

Governor Richard Lamm of Colorado and the first lady entertained at an elegant black-tie dinner in the Penrose Room of our hotel, the Broadmoor. This dinner had been arranged by my good friend and Beta brother, John Sommer, and his lovely wife Susie.

A two-day stop in San Francisco included a motor tour of the city, and a visit to Muir Woods. We had lunch at Ondine's in Sausalito, and a private cable car trip to Fisherman's Wharf. The evening festivities included a spectacular reception at the Palace of the Legion of Honor.

And there was more, without a moment for personal relaxation, for shopping. You were lucky if you could squeeze a moment into the hustle and bustle for a visit to the rest room. The speed increased on the last leg of the journey—Chicago—where a large community of immigrants from Luxembourg holds forth.

We had become accustomed to being everywhere on time, being moved at top speed by extremely well-coordinated traffic control and police escort. It became more dramatic in Chicago where massive traffic jams were avoided, or prevented, and everything moved with clockwork precision.

A Memorial Mass, in honor of American soldiers who lost their lives in Luxembourg during both World Wars, was held at the Holy Name Cathedral by Joseph Cardinal Bernardin, archbishop of Chicago. After the mass, our motorcade sped off to the Drake Hotel where we prepared for an American Luxembourg Friendship Reception and Banquet, organized by the American Luxembourg Society and the Consulate General of Luxembourg in Chicago.

Mayor Harold Washington received Their Royal Highnesses at City Hall the next morning. He presented Grand Duke Jean with the key to the city and proclaimed the day "Luxembourg Day" for the city of Chicago.

The State Visit ended officially at 7:30 P.M. on November 19. Winnie and I bade farewell to our distinguished guests at O'Hare International Airport, and after their lift-off we flew to Cincinnati with big plans for a special Thanksgiving in Ohio. After the holidays we headed for Washington to finish our consultations, and to wind up a never-to-be forgotten State Visit before returning to Luxembourg and our home on the Boulevard Emmanuel Servais.

Winnie and I reached a major decision in late spring 1985. After much soul-searching, rationalizing, and serious talking, we decided that four years of embassy life was enough. We had already served beyond the usual tenure of ambassadors, and ought to quit while we were ahead. Relations with the Luxembourg government were more than stable. Our agenda had been met. We had put Luxembourg on the Washington map of Europe, and had successfully engineered VIP visits far beyond our expectations. The embassy residence and the chancellery were in tip-top condition. And, we had reached the pinnacle of our tenure with the State Visit.

On the negative side of the ledger were the growing confusion and contradictions of a nonexistent foreign policy, coupled with an increasingly antagonistic attitude of the career foreign service people. Dennis Hays, president of the American Foreign Service Association (AFSA), the professional group that represents career diplomats, was publicly registering "fresh concerns about the degree to which U.S. Presidents dole out ambassadorships as political rewards."

Almost daily we were reminded that the United States had such an abundance of trained diplomatic officers that it amounted to what one careerist called "an officer glut." It was claimed the U.S. Foreign Service was having difficulty recruiting and keeping good professionals. Furthermore, career officers not promoted within a certain period of time were being "selected out" of the service and forced to retire.

There was a certain amount of sour grapes in all this complaining. Malcolm Toon, a former career ambassador to the Soviet Union, was leading the assault. What bothered him most was "the caliber of the political appointees chosen. The majority are not really well-qualified people, even in their own line of work," said Mr. Toon. He maintained the principal qualification of an ambassador should be competence. Loyalty, ideology, and reliability were not enough.

Of course, one couldn't argue with much of this kind of generality. But specifically, what good is a competent career officer whose loyalty rests with the party out of power, who disapproves of the policies of the administration he is to serve? And since when is reliability not related to competence?

The point is that there are political appointees who make exemplary ambassadors, and there are some who are total failures. But exactly the same is true of career officers. A careerist with twenty years of service as an economics counselor or political adviser in Zimbabwe, Zaire, and ten other exotic posts, is not necessarily qualified to be ambassador to Great Britain. I know career officers who don't know enough to tuck in their shirttails or to refrain from picking their noses in public, their years of service notwithstanding. Seniority in itself does not make for competence, nor does membership in the AFSA. Personally, I found all the bickering and posturing demoralizing. It was bound to affect relationships and peformance.

In light of the career and noncareer brouhaha, I wasn't surprised to receive a telephone call from Michael Deaver at the White House one afternoon in late April. I had heard that he was in charge of ambassadorial appointments during the second Reagan term, thus proving Ambassador Toon's point.

Our conversation was amiable. Would I be interested in a larger post? That question had already been answered by me earlier. No. I didn't consider myself qualified for a larger mission. I couldn't afford it, and I really had no interest in trying to stretch my appointment into a career. His question was academic anyway, a conversation starter.

"Well, we have a problem," said Mr. Deaver. "Shultz has convinced the president that political appointees should either be rotated or replaced after three years of service. He wants to make room for the many career people who want to become ambassadors."

I assured Deaver that this presented no problem in my case. I understood the need to provide advancement opportunities for professionals. He thanked me for my understanding. Then he went on to say that the president had asked him to call me to find out what my intentions were. Recalling President Reagan's conversation with me in November about staying with him through the next term, I smelled a little of what we'd become accustomed to in Luxembourg cow barns. Regardless of that, Winnie and I had already discussed the matter and had reached our own decision. Mistaking my momentary silence for concern, Deaver said: "Now the president doesn't want to create any personal hardship, so tell me if you have any problems."

I told him we had already decided this was our last year; so, I had no problem. As for timing, I told him that Luxembourg would take on the presidency of the European Community for six months on July first.

"I didn't know about that," Deaver said. "I'm not sure the State Department would want to change ambassadors in the middle of the EC presidency. Why don't you just sit tight and do nothing until you hear from the State Department. And if you do, be sure to mention this EC complication to them." With that, our conversation ended.

A week later, my secretary brought me a clipping from the *New York Times*. It announced the appointment of a new ambassador to Luxembourg, "replacing John E. Dolibois who has resigned." I nearly fell off my chair. We hadn't received a request for an "Agrément" from the host country for a new ambassador. And I certainly had not yet resigned.

What further confused the issue was that no one in Luxembourg had any idea of my future plans, not even my own staff. It is not proper protocol to announce an appointment of a successor until all the right steps have been taken, beginning with the request for an agrément—by which the host country finds a proposed appointment agreeable to them. This obvious leak to the media was embarrassing.

"Possession is nine-tenths of the law," I was told when I called the State Department for clarification and direction. "Just stay put until you're ready to move."

In the days that followed, other newspapers reported my resignation and the appointment of my successor. An official inquiry from the government of Luxembourg forced the issue. I checked with the department again. This time I was told that the person whom the White House was considering as my successor, if and when I resigned, was *not* a foreign service career officer, but another political appointee, a "hardworking party functionary and generous contributor." Deaver had fed me a line—just before he himself resigned as deputy chief of staff at the White House.

Meanwhile, the comedy of errors persisted. We were beginning to get invitations to farewell parties. The Luxembourg Communist newspaper gleefully reported that "Ambassador Dolibois got his ears boxed. He will be replaced by Jeane Kirkpatrick, former permanent representative to the United Nations. And soon after his successor arrives, Ronald Reagan is coming to Luxembourg on a State Visit." We got tired of explaining the inexplicable. I requested written instructions.

"Scheduling depends on the agrément, when the White House announces your successor, and the entire confirmation process," read the reply I received from the deputy assistant secretary for Europe. It continued, "The European Bureau is not consulted on the timing of any of these steps. Typically, once the confirmation process is completed, the incoming and outgoing ambassadors try to work out mutually agreeable dates."

I decided the next move was up to us. Apparently the State Department wasn't concerned about the embassy's involvement in Luxembourg's presidency of the EC. Winnie and I checked the calendar. We had a host of commitments for the weeks ahead, and decided September 15, 1985 would be a reasonable and fair date for us to leave Luxembourg. In accordance with the procedure spelled out in the Foreign Affairs Manual, I tendered my "resignation to the President by letter under cover of a letter addressed to the Secretary of State, marked for the attention of the Director General of the Foreign Service." My letter was dated June 3. President Reagan accepted my resignation on September 12, "the effective date to be determined." But our departure day was set.

The summer months sped by, filled with all kinds of activity. There were the traditional events, such as the Luxembourg National Day, July Fourth, Patton Remembrance Day in Ettelbruck, and our own mountain-hiking expedition to Lech, Austria, the fourth in a row.

In time for the summer tourist season, an article appeared in *Atlantica*, the in-flight magazine of Icelandair. It was a friendly story about "America's Man in Luxembourg." Based on an interview with us, the author described my functions and the various activities which had enriched our lives since October 1981.

Shortly after this article appeared, a call came to the embassy from a lady who wished to see the ambassador, her "uncle." She said her maiden name was Dolibois, and she hailed from Flint, Michigan. My curiosity was aroused no end. My secretary Janet made an appointment, and thus I came face-to-face with Renée, my brother's adopted daughter, whom I had last seen as a six-year-old in 1945. I was flabbergasted, even more so when I heard the full story.

My brother Charles and his wife Rose had adopted the little girl through an orphanage. I had visited my brother's widow and Renée in their apartment on the rue des Capucins just a week after the war ended. I saw them regularly during my assignment in Europe, and then lost touch when I returned to the States. Rose had died suddenly, and Renée was sent back to the orphanage, where she stayed until she was eighteen years old.

She was working as a salesclerk in a bookstore on the Grand Rue when she met an American airman, George Borek. They were married, and, in line with his duties as an air force engineer, were stationed in various parts of the world. They settled in Michigan upon his retirement. In the summer of 1985, they decided to visit Luxembourg. While on board their Icelandair flight, Renée opened a copy of *Atlantica* to the story of the American ambassador in her native country. She determined that this same ambassador was her uncle John, whom she vaguely remembered from her early childhood. Another circle in the pattern of my life was completed.

On Independence Day 1985 I was shaking the hands of hundreds of guests in the receiving line, when a charming, elderly lady appeared before me. Oblivious of the many in line behind her, she told me about the horrors of the German occupation. She wanted me to know that throughout those horrible years she never lost faith in the Americans who would some day liberate her country again, as they did in 1918.

"And when the Americans come," she had told herself back in 1943, "I'm going to have the Stars and Stripes hanging from my house to welcome them."

Possession of an American flag was against the laws of the occupiers. Such a crime would be severely punished. Nevertheless, Madame Madeleine Fischbach-Jost was determined. She made an American flag, with much difficulty, and in great secrecy. And when American tanks came rolling past her home on September 10, 1944, the Stars and Stripes waved gracefully and triumphantly in the evening breeze in front of her home.

Just before Winnie and I left Luxembourg, a package with a letter was delivered to the embassy. The package contained the flag Madame Fischbach had risked her life to make. The letter reads:

Your Excellency,

During the war I was sewing this flag with poor cloth and little thread. It meant for us the hope of liberation.

At the reception for Independence Day, you told me you would accept it. It is a token of admiration for your great nation and nobody better than you, with the close links you have to Luxembourg and our people, could keep it.

The very best wishes for many, many happy years for your Excellency and Mrs. Dolibois.

Yours truly,
Madeleine Fischbach-Jost

I cherish this flag as the most meaningful of the memorabilia of my ambassadorial career. Madame Fischbach stands out in my memory as typical of Luxembourg womanhood, charming, gracious, and courageous. A true patriot.

The clock was winding down. We made a conscientious effort to start reducing the number of activities, but even after my resignation, in just one month, we still had the Portuguese, Italian, British, and Spanish national days. We attended the opening of a new General Motors engineering center, and a new Inter-Continental Hotel. In our own embassy we had four receptions and three briefings. Meanwhile, each day, I watched for word from Washington about my resignation. Nothing!

I didn't know if the long silence meant the president wasn't accepting my resignation, or if he was so excited about the good news of our leaving that he couldn't put it in words. But, in retrospect, I believe Ronald Reagan had more weighty problems on his mind. First, the hostage crisis, and then, his own health. We decided to stay on schedule, and were soon immersed in farewell dinners, receptions, and the tedious task of packing.

Members of the American Luxembourg Society turned out in record numbers to give us a memorable sendoff. The ALS invited the country's mayors to a farewell dinner. Sixty-two Luxembourg community executives were able to attend. They represented over 70 percent of the total population. It was a sympathetic leave-taking, at which we realized that it *was* possible to have two homelands, that we were leaving a part of ourselves in Luxembourg forever.

While dining for the last time as the American ambassador with our good friends of the ALS, I reflected on the many occasions we had been together in my four years. Several hundred strong, the organization enthusiastically celebrates Thanksgiving, Memorial Day, July Fourth, and every other American holiday. They sponsor lectures, concerts, excursions to U.S. military bases, and frequent tours to the United States.

Under the leadership of Emile Weitzel, their president of many years, the ALS published a complete history of the society in its one hundredth year in 1983.

Jean Calmes, son of the marshal of the court, succeeded Mr. Weitzel in 1984, and immediately introduced a program which expanded the loyal support of the American embassy by his society. The ALS participated in the Chicago portion of the Grand Duke's State Visit. They published an attractive report by Marshal of the Court Christian Calmes of the entire State Visit. I'm convinced that every ambassador needs an organization such as the American Luxembourg Society.

Luxembourg's Prime Minister Pierre Werner invited Winnie and me to a day in the country at his summer home on the shores of a beautiful lake in the Ardennes. The Austrian Ambassador Gerard Heible and his wife Marie-Térèse were also invited. The Heibles were leaving Luxembourg on October 1. The six of us walked around the lake at Lultzhausen, reminiscing, recalling memories of our years together, knowing that this day we were enjoying so much would never come again.

Each tour of the Luxembourg countryside, each walk through a sloping vineyard, through emerald green woods, or across golden fields, now became rather poignant. Every meal in a favorite restaurant, and every visit with dear friends, stood out. We began to suspect that there would be many times back home when we would suffer genuine pangs of "verlaangeren"—homesick feelings—for the lovely little country that had been so good to us.

Our very last social function was the best of all. The marshal of the court called to ask if we were free for lunch on Friday, September 13. He quickly added that if we weren't, we should rearrange our schedule, because we were being issued a most unusual invitation. Their Royal Highnesses, the Grand Duke and the Grand Duchess, invited Winnie and me to a private luncheon at Chateau Berg.

I find no words to describe the occasion. Sitting informally on a sunny terrace with these two admirable persons, enjoying a relaxing aperitif; wandering through the beautiful gardens together, admiring and appreciating, while Her Royal Highness snapped pictures for lasting souvenirs. A delightful luncheon, just the four of us, recalling their visit to Ohio in 1979, the Miami connection, the weddings of their daughters, the births of their grandsons, the death of their beloved mother. We spoke of the important official guests from the United States, their own successful State Visit, and a highly successful helicopter journey over Luxembourg we had enjoyed together.

All of these experiences contributed to a personal, mutually satisfying friendship, which we deeply appreciated. We could admire and respect

Their Royal Highnesses, and share a common bond, even though we were miles apart in every other sense.

The Grand Duke excused himself for a brief moment, and then reappeared with a handsome little chest. He opened it and revealed the most elegant decoration I had ever seen. He presented it to me, the "Grand Cross of the Grand Ducal Order of the Crown of Oak"—an order going back hundreds of years to the days of King John the Blind.

For me the circle was complete. The barefoot kid from the Petrusse Valley, who fifty-six years ago had gazed longingly at the spires and towers high above the steep cliffs, was ending his journey on a most rewarding path at the top of the summit.

Being an ambassador of the United States was a fantastic experience, an immense ego trip. We were privileged to serve our country in an unusual, rewarding manner. We learned much about the rest of the world, and our outlook on many things has changed. The honors, courtesies, and respect accorded me as the president's personal representative to the Grand Duchy were mind-boggling. But I also realized that we lived on this high plane only because of my position as the representative of the greatest country in the world. At least, that is what the United States is to many people in Luxembourg.

We knew full well that once my credentials were returned, and I became a "former ambassador," all the glamour and preference would come to an abrupt end. "Get back in line, Buddy!"

Sometimes Winnie and I wondered if we shouldn't have stretched our luck and extended our stay another year or two. Such feelings were especially strong when we drove through a particularly beautiful countryside, or sat on our terrace and heard "Charlie," our neighborhood bird— a Merl—sing his heart out for us. But then we returned quickly to reality. Quitting while you're ahead is a smart move. We knew we had done a good job in Luxembourg. We'd reached all the goals we set for ourselves; it was the right time to leave.

Winnie and I were a good team. I wouldn't have accomplished one-tenth as much without her loyal support and very active participation. I know of no other diplomat's wife who has taken part in every activity involving her husband or her country, as Winnie did. Unless an affair was strictly business or for men only, she was at my side at every event.

How did Winnie really feel about her personal role in Luxembourg? She would never tell. But then one day she confessed that she occasionally made notes—very private notes—just for herself. I persuaded her to let me look at just one entry in her personal diary. At random, I came upon what she wrote to herself on February 29, 1984—leap year. It's honest, soul-talk. Winnie has allowed me to share it with you:

I am no longer the wide-eyed Cinderella who appeared on this doorstep October 11, 1981. There is a slightly jaundiced cast to the eye today. To my natural bent toward cynicism has been added proof of the folly of man (certainly my own). Without trying to sound pompous or overly confident, I must say I find people in so-called "high places" not too much different basically from any others I have known. The antics and posturing are more tolerated at the high level—but not terribly original.

The "semi-celebrity" status we enjoy, the lovely perks of this job, can give one an inflated idea about his or her own real worth. It is dangerous ground. It also presents the pitfall of emotional security—"do they like me for myself or . . . ?" Add to this, in my case, the language barrier, and a few thorns appear in the rose garden. Plus loneliness, yes, loneliness. I could organize all kinds of activity, but that is not my bent. I am a private person, who very often doubts her own usefulness and worth at this time. The years I spent doing all my own work in relation to my own family, plus working with John, were hard (and God knows I bitched enough). But basically I was challenged and busy, physically involved. Here, it is lovely to have such a competent staff—but I'm not in complete control, and sometimes I feel totally useless. It's not my nature to accept this. One has to live this life to understand what I am talking about. I'm not complaining. I'm just trying to analyze the whole feeling I have for this.

There are aspects of life here which we both dearly love, and these aspects are either non-existent or unavailable to us in the United States, and, vice versa. The only observation here, I think I'll find it easier to live in the USA as an ex-ambassador's wife, than here in Luxembourg.

So enough introspection! I'll resume recording events with only an occasional acid comment. . . .

My wife's innermost feelings, as of February 29, 1984, came as a surprise to me. I realized for the first time how great were the challenges confronting her, the personal hurdles she had to overcome. Yet, Winnie was the perfect wife for an ambassador, in spite of loneliness, language barriers, and the problem of being pampered. And there *are* problems with being made to feel totally helpless. I remember one former ambassador telling me that it took him two weeks before he learned how to open his own car door again. He said he'd walk up to his car, right-rear passenger door, and just stand there waiting for someone to turn the handle.

Our present life in Oxford, Ohio, when we are at home, is itself deeply satisfying. We have a need for close friends who understand our culture shock and tolerate occasional lapses when good humor fails us. Let's face it, a sense of humor sustains, but only when shared. I realized our ego trip had ended when, shortly after our return home, I called a prominent Cincinnati restaurant for a reservation. The lady with whom I spoke got it all right. The time, seven thirty. The number, three. "And what's the name, please?" she asked. Thinking if I tell her I'm an ambassador, we'll get a good table, I replied, "Ambassador Dolibois." There was a moment of hesitation, and then the question, "How do you spell your first name, please?"

We traveled to Washington to join in the observance of the fortieth anniversary of the Fulbright Program. How rewarding it was to see so many of my former colleagues of the Board of Foreign Scholarships again! Some of them, like Lyle and Corinne Nelson from Stanford, had visited us in Luxembourg. So did Dr. James Billington, who is now director of the Library of Congress. Jim and his son spent several days with us in the embassy, and contributed to our rich memories of great visits.

Senator Fulbright himself was on hand for the reunion of the "Fulbrighters." While along in years, his mind and memory were as sharp as ever. His pride in the program he had started inspired everyone.

Winnie and I spent July 4, 1986 with our friends Bill and Martha Lee Pulley in Cashiers, North Carolina. Their striking summer home is perched on the edge of Big Sheep Cliff, offering a spectacular view of the valley below and the mountains beyond. I can't think of a more fitting place to celebrate our national holiday. Sitting on the outside deck, drink in hand, watching the sun set, and listening to the birds sing their evening song, I found all right with the world.

Independence Day 1986 was particularly significant for me. You'll recall that the Statue of Liberty was rededicated on that day. Americans everywhere stood tall with pride and devotion as the president of the United States pressed the button that illuminated the statue, and turned New York harbor into a fairyland. Will we ever forget the Tall Ships, the fantastic fireworks display, the music, and the inspiring speeches full of promise and hope?

My eyes were glued to the television screen in our friends' home on that beautiful North Carolina mountain. I remembered the first time I saw that glorious statue of the Lady in the harbor—on the morning of July 4, 1931. I had been awakened to my future by the sound of fireworks, mingled with the shouts of celebrants. Therefore, this 1986 celebration had a special meaning for me. So much so, that I felt compelled to write to President Reagan, as I had on several other moving occasions as his ambassador. I received a prompt, personal reply:

Dear John:
   Thank you for your beautiful letter about the Statue of Liberty centennial weekend. Your kind words mean a great deal to me.
   You were kinder still to tell me of your and your father's arrival in New

York on Independence Day when you were a boy, and of how your ship anchored by the beloved Statue which personifies liberty so well. You had truly made safe harbor.

You are so right about the promise of America—how an immigrant boy could get an education, have the opportunity for a successful career, and, fifty years after his arrival in America, become Ambassador to his native land. May I simply say that the talents you've shared and the love for our land which you manifest are wonderful gifts to our nation—and no wonder someone who shares America's spirit so well was chosen to represent us.

You and Winnie have my best wishes and those of Nancy, too. From the bottom of my heart, thank you and God bless you.

Sincerely,
Ronald Reagan

Our lifelong friend and chronicler, my former mentor and colleague, Walter Havighurst, has written many books about Miami, about Ohio, and the Northwest Territory. I vividly recall how deeply I was touched by a story Walter wrote about the arrival of a Norwegian family in mid-nineteenth-century America. As their ship lay at anchor in New York Harbor, Ole Svenson was awed by the vast beauty of all that he saw, the height of the "skyscrapers" along the Battery—"buildings that reach up into the clouds."

He and his wife were overwhelmed by the thousands of people on the sidewalks and the streets of New York, and the wealth so obvious in that enormous city. They were struck by the beauty of the mountains, the lakes and streams, the vineyards and orchards, through which they traveled west on an Erie Canal barge. Later, on deck of a steamer that took them across Lake Erie to that part of the country where so many Scandinavians found a home, they were at once excited and bewildered by a land so vast and rich, with lakes as big as oceans, where you can't see the shore on either side.

"What a great and beautiful country," exclaimed Mother Svenson. Then her voice fell. She pointed to their battered chest and carpetbag. "We bring so little. What have we to give to this great land?"

"We have ourselves," said her husband, "we have our hands, our hearts, and our minds. With our minds we can learn to understand it, with our hearts we can love it, and with our hands we can serve it."

That question was also on my mind as a boy when I came across the sea from Luxembourg. My friend Walter Havighurst suggests that my journey is a pattern of circles. In the depth of an economic depression, I came from the old world to the new. A world war took me back to my starting point in the heart of Europe. With the oncoming of peace, I returned to the American scene of my young manhood, and then went back again to my native land as the representative of the only country in the world where the impossible dream can still come true.

Along my journey of personal growth and fulfillment there were many signposts pointing the way. They were put there by friends, whose hands also opened the doors through which I could enter. Like the Ulysses of three thousand years ago,

> Much have I seen and known, cities of men,
> And manners, climates, councils, governments. . . .
> I am part of all that I have met.

Here ends my essay in gratitude.

Index